Militia Stand Down

The First Objective Reading

Of The

2nd Amendment

By Geoffrey Smith

Copyright @ 2017 by Geoffrey Smith

All rights reserved. No part of this publication

may be reproduced or distributed,

or transmitted without express consent of the author.

Cover Photo by Geoffrey Smith

Cover Design by Geoffrey Smith

First Edition

ISBN 9780995099005

All Rights Reserved

Dedication

For
"We the People"
Future, Past and Present

Table of Contents

Militia Stand Down 1
Dedication 5
Preface 15
Prologue 19
1-Introducing the 2nd Amendment...23
    Progressive Hints on how to read the 2nd Amendment Objectively..............27
    Lead up to Reading the 2nd Amendment Objectively (Spoiler Alert!) 28
    The First Objective Reading of the 2nd Amendment......................................31
        Thomas Jefferson Letter to John Taylor May 28, 1816........................37
    Profound Implications 41
2-The Advent of Suspicion..47
    Approach to Discerning the Legitimate Meaning of the 2nd amendment.......47
    The Start of the Research..59
    Overview of the Book and "How to read it" 64
    Why encrypt the 2nd Amendment? 72
    Not a Deception 74
3-New History..77
    Early Beginnings 77
        A Tale " Passy, printed by Benjamin Franklin, in 1779?..................79
        The Gadsen Flag 85
        Pennsylvania Journal on December 27, 1775 87
    Governments are the Invention of Man 93
        Invention of Kings...93
        A Transfer of Power to Democracy 95
    New Constitution..96
        Life Liberty and the Pursuit of Happiness 105
        The Delegates and the 2nd Amendment...................................108

A Cabal Discovered	109
The American Philosophical Society	109
Benjamin Franklin Ciphering Institute	114
The 2nd Amendment is the Key to the Constitution	119
The Cipher Letter	122
The Damage of the Old Rhetoric	126
A Mystery of History Solved?	128
From John Adams to Timothy Pickering, 6 August 1822	129
Thomas Jefferson to James Madison August 30 1823	129
Thomas Jefferson to the John Adams June 1822	130
4-Major Discoveries – Yes it Gets Better	133
The Federalist Papers Revisited	133
Federalist Papers #84 , Alexander Hamilton, 28 May 1788.	137
|| Federalist No. 1 ||	142
Concluding Remarks on the Federalist Papers	148
A Benjamin Franklin Cipher	149
TO WILLIAM ALEXANDER (L. c.) October 26 1789.	150
TO WILLIAM ALEXANDER (L. c.) October 26 1789.	152
To Patrick Henry (unpublished) Oct 8 1785	159
The Bill of Rights	161
First amendment	165
Third Amendment	166
Fourth Amendment	167
Fifth Amendment	168
Sixth Amendment	170
Seventh Amendment	171
Eighth Amendment	173

- Ninth Amendment..174
- Tenth Amendment 175
- Concluding Comments..176

5-The Privately Held Hoards..179
- Benjamin Franklin-Sets the Board-Chess Theme Ciphers 183
  - "The Morals of Chess", [before 28 June 1779].......................................183
  - To Joseph Reed Passy, Mar 19. 1780...188
  - To Joseph Reed, March 19. 1780. 188
  - Om the Chevalier - (unpublished) Paris this 30 June 1785 190
  - From - Chevalier (unpublished) Paris on 16 May 1784..........................192
  - To the Chevalier — (unpublished) June-July, 1785................................194
  - From Feutry Paris, April 21, 1777. in the evening 197
  - Feutry: Verse for Franklin's Portrait April 27, 1777. 197
  - From Aimé (or Amé) -Ambroise-Joseph Feutry.....................................199
  - From Aimé (Amé) -Ambroise-Joseph Feutry Paris, this 8th of July, 1781.200
- Benjamin Franklin-Cipher Collection 203
  - From Alexander Small March 15th 1777 206
  - To Alexander Small July 22, 1780..207
  - From Alexander Small [before July 22, 1780] 211
  - From Alexander Small [after July 22, 1780] 212
  - From Alexander Small [before July 20, 1781] 212
  - From David Hartley July 27 1784 (up)...214
  - From David Hartley Aug 4 1784 (up) 214
  - Alexander Small (up) Philad Sept. 28. 1787 215
  - Mystery Letter- Pre 2nd Convention 219
  - Philadelphia Independent Gazetteer,30 April1788 219
  - To Patrick Henry (unpublished) Oct 8 1785 221

To Richard Henry Lee, April 12th, 1785. 223

To John Jay (unpublished)..224

From William Alexander (unpublished) Jan 22 1786 226

From William Alexander (unpublished) 10 June 1786...........................229

From William Alexander (UP) 30 May 1784 230

From Benjamin Franklin to Arthur Lee, 3 April 1778..............................236

From William Alexander (unpublished) 237

From William Alexander (unpublished) 30 July 1783 238

From A— B— (unpublished) June 3 1786...239

From David Hartley Rue Caumartin Wednesday Morning Aug 4 1784.....240

From David Hartley (unpublished) Rue Canmartin July 27 1784...........241

To John Adams (unpublished) Aug. 6. 1784. 241

To Noah Webster, Jr. (unpublished)..243

Philadelphia Independent Gazetteer, 30 April 1788 250

Benjamin Franklins last Speech Sept 17, 1787 254

Benjamin Franklins last Speech Sept 17, 1787 254

George Washington..257

William Milnor to George Washington, 29 November 1774....................257

John Milner to George Washington January 1776 260

George Washington to John Hancock, 20 Dec 1776.................................261

George Washington to James Madison, 30 November 1785....................262

George Washington Farewell Address 1796...266

George Washington to John Jay, 10 March 1787......................................269

George Washington to Alexander Hamilton, 18 Oct 1787........................272

Alexander Hamilton to George Washington, 30 Oct 1787........................274

Alexander Hamilton to George Washington, Nov 10, 1787.....................276

George Washington To Henry Lee, Jr.Sep 22 1788 278

John Adams 283

    John Adams to James Warren, 13 April 1783 284

    John Adams To Benjamin Franklin July 19. 1784 289

    John Adams (up) The Hague July 27th 1784 291

    John Adams to Benjamin Rush, 4 April 1790 294

    To John Adams from Benjamin Rush, 13 April 1790 300

    John Adams to George Washington, 31 October 1791 304

    John Adams to Benjamin Rush, 19 March 1812 305

    From John Adams March 8 1823 308

Thomas Jefferson 309

    Essay On Exercise August 19 1785. 309

    Thomas Jefferson to Noah Webster, Jr., 4 December 1790 316

    To Thomas Jefferson from Noah Webster, Jr., 12 Dec 1790 319

    To William Stephen Smith Paris, Nov. 13, 1787 322

    Thomas Jefferson to John Payne Todd, 15 August 1816 326

    John Payne Todd to Thomas Jefferson, 31 August 1816 328

    Thomas Jefferson Inaugural Address, Wednesday, March 4, 1801 330

    Thomas Jefferson Inaugural Address, Wednesday, March 4, 1801 330

    To Dr. Benjamin Rush Monticello, September 23, 1800 337

    Thomas Jefferson to James Madison 20 Dec. 1787 340

    Letter to James Madison November 18, 1788 341

    From Thomas Jefferson to John Taylor, 26 November 1798 345

    Thomas Jefferson Letter to John Taylor May 28, 1816 348

    Canons of Conduct Feb 2 1817 353

    Decalogue of Canons for Observation February 25 1825 353

    LETTER CLVII.—TO JOHN ADAMS, January 22, 1821 356

    To Justice William Johnson Monticello, June 12, 1823 359

John Jay 369
    John Jay to Thomas Jefferson 27 Oct. 1786 369
    To George Washington from John Jay, 7 January 1787 371
James Madison 375
    1778 to the General Assembly of the State of Virginia 375
    James Madison to Richard Peters 19 Aug. 1789 377
    The "Well-Regulated" Fallacy: (Jan 21, 1792) 382
First Important Findings Thomas Ritchie 387
    To Thomas Ritchie from James Madison Sept 15 1821 388
    John Taylor 390
    To Thomas Ritchie Monticello, December 25, 1820 390
    Thomas Jefferson to Archibald Thweatt, 19 January 1821 392
    To Thomas Jefferson from Spencer Roane, 25 Feb 1821 395
A Conspiracy Theory? 398
The Martyrdom of Alexander Hamilton 408
"We the People" 411
    To ——— (unpublished) [after July 4, 1786] 415
Colonel John Taylor 418
Construction Construed and Constitutions Vindicated 1820 John Taylor 419
The Cherry Tree Revisited 425
    Thomas Jefferson to Mason Locke Weems, Dec 13, 1804 435
TREASON 437
    From William Alexander 437
6-United States Seal 443
    The Eagle Side 444
    The Pyramid 446
    Connecting Benjamin Franklin to the Seal 448

From David Rittenhouse April 29th 1780	449
The Inner Chamber	461
The Key to the Plaques	463
The Presidential Seal	465
The Dorset Dies	471
The United States Seal Letter	472
To James Madison from Charles Thomson, 1 December 1801	472
The Concluding comments on the Seal	477
Plaque Trivia	478
7-Pre-Cabal Findings	**479**
An 18th century Massacre	479
Do Geniuses Go Hand Fishing for Lightning?	482
Joseph Priestley 1767	488
James Madison: Advice to my Country - ca 1834	491
From Joseph Priestley	494
From [Joseph Priestley]	494
Passages for Priestley's History of Electricity (II)	495
To Joseph Priestley London Sept. 19. 1772	496
The Grand Leap of the Whale	499
8-Conclusions and Reflections	**505**
The Narratives We Build	505
How we think	509
Racism	511
Choices	513
Some Closing Remarks	518
Benjamin Franklin was the Candid friend to Mankind	529
Overview of History's New Context	529

9-The Book Ends 534
   The Authors First Words 534
      Observations on Reading History 534
   The Authors Last Words...536
      The Epitaph...536
Reference and Sources 537
   The 12 Article Bill of Rights. 537
   The Bill of Rights (as ratified Dec 15 1791)...539
   Actors Reference 541
      Alexander Small (1710 – 31 August 1794) 544
      Noah Webster Jr. (October 16, 1758 – May 28, 1843) 545
      David Hartley (8 August[1] 1705 – 28 August 1757).................................545
      William Alexander, 1st Earl of Stirling (c. 1567– 12 September 1640) 545
      William Alexander, (1726 New York City – 15 January 1783) 546
      Mason Locke Weems (October 11, 1759 – May 23, 1825) 546
      Joseph Priestley (24 March 1733 – 6 February 1804)............................546
      Thomas Ritchie (November 5, 1778 – July 3, 1854) 547

Preface

    This is my first book. It is a history book. I have never had the aspiration to write a book before simply because I didn't have anything to write about. In turn, I'm not a credentialed historian so I have had to rely on my own ability to think and use a skill I have learned years earlier which is the ability to read. Historians are like detectives and for the most part will generally only be interested in the truth of history. To apply a preconceived bias towards it I suppose is fine but that depends on the source of that bias. Is the source of it emotion alone? Does truth care about our feelings? Does the truth of history require on a bias to the very consensus of known history? If this was true then why do historians even exist? Some history is of course recorded and some of it is not so it takes a bit more work to resolve it. It requires more thinking.

    I have 20 years experience in learning to think objectively. I have a background in software development. I'm used to both reading code but more importantly connecting it together in order to achieve a desired result. To go off on tangents and with no rhyme or reason has no value in its construction especially if I want to keep my job. I find it enjoyable because it is a highly creative process and requires problem solving in order to provide a solution. The problem is getting the code to work and connect together. Even if there is a bug in the code that causes it produce results that clash with the very purpose of it I then have to resolve the cause of the problem in order to eliminate the effect of it. It is only the perception of the effect that tells me that there is something wrong with inside of its code. I once had to "debug" some code that was written by multiple developers that was propagating incorrect values into a very large database for some widely used accounting software. What I discovered is that there was not just one bug, but about eight of them. Each one was introduced at different times. The issue was further complicated because the system had been running live for months. In order to fix the problem I first had to resolve where the bugs in the code were and fix that. In turn because I didn't think it prudent to shut down the live database during this process so I created some software that would clean the values across multiple tables. Once I was able to resolve that my code was working in order to achieve this goal I then had to put out a notice that the system would be shut down for about 10 minutes and kick about 100 people out of the system. I uploaded the new software, ran my program and everything was aligned. In the beginning of the process though, my manager instructed me to fix only one thing at a time. It is an awkward thing to tell a manager that there was no logic in that solution because the false values that values that were being propagated to the database were arrived at by about eight different sources of bag code attacking the veracity of the value itself. The point that I'm making here is that I'm experienced at drilling down to the very cause of a problem in order to stop its effect. While I may not like the truth what is involved in fixing it, that truth was the only solution to remedying the problem.

Give a man suspicion and his intelligence something to feed upon. Sometimes suspicion is something that is not easily arrived at because our own bias can get in the way of allowing it to take seed in our mind. I am a Canadian and while watching the news one night, that night being Dec 2 2015, yet again another gun related massacre was being reported on the television. It was the San Bernardino massacre. I got to thinking. I chose my bias very carefully. I viewed the United States Constitution as being very similar to software. It is similar to any software program because it's code describes a form of government that seemed to acknowledge that there was no cure for human nature. In order to accommodate for this it used the principle of checks and balances to guide human nature in spite of itself. With checks and balances oppression could be limited in a society by not allowing any one individual too much power which would enable him or her to become a tyrant. A tyrant can only be named AFTER their act of oppression has been witnessed. Before this time they are generally invisible to us. It was my view at this time that there was no way that James Madison would have written such a thing as the second amendment and yet there it was. Just like my manager, there are those that are far more credentialed than I that have explained this sentence in great detail. There was also a consensus on the history behind it. In spite of the opinions and research of others, I was still suspicious. It's just one sentence and I perceived it as something to be solved. The bias I chose in this regard was to the intelligence and education of James Madison. I saw truth in this. The 2nd amendment appeared to be a contingency to be used only after a tyrant was allowed to exist. In some manner the tyrant was able to navigate through the checks and balances of the very code of the constitution. The 2nd amendment appeared to be causing great oppression in the American Society which appeared to me to run contrary to the very code of the constitution. I saw the effect, and perceived I suppose you could call a bug. If was my view that not only would have James Madison have known how to construct a sentence which could be read with clarity but he would have done so in such an important document as the Bill of Rights. It was not that I had any preconceptions as to what this sentence might be, but only a feeling that it was not what it appeared to be. It has also been stated that the sentence is awkward in construction in that its front is not easily connected to its back. The Supreme Court has affirmed their own bias in their approach to interpreting this sentence by calling it's front half the "prefatory clause" and the latter the "operative clause". Their starting point was a bias to the 3rd clause the one that brands the 2nd amendment as "the right of the people to keep and bear Arms". My approach was different in that my bias was to the sentence itself and the education of James Madison. So I went about seeing if I could connect the front of it to the back. If I had any illusions of success in this matter I would have told you most certainly not. It is after all the most highly scrutinized sentence in the United States Constitution but scrutinized by people far more intelligent and educated than I. The thing about bias though is that it manages our intelligence. It dictates to us where our intelligence is allowed to roam. Now did I have any success in this? Consider the weight and thickness of this book as foreshadowing because it will throw a much wider shadow than a sentence alone. Oh yes, there is one area where the code of the constitution differs from regular software. In the final compiling of it the constitution must be voted upon by men of widely varied opinions, in other words, there was politics involved and in the vote , opinions and biases are rendered equal. The wisdom and intelligence as a collective had to first be essentially, averaged. I can tell you right now that it most certainly was not.

Prologue

In the year 1752 Benjamin Franklin sat down at his kneehole writing desk and dabbed a part of the re-purposed turkey he had eaten just days before into its future playground a 20 year old inkwell. Taking a sip of mead he then stared out his window toward the sky and saw the flash of lightning. In a few more seconds he heard the sound of distant thunder. A smile crossed his face as he began to cook-up a fable in his mind. Once again this feather was going to be at one with a draft.

He proceeded to draw a line on the parchment to represent a string or in other words a string to represent a line laying out a component of an experiment which was to be nested in another of a much grander design. Time was his friend in this a variable that was essential. The dynamic of suspicion was to be both a foe and a friend but tied in a knot to time itself. This particular experiment, the kite experiment would become a fable, and as such it would have every likely hood of travelling through time and reveal itself for what it really was, a component in a much grander experiment. Many more letters would be needed all crafted just as the one he was writing now in the hopes of stacking the cards in his favor, but more importantly in the favor of the future of his nation. He then drew a kite, as the wordsmith, knowing full well that a kite was also a person who preyed upon others. He then drew a key near the front of this line, which would unlock the door to this letter which would otherwise show no crack to give away its existence. He now had a line, with a key near its front, in anticipation of flashes and bangs in the future and a kite flying around almost at whim empowered only until a time when no power was due it.

At this time Benjamin Franklin had high hopes for his Albany plan in which he would nest a chameleon. A creature crafted in much the same way as his letters but with veracity of language itself as the key to his truth. One key tied to many others. His plan didn't transpire but his other labors would not be lost to time. They were now seeded to further support what he viewed was to be the inevitable joining of the colonies in the creation of a new nation. Human nature was at issue, a force which he could never compel to endorse his opinions in the early days. The only dynamic that was in his favor was that of experience a thing tied to reality itself and cared not for the opinions of others.

Years later with the war underway a new constitution was going to be required. More letters would be needed for its legacy. More wordsmiths to be allied in his plan would be needed. The chameleon would have to be ratified and put into a state of limbo. Once established it would put into motion the very scrutiny it would require. Suspicion would grow and it would take only one to discover it's secret. Once that event occurred then the cracks that were once invisible that defined the doors would begin to show light.

On December 15 1821, one of the men Benjamin Franklin had recruited to help him with his plan, the once much younger James Madison sat down at his own desk and he wrote the following in a letter to Thomas Ritchie.

> "In general it had appeared to me that it might be best to let the work be a posthumous one; or at least that its publication should be delayed till the Constitution should be well settled by practice, & till a **knowledge** of the controversial part of the proceedings of its framers could be turned to no improper account."

A few sentences later James Madison then scribed out the following.

> **"the legitimate meaning of the Instrument must be derived from the text itself;** or if a key is to be sought elsewhere, it must be not in the opinions or intentions of the Body which planned & proposed the Constitution"

James Madison has now provided instructions that would reveal the chameleon for what it really was. He could not be explicit though because this was against the rules of the grand experiment. Time was still required for the new constitution to cycle through presidents. It had to first be proven that the checks and balances against the tyrant would prove themselves effect. The check and balance of power against that of a kite would still have to wait to reveal itself as the instrument it was.

On June 12, 1823 Thomas Jefferson sat down at his own desk about 30 years after Bill of Rights had been ratified and started crafting his own letter to Justice William Johnson. He too was being aloof in his writing. He too was using symbolism and metaphors. He too was referring to a publication. He too seemed to referring to some sort of conspiracy at play. His letter was a bit more explicit though, in that it seemed to belay a context for the overall experiment. In that letter this passage was written, because in time it was hoped to be read for what it really was. It would be unlocked.

"History may distort truth, and will distort it for a time, by the superior efforts at justification of those who are conscious of needing it most. Nor will the opening scenes of our present government be seen in their true aspect, until the letters of the day, now held in private hoards, shall be broken up and laid open to public view. What a treasure will be found in General Washington's cabinet, when it shall pass into the hands of as candid a friend to truth as he was himself!

Jumping back in time a bit , on Dec 19 1801 history has provided us with a convenient tutorial that explains ciphers and keys. It is a letter between Robert Patterson, a member of Benjamin Franklin's American Philosophical Society, a society in which Thomas Jefferson himself was enrolled in the year 1780 and was also this tutorials recipient.

The art of secret writing, or, as it is usually termed, *writing in cypher*, has occasionally engaged the attention both of the statesman & philosopher for many ages; and yet I believe it will be acknowledged, by all who are acquainted with the present state of this art, that it is still far short of perfection. A *perfect* cypher, as it appears to me, should possess the following properties.—
1. It should be equally adapted to all languages.
2. It should be easily learned & retained in memory.
3. It should be written and read with facility & dispatch.
4. (Which is the most essential property) it should be absolutely inscrutable to all unacquainted with the particular key or secret for deciphering

Two hundred and Sixty Five years after Benjamin Franklin had composed his kite experiment a man from Vancouver Canada was watching the news on December 2, 2015. The San Bernardino event had just occurred being yet another gun related massacre 1300 miles to the south. He started to scrutinize the second amendment and almost like clockwork he became suspicious of this one line that seemed to be underlying source of this endless oppression. In studying it a crack appeared. Its' color vanished and it became black and white. There was a way to actually read this sentence from left to right like any other with clarity. It was self evident. The "prefatory" and "operative" clauses vanished. "the right of the people to keep and bear Arms" never existed. As he sat there and read it he was both astonished and horrified because all he was left looking at was the 2nd Amendment to the United States Constitution and it became quite apparent that it had been infringed for a very long time. He saw the purpose of its capital letters which were written mid sentence. He knew that this did not belong to him but to 320 million people. He had a choice to make and then perceived that there was none to make. He just got sucker punched by fate. While he didn't know it at the time, in about three weeks while trying to discern history, he was astonished to discover that history had discerned the future.

Almost two years later after much research the "public view" that Thomas Jefferson had alluded to now rests in your hands. Judge it for yourself and watch history become un-distorted.

1-Introducing the 2nd Amendment

A well regulated Militia, being necessary to the security of a free State,
the right of the people to keep and bear Arms,
shall not be infringed.

This is the 2nd amendment exactly as it was ratified with capitals, no hyphens, word for word on December 15, 1791. Sometimes you will see other versions of it where it is transcribed incorrectly. There is no capital "S", "A" or "M" in the incorrect transcriptions. They are important, as authored, because they are part of a riddle which only a select group of framers was aware of. It is quite common to see a hyphen inserted which of course re-authors the constitution it is found in "well-regulated". This was done to push someone else's interpretation of what this sentence says upon others which would of course rob them of an opportunity to interpret the sentence from source. It is not that others knew what this sentence actually was simply a tactic to enforce upon others what they wanted it to be. Early on in my research I have encountered many quotes that are attributed both to the 2nd amendment and to some framer. The quotes were completely contrived and never existed. Slapping the name "Thomas Jefferson" or "James Madison" on it does not make it true but just a fabrication of history which appears to nefarious intent to propagate a false narrative.

In researching the history of the 2nd amendment as it relates to being objectively read in a manner that has never been recognized before it as crafted as a literary sleight of hand. There are source documents that speak to this including why it was crafted in this fashion. On the next page you will find 10 progressive hints if you wish to work through what is essentially a riddle. This is just one sentence, however it was not James Madison who originally drafted this sentence but Benjamin Franklin. The veracity of that claim will be demonstrated with source documents later on. At the time that I read this sentence I had no reason to think that any other than James Madison was the original author.

There are many well crafted puzzles in this book which require solving but until you arrive at the path's destination they will be invisible to you. The destination will be your guide and no amount of intelligence or education will give you access to these puzzles in the absence of first knowing the 2nd amendment. This is how the secrets that will be shown to you here have remained unknown and for the most part unsuspected for over two centuries. It was not just for love of language that Thomas Jefferson wrote with such artistic flair. It was because he had too to the security of a free state.

. The following is a cipher and talks of the 2nd amendment, I have included it because it is relevant to what you are up against. While it may be true that the date itself conflicts with our current understanding of history, it adds veracity to the underlying dynamic of secrecy. Keep in mind that in just knowing that the 2nd amendment was kept a secret that has never been known till now you are now in the possession of a new context that no other scholar has had before. My advantage in seeing this letter for what it is was that I had already located over 400 ciphers in advance of it. I knew what a group of men were up too and how they were going about it. This letter was sourced from FranklinPapers.org

A Literary Sleight of Hand

From —— (unpublished) [1]

[ca. Dec. 1776]

In whatever business you may have to do with Foreigners, sign never any thing that is not in English let them take the Pains to express themselves. My reading has furnishd me with Cases where great Tricks have been playd by means of Foreigners giving a sense of their own to words not so taken by the others. There are Equivocal Expressions. One may take the gingerbread for the Baker.

In order to read these ciphers the information they contain must be mined out. Note that the letter has no one mentioned after "From". I believe that this pertains to "others" who were a small group of men who actually knew how to read the 2nd amendment. The "Foreigners" are those that were alien to its true meaning which can be read only in "English", or in other words, objectively arrived at. While subjectively read the interpreters of it will experience great "Pains" which relates to gun violence. The "Cases" refer to the Upper case letters used in the 2nd amendment and were put there to add to the veracity of reading the second amendment objectively. As I stated above the capitalization in letters in this sentence is important. Had I been using an incorrectly transcribed sentence then as you can see the reference of "Cases" would have escaped me. They can also be thought of as clues to emphasize the importance of

---

[1] www.franklinpapers.org

these particular words. "Tricks" relates to "A literary sleight of hand. A baker is like a wordsmith and knows the recipe to create the gingerbread, a thing most appealing to the consumers of the text. The gingerbread is of course the 3rd clause of the 2nd amendment which is argued most loudly by those that like it the most. Equivocal Expressions relates directly to necessity of choosing the correction definition for any given word in order to allow this sentence to behave like a sentence. When looking closer at the third line there is even more information that can be gleaned that points directly back to the 2nd amendment. Why? The 2nd amendment has often been referred to as a "natural right" and even a "god given right" which removes the Baker from the realm of the living. This is a false "interpretation" which Benjamin Franklin recognizes by using the word "take" The Baker does in fact exist and has in fact created a recipe for the success of the 2nd amendment being secreted into the Bill of Rights at the time of its ratification. Chef Boyardee he was not, though the shelf life of this sentence had to last at least 100 years.

Here are your hints which will help you to transform the 2nd Amendment into something you have never seen before. Prepare to engage minds with Dr. Benjamin Franklin

The Supreme Court while trying to make sense of this sentence, and in taking a bias to its 3rd clause as a starting point did not perceive a way for the word "regulated" to live harmoniously in the same sentence as their bias being "the right of the people to keep and bear Arms". In order to support the third clause they have argued, with the help of English professors that well regulated was viewed as being "well-regulated" at that time. There is however proof that the 18th century did use hyphens, the word "well" and the word "regulated". At this time both Benjamin Franklin and Thomas Jefferson were both very familiar with the correct usage of a hyphen. George Mason used the term "well regulated" in his drafting of the Virginia Declaration of Rights however this does not necessarily infer that he knew when to use hyphens. It is pretty much moot point in light of this research. At this time Noah Webster was drafting his dictionary to help the colonies with language and education was also being promoted by some. The colonies may have just been getting lax with their English and even today hyphens are often overlooked. That being said, while the intent of George Mason was to describe "well-regulated", it does not mean as well that this was the same intent as the well-educated James Madison. I have also discovered that George Mason was home schooled in law at his uncle, John Mercer's library at Marlborough Manor. The nuances of the English language may simply not have been in his toolkit. It also appears to me that for the first time in history "well regulated" was deemed "synonymous" with "well-regulated" but only because of this one sentence. The term "well-regulated" means well-ordered or highly trained when attributed to a Militia. The training however, especially in the public domain would be highly subjective if each man was to judge his own skills. In this sense it is almost meaningless simply because there is no clear standard to compare any level of well-ordered against. What one man may deem "well-regulated" may seem comically to the observations of another, especially one of military rank working under the government's command. In this sense the term itself is highly subjective further confusing the sentence if reality is to have any say in it.

Progressive Hints on how to read the 2nd Amendment Objectively

Hint 1: The 2nd amendment is a literary sleight of hand premise.

Hint 2: James Madison was well-educated. Make his sentence work from left to right.

Hint 3: Do not read well regulated as "well-regulated" (aka well-ordered)

Hint 4: Two words were used as a sleight of hand or misdirection. Find them.

Hint 5: It has been stated the front of the 2nd amendment cannot be connected to the latter half. See if you can find a way to do this."

Hint 6: The capital letters are there for emphasis. They are clues that can help you solve this riddle

Hint 7: Think objective and don't talk about what "it" was used for. Keep "it" simple.

Hint 8: Think scientist, Think algebra. Think psychology. Think "We the People" and not "Me the People".

Hint 9: Look up the word "Liberty" in Merriam-Webster dictionary. Think Butterflies and Bunny Rabbits.

Hint 10: Think of an equation with input and output. Apply the fourth clause to it.

Lead up to Reading the 2nd Amendment Objectively (Spoiler Alert!)

It is subjective to talk about what militias were used for, why they existed and how they were armed. While there may be truth in this history, no history is required to read the 2nd amendment objectively. Once you start talking about what Militias are for you are doomed to the wander in the realm of subjectivity. In the actual word "Militia" there are only two objects.

Militia = people & Arms. Agreed? Is this even debatable? This must be settled in your mind, in spite of the old dogma.

This is the encryption. The sales pitch is "the right of the people to keep and bear Arms". It fulfills a desire and appears to put control and power in the hands of the individual.

Benjamin Franklin was known to be a scientist so let's assume that he would have been very familiar with equations. He was a polymath and one thing he did most of his life was study human nature. This is consistent to the nature of the sales pitch. He predicted that people would like Arms. I have no doubt that he probably tested out the 2nd amendment on others in advance of its implementation.

The worm was "the right of the people to keep and bear Arms" and the hook was that it was a peoples right. It was with that that he went fishing for its ratification. People and Arms are variables, place holders to be populated with the people of the day, and the Arms of the day. We can read them as a Militia, or people and Arms. They are one and the same thing. The "trick" is to read it/them objectively and not to concern ourselves with what is further along in the sentence. Imagine trying to read a book with a similar approach. We have now connected the front of the sentence to the back. There is a new intelligence behind this one sentence that has never been witnessed before.

In 1790 there were about 3.25 million people with access to all types of Arms. Muskets, flintlocks, hatchets, swords and knives would all have fallen into this generic classification. Today, after 2 more centuries of man's relentless pursuit of new Arms technologies there is now a much larger and more lethal variety of these devices.

If we must create laws pertaining to the entire universe of people and arms then the latter must be a subset. Remember what James Madison had stated in his letter?

James Madison: "the legitimate meaning of the **Instrument** must be derived from the text itself" or if a key is to be sought elsewhere, it must be not in the opinions or intentions of the Body which planned & proposed the Constitution." (December 21, 1821)

The Merriam Webster Dictionary defines an instrument as being "a measuring device for determining the present value of quantity under observation".

30

The First Objective Reading of the 2nd Amendment

A well regulated Militia[2,]

(Create and or maintain laws as they pertain to the people and the Arms in the public domain aka Militia. "Well" means in real time with study and reporting of gun violence. Guns are put on trial immediately after an event in order to ensure the public safety. This is the REAL right of all the people in the United States of America)

being necessary to the security[3] of a free State[4],

Merriam Webster Liberty: "the quality or state of being free" is nested here.

(ensure that there is no anxiety in society due to the introduction of lethal arms. This is a filter and the nature of the measurement. It must be secure from the arms themselves)

the right of the people to keep and bear Arms,

This is the output of the 2nd amendment which is arrived at after moving through the first two clauses. The government must continuously filter out the dangerous arms. At this point the people who are allowed to use Arms and just what those Arms are have been resolved by the requirements of the 2nd clause through the creation and strict enforcement of regulations.

shall not be infringed.

This is an equation and every step must be followed in order. No clause can be ignored.

THE REAL RIGHT OF THE 2ND AMENDMENT IS THE 2ND CLAUSE.

> Think Butterflies and Bunny Rabbits and go with that feeling or state of mind. Think of the inalienable rights of Life and Liberty first before Pursuit of Happiness

---

[2] People and Arms from time period

[3] Merriam-Webster Security: "1 : the quality or state of being <u>secure</u>: as *a* : freedom from danger : *b* : freedom from fear or anxiety

[4] Merriam-Webster State: "a way of living or existing" also Liberty = 'state of being free";

This sentence is a reality based Arms Control Amendment and a check and balance against power now completely consistent with the premise of the constitution itself. It is a mandate on any government to keep the peace.

We now know what James Madison was referencing and have followed his instructions to the letter.

"the legitimate meaning of the **Instrument** must be derived from the text itself"

Objectively speaking, are people and Arms the constituent parts of a Militia? Yes or No?

Yes.

Is there a hyphen in the words 'well regulated"?

No there is not.

Does it matter that "shall not be infringed" is assigned to the entire sentence or just "the right of the people to keep and bear Arms"? It really doesn't make any difference because each clause in the sentence is completely contingent on the previous clause. This is how sentences are meant to be read from left to right in the English language. This sentence was not read in this manner before due to the confusion of two words, being "Militia" and "State", both which were capitalized. Perhaps we now know why these words were capitalized. History may currently report that this sentence had evolved from a few different renderings in 1788, but it is the renderings that evolved from the sentence for the benefit of nation in anticipation of historians. The secret had to be kept, and the future had to be "outwitted" for a time.

It does not make any difference because that part is ONLY arrived at after the first two related clauses have been completed in order, as written, and as read FIRST. The fourth clause only enforces things where the 3rd can only be read in the context of the all other clauses because this is where it lives.

The word "well" is similar to the word "shall" in that there is no wiggle room here. There can be no bias toward the wishes of industry or self defence because the 2nd amendment has zero to do with this. There is only one approach to gun violence and that is to put the gun class on trial. Diligence is required to report ongoing incidents that involve gun violence in society in order to secure the liberty of "We the People", where Liberty is defined as "state of freedom" straight from the Merriam-Webster dictionary. There is no wiggle room in this. This process must be ongoing and it is not up to the voters to decide upon because this is the constitution. If there are any Arms related incidents in the public domain such as accidents or massacres then the Arms must be put on trial. The people must be protected from themselves in spite of themselves. Think seat belt laws and butterflies and bunny rabbits. People may argue that times have changed since the 18th century which is of course a null starter. The 2nd amendment was created for the future to prove that harm to society will only increase proportionately to the introduction of both guns and newer gun technologies. If this was not the case then there would be no debates and there most certainly would not have been the current levels of gun violence related statistics. For over 200 years there has been a gradual introduction of guns to society. Owning a gun is a privilege and not an inalienable right regardless of what has been taught in school by any professor. No professor or teacher has ever been educated in this before. This does not mean that everyone doesn't have a right to self defence, and should not be interpreted as such. It is only the medium that is accessible to the public for that self defence that is the issue. Everyone may claim they have the inalienable right to mobility, where the medium to accomplish this are wide and varied from cars, to bicycles or even horse and buggy. This doesn't mean that everyone else in society has to put up your any horse manure you leave lying around. Seat belt laws, speed regulators, airbags etc have been put in place to protect the people in spite of themselves through government regulation. Of course people will still be allowed to hunt but no longer will opinion have a voice in this but only the truth of reality and the experience of society. While this may not seem like common sense to some peoples narratives of how their environment works, truth does not care about narratives, because truth just is.

The entire sentence is a right of all the people and the word "well" leaves no latitude for obstruction or conflation. The federal head is mandated to make common sense Arm control laws because the any introduction of lethal arms into the secured liberty of the public domain is unconstitutional. This is not an amendment written for gun owners but is one for all the people, including gun owners. I suspect the gun laws would probably come in line with those of France or Canada. If a particular class of gun is used to hunt humans, then they are put on trial immediately.

After discovering that the 2nd amendment was essentially the Holy Grail of Gun Control, I immediately attempted to figure out just how this had been misinterpreted. It was a rather astonishing thing to see such an important sentence transform right before my eyes. I'm not implying that the cipher was obvious, but was more curious as to how its encryption had been working so well, for so long. You can now make an educated guess regarding this. I have no doubt that those who were rather fond of this amendment will be arguing that it is returned to its subjective and dynamic interpretations. While the debate may rage on as to why people should have arms the 2nd amendment will no longer be playing a part in it. Fear is a very powerful motivator because the human imagination has no limits if one gives it free reign. The politics of fear are often used by corporations or tyrants to get their way because it is the easiest of sales pitches for the masses.. It is used by politicians regularly and all they have to do is show you an enemy imagined or otherwise..The misreading of the 2nd amendment was founded on fear and proves that if you let emotion rule reason then truth can easily be lost to time. This was America's first alternative fact.

> "Where is the Man to be found who wishes to remain indebted for the defence of his own person and property, to the exertions, the bravery, and the blood of others, without making one generous effort to repay the debt of honor and of gratitude?"

George Washington to John Hancock June 11, 1783.

The generous effort is to be brave like those that do not feel a need for guns. The blood is from gun violence and the generous effort is in choosing the real meaning of the 2nd amendment and to be part of a United States of America. Property is symbolic of greed, and person relates to fear which should never trump the life and liberty of all of society. "Others" is a reference to all of society as in "We the People".

We can now reconcile James Madison's letter with the 2nd amendment. There are two reasons for this. We now know why he was being aloof because he was trying to protect the secret encryption of the 2nd amendment. Remember that before the 2nd amendment was read objectively it was always read subjectively. This letter has never been tied directly to the 2nd amendment before. The 2nd amendment can now be viewed as an "instrument" because it is always measuring the state of the public environment as per the second clause. Arms must be immediately put on trial if the tranquility of the public domain is disturbed. If massacres are starting to trend due to arms in a society, then the offending arms must be removed from the equation.

Another proof is that this sentence can now be read from left to right as a sentence are normally both read and more importantly written. No assumptions should be made about tyrants because none are inferred, or at least not in the sense of the federal head. Put aside all other opinions and read it with your eyes and ONLY bias of a dictionary. You do not require the Supreme Court to tell you how to read English if it can be plainly read. It is they that have been fumbling with this and this reading has never before come up in any of their arguments. They just did not see it , as you do now.

We read it from left to right and as explained we make laws about Militias and then we find out what they must accomplish and with no backtracking required we then find out that some people get some arms but only in the context of regulations we already have made. Then we arrive at the end and it simple states that we must do, what we have just read, because this one sentence lives in the Bill or Rights and it must be obeyed because it has been ratified by the States and amended to the United States Constitution. This is how you read the 2nd amendment of the United States. Keep it simple and pretend the man that wrote it was both well educated and knew how to write a sentence. Our own biases can be our worst enemy and it is not a fault that can be cured, because we are all human, and we must struggle and cope with our own nature. If we let our bias be the very source of our ego then the power we receive from it has no foundation in reality. The power comes from the enlightenment of knowing that there will never be a cure for our own human nature. If we debate it within ourselves first before every single day of our lives then there will come a time when constitutions will become irrelevant.

It's very easy to see how the other delegates at the convention read what they wanted too and then passed on the lore of it to future generations. They literally jumped to the gun. The small group of men that knew how to read the 2nd amendment would have had mixed feelings about this and because a part of the "dangerous experiment" was not in motion. Part one had succeeded because "the tree of liberty" had just been established and this was the "from time..", in "The tree of Liberty must be refreshed from time to time with the blood of patriots and tyrants..." as written by Thomas Jefferson. The sand of time began to fall from a beach with its end beyond the horizon of their vision. I'm still brushing that same sand from my shoulders as I try to tidy up this book to present to you.

The Supreme Court Justices and Professors of English were not immune to this encryption either. How could they come back and say

"No, we do not understand the 2nd amendment so we will just have to put this on hold for a bit" Not discerning a people's right simply was not an option. There was logic in using the words "the right of the people to keep and bear Arms", but the problem was in order for this to make any sense language itself had to be manipulated."Well regulated had to be equated to "well-ordered". Regulations or

Laws and "shall not be infringed" were like oil and water. The only time in human history that "well regulated" has been seen as being synonymous with "well ordered" or "well-regulated" is in the context of the 2nd amendment. The United States Supreme court does not have jurisdiction in redefining the English language, only in reading it and attempting to discern what its authors were trying to say.

With that being said it should now be obvious that 'well-regulated' is not relevant to the 2nd Amendment in any way shape or form. To further substantiate this "vision based reasoning" I have located a letter that talks about this by the very man who wrote it. I have titled it the "Well-Regulated" Fallacy: James Madison to Edmund Pendleton (Jan 21, 1792). James Madison explains his reasoning for using "well regulated" in it. He explains that this similarity of English was used for the encryption because everyone was already discussing well-regulated Militias. It has been working its magic for over 225 years. If you choose to jump forward to this letter note that he "fabricates" this letter about 5 weeks after the Bill of Rights was ratified. I would recommend reading the section on Benjamin Franklins cipher school before jumping ahead. I say this because it is a summary of the collective observations and patterns I have thus far been able to resolve across 150 letters. These letters grew easier for me to both recognize and resolve over time as I observed the repeated techniques and styles and patterns in symbolism. They are in fact woven together across decades in some cases. When reading the 2nd amendment that one hyphen is a major crossroad and everyone has been making a right turn when they always should have been going left. It is a fact that that hyphen is not there, and was never there. I took that left and traversed that path and it took me to a brand new place that is the reason why this book even exists.

> **"The tree of liberty must be refreshed from time to time with the blood of patriots & tyrants. It is its natural manure"[5].**

The constitution "must be refreshed" because the 2nd amendment has finally been revealed to the general public for the first time in its history. It is exactly what it says it is. It now functions like any other sentence in the English language and can be read from left to right with perfect clarity. The days of its judicial or political "discernments" are over. The English of today verses the English of the 1790s are one and the same as far as the 2nd amendment is concerned.

---

[5] Thomas Jefferson to William Stephen Smith Nov 13 1787.

Thomas Jefferson Letter to John Taylor May 28, 1816

I can now explain the three capital letters that have always lived within the original transcription. The capital letters were put there for emphasis as a clue that the second amendment was more that what it appears to be. I have already explained the word "State", and it has nothing to do with the geography or colony/state, but rather is other definition as the inalienable right of Liberty under We the People as it pertains to a United States of America. Thomas Jefferson explains this in a privately hoarded letter[6].

> "What constitutes a State?
> Not high-raised battlements, or labor'd mound,
> Thick wall, or moated gate;
> Not cities proud, with spires and turrets crown'd;
> No: men, high minded men;
> Men, who their duties know;
> But know their rights; and knowing, dare maintain.
> These constitute a State.[7]"

The "M" in Militia and the "A" in "Arms" are capitalized. Can you figure out why?

From an objective stand point, "Militia" is the key encryption. It has been a literal launching point into the subjective interpretations of the 2nd amendment since day one. It is highlighted in conjunction with one of its constituent parts which are of course Arms. The words are tied together with capitals and are more intimately related than has ever been suspected before. It is the word 'people' though and the absence of a capital "p". Without the people there can be no Militia only an armoury. The reason the word "people" is not capitalized is because it is all about the Arms, not the people. Arms are the empowerment, where a person's motivation in a completely unregulated environment can never be harnessed through deterrence alone. Once a transgression has occurred, it's too late because death cannot be fixed.

It stresses the point that Arms are more than just a tool. It stresses the point that Arms are dangerous and lethal. It stresses the point that guns do in fact kill people. Deterrence can never stop human nature so why empower it? Put the Arms on trial. Some opinions matter more than others, because some are

---

[6] Thomas Jefferson To Justice William[6] Johnson June 12, 1823
[7] Thomas Jefferson to Colonel John Taylor May 28,1816.

derived from fear or greed. Some men are wiser than others and if you own an air conditioner on a hot day, be thankful for it. If you need insulin to stay alive why debate it? If the constitution has made America great why knock the wisdom of the men that wrote it?

2nd amendment discernments have been going on for at least 150 years. Since 2008 the judiciary has argued it is a right to self defence. The judiciary has also argued that guns are great for offence. It appears that the judiciary may be biased at times due to influences of society, industry or political needs as opposed to its actually meaning.

There were gun statutes in the State of Alabama which were in existence since 1839. In 1846 they were struck down as being unconstitutional due to the 2nd amendment. The case was State vers Reid 1846 and Chief Justice Colier who concluded the following in his closing arguments.

"And the acquisition of Texas may be considered the full fruits of **this great constitutional right.**"

This justice is arguing that guns are great for offence with respect to acquiring Texas. At the beginning of my research as I was flailing around looking for answers I went down what I later realised was a tangent. I did however discover a few interesting and possibly related threads in history. So correct me if I'm wrong but weren't the Mexican wars fought by the 'well-regulated' government forces? To acquire is to take and there is nothing defensive about taking. The point I'm making here is that for the past 170 years it appears that the 2nd amendment may have been exploited by the judiciary by forces related to something other than law. In the Alabama case, as you will see later, they seemed to make a rather good point of ensuring that the hyphen existed in the 2nd amendment as they miss-quoted it numerous times with a hyphen. Abraham Lincoln was 37 years old then and it was at this moment in time that he was destined to have a date with derringer 19 years later which was in part due to a hyphen that did not exist.

Cherry picking the constitution violates liberty and should not even be considered as an option. Case in point, "the president shall" <> "the next president shall".

This is a right for all the people. There is no such thing as a self regulating man once he is placed into a society. Men are self regulating until they are no longer self regulating. There usually isn't any warning to this because men are intelligent creatures, and as such, why would they be explicit in their motives that may be of a nefarious nature. The harm a man can inflict on his society is directly proportional to the very power that society allows him to have.

A man is like a time bomb in a sense. It does not mean that he will suddenly go off, even though he will get angry or frustrated throughout his life. He may become mentally ill or be mentally ill. The question is what magnitude of bomb should he be allowed to exist as? What transgression can society tolerate? Vote for deregulation and you roll the dice, because a man will always be running the show someplace. It is why there are checks and balances in government. The 2nd amendment has always been perceived as a deregulation amendment with the words "shall not be infringed" It is completely counter intuitive to the very spirit of the United States Constitution and the Declaration of Independence. The logic has been that the only man that can possess the title of tyrant is the president and the rest of society is immune from this ailment. This is why people don't trust government because in reality, nobody can be trusted. Those that are elected to government are of the people.

I will reiterate that if you add a hyphen, inferred or otherwise you are no longer quoting the 2nd amendment. You have changed it. When you change a sentence you have strayed from its author's intended meaning and have re-authored. This sentence is from the constitution and it doesn't care what your opinion is with respect to liberty. It only cares about liberty. The constitution does not allow modifications in the absence of a 2/3 house and senate vote. While it may be true that the justices are tasked with interpreting the constitution, it is not within their jurisdiction to actually change it. This started in the year 1846 and believe it or not, the gun industry may have had an influence in their bias but this shouldn't be confused with them actually knowing what the 2nd amendment actually meant. None the less, it was still done and once that was accomplished, then as far as the Arms industry was concerned, they had a goose that laid golden eggs. Their goose has just been cooked.

So is this enough to convince you? It both convinced me and it didn't'. A two hundred year old dogma is a difficult thing to erase from the mind. At the very least this is brand new. This is a discovery, a thing that now exists, where before it was never even suspected. In the balance of this book I will be explaining further narrative(s) that revolve around this sentence. Historical documents have been located which were also crafted in a similar manner as the 2nd amendment. These documents will be explaining what was going on behind the scenes of what you have just read. They are the very proof of it and I will be narrating those truths. I'm like a Marconi operator of sorts but deciphering messages which were purposefully sent through the ether of time.

Old School is in session and there are a number of narratives that must be explained. I will also be explaining just how it was that I even figured this out. At this time, I will say that it was both hoped for and anticipated that this secret would one day be found. I just happened to be the person to discover it in exactly the manner in which it was anticipated to be discovered. I was probably the first to suspect that the 2nd amendment could not be what it appeared to be. I can't of course know this for sure, but if this book has already reached the news by the time you are reading this, then that is pretty much the proof of it. I don't say this to afford myself any kudos in the matter, but only to acknowledge that I perceived this as being a discovery. I will also be revealing other actors who either knew or I suspect have known about this secret as well.

Profound Implications

There are 3 branches of government and anytime there is a disagreement the judiciary must discern the constitution. A big part of discerning the constitution is in trying to understand the intentions of the framers that wrote it. This is good thing but it infers a respect for the constitution. The bad thing is that the justices, while not always, tend to vote along party lines in their interpretation of the framers intentions. After some reflection on this it has occurred to me that one of the reasons why the Justices are sometimes so diametrically opposed is multifaceted. Further to biases, it's the nature of the highly symbolic letters that they have been reading which has allowed them much wiggle room in their discernments. What you will see in this book are many examples where history has been misinterpreted by scholars, including the justices and with good reason. Nothing has appeared to be explicit due to the highly symbolic language that was used by the framers, but this is about to change. This book is a primer on just how to go about reading those letters if truth is to be given any weight. Human nature will not change over the next 1000 years, but what will be exposed is the constitutions true interpretation on how to guide it's unrelenting service to "We the People. Bias will always exist because there is no actual cure for it because it is born from mans own imagination which in turn populates his own narrative. The proof of this is that the word "argument" exists in the dictionary and I don't believe that just this alone can be argued as an alternative fact. The very heartbeat of the constitution is about to be exposed for what it always was and yes this is my opinion, but a very well informed one as a result of the research that will be presented to you. Discern means interpreting or explaining confusing English into English. You have just seen that we neither discerned nor interpreted the 2nd amendment but only read it in plain English using only its text. The clarity of its very text cannot be denied even if it conflicts with all currently known history. History is after all established by historians and scholars all of which are in possession of their own wide ranging biases. There is no insult meant in saying this because nobody could have known what was actually going on in the absence of reading the 2nd amendment objectively.

If there is to be any conspiracy perceived here it is not from the eyes of James Madison. This wasn't a conspiracy in the sense that anyone actually knew what the 2nd amendment actually meant beyond the time of 1836. I believe the Supreme Court will recognize that they will have to be unanimous once presented with this research for two reasons. The first reason is that any one justice could be charged with Treason if they don't. The second reason is that if they cannot understand these findings then there is a good chance that the school they graduated from might charge them with defamation of character. A grade 6 student can now understand the second amendment. They will also come to understand the word myth. No court in the land will ever be able to convince the people that a "goat" is really "turkey". The wiggle room that was perceived to live within the 2nd amendment which appears to have allowed it to be exploited has now completely vanished.

The Supreme Court must be unanimous in their peer review of this book. I believe that congress and the executive have all sworn to uphold the constitution. In the past they may have perceived some wiggle room and taken advantage of it. The executive and legislative branches of government will have to fall in line with the Supreme Court's ruling if they decide to run the country under the rules of the United States Constitution... These are the exact words that Benjamin Franklin uses, and while he has his own opinion on the matter, he was also was VERY instrumental in writing the United States Constitution. He is a founder, and this is the cabal's intent. Ideology has no weight here because the wiggle room on the side of industry has just completely vanished. With respect to the gun laws, the shoe is now on the other foot and it's got "liberty for all" written all over it.

As a reference I've added the definition of treason from the United States constitution.

> "18 US code 2381 Treason
> Whoever, owing allegiance to the United States, levies war against them or adheres to their enemies, giving them aid and comfort within the United States or elsewhere, is guilty of treason and shall suffer death, or shall be imprisoned not less than five years and fined under this title but not less than $10,000; and shall be incapable of holding any office under the United States."

All Supreme Court precedents based on citing the 2nd amendment will have to be nullified and voided because they were never based on the 2nd amendment. They were based on a figment of the imagination in the absence of knowing it was a carefully crafted riddle in the first place. No political faction has any choice in this matter unless it is their greatest ambition to face a charge of high treason. They are outnumbered by "We the People" and those that respect both constitution and the flag.

Handguns banished. Large clips banished. Stand your ground laws banished. Open carry banished. Self defence arguments have zero purchase in the 2nd amendment because that viewpoint came from a Supreme Court ruling. The right to bear Arms never existed. The obvious transition to gun control regulations will not happen overnight. This is probably the understatement of the century, but the vigor in which they were introduced can easily be applied to vigor in their removal for those that wish to be known as patriot and law abiding under the flag. Courage is the absence of fear and that battle must be fought from within, because winning that battle will honour the wishes of the framers. Australia was able to do this. Will it be proven that they are a braver society than America? Is it to be supposed that the word "United" is nothing more than something yanked out of a Cracker-Jack-Box? United is forgiveness and understanding. United is the common cause for liberty, but only after it is understood for what it truly means. United was the dream of the framers, a dream that was never meant to be a nightmare. It was decided that the best teacher, regardless of opinion was the experience of reality. This transition is a divorce from fear and in the settlement fear would be awarded the pacification that only peace could provide.

It is unlikely that there would be any sudden moves on this because the safety of society is paramount. Guns have been gradually introduced into society and then normalized so they (the lethal ones) will be removed and then normalized just as they have been historically. In 1934 the National firearms act was created to remove automatic weapons from the public domain in light of the gangland shootings in the days of Al Capone. These are still just "guns", but when they were removed there was no push back from modern day organizations like the NRA. There will have to be a timeout of sorts because this revelation of the constitution is going to be quite a shock. There will be much discussion but the end goal cannot be debated because the because the 2nd amendment shall not be infringed in order to maintain the security of a free State. Remember that the 2nd amendment is measuring device and it was designed to only measure reality, in real time and forever put the Arms on trial as a check and balance to prevent the oppression of men. This will create jobs and new agencies will have to be formed and funded under the constitutionally mandate of "well regulated". It is the single most important amendment in the constitution if it was indeed written to protect the inalienable rights of the people because without life it is impossible for liberty or pursuit of happiness to be realized.

Japan has the courage to be in pretty much gun free environment. Australia reigned in their arms. If some believe that that did not work then you are welcome to your beliefs but your beliefs don't have any say in this. The only authority in this is a 2/3 house and senate vote through the democratic process. Democracy matters. America will know which arms are allowed in society when arms related violence becomes only an anomaly versus a way of life. Law abiding citizens should not be penalized by the fear of others to keep all of society armed to the teeth.

I have heard that over 90 percent of Americans desire common sense gun laws. The 2nd amendment now promises reality based gun laws. Only a good government with gun laws can take out bad guys with guns because the guns will be taken out. It would be much more difficult thing for a bad guy to enforce his will upon others throughout the span of his life without the utility of a gun he deems best suited for his plans. The guns that will be removed from society will also be removed from the very minds of men which are required to formulate their plan and can have no other effect than to reduce the plan in the first place.

Over 1,000,000 Americans have died due to gun violence which is more than all the American war casualties combined. There is a new war that must be fought now and it is not against guns but against fear. It's a rally for Liberty, forgiveness and common purpose. This can be fixed and it's just a choice. Australia did this to some extent. Japan exists on the same planet as the USA where guns exist and they have about 10 gun homicides a year. There is no question that guns are fun, and with fun, comes emotion. There is also no question that guns are very effective at taking life with great expediency. There are lots of ways in life to have fun but why have fun at expense of another's life? It may be fun to drive a car without speed limits but imagine what world would be like if speed limits did not exist? The carnage resulting from such a deregulation would be exponential. Are there still high speed car accidents? Of course there are, but far fewer than their might be. It may be true that guns are fun and there are ways to continue to enjoy them but in a regulated environment if need be. That environment cannot be in violation of the 2nd amendment as the constitution must have the final say in any matter with respect to guns. It is a right of the people. Fear is the enemy of liberty and a construct of the imagination which often cares nothing for reality. If there were NO hand guns in USA would the people feel less of a need to purchase one?. I've never in my life felt the need to purchase a handgun. Yes it's possible that I may get shot but it's also possible that I may get struck by a car or have a plane land on my head.

I have read that the domestic Arms Industry brings in about 43 billion dollars a year. On the flip side about 90 people are dying a day from gun violence. The answer has been thought to buy more guns because of this. The side effect of this is only camouflage of course because the police only have to pick out the shooter but it's not longer a scenario that his/her gun is the distinguishing factor. Is the expectation that the shooter, in all fairness, will raise his arm and say it was me? The shooter could even put on a face of wild eyed fear and go into a wild eyed open carry mode of the general public and simply walk away through the legions of open carriers who are even now looking at each other with suspicion.

The propaganda and marketing of gun sales is intense. It's my understanding that it costs America about 228 billion dollars a year for gun violence related costs. Not every shooting will result in a death and many are maimed for life. The collateral damage for a fear inspired contingency that has never happened is extensive. Relatively speaking terrorist related deaths in America since 911 amount If we extrapolate these numbers over the next 50 years in which your children will live you can be guaranteed that another 1,000,000 Americans will die and it will cost America 10 trillion dollars. For those that are fond of fiscal responsibility then this formula appears to be at least 5 times better.

Now if there was no gun violence by handgun, no suicides by handgun no police shooting citizens just because hand guns existed then they would still be allowed in society. The people would have to stop using these because they are convenient, a potential suicide victim would have to imagination another method and police would have to flat out stop worrying themselves about concealable weapons. That doesn't appear to be working, because before criminals are criminals, the mentally ill are the mentally ill and police are police we are all humans first. We all possess imaginations and intelligence. We will either factor in the best tools for the job or view certain tools as being of threat to us in our environment and act accordingly.

State laws and their constitutions must comply with this new revelation due to the Supremacy Clause of the United States Constitution.

The gun culture of the USA was built on the back of the 2nd amendment as it had been interpreted. I'm not saying this to put blame on anyone, because there is none warranted under these rather unusual circumstances. This is simply an issue of cause and effect. The 2nd amendment has also been commercialized because it can be tied directly to a product. The gun culture is not based on an American gene but inspired for some with the marketing campaign battle cries of "From these Cold Dead Hands" While Moses may have parted the Red Sea, it was for the liberty of a people to save them from oppression and not to lead them to it.

The 2nd amendment is the compass which will guide the people back to a secure State, which will include life and liberty. No longer will government hand be tied with respect to keeping the people safe from themselves. Accidents will always happen in a society but if carnage can be limited with a check balance against power then it is a choice for a civilized nation. Would America feel safer with 600 million guns, 1.2 billion guns or even more? What is the end game in this besides the bottom line on a balance sheet? The normalization of fear is a waste of energy and life, and without question the gun industry has been the worst form of terrorism to ever visit the homeland of the United States. It has been a very slow creep of anarchy.

This book is no conspiracy to take away the 2nd amendment but to align it with its only truth. The 2nd amendment is a sentence that was never truly read. The inalienable right of self defence will always exist. It's only the inalienable right of offence that will be completely removed from society over the course of time. There is nothing stopping any man from defending himself in any manner he sees fit within the confines of the law. It is the Arming of a man's free will which may cause it to visit the planning of nefarious acts. This is the worst kind of danger and there are over 1,000,000 graves to prove it. These are the true patriots that Thomas Jefferson has refers too because any man can be turned into a tyrant instantly if so empowered in the first place.

2-The Advent of Suspicion

A well regulated Militia, being necessary to the security of a free State, the right of the people to keep and bear Arms, shall not be infringed.

Approach to Discerning the Legitimate Meaning of the 2nd amendment.

"It is its natural manure[8]" goes to the heart of matter as to why I suspected the 2nd amendment was a complete fallacy. This quote is taken from a letter written by Thomas Jefferson to William Stephen Smith on Nov 13, 1787. Yes, it was my opinion that it made no sense in its construction and purported meaning derived from it. It was simply a riddle that people had been trying to solve for a very long time. It was simply my turn to give it a go. It was not arrogant on my part because I was doing this in the solitude of my own home, and if it helps any, I most certainly was not actually expecting to make a discovery, but I was armed with something no one else ever had before. The distinction between my approach and any other was that instead of taking one step back and looking at the 2nd amendment, I took about four steps back and made room in my mind for all its clauses and then pretended it was a sentence written by a man who knew how to construct them. Reading a sentence should be fluid as we read it from left to right. Why should we care about its ending in order to understand its beginning? I mean this is in the sense that if we read its end first, then its beginning becomes confused and must be re-authored to make it fit. Can you imagine attempting to read a book with sentences constructed in this manner?

The only reason it has taken over 200 years for 2nd amendment to be discovered is because of bias and suspicion. The day the Bill of Rights was ratified suspicion did not exist simply because it **was** ratified. There was a bias of distrust towards the government of monarchy is which is of course authority by another name. The war of independence had just been won but now the population was armed with the tools of war. And so it began because from this point forward the distrust of government prevailed and being taxed was forever perceived as a form of oppression. More on that point later. There was an appeal to the utility that arms could give a man, be it hunting, protection and most certainly to take down a tyrant. Within the general public this utility was of course

---

[8] The growth of suspicion is in this clause.

just proven. These were the same weapons the redcoats had used to enforce the will of the king on the population. And so there was a divergence after the war with respect to Arms because the Arms in hands of the redcoats were well regulated by government but the Arms in the hands of the people in America were not. All of the King Georges Army was well-regulated with ranks and mission but where the people of America were not. The moment however that people can be proven to be self-regulating would coincide that government itself is no longer required. Law abiding citizens are only law abiding citizens until they are no longer law abiding citizens. "Trust us, we will be good" doesn't fly in the context of a society where the bullets are simultaneously flying into the hearts of both life and liberty.

There are many influences that have kept suspicion at bay. As its ink dried over time the very lore of the 2nd amendment would take root in the American psyche. The fact that nothing had been discovered regarding it would further protect it from suspicion. Deferring to the wisdom of teachers, professors, historians the judiciary and ultimately the Supreme Court would steel it into a dogma. It is from their rulings and explanations that established a starting point in discerning the 2nd amendment. It was the premise that "yes the 2nd amendment was about a right to gun ownership" that the debate has been regarding only latitude that very gun ownership provides.

Perhaps there is a vanity at play here? If we look back in time we would like to think that the human race is making progress. We would like to think that we are at the pinnacle of its success. We would like to think that we are more "evolved" than our ancestors. We see all the wonderful inventions, advancements in medicine and perhaps there is a part of us that attributes this to raw intelligence, or at least the advancement of it? Perhaps we put off the 2nd amendment as being just a product of its period where that period would have no concept of its future. Something of a more primitive technology, and clearly not as advanced as what we produce today. It is one sentence though. This is not a thing made from parchment or carbon fibre, but rather of the mind with language. It was created with thought and is an invention of intelligence. This is only one sentence. What you will later see is that the 2nd amendment is also recorded in bronze and has had its very truth banked on by every man and woman in the United States.

The Arms industry has helped to generate the lore of the 2nd amendment by fabricating logic for its very need. There marketing have used slogans and propaganda with variations of the same arguments over and over again. This tactic was essential started with Samuel Colt and propelled him to become one of the richest men in America in his day. Two things were certain, money was flowing and people were dying. Nobody likes to admit that they are the victim of fear based politics but emotion has been a barrier to the suspicion. "Guns don't kill people, people kill people". "Guns are just tools" is a personal favourite of mine which I'd love to respond with "Water is just wet". That particular line is proof positive that some people's opinions matter more than other people's opinions. "We need more background checks" "We need better mental health care". These things are all based on only one premise which is of course that the people had a right to keep and bear Arms.

So these are all the reasons why suspicion has been kept at bay. It is a barrage of debate and noise coming from a singular point of view. Now I can't say for sure that others have not suspected what I did, but it was probably just a fleeting fancy which quickly succumbed to these influences.

Before I discovered that the 2nd amendment could be read objectively I didn't' have any reason to dispute its current dogma. As a Canadian I didn't grow up with the lore of the 2nd amendment other than hearing about it through US media. I don't fear guns in my society to such an extent that I feel I must own one. I think of getting shot as being akin to having an airplane landing on my head. Yes, I see from time to time there are anomalies of gun violence but nothing epidemic. I perceived that if there are more guns then there would be more gun violence. I have nothing against hunters in fact my own family hunts both moose and deer. I have friends that hunt as well. I shot a duck once when I was 14 and then ate it. I didn't use a 50 calibre gun to hunt this duck I had used a .22 of my grandfathers and since I wasn't yet a man I used the utility of my grandmother to pluck that duck and cook it for me. I viewed this as a symbiotic relationship because I was 14.

In later years I've been robbed while I slept in my condominium. I slept through it, lost a 2000 dollar digital camera, a 600 dollar watch and about 120 dollars in cash. I didn't own a gun at that time, but I did own a very large peppermill. Think bat. I love my pepper and I hate looking for my pepper mill. I am a man of logic. Is there any other kind? Now did I think to buy a gun after that? Nope, not even for an instant. Some may think me a fool but I wasn't concerned in the slightest. I made a point though of locking the door to my condominium. I moved on and bought a much better camera with the insurance money, took pictures of eagles as you can see on this books' cover. A book that I never imagined I would one day write to right a right. I'm sharing this experience just to show you the nature of fear in my environment and how I view it. I am trying to stand outside myself as I explain the influences that were in play that either helped me or didn't hinder me from discovering the 2nd amendment after 224 years. I viewed it as a bit of a curiosity myself only I was coming from the point of view of "Why me?" What helped me to discover this? I have not been living under a rock. I have seen the horror of the massacres in the news. I guess the first things that come to mind are presidential assassinations. The incidents that stood out the most are those which involved handguns. The only instances that I have ever seen a hand guns in Canada are those that are holstered by policeman. Ironically the first occurrence I recall was when I was in grade 6 and at the time was the Captain of the Safety Patrol or Crossing guards for my school.

There have been a few incidents of late where some mentally ill people have been shot by police officers. After hearing about these incidents I wondered if they were caused by Canadian police being trained by American Police who come from a completely different gun environment. In England many of the police don't even carry guns. Yes handguns are creeping across the border into my country and now so too are the methods to confront them whether they are there or not.

There has also been an escalation in the reasoning that more guns and peoples access to them will help to protect the people.

My background is in software development. I have designed and coded complex software from concept to implementation for about 20 years. I have reverse engineered software which basically means I had to figure out how the code was working in an existing program without any knowledge or a limited knowledge of its original code. I had to rewrite the code so that the software itself could be recreated to look and behave as close to the original software as possible. Code relates to the building blocks which must be arranged in such a way to achieve a desired result for the user. The user doesn't have to know how the code works but only how the program is to be used. There is virtually nothing subjective about this process in order to make everything fit together and actually run. Equations are used extensively in the code and are kept organized in things called subroutines. Think algebra and variables. At the moment I realized that Militia was just people and Arms an equation leaped out of the sentence. I was suddenly looking at input and output variables which I was already very familiar with. Now would an English professor have noticed the same thing if he rarely worked with equations? Would a law student be thinking of this or be thinking more about how this sentence could best serve his client? Would this pattern be something that would have been easily seen? Would judges have seen such a pattern? It's my opinion that they would not have noticed an equation quite so easily. Scientists would have noticed these things or mathematicians. How many scientists and mathematicians would have studied the 2nd amendment? Being more objectively minded they would probably have left it to the experts being the English majors, historians and law professors. I conjecture on this of course but it can't be denied that Benjamin Franklin was cross trained in all of these disciplines as he was a polymath. He would have known how to write a sentence like this including as we can see also incorporated human psychology in the process.

I bring this up because it goes to the very source of my suspicion. I viewed the United States Constitution as being akin to a well thought out piece of software. The input would be people and the output would be the American culture, but a culture protected from oppression in order to secure liberty. I had a rudimentary understanding of the constitution at this time but understood it had checks and balances so that power would be distributed evenly to prevent a tyrant from showing his face. With all that being said one of the outputs of the constitution was the gun culture that exists today. It was also very apparent that big money was very much tied into this culture because the 2nd amendment gave life to a massive market. It also appeared to take a lot of life too because if it affords people easy access to guns both in number and variety. It may be true that a very small percentage of people choose to take the lives of others or themselves for that matter but with a gun it is far easier and far less forgiving. Some I'm sure have resolved this to be the cost of liberty but in this I saw the cost as being far too high.

On Dec 2, 2015 the reporting of the San Bernardino massacre flashed across my television. I heard a law officer say the words I had heard spoken many times before, "We still don't know the motive yet". Everything always seems to be about the motive. While perhaps not 100 percent accurate it comes across that if the motive is found then people can move on. If the motive is found then the magic answer will be found. Motive of course comes from a man's imagination but that is the exact source of the guns. Some man had imagined the best gun for his plan, deemed it would work, and then proceeded. You also cannot get rid of a man's motive. Resolving a man's motive is after the fact. The problem was with the right to bear Arms. The 2nd amendment was restraining a fundamental governmental purpose of protecting its citizens with common sense gun laws. Isn't there something in the preamble of the constitution that promises to guard the people's welfare? The 2nd amendment was also fueling faction, fear based propaganda and the gun industry. If you have a closed system such as a fish tank full of guppies, and you introduce one law abiding shark to the tank what will happen? Then add another, and another and another and then wait. Say one law abiding shark goes to work, get's fired, comes home early, his car runs out of gas in the driveway, he then finds his best friend who he lent 2000 dollars too last week in bed with his wife while simultaneously drinking his last beer. It is my opinion, that this shark is going to have a motive, and it might have been better for his friend, his wife and the yet to be finished beer if this shark had been a guppy. It's a theory of course, but I think that it's worth a bit of pondering. Life is not easy, so why arm it?

I asked "How could men of intelligence have written such a thing as the 2nd amendment?" It is purported to have been written to ensure men had arms for the contingency of a tyrant. The 2nd amendment affords no protection to society from oppression on a day to day basis. Every other part of the constitution is very active where this one sentence appears to have been in limbo for over 200 years. At no time in the history of the United States were arms ever needed to be raised against the tyrant because the tyrant had yet to show his/her face. It did however keep the gun and lawn chair manufacturers busy. I went on the pretense that if there are more guns in a society then there would be more gun related deaths. Some of these deaths would of course be made up of homicides, suicides and accidental. So I looked up some statistics between the USA and another country where gun violence was less. Excuse any sarcasm here but I went on the pretense that both societies were composed of humans and each society had criminals. I've heard the argument that criminals would just get their hands on guns regardless. Seems to me though that there would be less criminals getting their hands on guns because there would be less guns. In 2008 the USA had about 12,000 gun homicides. You can add to this about about 584 accidental which probably included children. In 2008 Japan had 11 gun homicides for a population of 171 million people. It appeared that the criminals in Japan were unable to get their hands on guns even though they existed on the same planet in the same time space as the USA. There were other homicides in Japan of course where guns were not used, but even so, the homicide rate in the USA is still about 10x higher.

These were the same men that wrote the real checks and balances in the rest of the Constitution. The three branches of government, separation of powers and democracy were put into place to ensure there would never be a tyrant. These were preventive measures. So why would a 2nd amendment even be required? Surely these men must have known that there was no cure for death and in death, "Life, liberty and the Pursuit of Happiness" could be robbed by any random member of society in an instant. Further to this the 2nd amendment appeared to be awkward in its construction and yet was in a very important document. Is it to be supposed that it was constructed with a dram of whiskey playing the navigator?

I had a choice to make and that choice was very simple. James Madison was either an intelligent man or he was not. I decided to go on the premise that he was intelligent because he had written both the Constitution and the Bill of Rights. It is a rare thing for a man to turn off his intelligence in matters of great importance.

The checks and balances of the constitution have worked perfectly for 44 presidents. James Madison understood these checks and balances so why would he think the constitution required a contingency for just in case when it was never needed in the first place for the war of independence? Why would he cripple any future government to care for and protect its people in spite of the people's fears and concerns? There is a current argument that law abiding citizens should not be penalized by having their guns taken away. Why can't it also be argued then that a law abiding president should not be penalized by the checks balances to his power? Why can't it also be argued that law abiding nations shouldn't be penalized and allowed to have nuclear weapons? It is an undeniable fact that there is no cure for death and the quality of it is shared equally to those that experience it. A gun is of course empowering too, so why not a check and balance against that power? If for the sake of argument the 2nd amendment was solely in place to take down a tyrant why not use the current wisdom of deterrence? Why not take away all the checks and balances to power for a sitting law abiding president and if he oppresses the nation, then simply fine or jail him to set an example to future presidents. Isn't this the exact same logic which is currently used for criminals and is virtually impossible to prove? The problem is simply that by the time the oppression has occurred it's too late. The damage has been done. The avarice or motive of man is unpredictable other than it has been proven to exist in all recorded history, and probably pre-recorded history as well. A mind of avarice is not a liberal mind and cares nothing or very little beyond self where society is concerned. It is human nature for some to break the rules in the first place. Deterrence is nothing more than a "Wanted Dead or Alive" sign, and is more a demonstration of righteous power, than it is to the prudence of not allowing lethal Arms into society in the first place" A tyrant will never be known, until after the transgression has happened and anyone can become a tyrant through choice or accident.

Furthermore, how could the least liberal object in the constitution exist if the liberals of the day endorsed it? Why would James Madison construct this one sentence in such an awkward fashion? What manner of intelligence would construct something so confusing? At the end of the day though, and that day being Dec 15, 1791, the 2nd amendment was endorsed by all the delegates both the liberally minded and those that cared more for self than society.

It is a fact that the United States did not require a 2nd amendment to fight the war of independence. It just didn't exist at that time. A tyrant showed his face and the people rose up. They armed themselves because there was a purpose for those arms as tools of war and in war everyone was well-regulated through the ranks of men. The men became well-regulated with a singular purpose in mind that had nothing to do with a contingency. To put this in more modern terms "this was game on" and had zero to do with "what if".

The term well regulated jumped off the page when I started to scrutinize the 2nd amendment but I quickly found out that experts have said you can't read "well regulated" with today's English because it was different back in the 1790's. They said it must be read as 'well-regulated'. Both these terms appeared to be used back in the 1790s. James Madison being from Virginia and a politician would have been familiar with the "well-regulated" version because it was in the Virginia Declaration of Rights". Are we to suppose that James Madison, a man of intelligence make a booboo here? The Bill of Rights was in limbo for a few years until it was finally ratified. During this time why didn't James Madison, Benjamin Franklin or Thomas Jefferson catch this error? Being in the upper echelon of authors for their time it would be ludicrous to think that Benjamin Franklin or Thomas Jefferson would have missed this nuance? This is not the nature of reality. This is not the nature of truth. I was going to stick with the bias of believing James Madison was an intelligent and a well-educated man. It was my belief that these men knew exactly what "well regulated" meant and if they had wanted to use "well-regulated" then they would have used "well-regulated". There is no hyphen in "well regulated" and that is a point of fact and truth that cannot be debated. Yes, there has been an error made by well-educated men, but these men were not the authors of the 2nd Amendment. These were the men that were attempting to understand it, and in so doing, re-authored it without any authority from constitution in which it lives.

As I stated before I try to take my existing knowledge with a grain of salt. Too acknowledge that I might be wrong allows there to be a door to new knowledge and understanding. Why block in that door until it gets normalized and creates a foundation of ignorance? Why do that? I decided to apply "well-regulated" to the 2nd amendment. With a hyphen 'well-regulated' means "well ordered", "well trained" or even working perfectly as a clock might after a good cleaning. I decided to take that theory for a spin and see where it would take me. Is James Madison actually instructing the general population to have a 'well-regulated Militia' at all times? How is this supposed to be accomplished? Are the people expected to go to the range say every Sunday morning for 3 hours just to insure they are well-regulated? I decided that the "well-regulated" subjective interpretation was the stuff of fantasy and had no foundation in reality because James Madison, Benjamin Franklin or Thomas Jefferson would have thought this through. They may be dead now, but there was a time when these men were living, breathing and thinking men. There are none today that have any sort of intellectual advantage over them. Invention is inevitable over time and it's not because man is getting any more intelligent, but only because he is acquiring more and more things to think about, use and connect together.

I later encountered this in Federalist Paper #29 "Concerning the Militia" as written by Alexander Hamilton on January 10, 1788. This essay is from a wider collection which I will talk more about later. The key words here are "too oblige", which must be a direct reference to "A well regulated Militia" and its misinterpretation. When I say misinterpretation I pertain to "well-regulated'. Since these essays are commentary on the constitution, and in light of the fact that the 2nd amendment had been hidden in a riddle, it must be a context for this essay. Alexander Hamilton is making the same argument that I had in my observation of what would be required of society to maintain a well regulated militia.

> "The project of disciplining all the militia of the United States is as futile as it would be injurious, if it were capable of being carried into execution. A tolerable expertness in military movements is a business that requires time and practice. It is not a day, or even a week, that will suffice for the attainment of it. **To oblige** the great body of the yeomanry, and of the other classes of the citizens, to be under arms for the purpose of going through military exercises and evolutions, as often as might be necessary to acquire the degree of perfection which would entitle them to the character of a well-regulated militia, would be a real grievance to the people, and a serious public inconvenience and loss. It would form an annual deduction from the productive labor of the country, to an amount which, calculating upon the present numbers of the people, would

not fall far short of the whole expense of the civil establishments of all the States. To attempt a thing which would abridge the mass of labor and industry to so considerable an extent, would be unwise: and the **experiment**, if made, could not succeed, because it would not long be endured "

When reading the first two clauses as an instruction, in the context of its old meaning, James Madison appeared to be giving the people a **tip** that Militias could be used for security. If the right was to give people "hammers", would he then point out that hammers were good for building? Was he trying to ensure that the Militia was not to be used for quilting parties so he thought it best to add "to the security of a free state"? It's a nuance that I noticed and it seemed a bit too condescending. While many have argued that it is inferred that the militia required for the contingency of a tyrannical government it doesn't explicitly say that in this sentence does it? One must frolic through the pages of history to see if they can find something that may appear to stick to this sentence. Why would James Madison write a sentence that could not be understood clearly in such an important document as the Bill of Rights? I'm sure this question has probably already been asked but never taken to the next step. Yes, this man was from the past, but he is not so long dead that he could be classified as Neanderthal. He could read and write and I will say without any reservation that he could do both better than I. I know this because it has taken me six attempts just to create that last sentence.

There most certainly isn't any mention of "self defence" which was the recent interpretation In *District of Columbia v. Heller,* 554 U.S. 570 (2008). The Supreme Court claimed to have undertaken its first ever "in-depth examination of the 2nd amendment" Yes they dug deep and even had a professor of English explain the term "well regulated". As stated before I don't think well-regulated has ever been associated with "well regulated" except with respect to the 2nd amendment. It has been a false equivalency which enforced the very fallacy of the 2nd amendment and rendered it to a dogma. The professor was trying to make sense of the sentence but he really just re-authored it and changed language. The English professor sanctioned the term "well-regulated" to live within the 2nd amendment.

I have no doubt that the Supreme Court had gone to great depths but we now know they were digging in the wrong spot. The weight of their shovels came from the words, "the right of the people to keep and bear Arms", where the rest of the sentence was treated as clay, which was then molded into a pedestal on which the perceived right could then be showcased. It seemed to me that in that clay could be found the potters initials, "NRA", who then fired their creation and to be sold en masse. These are modern times though, and later I will be showing you a similar thread in history from over 150 years ago. There are other initials that predated the "NRA" by not even a decade with the exact same Modus Operandi. Ironically they are the initials of S.C. or the founder of today's Colt Manufacturing Company, Samuel Colt.

The sentence also seemed to be read from right to left. Is it to be assumed that this was the author's intent if he was skilled in the usage of the English language? Remember that the reader is not the author, and neither is the Supreme Court. It has been stated by some that the front is disjointed from the back. I discovered many explanations for this which all appeared to be highly subjective. Too put it bluntly this had to be a riddle of sorts based only on the premise that James Madison was intelligent. I assumed that he would have known how to construct a sentence because all of history has reported him as being well-educated. I figured that if I could somehow find a way to make the 2nd amendment behave like a like a regular sentence then maybe, just maybe it would reveal its true nature.

I did not like the word "Militia" because it seemed too period specific. I was ok with people and Arms because they appeared as generic terms independent of period. They could be anyone or anything, which was a good because they would be unshackled from either time or place. It was the observation that the second amendment had a front and a back and appeared to be separated was the biggest clue. This was perhaps the number one observation that led me straight to the truth. Every other discernment in history was always starting with "the right of the people to keep and bear Arms". My approach was simple to make this sentence, behave like a sentence. I would make it behave like a sentence first, and then I would read it. If James Madison was an intelligent man then he would have written a sentence and not something so cryptic. So how does one connect the front to the back? Then it clicked. People and Arms lived within the word Militia. The period specific word "Militia" vanished and suddenly I could connect the front of the 2nd amendment to the back. I then began to read it with this minor substitution for clarity.

"A well regulated people and Arms, being necessary to the security of a free State, the right of the people to keep and bear Arms, shall not be infringed".

I then saw the words people and Arms as being variables where the front ones were input and the back ones were output because if laws were applied to the first then the last must be a subset. It is because of my familiarity with equations as a software developer that I saw this pattern almost instantly. I was familiar with the logic of instructions to achieve an end result. The laws must be written to create a certain condition in society and no step can be skipped as stated by "shall not be infringed". This was the Holy Grail of gun control and it was based on the circumstance of any technology and the experience of that technology in any society independent of time.

The 2nd amendment is fine, it is timeless and it is perfect and there was no question in my mind that it had never been read like this before. I had just read English text. I didn't discern anything but it was very apparent why it had been misinterpreted before. People had read "the right of the People to keep and bear Arms" in a document called "The Bill of Rights" and simply assumed that this must be what the right is about. This is of course completely logical. The people had now been given the perceived gift of power and control, a thing that some would not want to give up. To further reinforce this is that "Laws" could not live in this sentence so "well regulated" had to be adapted to fit. A hyphen had to be added where none had existed before and only then could more sense be made from the sentence. The term at the end, "shall not be infringed" appeared to also solidify the logic of "the right of the people to keep and bear Arms". You can't debate a hyphen into this sentence though, because to do that would be to take over its authorship.

This was the discovery that compelled me to conduct the research.

The second amendment was just a check and balance against the power of arms measured directly from societies' negative experience of them. Just as the people were to be protected by the checks and balances of a tyrant having too much power so too were the people to be protected from the introduction of lethal weaponry. The people themselves could reach the level of tyrant if given too much power. The only thing however they needed to get elected was motive their own motive. The purpose of checks and balances are of course to prevent a society from being oppressed. If a tyrant is allowed to show his face, or lethal weaponry has caused carnage in a society then the constitution has failed in providing life and liberty to all of society. Society itself would no longer be punished or oppressed by lethal weaponry. This is nothing short of being the final legacy of the United States constitution.

There is more to this story than just the 2nd amendment. We have just learned something about the importance of regulation if the Liberty of society is to be truly guarded by the constitution. Life, Liberty and Pursuit of Happiness have now been given a new lease and meaning. They too are variables. They are supposed to be the output of the constitution providing that it is respected and adhered too. These inalienable rights have never before been truly understood and have resided in a place of limbo along with the 2nd amendment. Liberty, as shown was always buried within its second clause and not the third one.

The Start of the Research

On December 2, 2015 I discovered that the 2nd amendment in the United States Bill of Rights could be read objectively. If you are just learning of this and the findings of this book are not yet established as historical fact then I think you can agree that this is a profoundly important discovery. All other explanations of the 2nd amendment can now be grouped together, because this is the first time this sentence has actually been read like any other in the English language, from left to right and with clarity.

Pure and simple, this is the first Objective reading of the 2nd amendment.

The questions that came to my mind were.

> Why did James Madison hide the 2nd amendment?
> Who else knew about it?
> How was it lost to time?
> Why did I discover this?
> Why did no one else discover this?
> Now what do I do with this?
> How do I share this, and who would listen?

Some may wonder what would possess a man to attempt to research historical documents that would have obviously been sifted through by 1000's of scholars already. Well the profound importance of what I had discovered possessed me. I recognized that what I had read was a discovery. It is because of this observation alone that proved James Madison was particularly talented at hiding something in history. There also had to be an unknown narrative. Perhaps there was another avenue that was left to the future to discover what I had read? Was this lucky reasoning that I had used? I just couldn't' see James Madison simply encrypting the 2nd amendment as he did and letting it ride. It didn't make sense that he would write something so profoundly important and then just cross his fingers and hope for the best. I'm not saying he didn't cross his fingers only that he would have done far more than just cross his fingers.

I knew that without a narrative, what I had just read would be regarded as just "another interpretation". Some may even say this is just my "opinion", but the word opinion is perhaps one of the most meaningless words in the English language. It is often used as a defense mechanism by the monumentally judgemental in an attempt to bring down their target a few notches through an attempted flattening of intelligence and wisdom. That is just my opinion of course, for what is worth. Conspiracy theories, while intriguing, are generally not all that palatable to minds more grounded in reality. A truth had been hidden, but why? My experience in historical research was limited to genealogical searches on the internet. I will grace you later with that tiny piece of work but only as an analogy.

I was of course highly compelled to find answers to the questions above. While I had no expectations of actually finding the lost history, my expectations were equally low before I had read what I did. There was an interesting dynamic at play here, and just in knowing that it gave me hope of further discoveries. I had not option. This was not some "neat" thing I had just discovered..It was a profoundly important encryption that had been resting in limbo for a very long time. In essence this appeared to be completely on me now. I did not wake up that morning and think "This is the day I'm going to "debug" the United States Constitution.

I began to conduct internet searches and I was interested in the historical letters of James Madison. Any judicial interpretations ever conducted had no relevance in my searches because I knew that they could not have known what I had read. If the judiciary would have read what I have then it would have appeared in debate. I hypothesized that maybe Arms laws as mandated by the new 2nd amendment were not deemed necessary in a period when of Muskets and Flintlocks. This still did not explain away how its true meaning was lost and certainly didn't explain why it appeared to have been encrypted in the first place. I began to look for a period in the progression of Arms technology where guns would become so lethal that the 2nd amendment would have to kick in. Perhaps this was a bit naïve on my part, but it was something to work with at the time. That eventually took me to a six gun revolver known as the Walker-Colt of 1846. This particular thread of my research is more just a demonstration of my fumbling about but I have found some utility in it because it demonstrates the gun industry first wedding itself to the 2nd amendment.

I started searching for 2nd amendment quotes and looked at them closely. I was trying to resolve if they could be attributed to the 2nd amendment as I'd read it. The quotes led me to letters. I then realized that the letters were ciphers which required the next context of the 2nd amendment in order to understand them. Things started to pick up a bit after that.

The workflow that I developed was to discover the actors involved through the letters. I had to start with a completely clean slate, and on it I wrote just one name, James Madison. I couldn't rely on known history because what I was discovering was unknown history. Just because I encountered a new name, did not mean that this person knew about the 2nd Amendment, only that it was possible. I would then further interrogate the nature of this person. I was able to then go through their correspondences and see if I could find other ciphered letters and then other actors. There were of course many dead ends but also there were trails that lead me into new areas. Some letters were heavily ciphered, such as those written by Benjamin Franklin. I think with future study it will be acknowledged that his ciphers were perhaps the most advanced due the multiple layers he wove into them. From time to time though, he would throw out a very simple one, just to leave a trail of crumbs. Humour was interjected in these as well. It felt like he wanted to reward the efforts of a future historian. This in itself was probably an added strategy to help get one through the mental fatigue of actually deciphering these.

As I discovered actors I scanned through their letters because once associated with the cabal they would have written many ciphers. I just had to establish if one there letters was a cipher or just your basic letter. I'm pretty sure there were a few letters that I didn't recognize as being ciphers when I first came across them. It was only later, as I started to pick up different nuances, techniques or newly discovered themes in the ciphers that I was able to resolve a previously unresolved letter as being a cipher. I still have many letters that I've put aside that require more scrutiny. Once a new cipher was found I then added it to this book and deciphered it as best I could. I then learned more about the narrative and timeline in which these letters could be found. The narrative of history started to evolve, especially when some of the letter's dates began to predate the constitutional convention itself. The starting point in time in which these letters first appeared suddenly became a bit of a moving target. Currently I see it at as being at about the same time of the Declaration of Independence.

I think at this point in time, most will see that this is not just another book on the 2nd amendment. This book is different, because unlike every other book that explains the meaning of the 2nd amendment this one is purely objective. This book is not based on my opinions on the 2nd amendment, nor any preconception as to what I want it to mean. I didn't wake up one day and decide to write book on the 2nd amendment based on my education and historical knowledge. I woke up one day and was inspired to pay the 2nd amendment a visit after watching the San Bernardino massacre being reported on the news. I suspected something and in the lifetime of a cup of reheated coffee, I figured out how to read the 2nd amendment. I had not scrutinized the 2nd amendment so perhaps a fresh set of eyes helped. Call it beginners luck or lucky intelligence, it really doesn't matter. I guess the point I'm trying to make here is that I was not on a mission to take down the 2nd amendment, because I, like you would think it ludicrous. It is a fact that the 2nd amendment can be read objectively, but it is also a fact that it is going to be difficult to remove the resin of its dogma from your mind. Know only the source of that resin was painted with subjectivity. The subsequent discoveries to this are the letters and the "narrative of the letters".

These letters, while hidden in plain view have never actually been read before. This explains how I was able to learn the narratives I share with you now. I was empowered to read them because I had stumbled across the key which opened their secrets. The key was the 2nd amendment itself. It's not so much that the key was created for the secrets but rather that secrets were created for the key. I don't expect you to take my word for this though because I'm not trying to sell you anything here. I'm only showing you what I have discovered. Close your eyes and pick a page any page. Use the Table of contents if you wish. Jump to any letter to see this in action. Like a puzzle box I am going to first be showing you its cover so that you can get the bigger picture of what the individual pieces are going to build. I will be explaining to you the full narrative of history.

Now if you think these pieces are going to be explicit in their description they will not be. The first ciphered letter of Benjamin Franklins is undeniably a cipher. At first glance it appears to be an old bill of sorts that he is trying to resolve. Pretty nondescript, somewhat boring and a bit dry. I did however know what I was looking for and suddenly I saw that it was very descriptive. In a roundabout way two letters from the alphabet were described where one was small and one was capitalized that fit the 2nd amendment perfectly. Now both of these letters had to be a the front of a very specific word and the words had to be beside each other where one had to be in front of the other. I can't quite recall my math in series and probability calculations but it did appear to me that the odds that I had discovered 2nd amendment cipher was pretty good, which in turn made the odds of me being wrong in what the 2nd amendment actually meant being reduced to nil. It appeared to me that the 2nd amendments old meaning was being sentenced to capital punishment. In this particular cipher Benjamin

Franklin was also using variables to give its reader the ability to calculate the odds that this was in fact a 2nd amendment cipher. There was another method that he used to prove that this was a cipher which involved math and admitted that he was off by a bit. The bit that he was off by was 0.6 percent and when factoring this in the cipher could be related to nothing else. The utility in this can't be understated. The other ciphers I had encountered already were far more subjective, yet seemed to fit like a glove as well. This cipher was very objective in its construction to such a point that no longer could one disparage its true nature. It is the extrapolation from this that validated the other ciphers because there was no logic in reality that intelligent men would have written just one cipher and hoped for the best. If they wrote one, they wrote 1000. I had to keep this one cipher at the back of mind as I went in search of others. I had proven to myself that they exist and were being written. It was "simply" a matter of seeing if I could find others. I did manage to find more as you will see shortly. I'd pat myself on my back but my own ego is too busy shaking my hand.

So not only is it a cipher but a completely invisible one. Remember that no historian or scholar has even suspected that ciphers were written to explain the narratives behind the legitimate 2nd amendment so why would they be looking for them? Furthermore even if they did suspect it, in the absence of knowing what the 2nd amendment actually was they would have no context to work with. With no key we are only left with our imagination, and as we have seen, subjectivity has little value where the truth is concerned. For 14 months I have been hunting for the truth, and stumbling across these ciphers in my research. I even caught wind of one in listening to President Obama's farewell speech when he quoted George Washington's farewell speech. As president he revealed a cipher to me that was written to prove that at no time has any American ever had a right to keep and bear Arms.

Overview of the Book and "How to read it"

Why would I condescend to tell you how to read this book? This is after all just a history book is it not? Yes it is but it is a history book with a bit of a twist that will illustrate the ingenuity of the framers. In order to piece together the history that this volume reveals one of the biggest battles I found was that as I discovered "new" history I had to find a way to relinquish my knowledge of old history. It's a psychological thing of course but the dogma of over 200 years of history is not such an easy thing to replace.

Well yes it is but the history was hidden by design but while my explaining the narratives I have discovered will be more or less straight forward, the proof of how I went about discovering those narratives, being the attached historical documents will require a bit of thought. The key actors in this book hid what they were up to from the scholars of their day before, during and of course well after the Constitutional convention of 1788. While it may be unbelievable how such narratives have never been discovered before after almost two centuries, my first goal is to demonstrate that there is a very good reason why they have never been discovered before. How this book came to be requires understanding just how the letters were actually hidden and hidden by design. There is no letter that explicitly directs the reader's attention to the 2nd amendment but what you will find is that the secret of the 2nd amendment will give these letters new substance that has never existed before. While there are many letters in this book, as you approach each ask yourself just how anyone before could have attributed them to the 2nd amendment without knowing its true nature, including the fact that it was hidden in the first place. You, like I will eventually reach a point which may take 5 letters or perhaps 10 before it will settle in your mind just why it would have been impossible for anyone to guess the true meaning of the narratives that they reveal. Once that bias alone is removed, be it a perceived insult to your education or intelligence then it will be easier to work through them. Any feelings of being incredulous will quickly replaced with an Indiana Jones hat as you whip your brain into a place of intellectual wonder. The new narratives that are going to be exposed are from the new substance of the letters which was hidden for the very same reasons the 2nd amendment was in the first place.

Thomas Jefferson speaks of what surely must sound like a conspiracy theory because it is very book that he references in a letter he wrote about 190 years ago which he calls "the public view". He references the letters that I'm going to be presenting to you as those that were in privately hoarded. How could any scholar in the past 200 years have even known what he was actually talking about without first understanding what the 2nd amendment actually said? In just knowing that alone a person would have taken the time to do the research and find these letters as I have done. You see, by the time I found this letter, I already knew full well what the framers were up too, because I had already located about 100 ciphers. This was most certainly a good letter to find because either this is one hell of a coincidence or this narrative that I'm describing to you is real.

> "Nor will the opening scenes of our present government be seen in their true aspect, until the letters of the day, now held in private hoards, shall be broken up and laid open to public view"

In order to accomplish the task of breaking up the letters and laying them open I must explain how to read them. I must explain the narratives behind their very construction which shouldn't be confused with what they actually say. This is what "broken up" means. It means deciphered, I have already deciphered over 100 of these letters. I have included a section in this book which explains the nuances, techniques and patterns that were employed in the ciphering as a collection. These were collectively designed primarily by Benjamin Franklin with probably the helping input of others such as Thomas Jefferson. I have no doubt that it was a team effort and a highly regimented one at that. The letters were more than likely tested, before archived and placed into a limbo where they were required to begin their journey. This book is their final stop and ultimate destination, because it is the "public view"

The narratives that I have discovered are derived from real historical documents which span a 82 year period of time starting in 1752. These documents explicitly prove the legitimate meaning of the 2nd amendment and the narrative around it. When I say explicit they only become explicit once a key is used to unlock their secrets, otherwise they are invisible. With that being said, how was I able to locate these letters? I analysed letters to see if in fact they were ciphers first and if the evidence steered in that direction then I proceeded to decipher them. It's like discovering at the Easter Bunny was real, and in knowing that alone, I then knew that eggs were hidden, and out there somewhere for the cracking. Once I located one, I then stewed on it for awhile and attempted to separate the meat from the broth.

The transcribed documents in this book are all ciphers, unless otherwise stated. The ciphered letters span a period of time from 1774 to 1837. One of these historical documents is actually a tutorial on keys and ciphers. This document is a letter written between John Patterson and Thomas Jefferson which I have called "The Cipher Letter". It will help you to better understand the exact relationship between keys and ciphers. When I first located I thought, gee isn't that a coincidence, because I had been seeking out letters and deciphering them with a key. Then I thought, gee this is no coincidence, what a sport. The utility of such a letter would be extremely important because I could use its existence help reinforce that these letters are not a figment of my imagination. Thomas Jefferson is telling us that "they" were very familiar with writing ciphers and ciphers have explicit clarity when their crafted key is used to unlock their secrets. This is perhaps one of the biggest hurdles to get past in trying to resolve how a complete nobody as myself was able to uncover so much while simultaneously inferring that others had failed. Nobody failed because there was nothing to see in the first place. There still may yet be cheese on the moon, but why would anyone even look for without a reason? No, my cheese is still firmly lodged on its cracker, but it was heated a bit too much for my liking. You see, Benjamin Franklin had no choice in who would discover this any more than I did.

    This is essentially a puzzle book which in itself poses a bit of a dilemma. Not everybody is going to understand it and they are going to be the ones who will be exploited by those who want to classify these findings as both myth and conspiracy. A National understanding of this is going to be required because everyone must live under the constitution. The passion must be for the truth in these findings. Just remember, Thomas Jefferson has referred to the person that puts these findings as the Candid a friend to Truth which I think puts me into a rather unique position as one who is able to discern both the intent of the founders and the constitution that they wrote. He is explicitly saying that this information is correct.I will submit that there can be nuance to truth but I will not submit that the narratives that have been discovered are alternative facts. The alternative facts have been spelled out very clearly by Thomas Jefferson when he states "History may distort truth for a time" and it is this book that has uncovered the truth. Too be clear nobody has as of yet been educated in these discoveries and if they have, it is from the public view.

    I have located a rather large collection of the letters from Government digital archives which is the repository of the letters that Thomas Jefferson referenced. I selected and transcribed about 25 percent of them into this book that I thought would be most beneficial demonstrating what a small group of the key framers were up too. I will also be sharing with you their actual implementation of the ciphering. Beyond just the symbolisms I also noticed patterns and techniques that they had employed across eight decades. It is from these historical documents that a previously unknown truth of history and a new dynamic of it that has been found where each letter both explained the history and due to their very existence as ciphers was part of the dynamic that is described. Since the framers had no guarantee that any of their letters would survive the passage of time as well as knowing just how long that time would take before they were discovered last, let alone discovered for what they were to increase the likely of success they wrote many. The final legacy of constitution was far too important to leave to chance alone so they stacked the odds in its favor. Unlike a puzzle though, there had to be back up pieces and overlapping pieces because there could be no certainty short of clairvoyance in knowing that any one letter would survive the passage of time. While I may have resolved the name of the actors, I had no idea what part of a puzzle any one of their ciphered letters would reveal to me. I must admit it was always exciting to resolve that a letter was a cipher, because even though it was likely to overlap with what I may have already discovered, it was equally likely that here may be something new in it, be it the nature of its crafting or what it revealed. Perhaps it was a nuance in history, or a reinforcement of something that was previously just inferred. Case in point, the "Cipher Letter", was a bonus because it was reinforcing what I already knew. I was collecting evidence to share with you now, and it was written to be shared, and put into the public view.

While I could certainly choose to look for a letter under any given name, I did not have a choice as to the nature of its content. Who, had written the letter was to some extent of no pertinence other than to tell me that they were cipher authors. The counterpart in the letter, the receiver or the sender may in fact be part of the cipher itself. This will be demonstrated to you in a few different ways.

For the most part I have organized the letters by key founder though sometimes you may find the particular founder filed under another's name because there was no need for duplication. A quick scan of the table of contents may be required to locate a particular individual. There are some letters which were pertinent to a particular thread that I was following so I opted to keep the letter in the thread itself for enhanced readability. This can be seen in the United States Seal Section where you will find letters written by Benjamin Franklin, James Madison and Thomas Jefferson.

I have not deciphered every letter in its entirety simply because my primary purpose was to establish that what I was reading was in fact a cipher to begin with. Once I was able to do that, then I would glean the information it provided. If I saw something that was new, I would keep mining this new vein of information until I found no more. Sometimes I would encounter more of what I had already discovered and didn't bother to keep digging. It would also be difficult to take any one letter to its full conclusion without having any way of knowing if I had in fact gleaned all the information that was there. There was no answer book to these ciphers other than the one I was writing, so how could I possible know if I had actually succeeded in resolving everything.

Some of the references or symbolisms are period specific and I have no degree in history so I have no doubt that some references would have been invisible to me as well. My approach though was to look at nuance from about 3 steps back and see if I could observe a ripple in the pattern. If I perceived one, then I would research that area as best I could. The ripple you see, I perceived as a clue of sorts. I don't think they would have used a reference that would easily have been lost to time, because it would have defeated the entire point of the cipher itself. Some have come close though. An example of this would be "papers and effects". Jot that down on a sticky note, the context of it as I've just explained with this current page number and you will see what I mean later. My knowledge of history is somewhat limited and the research I present to you here is what I have had to learn along the way. I would discover a thread here, a thread there and follow it as best I could. I would then research battles, scenarios, biographies, timelines anything that seemed pertinent to what I was currently working on. So with all that being said, the ciphers I have discovered are indeed just that, they are ciphers. Outside of the importance of the research, I did find the research fun simply because I felt like I was hot on the trail of something important. So try one out if you wish. Treat a cipher as a crossword puzzle. There is still much left to be discovered and completed. Just go through the list of letters in the table of contents and know that they are ciphers. The cipher letter and perhaps one or two others are not ciphers, but were written and published to future in the sense that the entire letter was symbolic in its nature. Now if you decide to decipher these letters, they must decipher back to the key of course, which is the 2nd as it is read objectively. If you use any other context than the key itself then I would suspect the only key you are using is your own ideology. The cold hard truth is that the founders did not use your ideology to write the constitution or these letters. The ideology you may be using perhaps didn't even exist two centuries ago and only developed from a slowly evolving fallacy of the constitution itself as it was slowing and subtly manipulated over time due to faction. If your interpretation strays into "known" history just remember that there is a very good chance that it is the "distorted history" as per Thomas Jefferson. Very early in my research I was talking to a man in the comments section and I was explaining some of my research. He stated that the commerce clause of the constitution was in conflict with the 2nd amendment as being within the complete jurisdiction of the federal government. I made the point to him that that clause was not applicable to the 2nd amendment because the 2nd amendment existed before that particular interpretation of the commerce clause itself. The chronology of the constitution must be factored into any and all amendments or rulings that have been created on top of the 2nd amendment beyond its original inception into the Bill of Rights as ratified December 15, 1791. The new 2nd amendment as it has now been revealed must be prevailed simply because the "old" one never existed in reality. It was discerned and interpreted subjectively and under the duress of political and perhaps industrial motivations towards its utility as being integral to their business model.

The pathway for each person to find their way to the truths in this book will probably be different. I have shown you my path to get there and have attempted to be as transparent as possible. You will want to validate the narratives that I will be presenting to you simply because they are brand new, so there will be some back and forth, between the source documents. Unfortunately the documents are not explicit, however they are not to be subjectively interpreted either. You must first learn how to read the ciphers, and while each one may have a different author the pattern you will see is that they all had the same key to unlock their message. What has to settle at the back of your mind, as it did mine, if you are trying to resolve a letter as being a cipher, remember that the author knew he would be writing ciphered letters anytime after about 1780. The ciphers were never meant to be easily discovered and just because you are unable to solve it is in no way evidence that it is not a cipher. If you see symbolisms, nuance and if the letters construction seems "off", then usually this is evidence of cipher sign. With a bit of practice you will see the patterns across the ciphers and you will be able to recognize them with greater ease.

The path I have taken followed in the footsteps of others, because they left footprints that have never been seen before. They are the letters and the essays which move in a straight line. Any one footprint on its own can always be debated, but after seeing a few, stand back, and study them. Where are they going? Can you honestly say that others have seen these footprints collectively? The thing about the footprints, which will be most confusing, is that each one was made with a different shoe to foil suspicion. You will see that far more thought has gone into their letters than initially believed. Two separate stories had to be told with the same exact words. Picture a founder with a backpack full of shoes, and with each step he would then change one while standing on one leg, and then take another step. While the shoes themselves may appear to be different, the path they take will arrive at the same destination. The destination is this book, as the "public view", as written and laid out 180 years later.

The logic you must use is similar to the shoe analogy. Is it possible for someone to change shoes with each step? In order for that to make sense you must also understand the motivation for the steps in the first place. The footprints have all been created over a period of about 61 years and stopped either to inevitable slowing down in the twilight years, be it gradual, or sudden. Study the footprints and forget about the shoes that made them. Follow the path because it will lead you straight to the narrative and legitimate meaning of the 2nd amendment. I'm just a scout that happened to notice the path, its direction and resolved the owners of the shoes that made it.

A brand new dynamic in history has been exposed and with it be shown the cabal behind it. It consisted of Benjamin Franklin, George Washington, John Adams, Thomas Jefferson, John Jay, James Madison and Alexander Hamilton. Thomas Jefferson speaks of this very dynamic when he writes

> "Nor will the opening scenes of our present government be seen in their true aspect, until the letters of the day, now held in private hoards, shall be broken up and laid open to public view".

Well, I'm the guy that just happens to be breaking open these letters and I couldn't' help but notice that some historians have gotten it wrong. Without knowing the true nature of the 2nd amendment it would have been impossible for anyone to have gotten it write. We now have a group of men that you will soon see orchestrated the constitution. These men were very busy both during and outside of their political careers. These were not men interested in kissing babies just to get elected. These were not men that used the politics of fear for reasons of avarice. These were collectively liberally minded men that cared far more for the future of their nation than they did for their own time. Their letters collectively spanned a period of 61 years and they all wrote them up until either their deaths of loss of faculty. These are the types of men who would have been concerned about things like global warming. While it may be true that they were tasked with the business of the day, they were also demonstrating the constitution's usage for future generations. With that being said, there would also be utility in the illusion of faction so that future generations could observe how faction was controlled by the constitution itself. They were very wary of suspicion so breaking up the cabal into two factions would have the appealing side effect of reducing suspicion. Suspicion was the enemy of the nation for at least 100 years so it also had to be kept from future historians during this period. As James Madison put it earlier, it was to be a posthumous work.

You will see examples of this later, though I think scholars and historians will be more familiar with them.

Why encrypt the 2nd Amendment?

The 2nd amendment was crafted to be read subjectively in the 18th century so that the "other" delegates would ratify it into the constitution. It was literally ahead of its time. Being over two hundred years later we now know that this plan has now worked. The repercussions of this plan could never be truly known but only anticipated. These men were very leery of this plan but felt they were trapped into it. George Washington "clearly" states this now when he says

> "It is a **dangerous experiment**[9]—once slacken the reins and the power is lost—and it is questionable with me whether the advocates[10] of the measure[11] foresee all the **consequences**[12] of it.",

in his letter to James Madison. I repeat this again to drive the point home that this was not some cruel joke on their part. Mans inability to control his fear as well as industries desire to exploit it for profit are the forces that have been the primary causes of this environment. Once the 2nd was instilled, it would be protected because it would now take 2/3 house and senate vote to change it. It would also enjoy the supremacy clause of the constitution so that it would ensure that the right of the people to common sense gun laws would be enjoyed across the nation.

Benjamin Franklin realised that if he was going to architect the perfect constitution then he would have only one shot at it. With no disrespect to congress itself, but rather an observation on human nature how long would it take Congress to create a constitution from scratch? It would have to be the perfect constitution and its output would be liberty for all. You will be finding out shortly that the 2nd amendment was crafted well before the constitution

---

[9] Experiments have a hypothesis and variables Sociological experiment The hypothesis is multifaceted and relate to hiding the 2nd through human nature, and then suspicion growing over time until it is cracked.

[10] Benjamin Franklin, George Washington, John Adams, Thomas Jefferson, James Madison, Alexander Hamilton and John Jay

[11] What James Madison calls an instrument is George Washington's measure, which are just symbolisms for the 2nd amendment.

[12] For the most part the consequences have culminated in today's current level of gun violence, but also include a booming gun industry which has utilized a false interpretation of the 2nd Amendment to promote its sales and then attribute it to patriotism.

convention in its current form. From this point forward I will be referencing Benjamin Franklin as its original author as well as the mastermind behind what was going on. It is only my hypothesis that Benjamin Franklin was the original author of the 2nd amendment. It is a fact that it existed well before the constitution convention though.

He and a small group of his allies put into motion what will soon be known as the longest running sociological experiment in human history. I say this only in the context that it was conducted in complete secrecy. Just the fact that you are now reading this book is actually part of that very experiment. This book was meant for you simply because you are the current society it was meant to inform. You are part of the society that had to be born out through generations against the variable of time.

Not a Deception

It's important to clarify that these founders did not deceive the other delegates with respect to the ratification of the Bill of Rights. As one can imagine the pushback on the discoveries which will be revealed in this book is going to be in a word, ferocious. That pushback will no longer have the constitution arguing in its favor. The cabal thought this through and did so in a rather clever way. Benjamin Franklin had to ensure that the encryption was based solely on the bias of the reader. Lawyers use a less sophisticated method today which is generally referred to as fine print. Just hide it in plain sight but make it difficult to read. The delegates simply did not read the contract. They read what they wanted to read AND they did not question it. They didn't require any clarification, because they took from the 2nd amendment what they wanted and they were perfectly good with that. Some may have seen it as being a bit awkwardly constructed, but not so much that it was worth questioning. They also didn't suspect that something was going on.

The reader gives up trying to make sense of the sentence by reading it from left to right. They read the third clause which is the misdirection and use that as a starting point. The reader has now become the author and is doomed to exist in a realm of subjective interpretation. Some may argue that the sentence clearly states what it is, however it is quite clear that the 3rd clause of a sentence be it in the second amendment or any other does not a sentence make. The misdirection is solely in the mind of the reader in trying to extrapolate perhaps what they wish for the most. It is the reader that must own this, because it is the reader that has turned this into an alternative fact. One must admit that the crafting of this sentence is ingenious. It is and always was a literary magic trick which used a slight of mind to its advantage. I could not see any truth in it and I kept looking, until I did. I don't believe in magic and I saw the misdirection and refused to go down that road.

In part, writing this book involved research with modern day people who had the 2nd amendment now well established in their minds after almost 10 generations of its existence. Due to the importance of the discovery it appeared to me that it would be best to establish that I was presenting the information in the best way possible, and in turn, recruit people to help share this discovery upon the books release. I had to convince people as to the veracity of my claims. This took a bit of practice because such a claim is of course unbelievable especially from a complete stranger. What ultimately surprised me is that those who knew me best were far less likely to believe the discovery. The opportunity for benefit of the doubt had run its course decades earlier which I believe was due in part to their narratives on who I was or what I was capable of. A stranger however, would hear me out, without debate or argument, and seemed far more able to understand that while related, an objects existence is not dependant on the nature of its discoverer. So even though I had it in my hands, as if I had picked it up off the ground, those closest to me were not even interested in seeing it, but seemed to take far more comfort in disputing it. They will have to learn about this by others, even though they were witnessing the very genesis of the discovery. Outside of it being irritating because I was attempting to get support in this matter, it was an interesting psychological phenomenon. I was simply trying to share with them as I do with you now on how to actually read the 2nd amendment. My success rate with strangers, for the most part has been about 90 percent. In the process of sharing this with a young health care professional, at the moment she understood how to read the 2nd amendment, when it clicked she said. Her mind was not cluttered with what she wanted the sentence to say but only with your knowledge of language. She said.

"Ok. That's so simple. In front of my nose simple"

She pretty much summed up what I felt too. It was unbelievable that it had been hidden for so long and yet just as equally believable that it in fact was. Benjamin Franklin believed in both scenarios, but he had English on his side with respect to the truthful one. The key to the 2nd was to suspect it had to be a riddle. It also had to be read from left to right because that is how sentences are meant to be read. The end of a sentence should not be a clue as to the nature of its beginning because an educated person would not construct a sentence like that. By reading the 2nd amendment from right to left would be to take ownership and transform it into an alternative fact.

The point here is that when the Bill of Rights was actually ratified the only people that were doing the deceiving were the delegates who chose to read the 2nd amendment subjectively. They chose to read the sentence from right to left. They chose to read "well regulated" as "well-regulated". They chose to assume that the James Madison was incapable of writing a well constructed sentence. They chose what seemed logical to them and what suited their own preconceived narratives. They did not however choose right they chose something that was nothing more than a figment of their own imaginations. They fell for this literary magic trick, because it wasn't perceived to be a trick in the first place.

3-New History
Early Beginnings

It's my belief that Benjamin Franklin had a far greater influence on the design of the United States Constitution than may have ever before been suspected. It appears that there was more encoded in it than just second amendment. These truths were ahead of their time because much of society and their currently established institutions would have felt threatened in the 18th century. Perhaps they are still ahead of their time today or just in time. It can't be denied that the people are now in a position where they have experienced the constitution for over two centuries. It's really just all about human nature, experience and observation. Things get normalized in a society and it takes time to change it. Perhaps in 200 years some people may look back to the 1980s and think that everyone thought guns were ok. They may paint an entire society with only one brush. They will assign a collective blame to society, and then in turn conflate it to ever single individual within it. So if you the reader, have a calendar on your fridge with the year 2217 imprinted on its top then know at least one person did not believe that "a right of the people to keep and bear Arms" never existed. Hopefully you did not sign out this book from the fiction section of the old book repository. Just because something is normalized in a society does not mean that others cannot see the folly in it. It is the others, the few that stand up and effect change because they possess the weapon of truth, which sometimes is only arrived at through the harsh lessons of experience.

With that being said let's look at what was normalized back in the 18th century. The Salem Witch trials finished up just 13 years prior to Benjamin Franklins birth in 1706. The Spanish Inquisition was still winding down ending in 1824. Slavery was normalized in the southern states. Racism was normalized and the American Indians also felt its wrath but were lucky enough to escape slavery simply because their skin was lighter. Men were discerning the nature of other men based on skin color alone. Dueling was on the way out as organizations were created to ban it. Are we to paint all men deplorable in this society because these things were normalized? I would answer no to this. I also don't paint all men as being less intelligent then men are today which allowed me to make the discovery that I did.

Pennsylvania started the process of abolishing slavery in 1780. Benjamin Franklin had slaves but does this make him a cruel man? Does this make him a hypocrite? Benjamin Franklin was a slave to his time and he could not just flip a switch to turn off slavery. Nobody was singularly in a position to do that for the simple reason that they were outnumbered. Even then, people were probably using the ridiculous phrase of alternative fact based knowledge, "It's just your opinion". Would it be better to not "own" a slave and let one fall into the hands of one born to the reasoning of bigotry? The slave would only be playing the part of the slave for appearances sake, because a free black man was not yet the norm. I'm talking more about a symbiotic relationship. Surely there must have been some slave owners that were kinder than others. These are the seeds of a transition that had not yet reached abolition. Thomas Jefferson I believe is rumoured to have fathered a child from one of his slaves. Is he also to be thought of as being a hypocrite? While being somewhat knew to historical research it is my belief that men back in the 18th century were not immune to their own obligations to the female gender. Love also existed. One of my own ancestors was 23 years of age when he took at 13 year old as his wife in 1819 Livonia Township. She had her 8th child in 1831 who was an ancestor of mine and I'm actually in a 5 generation picture with his daughter, who was born 5 years after Abraham Lincoln was assassinated with a very concealable handgun known as derringer. My point here is that the founders were not so far removed as they may appear to be. I was in the arms of a woman who may have talked to her grand-father-in-law at when she was of 20. About 46 years before this time he would have been 40 years of age in the year of James Madison's passing. I was in the arms of someone, who could have talked to someone who could have easily talked to Thomas Jefferson, John Adams, James Madison and John Jay at the age of 20 if given the proximity. The point here is that seven generations is not so long ago and if there is in anyway a bias that our raw thinking power in terms of intelligence has increased from then too now, I would doubt that. The question is as humans can we learn from our experience over time? This book proves yes, but also proves that normalization is nothing more than a crowning achievement of propaganda. How we think is an individual choice.

Now that we know that the constitutional convention was orchestrated in advance can we traverse back in time to see if we can resolve its initial ideas? Which one of the cabal was best educated in understanding of human nature?

So let's jump back to 1730. At this time Benjamin Franklin was 24 years of age. I pick this date because this is when he became a freemason. I have located evidence that his membership in this organization has had a direct influence on the drafting of the United States Constitution. Freemasons are known to be a very secretive society and with good reason. The churches views were normalized and their own power and influence on society well established.

The freemasons practiced virtuous thought in the absence of the bible. Their teachings, like those of the bible, recognized mans free will and with that came choice. This does not necessarily mean they were atheists but rather a society that practiced altruist thinking. If one exercises the body through riding a bike, why not also exercise through hiking as well if a goal of fitness is to be achieved? They kept their exercises of the mind pure and uncluttered by scripter which at times could have many subjective interpretations. The church would prefer that this kind of thinking and teaching be exclusively in their domain. Church donations would also diminish. Imagine if there as a sudden migration to the society of freemasons because there was more enlightenment found there. There has always been faction due to religion. Wars have been fought. The freemasons were not a religion though. They didn't want to take over the world with their thinking, but rather to affect it positively with their deeds. It was essentially a society that practiced mind yoga, and it appears to have been the very source of separation of church and state and the very code of the United States Constitution.

Benjamin Franklin went on to become the Grand Master Freemason to Pennsylvania. In learning about ourselves, we also learn about others and human nature. This is the kind of knowledge that would be invaluable to a constitution that was to be governed by the people for people. We learn about our own human nature and the choices we make and recognize that it is never a thing that can ultimately be cured to the benefit of all. Now at this point in time it should be observed that Benjamin Franklin was the first man to be exposed to these ideas because the others in the cabal have not even been born yet. While it would still be 55 years before the constitution was written it would be only 40 years until things started.

There is a ciphered letter written by Thomas Jefferson which I've transcribed where he talks about exercising with a gun. The exercise is in thought only and the thinking is in the benefit of giving up your own guns for the sake of society. I note it at this point because it ties into a little story that was authored by Benjamin Franklin. It was originally written in French and I had it translated. It also ties into the church and the idea of separation of state.

A Tale " Passy, printed by Benjamin Franklin, in 1779?
(TRANSLATED from french)

[December, 1778?]

Tale.

There were an officer, a good man, called Montresor, who was very ill. His pastor thinking he was going to die, advised him to make his peace with God, to be received in Heaven. I have not much to Worry About, said Montresor; as I had, the last night, a vision which I entirely made reassures. What vision did you have? said the good priest. I was, he said, at the Gate of Paradise, with a Crowd of People who wished to enter. St. Pierre and demanded everyone to what religion he was. One answer, I'm a Roman Catholic. Well, faid St. Pierre; Enter, and take your place there among the Catholics. Another said he was of the Anglican Church. Well, said St. Pierre, enter, and you place there among Anglicans. Another said it was Quaker. Enter, said St. Pierre, and take place among the Quakers. Finally he asked me what religion I was? Alas! I said, unfortunately the poor Jacques Montresor has none. It's a shame, says the Saint, 'I know not where to stand; but still enter, you will begin where you can.

The message here is not only do you not require religion to be good in life but there is no "winner" religion in the eyes of god. The moral of this story are the morals of man. The observed utility of religion is to help people find the path to goodness. You can't buy your way into heaven by making bigger donations to the church. It seems to me the atheist that made it through the gates was pretty fiscally responsible. When you pay at the church it is to pay the priests, cover the heat, the hydro and that sort of thing. These donations shouldn't necessarily be viewed as an advance on heaven rent. You will also notice that in heaven there are no nations, but only people who just happened to be of a religious persuasion. Nation is simply the invention of man. Religion is often exploited and can cause wars for the advancement of a nations boundaries or the complete demise of a society.

In this one little story I think it should be pretty clear why church and state should be separated. I don't believe Benjamin Franklin's views were to downplay any religion. He is simply pointing out that religion isn't the sole harbinger of a moral existence. It's not too likely that these particular founding fathers would have endorsed the current wording of the pledge of allegiance. Separation of church and state should be pretty cut and dry if one understands the constitution. It is my belief to include it is to re-author it and why do that if religion has been shown to be the very source of faction among men for the past

1000 years? Anyone can have values. There are Christian values, Jewish values, Muslim values and Atheist values.

One year after becoming a freemason it appears that Benjamin began to put into practice the teachings of his "brain yoga for good". He began to publish a yearly book under the pseudonym of Richard Saunders. The book was titled "Poor Richards" Almanac which was started to enrich societies own viewpoints on their own human nature. It was an attempt to undo the harmful effects of some things that are normalized. These writings contain many one liners to get people to think about life. There was humour in them. There was a gentle prodding of the intellect to keep things compelling without too much insult to ego. Apparently these books sold so well that he could have retired from their proceeds at the age of 53 sales of these books writing was highly successful and he produced these for the next 26 years. In order to solve one cipher I had to look into these almanacs as per his direction. It was in perusing them that I couldn't help but notice their construction appeared to be somewhat similar to that of the 2nd amendment. They also had something else in common with the 2nd amendment, which was only crafted after 26 years of practicing these. They both "toyed" with human psychology.

> Three may keep a secret, if two of them are dead."[13]
>
> "We may give Advice, but we cannot give Conduct."[14]
>
> "The World is full of fools and faint hearts; and yet every one has courage enough to bear the misfortunes, and wisdom enough to manage the Affairs of his neighbor."[15]
>
> "The first Degree of Folly, is to conceit one's self wise; the second to profess it; the third to despise Counsel."[16]
>
> "If you would not be forgotten, as soon as you are dead and rotten, either write things worth reading, or do things worth writing."[17]

---

[13] This genius was pondering methods for keeping a secret effectively

[14] This genius saw the folly in debate and devised a way to get around it in order to achieve his goal. He knew experience was the best teacher because a clash of egos is not involved.

[15] The very foundation of the 2nd amendment to think of your neighbours first and they shall think of you.

[16] It would be tough to Trump this one.

[17] I couldn't help but noticing 4 clauses. The pattern demonstrates a writing style that he was familiar with. The idea of writing something very important fits

The last edition of the Albamacs was printed in 1758 when Benjamin Franklin was about 52.
In the year 1743 Benjamin Franklin founded the American Philosophical Society, which I will discuss some more later.
  In the year 1752 Benjamin Franklin discovered electricity

   In the year 1754, at the age of 45, Benjamin Franklin had proposed the "Albany Plan which scholars have said inspired many of the Articles of Confederation.

   Benjamin Franklin drew this cartoon for his newspaper the Pennsylvania Gazette on May 9 1754. The population of Philadelphia at this point in time was about 18,000. I'm showing this to you to further illustrate his viewpoints on human nature. The snake represents the influences that human nature will always have on each of us in a society which is temptation. He has borrowed this snake from the Garden of Eden. I don't believe that he explains this which is in itself rather telling. I don't believe that he would have explained in Poor Richards diary either that what he had written was written to help improve your thinking and stop taking yourself so seriously. He cannot explain it because he is being prudent, because in his day, it might add insult in exposing the very hypocrisy of

---

like a glove with the 2nd amendment which we now know has been living in the Bill of Rights waiting for its the future to arrive.

religion. There were many church going god fearing slave owners who felt they had every right to own humans. All they needed to tell one from the next was skin pigment.

Black and grey squirels are both of the same species and surely they must also use contrast to differentiate things in the each other. To the best of my knowledge it doesn't appear that they have ever enslaved their darker side of the species? Perhaps they did not do this because they didn't have the intelligence to see the utility in it? Perhaps they didn't do this because they possessed more compassion than humans? Perhaps they preferred to collect their own nuts as opposed to having others do it for them? It's interesting though how man chooses to use his own intelligence to prop himself up against others. While one species spends most of its time collecting nuts, the other seems to spend most of its time proving that they are totally nuts. It's no wonder that squirrels never saw the need to create a constitution, unless of course it's a pile of nuts.

Benjamin Franklin knew that to expose his snake symbolism for what it truly was would just stir up controversy. He was a scientist and a philosopher and he liked to segregate the building blocks of nature to best see how they fit together. He did not invent this snake but only transposed it, because its symbolism was based very much in reality. He could always use plausible deniability if he ever felt pressed to discuss it from someone he might perceive as an enemy to his cause. Benjamin Franklin had been observing human nature and this is simply a representation of man being constantly tempted to make choices that are only of benefit to self over society. The full weight of temptation is a survival of the fittest attitude in its rawest form. It is a rationalized entitlement to the collective accomplishments and resource of a society. Man requires man just to survive both among each other and for the very protection of the planet. Those that fall to this temptation have done nothing more than simply substituting God for Progress. Everything these people do is in the name of progress. It is an excuse and a sales pitch. So the snake is in pieces where each piece represents a colony so now we have teams of people who are more interested for the progress of their states than perhaps others. Yes, Benjamin Franklin knew that the temptation men encountered throughout their lives could never be stopped, but he began to device a way to protect society from itself with checks and balances. Perhaps the harm could be kept to a minimum. While children can be taught to share by adults and parents, who is to teach the adults who have now escaped the bonds of authority?

It is only when the snake is joined can progress truly be made. It is the Supremacy Clause of the United States Constitution that stitches the snake together and gives it life, mobility, direction and strength. Its direction is steered by the degree of temptation which exists in the any of it parts, be it the individual, a state, or its head. True Liberty is a respect for the whole and the complete absence of oppression which requires that temptation be regulated from its relentless ambitions. Not only regulated, but well regulated. The head is chosen only through the vote of the parts so vote wisely if you wish for the nation to take all the parts to a place of liberty. It would be best that the head be an adult though, or at least one who sees liberty as the promise of the constitution.

He likes the symbolism because he has a scientific mind and it fits with his almanac as well. His almanac after all is trying to get us to look at ourselves and our views and put some thought into how we work. He is using the almanac as a tool to help society in that it may influence peoples choices, just has his own thinking has influenced his own. It's my belief that it is only in his understanding of man, was he able to create the perfect constitution for mans direction. Man must be protected from himself if the whole is to survive. There will be many in society that will not like the revelation of the second amendment but the snake must remain whole. Replace fear with courage and think of the whole of society. Get behind the constitution and the constitution will get behind you.

Benjamin Franklin has used both the concept of choice and the snake with respect the United States Seal. There is a very special hoarded letter which has a snake embedded within it. It is a "letter" carved in bronze which I will show to you later. The snake is there to solve a puzzle and that puzzle is the encryption within the United States Seal. The snake here is not broken, but rather whole. The symbolism is at a point in time where the snake has now joined to form a United States of America. This snake, the same snake, was rendered almost 3 decades after Benjamin Franklin's original doodle. The snake though is biting its tail as if it is causing itself harm even as it is completed. It is a clue that with more scrutiny the solution to this problem is nearby. There are two other objects nearby but don't worry, I won't pass the buck on this one even though it is about to change.

This is getting interesting, isn't it?

It proves much more as well. You will also see that the eye of providence is related to this snake. I think it has been interpreted as being a "free pass" by god as we live in the human invention of nation. The only free pass that god has ever promised was freewill. Free will is choice which I suppose could be debated, but it is the debating of it , that is the very proof of it.

Three years after his "Join or Die" drawing appeared in his newspaper Benjamin Franklin published his last Almanac. At this point in time he had also risen to the title of grandmaster freemason for Pennsylvania. He was practicing to make society a better place for all, doing what he could and where he could. This man was collecting the very code of human nature and his observance of how it can exploit others. Two decades from the time he doodled this cartoon takes us to the year 1774. I believe this is when the 2nd amendment as it has been revealed first existed. Choice is of course integral to the constitution. He knew no one would choose its real meaning and have it ratified into the constitution because of both fear and mans lust for power. I have located two letters that appear to be the beginning of the ciphers. The plan for the ciphered letters started and would continue for 61 years. The ciphers are all directly related to the 2nd amendment either in its current form or the idea of it as it has been revealed to you.

The Gadsen Flag

The Gadsen Flag was designed by General Christopher Gadsen in 1775 during the American Revolution. It was flown by the Continental Marines. Is it possible that General Gadsen borrowed the snake from Benjamin Franklin's symbolism but only in so far that the snake represented the now joined United States? It appears that General Gadsen uses the symbolism of this snake to represent its striking power if angered in conjunction with the its symbolism of it representing the United States. There's nothing wrong with this of course because this is exactly what has happened with the 2nd amendment. Perhaps Benjamin Franklin observed this tendency of human nature through this flag alone to extract power where one sees it? This may be the case but chronology is very close. The symbolism of the snake, as taken from the garden of Eden escaped General Gadsen's scrutiny of its true purpose. It is simply a representation of human nature, a thing that can never be cured. It is a symbolism of choosing to sin or not to sin or in other words to be in gods favor or not.

Here is another rendition of Benjamin Franklin's original cartoon from 1754. As you can see it was printed just prior the General Gadsen designing his flag which appears to infer that it is the same serpent.

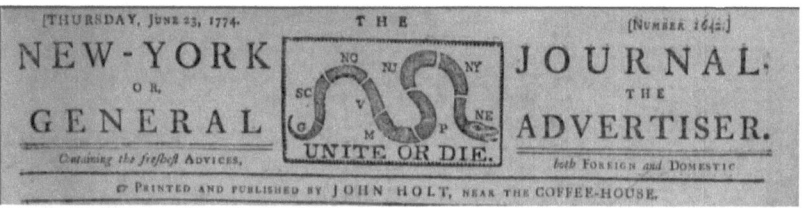

The period in time for this research started around the Dec 15,1791 but ended much further back in time as I tried to frame in the full period for these ciphers. Before I could even do this though I had first discover the narratives of the ciphered letters which could be resolved back to the 2nd amendment. The ciphers provided me with new actors involved and began to further expand out the time period in which they were being created. In order for a plan to exist its precursor is of course the idea of it and an idea usually starts with just one man. One major part of this hidden narrative is the fact that it was hidden, and the reasons behind why it was hidden. Just because someone is hiding something from the public view though doesn't necessarily mean it is related to the 2nd amendment narrative but it does demonstrate that someone is practicing the art of hiding information to begin with.

The next letter has been attributed to be that of Benjamin Franklins. When Benjamin Franklin was 16 years of age he apprenticed as a printer under his older brother. I guess he had a hankering to write, working with letters and all, but was denied this opportunity by his brother. So at the age of 16 he devised a way to get around this. He created the pen name "Silence Dogwood" and proceeded to write about 15 contrived letters to the paper.

Ironically after 300 years I now find myself in a bit of a similar situation. I am an unproven author or historian though I have been compelled to write in light of the discovery. This is a bit of a crash course for me and I'm only driven by the substance of a profoundly important discovery. I had notified over 30 different people and organizations in December of 2015 in attempts to share how to read the 2nd amendment objectively. It soon became apparent that the only way to share this was through a book to give context to the research. There was no value perceived in what I had to say do to the unbelievable nature of the discovery. It seems that strangers have been far more likely to listen to me than family and friends. I must say that it's a refreshing thing to be able to write without the noise of debate when all you are trying to do is share a discovery of profound importance. Oh, and just to clarify I did not mean to infer in any way that I now being at least three times the age of Benjamin Franklin at 16 have anywhere near his skill as a writer. I only write to write a right, where he wrote to right his rote.

Sorry for jumping around there a bit but this does tie into the Gadsen flag. I needed to illustrate Benjamin Franklin's habit of using pen names because this next letter was written by someone who did not wish to be named. The Pennsylvania journal   To put things into perspective I'd like to point out that the population of Philadelphia in 1790 was about 28,000 people. I have located this letter from Franklinpapers.org which discusses the Gadsen flag and was written anonymously by "An American Guesser". So in reading this letter I'm trying to see if there is anything in it that may reference the Garden of Eden, temptation symbolism. What is interesting is that there is no mention of this symbolism with respect to the serpent?

Pennsylvania Journal on December 27, 1775

I observed on one of the drums belonging to the marines now raising, there was painted a Rattle-Snake, with this modest motto under it, "Don't tread on me." As I know it is the custom to have some device on the arms of every country, I supposed this may have been intended for the arms of America; and as I have nothing to do with public affairs, and as my time is perfectly my own, in order to divert an idle hour, I sat down to guess what could have been intended by this uncommon device – I took care, however, to consult on this occasion a person who is acquainted with heraldry, from whom I learned, that it is a rule among the learned of that science "That the worthy properties of the animal, in the crest-born, shall be considered," and, "That the base ones cannot have been intended;" he likewise informed me that the ancients considered the serpent as an emblem of wisdom, and in a certain attitude of endless duration – both which circumstances I suppose may have been had in view. Having gained this intelligence, and recollecting that countries are sometimes represented by animals peculiar to them, it occurred to me that the Rattle-Snake is found in no other quarter of the world besides America, and may therefore have been chosen, on that account, to represent her.

But then "the worldly properties"[18] of a Snake I judged would be hard to point out. This rather raised than suppressed my curiosity, and having frequently seen the Rattle-Snake, I ran over in my mind every property by which she was distinguished, not only from other animals, but from those of the same genus or class of animals, endeavoring to fix some meaning to each, not wholly inconsistent with common sense.

I recollected that her eye excelled in brightness, that of any other animal, and that she has no eye-lids[19]. She may therefore be esteemed an emblem of vigilance. She never begins an attack, nor, when once engaged, ever surrenders: She is therefore an emblem of magnanimity and true courage[20]. As if anxious to prevent all pretensions of quarreling with her, the weapons with which nature has furnished her, she conceals in the roof of her mouth[21], so that, to those who are unacquainted with her, she appears to be a most defenceless animal; and even when those weapons are shown and extended for her defense, they appear weak and contemptible; but

---

[18]. Worldly properties are the physical snake. The non worldly properties are related to temptation in the context of the Garden of Eden snake. Selfish versus altruist choice.

[19] Eye of providence never blinks and is always watching.

[20] Takes courage to give up Arms for all of society.

[21] Two teeth are concealed just as People and Arms are concealed in the word Militia.

their wounds however small, are decisive and fatal[22]. Conscious of this, she never wounds 'till she has generously given notice[23], even to her enemy, and cautioned him against the danger of treading on her.

Was I wrong, Sir, in thinking this **a strong picture of the temper and conduct of America**? The poison of her teeth is the necessary means of digesting her food, and at the same time is certain destruction to her enemies[24]. This may be understood to intimate that those things which are destructive to our enemies, may be to us not only harmless, but absolutely necessary to our existence[25]. I confess I was wholly at a loss what to make of the rattles, 'till I went back and counted them and found them just thirteen[26], exactly the number of the Colonies united in America; and I recollected too that this was the only part of the Snake which increased in numbers. Perhaps it might be only fancy, but, I conceited the painter had shown a half formed additional rattle, which, I suppose, may have been intended to represent the province of Canada[27].

'Tis curious and amazing to observe how distinct and independent of each other the rattles of this animal are, and yet how firmly they are united together, so as never to be separated but by breaking them to pieces. One of those rattles singly, is incapable of producing sound, but the ringing of thirteen together[28], is sufficient to alarm the boldest man living.[29]

---

[22] This is an interesting take on a snakes weapons. This is now a cipher but related to the 2nd amendment because the author is now attempting to make his reader think about weapons being dangerous in a society if you really think about it.

[23] Noticing that Militia = people and Arms. The serpent is like a line.

[24] Arms laws are poison to those that would want to use guns as weapons against fellow Americans.

[25] It's necessary to have a well-regulated Army to defend then nation.

[26] Colonies of course or the current size of America.

[27] He knew a Canadian would one day figure this out. (Hey, what can I say, I'm biased, but I didn't say that to rattle you).

[28] 13 Colonies

[29] The strength of the people comes in numbers but United if war is necessary.

The Rattle-Snake is solitary, and associates with her kind only when it is necessary for their preservation[30]. In winter, the warmth of a number together will preserve their lives, while singly, they would probably perish. The power of fascination attributed to her, by a generous construction, may be understood to mean, that those who consider the liberty and blessings which America affords, and once come over to her, never afterwards leave her, but spend their lives with her. She strongly resembles America in this, that she is beautiful in youth and her beauty increaseth with her age[31], "her tongue also is blue and forked as the lightning[32], and her abode is among impenetrable rocks."

– An American Guesser

"American Guesser" is a curious pen name for this essay.8 Benjamin Franklin would most certainly have noticed this flag had he seen it. It would probably have been irresistible for him to make some commentary on it to get the people to think. This is one of his ciphers. American guesser is anyone who is scrutinizing the language of the 2nd amendment. I believe his take on the snake was from the Garden of Eden. He says "worldy" when referencing the snake as a symbolism. The not so worldly would be its symbolism of temptation in the Garden of Eden. He is making a distinction from two completely different viewpoints. Not so much for the reader though or at least not in the 18th century. He has already started writing ciphers for the future at this point in time. It is related to the 2nd amendment. He talks of things hidden in the snake as weapons. The 2nd amendment has a weapon in which is to defend liberty for all.

---

[30] "the right of the people to keep and bear Arms" is the singular phrase in the 2nd amendment that can only be preserved by those that want power most. It can only be preserved by those that are fearful and for want of power even though it would harm their very society.

[31] The true second will begin to reveal itself.

[32] Forked tongue may come from the story of Milton's Paradise lost and is a reference to the snake from Adam and Eve. The temptation to want to protect oneself in spite of the general welfare of society exists in the old interpretation of the 2nd amendment. This being the final sentence in this article appears to drive the point home. The symbolism of the snake has been reattributed to the 2nd amendment otherwise why would the concluding sentence about the gadsen flag observation be directed to this completely unrelated place?

In the mid 18th century Virginia, Pennsylvania and New York had Militia laws which allowed people to form Militias. This was observed by Benjamin Franklin and he makes note of it in a letter to an acquaintance, Peter Collinson, on Dec 19, 1756. This is just an excerpt from that letter but it is fully transcribed further along.

"let me acquaint you, that if every Man in the Country was a Veteran Soldier, our sparse Manner of Settling on so extended a Frontier, would still subject us to Mischiefs from the Depredations of such an Enemy as the Indians are, who do every thing by Surprize, and lurk about for Opportunities of attacking single Houses, and small weak Neighbourhoods. But all that Pensilvania has suffer'd is charg'd to the Account of our not having a good Militia Law; tho' Virginia that has such a Law has suffer'd *more;* and New York, with such a Law and all the King's and New England Forces to assist her, has not been free from Scalping, besides losing Oswego. One might as justly charge to your Want of a good Militia Law in England, the Highway Robberies and Housebreakings which sometimes fill your Newspapers; and even blame your regular Forces for not preventing them. We have now near 1500 Men on our Frontier, and yet People are sometimes scalp'd between Fort and Fort, and very near the Forts themselves. And if these Soldiers who have Arms continually in their Hands cannot always secure themselves, why should the Mischiefs done to the Farmers occasion a Doubt of the Truth of what I told you of our People's learning military Discipline under our Militia Law. For the Militia cannot be always under Arms, the Land must be till'd and Business follow'd; every House and Plantation cannot be guarded, and on the Frontier they are Miles distant, and so can afford little Aid to one another"

He states that Virginia has suffered more because of having this law which in the context of the overal dynamic that this research has discovered must mean that the guns in society produced more harm to it among its citizenry then its ability to save the public from an epidemic of hair loss. This is simply another source of fear for most men including myself if you will permit me a moment to brush over my own. .In any event it was almost impossible to prevent from being scalped in the first place do the cunning of the Indians. Indians are of course men and men with motive and a plan are generally get their way with it. Criminals in society are also humans and if they really wanted to shoot you, you would probably never know it. So why arm them in the first place on mass? It appears that Benjamin Franklin was against these laws because he saw them doing more damage than good in the mid 18th century.

An 18th century Massacre.

At the age of 58 Benjamin Franklin would have read about a rather horrible massacre in the papers. I was looking for evidence of gun violence in the 18th century and found this.

"The Narrative of the Late Massacres Jan 30 1764" at FranklinPapers.org.

> "On Wednesday, the 14th of December, 1763, Fifty-seven Men, from some of our Frontier Townships, who had projected the Destruction of this little Common-wealth, came, all well-mounted, and armed with Firelocks, Hangers and Hatchets, having travelled through the Country in the Night, to Conestogoe Manor. There they surrounded the small Village of Indian Huts, and just at Break of Day broke into them all at once. Only three Men, two Women, and a young Boy, were found at home, the rest being out among the neighbouring White People, some to sell the Baskets, Brooms and Bowls they manufactured, and others on other Occasions. These poor defenceless Creatures were immediately fired upon, stabbed and hatcheted to Death!"
>
> "When I mention the Baseness of the Murderers, in the Use they made of Arms, I cannot, I ought not to forget, the very different Behaviour of *brave Men* and *true Soldiers,* of which this melancholy Occasion has afforded us fresh Instances. The Royal Highlanders have, in the Course of this War, suffered as much as any other Corps, and have frequently had their Ranks thinn'd by an Indian Enemy; yet they did not for this retain a brutal undistinguishing Resentment against *all* Indians, Friends as well as Foes."
>
> "The only Crime of these poor Wretches seems to have been, that they had a reddish brown Skin, and black Hair; and some People of that Sort, it seems, had murdered some of our Relations. If it be right to kill Men for such a Reason, then, should any Man, with a freckled Face and red Hair, kill a Wife or Child of mine, it would be right for me to revenge it, by killing all the freckled red-haired Men, Women and Children, I could afterwards any where meet with."

This group of men came back to finish the job a few weeks later and killed the balance of Indians that had been in the town that day to sell their wares. A total of 20 Indians were massacred which consisted of 7 men, 5 women and 8 children. A fifty man militia decided to use the power they possessed to proceed to massacre some people based on their race. Race and religion are often used to classify groups of humans. So now we have 50 men that used this logic then massacred this group of Indians under a consensus of opinion and such is the way of self regulating men with too much power, who may otherwise have been law abiding citizens. This is human nature at its worst and was perhaps not an anomaly in Benjamin Franklins' day. Virtually nothing has change from the 18th century to the 21st century as far as this logic of labelling goes. Race and religion are banners of the tyrants to enforce their will on others and build a consensus. Were the Indians oppressed or the women who were burned at the stake in the name of god in the late 17th century? The only difference between the 21st century and the 18th century is invention. Human nature is exactly the same.

Governments are the Invention of Man

Until every man agrees with every other, all the time, then governments will always be needed to keep the order. Regardless of the form of the government it must be sold to the people, and usually the best way to do this is with fear. The people will always outnumber their leaders. Keep the people busy and normalize their existence and poof, you have a fine tuned machine. Different governments have different approaches as to how to keep their machines running.

Invention of Kings

My previous experience in historical research involved genealogy. I was inspired after a cousin mine had supplied us with some of her own research into our shared family tree. This was on my paternal side of the family which went back to my gggg grandfather who was born an Ebenezer in 1796 Vermont. As a point of trivia the name "Ebenezer" went out of vogue after Charles Dickens publication of "A Christmas Carol". As of yet I haven't discerned just why but I suspect it may have been due to his high spirited writing. I also have the same DNA marker as Alexander Hamilton and after 45 minutes of study it appears we have the same nostrils as well as a desire to proving the veracity of the objectively read 2nd amendment.

On the maternal side of my family things became more interesting. Being half French it was far easier to pick up the trail. Someone had completed a genealogical record that took me to the door step of France. My starting point here was 12 generations back and the year was 1645. Somewhat bored that evening the genealogies were much easier to locate due to that nation recording much of it in bibles and churches. I was trying to see how far back I could go through either maternal or paternal bloodlines. Eventually the bloodline found branched into royal blood in the year 982 AD. These bloodlines are meticulously recorded and soon I was about 85 generations back and it stopped at just one individual by the name of Zeus. The year as 3300 BC, or AZ in this particular context.

There is a point to this because I had just researched something to such an extent that I had crossed the interface of reality and fantasy. As I write this I'm making sure I'm well grounded. Someone had given someone else an alternative fact in order to procure a blood based rationalization to entitlement. Some dude, perhaps a big guy, charismatic for his day, came strutting into some village and said, "Hello, I'm the son of Zeus", "He sent me here to govern you and help to keep the order. I'm also here to protect you and show you how to protect yourselves from our very bad neighbours to the west. You can see that they look different than us and if they look different and we are good then they must be bad"."Let's work as a team and be united in this effort for the greater good, which is of course us." There are many other enemies out there that I can also help you with, but I will tell you about them later"."So due to the nature of my genes and as you can see they are very good, I would like to put into place a form of governance to maintain order which we will call Trickle down Ruling." "It will benefit us for 1000s of years. So the first thing I'm going to need is a castle, some live stock and some beer to quell my thirst. In order for me to rule though, we all know that money does not grow on trees, so I'd like to introduce you to something called taxation. This will be for the benefit of all of society and my genes will know best on just how to distribute them.

The people had no choice over their own destinies because this form of government has been normalized. Having a good king in your lives or a bad one is really just a matter of blind luck. The power a king has gives him the ability to maintain his reign. Sometimes the people have had enough when they see the wealth squandered by the few. They come to realize that they are just a tool to their leaders and nothing more. France is a good example of this and after King Louis arrogantly flashed his wealth the people rose up. He ultimately stopped his nonsense and quit while he was a head. The moral of this story is that governments are nothing more than the invention of man and the people get what they endorse.

A Transfer of Power to Democracy

This is the period of the revolutionary war and the genesis of a brand new type of government. It is even referred to as being an experiment however that context may have been misinterpreted by previous historians. Benjamin Franklin had already thought through a template for a new constitution with respect to his the Albany Plan of 1754. Remember the Join or Die cartoon of the snake? If not there is a picture of it in the United States Seal section. The only difference now though is that there would no longer be a king, but a president who was to be selected from the people themselves. Royal blood would no longer be a factor and terms could be limited through the vote of the people. As an extra safeguard, limited terms have been put into place to safeguard the liberty of all. Whether it was 1754 or 1776 Benjamin Franklin still liked the synergy that could be achieved in joining the colonies together. The problem was politics though. In a transfer of power from the King of England to the Colonies, the colonies themselves would instantly become their own little kingdoms. Some men like power which has caused the 2nd amendment to be misinterpreted to a great extent as demonstrated. The governors of some states no longer had to report to a king, whose ONLY claim to power was royal blood. Suddenly the governors of the colonies had even more power and without any checks and balances against it there would also be much opportunity. This is just human nature, and it was very well studied by Benjamin Franklin

In Benjamin Franklin's final address on Speech Sept 17, 1787 he states the following.

"For when you assemble a number of men to have the advantage of their joint wisdom, you inevitably assemble with those men, all their prejudices, their passions, their errors of opinion, their local interests, and their selfish views[33]. From such an assembly can a perfect production be expected?"

Seems like a reasonable observation of human nature. If you were to dispute this, you would actually be adding to the veracity of it. You can't really sugar coat

---

[33] This is exactly why the convention was orchestrated in advance. This is also why this letter was written. It was too clarify just why the convention was orchestrated in advance for a time when it was to be needed most, scrutinized and then discovered. He is saying that some opinions do in fact matter more than others where truth is concerned. If a perfect constitution is to be constructed then don't allow lesser opinions a voice in it.

human nature because its limits are defined only by the imagination. Human nature also creates faction which is easily seen in 2nd amendment debates today. In the faction exists, fear, patriotism, religion, racism, hypocrisy, ignorance, wisdom, intelligence, avarice, frustration, heart ache and vitriol. Faction was alive and well back then and to assume that all the founders all had the same interests in mind is, to put it mildly, simply silly. You will note the expression "errors of opinion". It seems that "it's just your opinion" would not fly with this man. He was smart enough to observe that like it or not, some opinions are of more value than others. Some opinions are in fact, alternative facts, or "errors of opinion". While this may not seem fare, reality doesn't particularly care, because reality does not think, it just is.

Thomas Jefferson also stated his own observation on the bill of rights for this period.

"The declaration of rights is, like all other human blessings, alloyed with some inconveniences and not accomplishing fully its object. But the good in this instance vastly outweighs the evil." -Thomas Jefferson to James Madison, 1789. ME 7:309

We now know that the object Thomas Jefferson is referring to is the 2nd amendment. The "inconveniences" have played themselves out for over two centuries. The "good" is related to the 2nd amendment being discovered that it is a gun control amendment.

New Constitution

For the past two hundred years the people have been fearful of a tyrant taking control of power and oppressing the people. To the extent of taking to Arms this has never occurred so as of yet this contingency has not been required for about 10 generations of people. How many more generations will it take to suppress the will of the human imagination? Will it take 50 more, 200 more, 1000 more generations? The current generation will have to revisit this logic, though now the very rhetoric of the 2nd amendment has given the imagination something new to feed on, that being a right to self defence. The rhetoric itself has been rebranded, and when something is branded it is usually associated with a business model. What is oppression though? Oppression is still alive and well in the United States and perhaps its worst form in history comes from slavery. Slavery was one reason why the people wanted a right to keep and bear Arms. This "right" if preserved the constitution continue to empower the slave owners to force their will on the slaves. If slavery could be maintained then the slave owners would be able to make more money with very cheap labor. Religion has much the same utility because it justifies our very existence upon this earth. The bible itself can be considered a constitution of sorts. Some have even tried to infer that the right to keep and bear Arms was a god given right. So why would men, oppressors and surely tyrants in the eyes of the slaves wish to give up a power that allowed themselves to profit on the labor of their fellow man with complete impunity? Why would they give up a power that quelled their worst fears and threatened the very narratives they fully endorsed and profited by?

We now know that the actual 2nd amendment is a check against power. A tyrant is sourced from the population and is nothing more than a criminal where both can cause a society oppression in proportion to the power that they are allowed.. Remember Thomas Jefferson's quote from 1789, which was directed toward tyrants and people?

> "The tree of liberty must be refreshed from time to time with the blood of patriots and tyrants"

Patriots and tyrants are both people, but the tyrant is the one that has been empowered through the usage of a gun and has chosen at whim to use it to harm any other. A tyrant is of the people and does not have to be elected to power through the vote. A patriot is a man that has died for his country simply by being a victim of gun violence. A patriot is the man that puts aside his fear and puts his society ahead of himself. Where it may have been thought the 2nd amendment was a contingency to quell a tyrant, which has yet to be named, it is now a pro-active measure to not empower one to exist in the first place. The patriots are the victims of gun violence which now number over 1,000,000. While this number most certainly was not anticipated, harm was anticipated which was required for the 2nd amendment to be scrutinized in proportion to it until finally its secret was revealed. The blood is created directly from the constitution, which is the tree of liberty, or that mechanism that is "necessary to the security of a free State". Liberty can only be secured for "We the People" if the constitution is not cherry picked. This is clarified by another cipher that was written by Mason Loche Weems in his story of George Washington and the cherry tree towards the end of this volume. Life should always trump the Pursuit of Happiness which in part is demonstrated by those that find enjoyment as hobbyists in the plethora of Arms that are currently available to them.

So what we have here are some people in power who were able to enforce their will upon others. The slave owners had power over their slaves and the king had power over the colonies. There were varied degrees of oppression being experienced. The experience of oppression itself does not particularly care as to the source of it only that those that experience it want it to stop. Removing the source will of course remove the effect. It is like a bug in a software program and the program in the context of this study is of course the United States Constitution. The bible or the Koran can also be thought of as being constitution as well. Some who follow these scriptures may be cherry picking from them what they wish. In turn the existence of another religion may be perceived as an assault a bias to one's own. In this respect to vote in the defense of one's own religion is in effect introducing a second constitution which must now exist harmoniously with the one which is to dictate how society is to function. If the goal is have the scriptures of any religion define the code of the Constitution then one has to win out. To go against the wisdom of the Constitution is in itself unconstitutional. People must be allowed the liberty of choosing the comfort of their own religion and not be oppressed in its practice. This is why there is separation of church and state. In the exploration of the United States Seal the myth of "In God's favor" is reduced to the simple concept of the promotion of Liberty for all, irrespective of a man's chosen religion. I have no doubt god would fully endorse the constitution, but any god whose scripture promotes the peace among men. It is a choice of respecting the liberty of others or not who in turn support their own religion with equal passion. There are other factors in this as well, but as far as Benjamin Franklin was concerned he was more interested in cause and effect. If a man has too much power the effective of this by some is the inevitable oppression of others. In the vote oppression can be promoted or not. Vote for "We the People" and there will be Liberty without concession in a United States of America or in effect any real democracy.

If this power can be limited in some manner, then so too will the oppression experienced in Society. It's my understanding that in the year 1780 Pennsylvania began to phase out slavery. This was the year that Benjamin Franklin started to ramp up his plan for the United States. He wasn't getting any younger, and he was going to need some help in his plan. This will be elaborated on in the section titled "A cabal Discovered".

The 2nd amendment appeared to have been borrowed from the Virginia declaration of Rights, as written primarily by George Mason on June 12. 1776. It was in that document that the term 'well regulated' was used and appeared to be transcribed with some changes into the Bill of Rights. Immediately after the Virginia Declaration of Rights was published the Declaration of Independence was both drafted and read. There are subtle differences in these two documents because the Declaration of Independence had a far more liberal view on how society should work

George Washington and the other men in the cabal viewed George Mason as being a man of avarice. One of the ciphers refers to him as the "duke of Marlborough". He apparently did not sign the Constitution because he wanted it to have a Bill of Rights. The greedy saw a place of sanctuary in the Declaration of Independence and while not explicit, it was there. They liked the words, "Liberty and Pursuit of Happiness". In these words there did not appear to be regulations or restrictions. Perhaps the words Life, Liberty and Pursuit of Happiness have been viewed as being synonymous? I can't comment on modern day interpretations or discussions about them because I haven't researched this. I do however have my own take, on them, but only in the light of the new dynamic. Remember that one of these words is associated with the 2nd amendment. The word is "Liberty", and to achieve that state, A well regulated Militia is required. Now it is clearly demonstrated that there are checks and balances against the common man, just as there are against a federal head. Liberty and Oppression are directly related, and so too are all men, because all are not immune from their own human nature.

The United States Constitution was created from scratch. No longer would bloodline alone determine the governance of a nation. A king isn't so bad but only if he isn't a bad king. If he governs without exploiting his nation's wealth to satisfy his own vices then in theory the people would all have their own liberty. He would live a long life and there would be stability within the nation. It's pretty rare though for a man, any man to live his life with power and not grow drunk in it. Once a man has established power and status just based on his life's own hard work this can become a part of his very identity. He may measure his own value as greater than those that are just not as far along as he is. He may at times, become oppressive to others simply because he can. Some men are born to wealth and have never learned the lessons that can only be provided from hardship. They may view others in hardship and think that is just simply their station in life.

Some men generally like the idea of being kings and the governors were probably not immune to the idea of this regarding this permanent transition of power after the revolutionary war. The federal head which is tasked to look out for "We the People" sets up a possible condition of conflict with the governors who have their own ideas just how much Liberty their people are entitled too. Governors to some extent would instantly become kings if they were no longer reporting to the crown, and in order to limit any power coming from above they became anti-federalists.

It is common knowledge that some of the founders had studied past civilizations in order to form a new government by taking what appeared to work and what did not.. This can easily be seen in the extensive commentary in the Federalist papers. Different forms of governments were looked at and studied. They all agreed on one thing though, that a government was going to be needed and they knew this because of one very simple observation of mankind. In the absence of government there is there is no such thing as a self regulating man whose opinions would mirror all of his neighbours.

This passage was taken from the Federalist Papers has been attributed to the 2nd amendment. It is most certainly related to it and in this regard nothing has changed. The explanations of it may be argued to be only an interpretation of my own however I did not interpret the 2nd amendment itself. I simply found a way to actually read it. Now the context of this one passage can be read as well, but this time with clarity. It's very essence is that there is no such thing as a self regulation man. History proves this, the present proves this and there is no reason that the future will line up with this very simple fact of reality. It is the very reason why the Constitution has checks and balances against power. To deem ourselves an "angel" is not up to us to decide because the more we do that, the more apt we are to deem all others devils. It is our own ego that can be a great source of oppression for others. I anticipate a pushback on this book by some groups in academia as being inevitable. They must only ask themselves the "why of it" because I suspect it will come from a place of emotion which will further add to the veracity of an observation on human nature. This book was not meant to be political in any way, but only a study of the code of the constitution, the intent of the framers and the truth of history.

THE FEDERALIST NO. 51,
The provision[34] for defense must in this, as in all other cases, be made commensurate to the danger of attack[35]. Ambition must be

---

[34] Arms

[35] It is observed that Arms can be used for defense, but it must be recognized that the arms allowed can also be used for offense or "attack". There must be a balance between what the people are allowed to possess, because in the people will also reside the attackers

made to counteract ambition[36]. The interest of the man must be connected with the constitutional rights of the place. It may be a reflection on human nature, that such devices should be necessary to control the abuses of government. But what is government itself, but the greatest of all reflections on human nature? If men were angels, no government would be necessary. If angels were to govern men, neither external nor internal controls on government would be necessary. In framing a government which is to be administered by men over men, the great difficulty lies in this: **you must first enable the government to control the governed[37]; and in the next place oblige it to control itself.**[38]

This is why the 2nd amendment was put into the United States Constitution. It demands that any government must create arms laws regardless of opinion or ideology. Oblige is rather explicit in the 2nd amendment because it can be found in the words "well regulated" and "shall not be infringed". Opinion simply does not matter, because opinion is fueled by human nature and the 2nd amendment was created simply as a check and balance against in spite of it.. The opinions of the voters do not count when it comes to the constitution itself. Democracy is not the most important thing but it is the best solution with respect to keeping oppression at bay. The most sacred thing is the constitution itself because only it can provide liberty, providing that the people vote for those that respect it in the first place..

It is because of democracy that the 2nd amendment had to be crafted in the way it was. I bring up Benjamin Franklins observation on human nature in his final address on Sept 17, 1787.

---

[36] What is more dangerous to a society, the ambition of a killer who is armed, or the ambition of a man to fear the killer and have a desire to be Armed? Which man will be taking the first shot and how many will he be so empowered to take before only one man is able to stop him? Use the objectivity of math.

[37] To enable is to give the government a way to control arms in society to protect the people.

[38] Since the 2nd amendment is in the constitution and due to its construction any government

is obliged or must control arms through the mechanism they are given for the first task. It is not an option.

"For when you assemble a number of men to have the advantage of their joint wisdom, you inevitably assemble with those men, all their prejudices, their passions, their errors of opinion, their local interests, and their selfish views[39]. From such an assembly can a perfect production be expected?"

It was in the recognition of mans nature that Benjamin Franklin devised a plan to bypass its very participation in the vote. He used it, it being human nature to hide it, it being the 2nd Amendment.

Ideology and Opinion are nothing more than words that democratize and average the collective wisdom, removing from it the very quality of it. While all men are born with their own splash of intelligence in reality some have been proportioned with a bigger splash than the next. In turn if logic is derived from emotion alone then the areas where any intelligence will be allowed to roam will further diminish quality the wisdom that it perceives. While all opinions should be respected, the respect should only be attributed to a person's own journey in increasing the quality of their wisdom. It is a process that will never end. In our younger years, emotion alone was our sole source of wisdom. I speak of the temper tantrum of course. Do we then attribute the opinions of a scream with equal weight to that of our own? If we do, then we have the makings of a spoiled child, leaving it no opportunity to grow and evolve because the child has not only had its own narrative validated but is quite happy with it and then has no motive to change it. Nobody can be faulted for being human, but this is not an excuse to presume that all opinions are "created" equal.

All opinions are not created equal and opinions fuel the vote. The motives behind a vote can be wide and varied, fueled by emotion or the fallacy of certain ideologies, which is nothing more than a cult of shared opinion which is further perceived to be validated by the very consensus of it. I am just one person and it is my opinion that the right to keep and bear Arms never existed. It conflicts of course with the current wisdom of over 320 million people. I chose a bias that aligned with reality where I perceived it to live. I have achieved success in this approach to thinking. As arrogant as that may sound for me to say, I am simply

---

[39] This is exactly why the convention was orchestrated in advance. This is also why this letter was written. It was too clarify just why the convention was orchestrated in advance for the time when it was to be discovered. He is saying that some opinions matter more than others, if a perfect constitution is to be constructed, so don't allow those lesser opinions a voice in it.

trying to demonstrate the very point that Benjamin Franklin is making in his letter. If this alone is not the proof of this concept, then it is my opinion, for what it's worth in this regard, that nothing can be proved. While our species is highly intelligent, it is whim that guides it and in turn will be the destroyer of ourselves which is now being demonstrated with the ideological views of climate change. In the 18th century the average of each vote included the normalization of slavery, fear, ignorance and greed. Why would these choices of human nature vote for a check and balance against themselves if it would dramatically affect their currently perceived station's in life in order to secure the Liberty of all

Sometimes a vote is based simply on a good haircut and nice set of teeth. Haircuts and nice teeth did not create the constitution. Intelligence, wisdom education and a respect for "We the People" did. "Me the People" is just the opinion of the entitled, like kings and corporations whose only priests are accountants.

Once a narrative of history is exposed then we can make better sense of history itself. The narrative in this case is that the Constitution itself was orchestrated in advance of its drafting by the liberally thinking men of the day. How long would it take congress, being simply a body of men with their own opinions, to draft a Constitution from scratch? If that could even be accomplished what would it even look like? In the 18th century coding of the constitution it is my belief that it had to have a degree of ambiguity in it very code so that it would be ultimately ratified. The second amendment is an example of this but I don't believe that this is the only place in which that was done. The "treasure" that Thomas Jefferson refers to in his letter to Justice William Johnson of June 12, 1823 I believe is directly related to the removal of that ambiguity through the revelation of the Constitution's code and consistency of it in order to achieve a desired result. If the code was ambiguous then differing ideology and opinion could of course gain purchase in it further stacking the cards in favor of its ratification. Today it is well studied by highly intelligent men. Both civil and not so civil debates as to what that code says can be found in court rooms, in university forums and in pretty much any medium available to us. This is not a dynamic that is associated with just the United States but one that is associated where human nature lives.

In exposing the code of the 2nd amendment something else has been exposed as well. It is that word "regulated". It is "regulated" that had to be re-authored in order to support the third clause known as "the right of the people to keep and bear Arms". At no time prior to this did the wisdom of the Constitution give advice to the people on how to vote. Where before that wisdom was always sourced from political ideology it now it can be sourced from the Constitution itself. The Constitution was put in place after all to limit the political shenanigans of party ideology. Sometimes these shenanigans are aligned with the code of the constitution and sometimes they are not. A recent example of this is in the recent assumption by the GOP that James Madison had provide a loophole in the code that says "on advice AND consent" with regards to their ignoring the constitutions mandate for a president to ensure the check and balance of the judiciary was operating as intended by the framers. There is no either or in this code, because the word "AND" is there for all to see. Cherry picking at its finest but in so doing had disenfranchised the votes of millions who had elected a president to whom this power would be assigned throughout his term of office. There is of course only one remedy for this and to argue otherwise would be to only cherry pick the constitution some more.

The word "regulated" is now to be associated with laws but more importantly is a mandate of the constitution to ensure regulations. The rhetoric of this could not be any clearer. To preserve Liberty regulations must be in effect. Arms are of course associated with power, and if misused or exploited will in turn cause a society great oppression. Power is the ability to enforce ones will upon others. Power is also money and to enforce ones will is to bribe another with it. If given enough power Corporations can of course now dictate the value of a living wage or ignore it altogether in their own quest for money. If a Corporation has no regulations then they charge what they wish for drugs. If a corporation has no regulations then in their quest for money can market these drugs in any manner they choose too. Opiod's and cigarettes would be an example of this. To oppress a society for self gain is to be the tyrant to a society. The ultimate check and balance is the vote itself. Vote for de-regulation then you are simply empowering others the ability to oppress. This does not mean that all corporations are oppressive. The political sales pitch for de-regulation is often referred to as "Trickle Down Economics" and "Free Markets". There is of course some truth to this but both have a message of "Trust me", and in trust me, there is no accountability because the parameters of accountability can come only from the regulations that provide a framework for it. The promise of lower taxes is the same of course. It points the finger back at government as being the tyrant. With taxes only being a portion of your wage would you prefer a wage increase or a tax decrease? Would you like to have more to begin with , being a living wage or greater, or have a fraction given to you in lower taxes against a wage that ignores your most basic of needs just to survive? This is the lead up to the ambiguity of the code "Life Liberty and the Pursuit of Happiness".

Life Liberty and the Pursuit of Happiness

The promise of the constitution can be found in "We the People" and not "Me the People". The concept of checks and balances can be proven to predate the constitution by at least 35 years which of course predates the Constitution. This new dynamic of the orchestration of the constitution also aligns with the principles encoded into the Declaration of Independence. The new dynamic is the ambiguity of the code itself in order to achieve a desired result for a self governed people.

> We hold these truths to be self-evident, that all men are created equal, that they are endowed by their Creator with certain unalienable Rights, that among these are Life, Liberty and the pursuit of Happiness. — That to secure these rights, Governments are instituted among Men, deriving their just powers from the consent of the governed, — That whenever any Form of Government becomes destructive of these ends, it is the Right of the People to alter or to abolish it, and to institute new Government, laying its foundation on such principles and organizing its powers in such form, as to them shall seem most likely to effect their Safety and Happiness

George Mason had just drafted his Virginia Declaration of Rights prior to the drafting of the Declaration of Independence and in his declaration of rights which were to be associated with his "kingdom" of Virginia he described property ownership. The concept of property ownership appears to have been stripped away from the Declaration of Independence and replaced with the ambiguity of Life Liberty and Pursuit of Happiness. I a man generally reads what he wants to he would easily be able to perceive that this is the place where his own pre-conceived narrative must live. This is same psychological dynamic that has occurred in attempting to discern the 2nd amendment. The men that were charged with writing the Declaration of Independence fell upon Benjamin Franklin, John Adams and Thomas Jefferson. Just as the Virginian James Madison was enlisted to draft Constitution so too was the Virginian Thomas Jefferson where John Adams was not. Benjamin Franklin however was sitting in the side lines where he always had been to some extent. I believe however his attention in these matters was highly focused, but not blatantly so because suspicion was after all an enemy to his plan.

So let us now take a closer look a these words but use them in the context of "We the People".

They are in a very specific order. We now know that Liberty is defined in a dictionary as 'the state of being free". Once nested into the 2nd amendment it is now associated with a check and balance against power. It can now be easily and rather explicitly viewed as a razor thin line were oppression even stops or it begins. Think of it as a line of demarcation. One side of it resides "Life" What does Life require for it to exist? Can Liberty or the Pursuit of Happiness exist without life? Of course not, it is the precursor to them and because of this is word, as ordered in these inalienable rights. Life requires food. Life requires shelter. Life requires the means to achieve these things which is usually through the medium of money. Life requires health care can only be provided by the collective resource of We the People, both intellectually and otherwise. Roads and bridges and fire departments are no different if one is to have Life. If one is to have life then an education is of course required in order to sustain it and allow any person the dignity to provide for one's self if a dignity. There is of course anomaly in this as there is in anything but anomaly should not in any way detract from the bigger picture in the very structure of society as defined by the constitution itself. It should not be an excuse which would detract from the liberty of the masses. If a person can achieve all these things for himself he will of course require a living wage to do so. In the absence of any of these things then this individual will be experiencing oppression because their most basic needs for Life. A job is meaningless if one cannot afford to garnish from his wage the very necessities for life. The slaves had jobs. There masters were rich. Where was the trickle-down economics for them if men are to be trusted? Has human nature changed one iota in the past 5000 years?

So now we have the Pursuit of Happiness. There is perhaps the most ambiguity in this, as there should be and as it is inferred. Happiness is highly subjective to the individual. The word Pursuit infers both direction and speed. This in turn is up to the individual. Some choose money, status and power where others do not. Everyone has these rights but only in the context of "We the People". The word Liberty is the line of demarcation because it is when one man's Pursuit of Happiness crosses over and affects any others right to life then oppression is realized again. One man's pursuit of happiness has infringed upon the Liberty of another. There is no ambiguity in these words. Everyone is entitled to the opportunity to better their own lives, but in the betterment of them it doesn't infer that you have the right to destroy the lives of others.

Life, Liberty and the Pursuit of Happiness are in turn the final legacy of the United States Constitution and they provide the rules to live by not to die by. This is perhaps the most important code ever devised and it has existed from day one if a United States of America or any other democracy is to in fact be realized. There is no cure for human nature but there exists a formula to save humanity in spite of its nature.

The Delegates and the 2nd Amendment

Historically many people have cited the quotes of Patrick Henry, Richard Henri Lee, Tench Coxe and George Mason to validate the 2nd amendment. There are some quotes that are used by gun rights advocates that simply do not exist. It true that that people feared government and oppression, but this is not a proof of dogma of the 2nd amendment but rather a proof that it had to be hidden in the first place. Many of the same arguments for guns have persisted for over 224 years and may well persist after this book is released. As I combed through the quotes I came to realize that only some of the delegates knew the truth of the 2nd amendment where others did not. It was in the Federalist papers were the full story was told, but there were far more letters that validated the true meaning of the 2nd amendment as well.

James Madison is "debunking" all known arguments for the "previously understood 2nd amendment when he writes this..

> James Madison: "the legitimate meaning of the Instrument[40] must be derived from the text itself" or if a key is to be sought elsewhere, **it must be not in the opinions or intentions of the Body which planned & proposed the Constitution**. (December 21 1821)

This was taken from one of the first letters that I had located. The "opinions" are those of Patrick Henry, Richard Henry Lee, George Mason and others. The instrument is the 2nd amendment. The legitimate meaning implies that there can be an illegitimate meaning which the courts have been concluding. There are not that many lines of text in the constitution that are more controversial than the 2nd amendment. We have in fact completely changed the meaning. Is it likely that the founding fathers loaded the entire constitution with cryptic riddles? I will answer that question with a yes, however not to the extent of the 2nd amendment. The other riddles are more "supplementary" and in no way change the meaning of the constitution itself or the bill of rights as best I can tell. When the Bill of Rights was ratified most of the men read what they wanted too from the 2nd amendment, where the men who knew its truth, quietly had their fingers crossed as they watched human nature perform

---

[40] Merriam-Webster Dictionary Instrument: "a tool or device used for a particular purpose; *especially* : a tool or device designed to do careful and exact work"

A Cabal Discovered

The American Philosophical Society

Early in my research while I was trying to resolve who else knew about the 2nd amendment I stumbled across the American Philosophical Society. Besides James Madison I had further resolved that Alexander Hamilton, John Jay and Thomas Jefferson also knew about this through "2nd amendment" quotes which had primarily come from the Federalist Papers. After resolving an individual I would start to sift through their letters to see if I could locate further ciphers and it was one from John Jay that first made me aware of the existence of the American Philosophical Society. The first cipher that introduced me to Thomas Jefferson as a cipher writer was the following.

> "the tree of liberty must be refreshed from time to time with the blood of patriots and tyrants. It is its natural manure".

In wikipedia you can find information on the American philosophical society.

> "The **Philosophical Society**, as it was originally called, was founded in 1743 by Benjamin Franklin, William Alexander, Francis Hopkinson, John Bartram, Philip Syng, Jr. and others[2][3] as an offshoot of an earlier club, the Junto. It was founded two years after the University of Pennsylvania, with which it remains closely tied."

> "The **American Philosophical Society** (APS), founded in 1743 and located in Philadelphia, is an eminent scholarly organization of international reputation that promotes useful knowledge in the sciences and humanities through excellence in scholarly research, professional meetings, publications, library resources, and community outreach. Considered the first learned society in the United States, it has played an important role in American cultural and intellectual life for over 270 years."

This seemed to me to scream out the word think tank. I then discovered this organization has a website with searchable membership records. I began to query the years in the year 1780 up popped the names John Jay, Alexander Hamilton and Thomas Jefferson three of the men I had already resolved to be writing ciphers. In the year 1785 James Madison's name appeared. It appeared that a cabal was forming and in it there appeared to be a few more members. Benjamin Franklin was now on my list of new suspects but in addition so too was George Washington and John Adams. What is also interesting is the grouping of five of the enrolments because they all became members in the year 1780. It appeared that a well planned recruiting drive was in motion which you will see to be verified with further analysis of this research.

While physically in decline it is reported that his mind was still sharp as a tack. You can judge this for yourself in reading one of his ciphers that he had written on October 26 1789 and the age of 83, about 6 months before his passing.

The Federalist papers I had never heard of either and I learned that they are volume of 85 essays written for newspapers in order to promote the Constitutional Convention of 1788. I had just learned that those papers are not all that they appear to be. I also discovered that this collection had the full endorsement of Thomas Jefferson as being very important. In having just learned what they actually were I don't even think you can call this the understatement of the century. I write more about this later but still just touch on it because that volume of research would be impossible to fit into the confines of this book. I have created this little graphic to illustrate what I'd like to refer to as the primary actors in my research. Being among them the first four sitting presidents of the United States I think adds a bit more clout to the importance of these narratives I'm now sharing with you.

Born Jan 17, 1706.
Passed April 17, 1790.
Founder of APS 1743

" The *Philosophical Society*, as it was originally called, was founded in 1743 by Benjamin Franklin, William Alexander, Francis Hopkinson, John Bartram, Philip Syng, Jr. and others[2][3] as an offshoot of an earlier club, the Junto. It was founded two years after the University of Pennsylvania, with which it remains closely tied. "

"An eminent scholarly organization of international reputation, the American Philosophical Society promotes useful knowledge in the sciences and humanities through excellence in scholarly research, professional meetings, support of young scholars, publications, library resources, a museum and community outreach. This country's first learned society, the APS has played an important role in American cultural and intellectual life for over 250 years."

George Washington
Born Feb 22, 1732.
Passed Dec 14, 1799.
Invited and Joined 1780

John Adams
Born Oct 30, 1735.
Passed July 4, 1826.
Invited and Joined 1780

John Jay
Born Dec 12 1745.
Passed May 17, 1829.
Invited and Joined 1780

Thomas Jefferson
April 13, 1743.
Passed July 4, 1826.
Invited and Joined 1780

Alexander Hamilton
Born January 11, 1755.
Passed July 12, 1804. (pistol duel)
Invited and Joined 1780

James Madison
March 16, 1751.
Passed June 28, 1836.
Invited and Joined 1785

The historian Richard B. Morris identified these exact men as the key founding fathers of the United States. According to my research I would agree with him completely and am compelled to read his book at some future date. I'm certain there would be additional discoveries made in merging of his discoveries and commentary with these. He could not possibly have known this new dynamic of history and may have recorded other letters that were actually ciphers which in turn would also have been invisible to him.

James Madison may not have been privy to Benjamin Franklins experiment until he was invited to join this organization in 1785. His primary purpose would have been to draft the Constitution and to help with the subtle orchestration of the inclusion of the Bill of Rights which of course was to contain the pre-existing 2nd amendment.

I would also like to point out that I located a quote of John Adams where he stated

"The Philosophers are speculating upon our Constitutions and I hope will throw out Hints, which will be of Use to our Countrymen".

All of these men have written ciphers or letters with symbolisms that point directly back toward the 2nd amendment. This statement is telling us that in our search for these letters to look closely at letters associated with Philosophers. If we were aware or became aware of the American Philosophical Society then philosophically speaking, we would understand that its' members could be construed as being Philosophers. Note the usage of capitals in this quote because they are important. What purpose could there be in capitalizing the word Hint? I don't know how else to say it but this is a "Hints" with no disrespect to this man who appears to have been a bit of a smart ass. This little play on a word must have produced a sly grin on this man's face. He was sharing humor and could only imagine its affect on an audience he would never know. It's perhaps a joke, though with utility, that was pitched across a span of time that can now be measured in centuries.

To capitalize or not to capitalize that is the answer.

Let's look at the other capitalized words in this sentence. We have "Constitutions", "Hints", "Use" and "Countrymen". The context of "Constitutions" is that there are in fact two of them where one contains the subjectively read 2nd amendment and the other does not. "Hints" give those with knowledge of this new dynamic a compass of sorts to locate further letters. "Use" is associated but drives the point home that the utility in these ciphers is to further prove the validity of the objectively read 2nd amendment and of course the narratives behind it. This is the very foundation of this volume as it evolved due, in part to me using the "Hints" that John Adams has exposed. "Countrymen" are of course "We the People" who are now going to be protected from the oppression of gun violence. The vast majority of the letters I have located were indeed written by men who have been thought of as being philosophers.

In 1780 Benjamin Franklin recruited 5 key founding fathers into the American Philosophical Society. Five years later, James Madison a shy and relatively young Virginian, 5'4 in height and 100 lbs was also recruited. I point out these attributes because I suspect there utility did not go unnoticed to the other members in this cabal. As the key framer in the convention, the other delegates who weren't in the know would have perhaps seen him as being less of a threat. Benjamin Franklin knew very well the power of a first impression and in knowing human nature, the first impression is a thing men take pride in. To sum up someone in a very short period of time is by some, viewed as a finely honed skill. Sounds a bit like the 2nd amendment, doesn't it? It has been my observance that some people choose to believe in conspiracy theories. Generally speaking they view things in black and white, big and small, weak and strong while rarely visiting any region in between. James Madison would have been categorized perhaps as being weak, because if something looks weak, the logic would be that it must be weak. This is not a reflection of intelligence but rather a reflection of choice. It is easier to think in black and white if it suits a person and in part is done to prop up our own egos. A sales' pitch is really nothing more than taking away the "work" of thinking in the hopes that a concept will be bought. Benjamin Franklin knew this so he used it to hide the truth by weakening any opportunity for suspicion to grow. Truth rarely lives in extreme viewpoints because they are just goal posts which contain truth in a field of reality. It's much easier to use a static goal post, than to follow the players on the field. One is either in the game of reality, or one is not. To play in it takes practice and effort. There is no better muscle that can be exercised than the one which allows ourselves to be wrong. The ego is usually just the mascot blowing a tuba. I need a bit more practice at this philosopher stuff. It appears though that I was deep in the field when I caught a pass that I never saw coming.

We can look at the membership from another viewpoint as well. Since we know that the letters were written for the future then these men were trying to provide as much information for the future. The membership records resided behind closed doors in an society under Benjamin Franklins' control. How much would there be to glean from a list of these names? Did these men actually have to belong to this society or any other for that matter to discuss their plans? Of course they didn't. There is an invaluable utility in this list which I conjecture that Benjamin Franklin recognized. It does after all tie directly to John Adams quote above. It is the fact that these men are on the membership list that would provide a future historian that is trying to hunt down these specially crafted letters. If there was no membership list then perhaps we would not see a grouping of Alexander Hamilton, James Madison and John Jay. These men just happen to be the authors of the Federalist Papers, and it could have been possible that that collection of essays could have been missed. A hint after all is not an explicit solution but only infers the existence of one. The ciphers are hints in that once we recognize them as ciphers then we are tasked to figure them out.

This "list" appeared to be a cabal. In light of the new dynamic exposed and fact that the shy young James Madison, a man who stood 5'4 in height weighing in at 100 lbs was leading the Constitutional Convention of 1788 his utility takes on a new light. He was also a Virginian and would appear more allied with George Mason. The cabal didn't like the way George Mason was attempting to steer the Constitution which will be illustrated in a few ciphers which I will be talking about in the next section. His Virginia Declaration of Rights was slanted toward property ownership where the Declaration of Independence, a document produced by the men in the cabal appeared to be not so explicit in this regard. Property ownership would have been perceived to be nested in the words "Life, Liberty and Pursuit of Happiness. The context of these words aligns with preamble of the Constitution because there can be found in "fine print" "We the People" and not "Me the People". Remember too that James Madison was invited to join the American Philosophical Society five years after the other men and only three years before the Convention began. I don't think it was lost on Benjamin Franklin that James Madison would have been the best fit to "run" the Constitutional Convention if one of his primary goals in his plan was to keep suspicion from gaining purchase in the minds of his opponents and in this particular matter even future historians. While human nature was the enemy of Liberty because from that can spawn the criminal or tyrant, human nature could also be used to get what he needed into the constitution right under the noses of the "human nature" that would oppose it. This was the "silent" pro gun control side of a gun debate that was barely perceived simply because it would have been suspicious and would have created more faction and most certainly suspicion. That same human nature is of course demonstrated today be its roots in fear, patriotism to the perceived wish of these very framers or in some cases avarice.

Benjamin Franklin Ciphering Institute

This is perhaps the most important section of the book with respect to the letters that I will be presenting and interpreting. It is based on the study of them collectively and the motives behind them with respect to the greater narrative that they actually describe. They expose a dynamic of history that surpasses politics in order to support the constitution itself and the intent of its chief architects. The difficulty in explaining them is that they are foreign to us to such an extent that it is almost like having to learn a new language.

Today if we want to share a secret with another we don't have to even think about how to go about that because encryption software is available to us at the push of a button. We can write what we wish, encrypt it and send it across the world in the span of 5 minutes. The 18th century had no such luxury in this matter and if people wanted to share secrets then it was up to their own ingenuity in encrypting the written word themselves. The quality of the ciphering is of course related to the quality of the mind that produced them just as the sophistication of encryption software is proportional to the labor and thought that has gone into its own design.

Now Benjamin Franklin as a scientist and as one he carefully design an experiment to test a hypothesis or achieve a desired result. He was also a very skilled author and love to write and even did so starting at the age of about 16 under a false name to become published in his brother's newspaper. This was a man who knew the utility of keeping a secret in order to achieve a desired result and was successful at it much to his brother's chagrin when it was later exposed that his successful articles were of his construction. So here we sit, 224 years later and once again he is being exposed as not only the author of secret letters but also the mind that was behind them. This man was relentless. The sophistication of his ciphering techniques will probably be viewed as his crowning achievement in this regard because the result he desired was the exposure of the final legacy of the United States Constitution. His secret letters have been hidden in plain view for centuries.

His desired result was to reveal the final legacy of the United States Constitution with the written word. The dilemma he had was that the written word had to be hidden for the span of at least 100 years. The people required time first to experience the checks and balances of the Constitution. The legacy in turn, being a legacy had to be hidden in the constitution itself so that the utility of it would be available at a future time. The primary component of this experiment if it was to succeed was human nature itself. Suspicion was to be both his enemy and his friend in this regard. Give a man suspicion and he will perceive that there is something to be studied. If there is no suspicion then there is nothing to perceive. As long as suspicion was in play then so too would a man's motivation be in play inspiring one to scrutinize that which is perceived.

He used human nature as the primary encryption to get his final legacy into the constitution. Now he had to tell the future just what was going on in history to further support it over and above its English. He had to share the intentions of framers, or at least the primary architects of the constitution. These are the rules for the crafting of these letters which had to be hidden in plain sight. They had to be immunized from every level of both intelligence and education if there was to be success in his plan. To keep these letters hidden forever would have no value to achieving the result he wanted. The letters at some point in time had to be put into the public view otherwise his experiment would fail.

Now he could have just written just one letter and hoped for the best. The problem with that is, is that it would have to be put into the view of a person who suspected. Benjamin Franklin could not tell the future destiny of any given letter. Would it survive time, and even if it did would it eventually reach the right hands? If his plan was to work he would need many letters. There was no such thing as enough in this regard. Each letter can be thought of as being many lines in a pond. If he could get just one bite by someone's scrutiny then motivation would come into play. He would require assistance to get both his final legacy into the constitution and also to craft these letters. He would need men who could be trusted and allied with his plan, but also men who were skilled wordsmiths in their own right. The men he recruited would have to be dedicated to the goal and very purpose of the constitution in promoting and securing the inalienable rights of Life, Liberty and Pursuit of Happiness. The 2nd amendment describes the inalienable right of Liberty but it was ahead of its time. It was the final piece of code to guard a nation against the oppression of a criminal.

These letters in turn could only be written by men who were alive so younger men would maximize the time in which these letters could be produced.

Background Dynamic Rule

Some may choose to argue that there is not historical evidence of gun control

There must be no perceived gun debate from a gun control point of view! In light of the first cipher being located from 1752 the men involved in the cipher writing could not be passionate in a gun control debate with others. As primary architects of the constitution this was particularly critical. In my research I have observed that many historians were looking for evidence of gun control in this period to establish the very existence of this bias. If these men had taken part in a gun control debate then it would have been extremely suspicious to suddenly cave and endorse the 2nd amendment as being "the right of the people to keep and bear Arms". This not only had to be kept hidden from the delegates but ALSO from future historians in "the sensitive period" which through a cipher of John Adams I believed has been quantified as being at least 100 years. He stated the following While today it may be perceived by the general public that common sense gun laws are necessary in light of the gun violence in the American Society, in the 18th century it was much different, especially with musket and flintlock technologies. They did indeed have stand-your-ground laws in the form of duels which is really just sanctioned murder where the only thing being defended was a man's honor.

Benjamin Franklins Golden Rules of Ciphering

Rule number 1 <u>The ciphers must appear to be regular letters to deter any suspicion</u>

In order to keep suspicion at bay the letters had to be invisible and not perceived as something that required solving.

Rule Number 2: Letters must NOT be explicit in referring to the 2nd amendment

Use symbolism and metaphor to hide the encryptions. If there is no context then they may

appear to be only the writing style of the author, or the period.

As letters they would be perceived as being a bit of correspondence between one person and another. There would be perception that they would be meant for anyone else. They would be further be hidden from scrutiny in that they would be based on current events.

Rule Number 3 Use common symbolisms and themes

In doing this the ciphers would be more easily recognized. In doing this red flags would provided to anyone seeking out these ciphers once it has been established that they actually exist. Each subsequent ciphers veracity would in turn be established do to a line of coincidences that all pointed back to the 2nd amendment

Rule Number 4 Use brute force failsafe.

Since any one cipher was not guaranteed to either survive traversing time or being located in the time that they were being searched out then repeat the narratives that the future was required to know to add further veracity to the objectively read 2nd amendment.

Rule Number 5. Where possible choose documents that were most likely to succeed in being preserved.

Examples. Presidential addresses, the Bill of Rights, the United States Seal, Legendary experiments or stories such as "The Kite Experiment" or "The Great Leap of the Whale".

Rule Number 6 Use the Naming Conventions of a letter or work of literature to provide a hint as to its true nature.

Colonel John Taylor wrote a book titled "Construction Construed Constitutions Vindicated". This appears to be pretty blatant if one knows that there are in fact TWO constitutions where the meaning of the 2nd amendment has in fact been construed to mean something due to the nature of its construction but once revealed for what it actually is it vindicates the constitution in its goal to protect a society from oppression, just like the other checks and balances. In Benjamin Franklins massive collection of letters the ones that stood out were the ones that had strange titles or no title at all. About 80 percent of these were ciphers. It certainly saved quite a bit of time. The name "William" was often used as well because there was utility in that which will be explained further along.

Rule Number 7 Use excessive detail to highlight the nature of the letter.

On this particular rule I conjecture a bit, but I believe it to be more valid than not. If an author goes a bit overboard in the subject matter of the letter then this in itself would convey a message that there is more here than meets the eye. As far as giving rise to suspicion it could easily be attributed to the passion of the of the author at the time. This observation of many letters was of great utility to me in recognizing an indication of a ciphered letter and more often than not, it was indeed a cipher upon closer inspection. As a disclaimer, I myself have not attempted to craft any ciphers of my own in this volume. I'm more the reading type.

Comments on these Rules

This list these rules that I have put together are based on the patterns that I have perceived across over 400 letters which had varied authors. In order to recognize the validity of them will require study. I believe it can be used as a primer of sorts to locate "new" letters for yourself if you are so inclined. They can in turn be used to establish the veracity of any one letter as being a cipher on your own. There is more objectivity in a consistent pattern than from the scrutiny of any one letter in the absence of using the pattern to in turn support the letter.

In light of this dynamic this may also explain, in part, why Thomas Jefferson was so eager to get his hands on a copying machine the [Hawkins & Peale's Patent Polygraph](#) in 1806. There would have been great utility in him keeping an archive of his ciphers in order to use them as a baseline to propagate more. I suspect there is a vast wealth of ciphers yet to be discovered in his library. Just now as I'm completing this I had located another written from him to Benjamin Hawkins on Feb 18 1803. While I haven't as of yet gone through it all, there is a line where he states

> "I shall avail myself of this private letter to state them generally"

In his letter to Justice William Johnson dated June 12, 1823 which I have used on the back cover of this book he clearly says

> "History may distort truth, and will distort it for a time, by the superior efforts at justification of those who are conscious of needing it most. Nor will the opening scenes of our present government be seen in their true aspect, until the letters of the day, now held in private hoards, shall be broken up and laid open to public view"

As you can see these two letters appear to be linked together. While it may be true that Thomas Jefferson was eager to purchase this copying machine after the above 1803 letter was drafted he was most certainly copying letters in the years prior to its purchase.

The 2nd Amendment is the Key to the Constitution

When I started my research I possessed a new context which I was convinced were undeniable facts.

> The 2nd amendment described right of the people to reality based Arms Control
> The 2nd amendment was most certainly encrypted.
> There had to be unknown history.

As I started into my research I had no knowledge of keys and ciphers as a mechanism to actually hide the narratives that is partially described in the prologue. I was able to resolve certain letters because I now was empowered with points A,B and C as mentioned. I was blindly looking for clues as to why the 2nd amendment was hidden. It was shortly after locating James Madison letter where he gives the instruction of discerning meaning from the text itself that I came across an even more astonishing letter. At this point I wasn't all that familiar with the Federalist papers but I had read that number 84 was said to be the related to the Bill of Rights. The reason I was perusing this collection was a result of searching for 2nd amendment quotes. Some of the ones that popped up had come from these papers and appeared to fit the new 2nd amendments new meaning better than its old one. In reading the 2nd amendment objectively we now know that "the right of the people to keep and bear Arms" really and the actual 2nd amendment Right as written are diametrically opposed.

> "The only use of the declaration was to recognize the ancient law and to remove doubts which might have been occasioned by the Revolution. **This consequently can be considered as no part of a declaration of rights**, which under our **constitutions** must be intended as limitations of the power of the government itself."

The ancient law is often referenced as a right to self defence. It is argued as being an inalienable right or even a god given right. To remove doubts was to pacify the people who were still angry at King George and the oppression he put the colonies under. The general population would have wanted to keep their Arms even after the war as a measure of personal security against the possibility of a tyrant. Once a man is given power it is not an easy thing to relinquish it because it can immediately put him in a mindset of the individual versus an enemy. It then says that the "right of the people to keep and bear Arms", is not the meaning of the 2nd amendment, and is not a right of the people. The right of the people is the mandate for government to create arms laws to protect the people in spite of themselves. It is well understood that the there is a separation of powers in the structure of government as checks and balances. It is then stressed that that the 2nd amendment is the only place where the separations of powers are not applicable. It is not just the federal government's jurisdiction but its constitutional mandate to create Arms laws until the society itself is no longer experiencing the harm that weaponry can create. Just as there are checks and powers to prevent a president from having too much power, the 2nd amendment is not thing more than a check and balance against the individual, in order to limit harm. If there were no checks and balances against power in government then there would have been many tyrants by now. If there are no checks and balances against arms in society then there would be about 117,000 people getting shot every year, 13,000 homicides, 18,000 suicides and even 500 accidental shootings a year. If you limit the power of something, then you limit the destruction it can cause. If death is not oppression then what is in the context of society itself? It appears that the Pursuit of Happiness of some has been infringing upon the liberty of the many. The constitution cannot be voted upon but it appears that this has even been discovered in the hypocrisy of some judicial appointees who are tasked with the job of interpreting the constitution and not re-authoring it and in so doing attacking the very premise of it, being of course checks and balances against power. The very heartbeat of the constitution has finally begun to beat which is of course its final legacy.

With the usage of this key, being the 2nd amendment, I have located other actors who knew about the 2nd amendment. Colonel John Taylor was one of these men and had authored a 300 page in 1820. It is another one of the hoarded letters hidden in plain view but in the form of a book. Letters, Federalist Essays, Inaugural speeches, the written word where ever it could be found was utilized. The utility of its packaging cannot be understated because it could increase the odds of survivability if it was perceived to be important. So , like the other letters this books symbolisms inside would have been completely invisible without the 2nd amendment key. If you read the title of the book though, I think it would be obvious to you why it made my eyebrows rise a bit. The title of the book was "Construction Construed, Constitution Validated". Now give that a toss in your coconut for a few moments. The 2nd amendments very construction had to be construed in such a way that the constitution would be finally validated. To put this in other words, the words of Thomas Jefferson, "the tree of liberty must be refreshed from time to time.."

John Taylor was allied in this mission, but he was also an actor in the early 19th century as their own politics raged. It is recorded in history that John Taylor called for both the Virginia and Kentucky Resolutions, which were written anonymously by James Madison and Thomas Jefferson respectfully to counter the Alien Act of John Adams. I couldn't help but notice that we now had 2 men in the primary cabal now reinforced with an enlisted secondary man taking sides against another who was of course John Adams .This too raised my eyebrows so now we have four. I have glanced through these resolutions and believe that there was a purpose for them other that what they appear to be. Their true utility appears to be a demonstration of the usage of the new constitution as it is being put into practice. Faction had to be created first off with John Adams setting up his Alien act in order to put this particular play in motion. I'd like to explore this theory a bit more but it is a bit of a sideline. It cannot be denied though that what these men were up to was for the future their nation. That came first, where the politics of their day, while important was probably far more demonstrative than has ever before been suspected.. Colonel John Taylor was also a friend of George Washington, He was very much a both a confident and am active participant in the "dangerous experiment".

There are many kinds of ciphers, but one thing they all have in common, is that they require a key. A cipher is not interpreted or discerned by its reader in any subjective fashion. The thing about a cipher is it holds a message which was intentionally hidden by its author. The only way that this message can be read is with a key which is also provided or was used to encipher the messages meaning in the first place. The message becomes explicit only when the key is used, otherwise it is not.

The genius of Benjamin Franklin was that his ciphers were completely invisible and unsuspected. His ciphers appeared as regular letters. It is through these ciphered letters, these previously invisible and now suspected ciphered letters that I have been able to uncover the narratives I am now disclosing to you. Just as I am explaining to the nature of ciphers right now you are about to see where I got that from. The utility of this letter to a historian, or to the future of Thomas Jefferson can't be denied if in fact they were creating ciphers. It is an explicitly written understanding and demonstration of ciphers as known in the late 18th century. If there is anything that can't be debated in this book, it is that alone. Benjamin Franklin's ciphers were so effective that all of American Academia was unable to penetrate or even perceive the encryptions for over two hundred and twenty five years. The proof of this is that you are reading it for the very first time now, and it is through the collective view of the documents that I will be presenting which cannot be denied. Think of each cipher/letter as being a "dot". As you read through the letters each one is another dot. It is only in collecting these dots that you will be able to connect them, and they all point back to the key, which in turn proves the message that they tell. This next letter is a dot, so see if you can resolve the point of it.

The Cipher Letter

Here is an excerpt from a letter by Robert Patterson to Thomas Jefferson in which he explains the nature of ciphering

> "To Thomas Jefferson from Robert Patterson, 19 December 1801
> Sir
> The art of secret writing, or, as it is usually termed, writing in cypher, has occasionally engaged the attention both of the statesman & philosopher for many ages; and yet I believe it will be acknowledged, by all who are acquainted with the present state of this art, that it is still far short of perfection. A perfect cypher, as it appears to me, should possess the following properties.—
> 1. It should be equally adapted to all languages.
> 2. It should be easily learned & retained in memory.
> 3. It should be written and read with facility & dispatch.
> 4. (Which is the most essential property) **it should be absolutely inscrutable to all unacquainted with the particular key or secret for decyphering.** "

Further down in this letter, Robert Patterson illustrates a cipher for Thomas Jefferson.

> "1 b i n l e i h t s h e e e n a e e a r 2 u v c l s t i h i e d c f i n s x n
> a 3 o e e t h h n p a l a e r n n o t n t 4 n n i h a t t o a a t i e e o n d o i
> 5 a p s e v h h r n t p v n t u t a n o 6 p e n w e e r t d t a e c e n h y a
> n 7 a a o o b c e u t e r d h e c e b n s"

In the Wall Street Journal there is an article dated July 9 2009 and is authored by Rachel Emma Silverman. The article pertains to this letter and its cipher and in it she states...

> "The cipher finally met its match in Lawren Smithline, a 36-year-old mathematician. Dr. Smithline has a Ph.D. in mathematics and now works professionally with cryptology, or code-breaking, at the

Center for Communications Research in Princeton, N.J., a division of the Institute for Defense Analyses.

A couple of years ago, Dr. Smithline's neighbor, who was working on a Jefferson project at Princeton University, told Dr. Smithline of Mr. Patterson's mysterious cipher.

Dr. Smithline, intrigued, decided to take a look. "A problem like this cipher can keep me up at night," he says. After unlocking its hidden message in 2007, Dr. Smithline articulated his puzzle-solving techniques in a recent paper in the magazine American Scientist and also in a profile in Harvard Magazine, his alma mater's alumni journal."

So end of story? Case closed?

No, there is more to this letter than meets the eye.

In order to accomplish what I have I had to first discover the key that I did not know existed and then discover the ciphers which I had never suspected. This letter is a tutorial on how ciphers and keys work.

Dr. Smithlines approach to this cipher was the exact opposite of mine. He had to work far harder than I did for his cipher. He recognized that there was obviously a cipher embedded within this letter but he had no key. I on the other hand came at this letter with a key and recognized the entire letter in itself was a cipher. It was the utility of the letter that was apparent to me, because it fit a narrative that Dr. Smithline was not yet aware of. As I glanced over the letter I knew it was no coincidence that it existed and it took me perhaps 10 seconds to establish the very purpose of its existence. I knew what the actors were up too. I knew Thomas Jefferson was an actor. I suppose it's possible that Thomas Jefferson suddenly received a letter like this out of the blue. What is absolutely not possible is to assume that he was unable to make the connection between the utility of this letter and the over 300 ciphers that were currently seeded for a future time. He was part of the cabal that was producing these documents. History is telling us explicitly "Yes, we know about keys and ciphers and the guy trying to explain them to you right now is imagining nothing."

Dr. Smithline is obviously far more educated and intelligent than I. What gave me advantage in this business was that I chose to study the 2nd amendment and in so doing also chose my own bias towards it. This one letter explains just how it was that I was able to discover the narratives that I have where others have failed. The ciphers I have located have been completely invisible to every level of intelligence and education of others because they have been "inscrutable to all". This is a testimony to the genius of Benjamin Franklin and his cabal. They managed to create completely invisible ciphers, and a completely invisible key that would gradually hint at its existence with only the passage of time.

You will see that I have stated "the narrative of the letters". The narrative is that letters were hidden in the form of ciphers and which had to be hidden for a period of at least 100 years.

"4. (Which is the most essential property) it should be absolutely inscrutable to all unacquainted with the particular key or secret for decyphering. "

This is the heart and soul of this letter. It could be no less explicit than this and Thomas Jefferson/John Patterson tell us so with the words "Which is the most essential property".

To be unacquainted with the key is to not even recognize something as being a key in the first place. This is the 2nd amendment itself and would remain hidden as long as it was interpreted subjectively. Each cipher had two meanings. It was actually a cipher that was disguised as a regular letter rendering it completely invisible and in so doing keep suspicion at bay. The best case scenario would be that it was viewed as being a bit awkward in its construction, as was the 2nd amendment and for the most part the Federalist Papers. The only thing that is black and white here is the concept of keys and ciphers.

The actual cipher in this letter was the first few lines of the Declaration of independence, which is of course "no great secret". The cipher was meant for demonstration purposes only. In the context of the greater narrative this particular letter has now been tied to it.

> "In Congress, July Fourth, one thousand seven hundred and seventy six. A declaration by the Representatives of the United States of America in Congress assembled. When in the course of human events..."

You may notice that I will often try to place any given letter into its chronological order of discovery. The narrative evolved with each discovery and sometimes subsequent discoveries will enhance previous ones. I've done this establish a basis for my reasoning at any given point in time. Since the discovery of the 2nd amendment is not a common event I saw the utility of the transparency in order to demonstrate my own motives. I have observed that some used the motive of an individual to disparage the result of a mans labors. The labor however produces something which in this case is the results of the research. The research speaks for itself, and my motives are irrelevant to the exposure of history that the labors have produced. My credentials are do not take away from the results either. Judge the results and not my credentials. A discovery does not care about a man's credentials and nor does the English language itself.

It was a process of learning the patterns, not just how to read the letters, but how they were to stand out in the first place. To add further veracity to the letters as being ciphers I came across the "Cipher Letter" which probably numbered 100 in the order of discovery. While 100 may seem high, within this group is a collection of 85 which are known as the Federalist Papers.

It appears Thomas Jefferson had a bit of sense of humour. He must have known that in some future time someone would also recognize the irony in him writing a letter about ciphers which was in its self a cipher of sorts. I say this in the sense that it has another context that can be applied to it now where previously this context was never perceived to even exist. There is a second irony now too, and if you will forgive my bias, it appears that "Smiths" seem to have a propensity to decipher letters as well.

There should be no indignation in this as far as academia is concerned. It should be apparent that a man of any level of intelligence would have no reason whatsoever to even suspect that this entire letter was a cipher. What reason? Why? It would be the stuff of fantasy. We have read the 2nd amendment as one sentence and it transformed. It was one sentence that has never been read like that before, simply because it had never actually been read. It had not been read because it was its own cipher, but it used many encryptions where its most powerful was human nature itself. People will generally read what they want to read. Benjamin Franklin had confidence in human nature and it almost never let him down. It was a force bigger than he was, so he simply decided to use it.

The Damage of the Old Rhetoric

When someone is told that something is their right, then it is a thing they can own. It is a thing they can own which can never be taken away. If it is perceived as an inalienable right then it is a thing that cannot be up for debate. It would even be more powerful than a birthright. A king may have a birthright after all which he acquired through the luck of heredity.

Now if one has something, then one may want to understand the utility of it. They may want garnish as much value from it as they can perceive. The 2nd amendment is particularly powerful because it can be tied back to the framers. but only through the constitution.

Much of the 2nd amendments rhetoric has been completely fabricated by the Supreme Court who have attempted to tie it back to the founders. They know that it is not within their purview to change the constitution, but only to argue its interpretation, and then vote upon it. Lines get blurred pretty fast between actually discerning the constitution and voting on its meaning in spite of it. It's a convenient way to bypass the 2/3 house and senate vote.

The "old" rhetoric of the 2nd Amendment

"You cannot trust your government to such an extent that they endorse you being armed and standing vigilant for the contingency of a tyrant."

"Freedom is power"

"Be Afraid"

"Every man for himself!".

"This is your right, and the government cannot take it away because they cannot be trusted".

Now run that rhetoric through a society for 10 generations.

This is the very seed of faction. It is patriotic to observe the wisdom of the constitution if it infers that you should be armed as a contingency to handle the possibility of the advent of a tyrant, This line of thinking would of course cultivate a distrust of government in the minds of those that felt this contingency was important. There are now two teams, where one is perceived as We the People and the other is the government. In reality "We the People" that cannot be trusted though, because in "We the People" lives human nature. The government is of the people, and no longer of royal blood. The ultimate check on power is in the vote of "We the People", and if the people choose to elect a tyrant then it is on the people themselves.

In theory, if it is patriotic to respect the constitution then there is no reason to abandon it unless it is deemed to be more important to maintain an involvement of the gun debate. The Constitution however can no longer be used as any source of this debate. Since laws must be created to enforce gun control then the only choice left is to be either law abiding citizen or not to be a law abiding citizen. People will of course still be able to hunt but as far as the right to self defense is concerned, it never existed under the constitution.

The days of hiding statistics are going to quickly come to an end because it is in the word "well" that such a cover up would be unconstitutional. The NRA may or may not continue to defend the 2nd amendment but they will no longer have an argument for self defense. It would be an act of high treason to attempt to enforce it, according to Benjamin Franklin in one of his letters.

The new rhetoric of the 2nd Amendment

"The government is now in charge of reality based gun control just as they have regulated seat belt laws.

Gun control is not an all or nothing proposition but their utility will be strictly for hunting.

The framers fully endorse this, and the full weight of the constitution is behind it.

A check and balance is now exposed in the constitution and forces the government to create regulations around power. Money is synonymous with power, and the people can enforce a check and balance against that if they wish too. The formula is simple, and transcends any incarnation of party or ideology because it goes to the very heart of the constitution. No man can be trusted so vote for the party of regulations without fail. If the people want the free market system to include the liberty of We the people, then We the people must vote for that liberty.

A Mystery of History Solved?

In a 1996 essay written by Professor Robert E McGlone titled "Deciphering Memory: John Adams and the Authorship of the Declaration of Independence" he references John Adams clarity in his recollection of earlier events. The reason that deciphering is required is because Thomas Jefferson recollection is much different. Thomas Jefferson was of course the man that drafted the Declaration of Independence. As we now know there was a completely unperceived mystery in history which is the full story of the 2nd amendment. Perhaps this is not totally accurate in light of the debates and ongoing discernments around it. Professor Cass Sunstein has even called the Second Amendment "The Constitution's Most Mysterious Right". We now know that these two men are actors in the cabal as discovered but are these two mysteries related? After a bit of thought and some more research I believe they are, but I will admit, I conjecture on it. I cannot prove it, because it was not revealed to me in any ciphered letter. I have only attempted to discern it. I will however be using reality as my guide and it seems to fit.

In addition to the essay above I've located a book that utilizes this same mystery. It is titled "Fundamentals of Cognitive Psychology by Ronald T. Kellogg 2016 3rd edition" in which he references Professor McGlone's essay. While I have not yet read this book I suspect due to the nature of its title he is using the essay to demonstrate how our memories can become a bit "tainted" over time and yet seem very real to us. Thomas Jefferson refers to this same observation of age when he says "it is at most but the life of a cabbage". If I may defend him the document in which he writes that was written in 1821 and references a man named Charles Thompson who was then in his 93 year of life. As a point of interest Charles Thompson was the secretary to the continental congress and was tasked to head up the fourth and final committee which rendered the final version of the United States Seal. It was completed in 1782. Ironically John Adams, Thomas Jefferson and Benjamin Franklin were on the first committee and were tasked to create a seal on the exact day the Declaration of Independence was read. History seems to report that they had failed in this particular Endeavour of intellect. You didn't honestly think these men did everything did you?

With respect to reality we now know that one of the cardinal rules that Benjamin Franklin had made was that suspicion must not be allowed to exist. It's my belief that John Adams recollection of events was bang on. His memory was fine. They mystery is why did Thomas Jefferson feel the need to appear to correct it? I believe that there was a nuance to what John Adams was revealing that was dangerous. He was exposing a tactic. Shortly after this Thomas Jefferson responded to the letter and disputed John Adams claims. He used John Adams age to give excuse to falsehood. It was not John Adams memory that was at fault though, or at least not in the context of the events that had transpired. Both these men knew that suspicion was the enemy. These men had to take this secret to their graves. It's astonishing that this cabal had pulled this off. Remember the rules of the ciphers. There could be no suspicion. It was a cardinal rule. Thomas Jefferson caught this faux pas where John Adams did not. I suspect it was missed because of his age but when you see what I'm about to reveal I think you may acknowledge its subtlety. Before I get too far ahead of this, I now present you with the pertinent excerpts from these letters. Overlay them with each other. Can you see the danger that Thomas Jefferson saw?

From John Adams to Timothy Pickering, 6 August 1822

The Sub-Committee met; Jefferson proposed to me to make the draught. I said I will not; You shall do it. Oh No! Why will you not? You ought to do it. I will not. Why? Reasons enough. What can be your reasons? Reason 1st. You are a Virginian, and Virginia ought to appear at the head of this business. Reason 2d. I am obnoxious, suspected and unpopular; You are very much otherwise. Reason 3d: You can write ten times better than I can. "Well," said Jefferson, "if you are decided I will do as well as I can."

Thomas Jefferson to James Madison August 30 1823

You have doubtless seen Timothy Pickering's 4th. of July Observations on the Declaration of Independence. If his principles and prejudices personal and political, gave us no reason to doubt whether he had truly quoted the information he alledges to have recieved from Mr. Adams, I should then say that, in some of the particulars, mr. Adams's memory has led him into unquestionable error. At the age of 88. and 47. years after the transactions of Independence, this is not wonderful. Nor should I, at the age of 80, on the small advantage of that difference only, venture to oppose my memory to his, were it not supported by written notes, taken by myself at the moment and on the spot. He says "The Committee (of 5. to wit, Dr. Franklin, Sherman, Livingston and ourselves) met, discussed the subject, and then appointed him and myself to make the draught; that we, as a subcommittee, met, & after the urgencies of each on the other, I consented to undertake the task; that the draught being made, we, the subcommittee, met, & conned the paper over, and he does not remember that he made or suggested a single alteration." Now these details are quite incorrect. The Committee of 5. met, no such thing as a subcommittee was proposed, but they unanimously pressed on myself alone to undertake the draught. I consented; I drew it; but before I reported it to the committee, I communicated itseparately to Dr. Franklin and mr. Adams requesting their corrections; because they were the two members of whose judgments and amendments I wished most to have the benefit before presenting it to the Committee;

We now know that the constitutional convention was fully orchestrated well in advance. What you will see later is that the 2nd amendment was actually drafted when James Madison was only one year of age and has existed in the year 1752, though not yet implemented in a Bill of Rights or any other means yet. I have previously conjectured on James Madison being used in the sense that others would be less suspicious of him than they would of a man like Benjamin Franklin. The other delegates would be less suspicious of him in the oral arguments and discussions if the some of the ideas appeared to come from him. Some of ideas would appear to be "fresh" and "just invented" under a collaborative effort of the delegation. James Madison was after all a young man, and anything he had "in the works" could only have been but a few years old. Benjamin Franklin on the other hand, well that would be a much different story.

Oh yes, a much different story indeed, hence this book.

Thomas Jefferson to the John Adams June 1822

"the papers tell us that Gen! Starke is off at the age of 93. Charles Thomson still lives at about the same age, chearful, slender as a grasshopper, and so much without memory that he scarcely recognises the members of his household. an intimate friend of his called on him not long since: it was difficult to make him recollect who he was, and, sitting one hour, he told him the same story 4. times, over. is this life?—with lab'ring step to tread our former footsteps? pace the round
 Eternal?—to beat and beat
 the beaten track? to see what we have seen

To taste the tasted? o'er our palates to decant
Another vintage?—it is at most but the life of a cabbage, surely not worth a wish."

There is a certain bit of irony in the next part of this letter as it relates to current events. It seems that even two hundred years ago Thomas Jefferson was observing the shenanigans of Russian rulers. A kite is defined as a person who preys upon others. He goes on to say this in the same letter. His observance isn't so much on governments as it is mans nature. This is why the checks and balances of real constitutions are so important within the context of real democracies.

"To turn to the news of the day, it seems that the **Cannibals of Europe** are going to eat, one another again. a war between Russia and Turkey **is like the battle of the kite[41] and snake[42]**. whichever destroys the other, leaves a destroyer the less for the world. **this pugnacious humor of mankind seems to be the law of his nature,** one of the obstacles to too great multiplication provided in the mechanism of the Universe. the cocks of the henyard kill one another up. boars, bulls, rams do the same. and the horse in his wild state, kills all the young males, until worn down with age and war, some vigorous youth kills him, and takes to himself the Haram of females. I hope we shall prove how much happier for man the Quaker policy is, and that the life of the feeder is better than that of the fighter: and it is some consolation that the desolation by **these Maniacs** of one part of the earth is the means of improving it in other parts. let the latter be our office. and let us milk the cow, while the Russian holds her by the horns, and the Turk by the tail. God bless you, and give you health, strength, good spirits, and as much of life as you think worth having"

At this point in time John Adams was 86 years old and Thomas Jefferson was still a spry 78.

The Declaration of Independence was drafted in 1776.

---

[41] See Kite Experiments of Benjamin Franklin. Thomas Jefferson is stitching his ciphers together.

[42] See United States Seal Section, Join or Die doodle of 1754. More stitching here.

John Adams letter was apparently reprinted in the Richmond Enquirer on July 4th 1823 to help illustrate the drafting of the Declaration of Independence. Just to put you into the current headspace of Thomas Jefferson, he had written this only about 3 weeks earlier. He has explicitly stated that there are some aspects of the opening scenes of government that are not yet known. It's very unlikely that this letter would have been public knowledge at that time, but more than likely archived just as the many Benjamin Franklin had. Privately held hoards.

> "History may distort truth, and will distort it for a time, by the superior efforts at justification of those who are conscious of needing it most. Nor will the opening scenes of our present government be seen in their true aspect, until the letters of the day, now held in private hoards, shall be broken up and laid open to public view."

4-Major Discoveries – Yes it Gets Better
The Federalist Papers Revisited

My initial approach in my research was to look up 2nd amendment quotes that people had been using to validate or explain it. In doing this if I could find a "match" with what I had read then there was a good possibility that I would have resolved another actor's name, thus giving me another trail for my research. The one other thing I knew that no one else would have known was that there seemed to be some sort of conspiracy going on because the 2nd amendment was most certainly a riddle. In reading a 2nd amendment quote that seemed to support the old meaning then that in turn would tell me about a delegate that did not know its true purpose.

Many of the quotes that I was finding that were of value were emerging from a group of essays known as the Federalist Papers. I was not familiar with these papers, but discovered that James Madison was among their others. Two more men were also involved in the writing of these essays, being Alexander Hamilton and John Jay who we now know were all members of the American Philosophical Society.

The authors of the Federalist Papers were James Madison, Alexander Hamilton and John Jay who were un-coincidentally members in of the American Philosophical Society. It was decided that there be a Constitutional Convention in Sept of 1786, which eventually began on May 14 1787. The Federalist papers are collection of 85 essays with a collective word count of 190,000 and were written from 1786-1787.

I had noticed that these essays were quite cryptic, flowery and poetic. They are loaded with footnotes and symbolisms. They seemed to have a similar style to some letters that I had read which were authored by Thomas Jefferson and later by George Washington and John Adams. I shared this observation with an American friend of mine from Chicago. In conversation I mentioned that students must have found these papers quite a chore to go through due to the nature of their construction. She responded saying that her older brother, now a retired from lawyer, had said the same thing when he was going to school 40 years earlier. Now if they are cryptic today, cryptic 40 years ago, then they was probably a good chance that they were also cryptic on the day they were first published. So even though this is a sampling of one, I take pride in knowing a chore when I see one. This book for instance, has been a bit of a chore which has been doing battle with my first discovery, and its profound importance from day one. So far that discovery had been winning.

As I started to research these papers the late Justice Scalia's name came up as being extremely familiar with the Federalist papers. There is a video of him talking on CSPAN where he recommends that everyone should be reading these papers to better understand the constitution. He is surprised that many law students had hardly studied these papers before. I also discovered that many Supreme Court decisions in the hopes of discerning the secrets and latitude of the constitution were based on interpretations of these essays.

At the time of Justice Scalia's passing on February 13, 2016 I had already resolved how to read these essays rather quickly because I had the key to them. I was of course also hearing the political speeches talking of the 2nd amendment, it being protected, Supreme Court Nominations and gun violence. At first I thought only a few of these were ciphers, but as I read a few, regardless of the order in which I picked them, cipher, cipher, cipher, cipher. I was astonished and then it hit me that these were written as a full on help document for the 2nd amendment and arguments around it. Yes, they were very much written to support the constitution, but they were not written for the 18th century, they were written for the 21st century. I then proceeded to go through about 30 of them, spot checking them, and while it would be boastful of me to say it was like reading a popup book, it was close. There were certain themes and key words that were spread throughout. Also each one had its own little spin on the nature of the encryptions that were employed. This was just another discovery though, and there was no way I would be able to share this information with the Supreme Court. How exactly does one call up Justice Scalia and offer to teach him how to read the Federalist papers without causing his nose to audibly snap? Besides, I was unable to locate a "help line" phone number or email address. The same of course holds true for explaining the 2nd amendment, hence the labor of this book. This most certainly was not going to be a snap

Another small wave of horror lapped to through my mind when I discovered that that these essays were actually used for discernments. I think about 250 court cases were argued with them as evidence. Just as the 2nd amendment had been misinterpreted subjectively for the advancement of industry, so to could the Federalist papers have been used to champion States rights, because every tyrant needs his own kingdom. The biggest transgression of justice is that the Federalist papers are not the constitution at all. They are simply commentary on it, but commentary of a nature that isn't altogether clear, expect by those that have sold it to others, that they are experts. These papers would have provided a great amount of wiggle room to lawyers, judges or scholars. To explore this is beyond the purview of this book, and a chore that gives me the shivers. This is beyond the purview of this book, and would probably take years to explore. I have no expertise in case law but I do sense that lawyers on both sides of an argument argue to win and will generally attempt to get a footing wherever they can. I'm sure there were many handholds used with respect to the utility of the Federalist Papers. I just figured I'd point this out. It's actually even possible that further amendments could have been based on these papers. To be clear though, this is not finger pointing towards anyone having nefarious motives, because there is logic, if had been stated by Thomas Jefferson that these are important papers.

I mentioned before that I had located 2nd amendment from within the Federalist papers which would have been completely invisible before knowing its secret. Here is one such example.

> "Among the many objects to which a wise and **free** people find it **necessary** to direct their attention[43], that of providing for their safety seems to be the first."
> Federalist Papers #3 -John Jay.

The object is of course the 2nd amendment. It is a thing. It is sentence. It is also the only object that was secreted into the Bill of Rights under the noses of the other delegates written and written in plain English' It was hidden by their fear and distrust of government. Wisdom comes from knowledge and after 224 years, the extensive gun violence that is currently ravaging the United States.

> "Distrust naturally creates distrust, and by nothing is good will and kind conduct more speedily changed."
> Federalist Papers #5 - John Jay,

If everyone is armed then everyone is scared of everyone else, but if far fewer are armed then there is far less to fear. Gun violence will be reduced which is of course a bill board of fear and excellent for gun sales. The pattern can be reversed, but it will require good will It can be reversed. Cause and effect. Remove the cause and there will be no effect.

> "In framing a government which is to be administered by men over men, the great difficulty lies in this: you must first enable the

---

[43] "necessary to the security of a free State".

government to control the governed; and in the next place, oblige it to control itself."
Federalist Papers #51 -Alexander Hamilton

The enabling is a reference to the 2nd amendment and its true utility. Obliging it is that there is no choice now but to obey the 2nd amendment. This point is driven home with the words "shall not be infringed".

The word "shall" is also used in the constitution to direct a president to nominate a justice. There is no choice in the matter. In the construction of that sentence the word "shall" is used at the front of the process where it is used at the end in the 2nd amendment. The entire process must be completed "toot sweet", capiche? Perhaps that sounded arrogant to say it, but I don't say it on my behalf but on behalf of the founders and their hidden labors to prove a truth. In one letter, Thomas Jefferson seems to value my opinion in this matter because he has referred to the author of this book, "the public view", as the "Candid a friend to Truth". He is joined in this viewpoint by the men George Washington's "cabinet" or cabal in this matter. I know what an alternative fact looks like, smells like and what makes it blossom. To disobey the constitution gives license to name the tyrant(s). A tyrant is the oppressor, a person that takes themselves far too seriously and puts themselves above all others. They put their own pursuit of happiness above the liberty of a nation which was always meant to exist under "We the People" and not political faction alone. The great difficulty was setting up the entire experiment, crafting the Federalist papers among the other private hoards of letters that span an 84 year period.

The quotes I've referred to are just some of the quotes that I had been finding and then resolved back to their source documents. The documents seemed to be primarily a collection of essays known as the Federalist Papers. I had never heard of these papers before, but in light of the pattern I was seeing, they seemed to speak of a mother lode in my research. A vein began to pulse in my neck, as my truth sniffer demanded more oxygen for what appeared to be an up and coming marathon. This was to be my first visit to the Federalist Papers, but also a first visit from one in the general public who suspected they may be more than what has previously been known.

When I began to look at the Federalist Papers themselves the first one I looked at was number one and I was stunned with what I was reading. It seemed directed to the 21st century, because for the 18th century it seemed a little bit over the top. I have transcribed it just ahead so that you can see this for yourself. These essays were different in that I could not think of any manner in how they could be written more accurately. They could have only one context and no other, because they seemed to line up perfectly with the reality of today. After some more research I discovered that other historians had stated that Federalist #84 was related to the Bill of Rights. Since the 2nd amendment belonged to that document I then jumped into it to see if I could glean any explanation about it.

At this point in my research there was nothing I was finding that seemed to be explicit. This would of course explain why what I was finding was never noticed before. This was like looking for Easter eggs hidden on a lawn that were all painted grass green. In light of the importance of what the 2nd amendment legitimate meaning was, it should be apparent why I was motivated to take a crack at these. It was still very confusing, and if you will forgive my final comment in this, I was still trying to resolve if these eggs I thought I was seeing were hatched up by my own imagination, or were they laid their through the genius of the framers?

I ask you this to demonstrate where my motivation was coming from including my frame of mind. The evidence I was uncovering ranges from flimsy to strong at this point. The quotes above are not too bad. My mind was in a constant tug of war though as the old dogma of the 2nd amendment tried to pull me back to a place of comfort. I was constantly wondering if my imagination was being overactive in what I was reading. I have no doubt that people reading this now will in turn be experiencing the same "disbelief" that I was. The source of the disbelief is of course multifaceted and is a personal thing to each reader.

The first and strongest quote seemed to substantiate that I had actually read the 2nd amendment objectively was validated by James Madison with respect to "the legitimate meaning of the instrument". The John Jay quote above that speaks of "Distrust naturally creates distrust.." was very good as well. Then I read this next quote. I knew without question what these men were up too, and it told me the true nature of the Federalist papers, or at least this one essay. This had to be a cipher, because it fit perfectly.

[Federalist Papers #84 , Alexander Hamilton, 28 May 1788.](#)

"**To the second**, that is, to the pretended establishment of the common and statute law by the constitution, I answer, that they are expressly made subject "to such alterations and provisions as the legislature shall from *time to time* make concerning the same." They are therefore at any moment liable to repeal by the ordinary legislative power, and of course have no constitutional sanction. **The** only use of the declaration was to recognize the ancient law, and to remove doubts which might have been occasioned by the revolution.** *This consequently can be considered as no part of a declaration of rights, which under our constitutions must be intended as limitations of the power of the government itself."*

Within a day or two of having discovered James Madison's letter where he states that the "**the legitimate meaning of the Instrument must be derived from the text itself;** I then come read what you see in bold. I knew this information prior to Barack Obama's town hall speech on January 6th of 2016. Again we see the "from time to time" reference which appears to mimic Thomas Jefferson his letter to William Stephen Smith "The tree of liberty must be refreshed from **time to time** with the blood of patriots and tyrants". Now Thomas Jefferson was not an author of the Federalist papers , but he was part of the cabal. He was writing his own letters, just as the Federalist authors were writing their own essays. These letters are all woven together with common themes and literary devices to prove the truth and tell the narrative through symbolisms. This essay was "originally" published on on July 16, July 26, and August 9, of 1788. Thomas Jefferson's letter was written on Nov 13 of 1787 about 8 months earlier from those publication. In light of what you are about to come to understand, these letters were more than likely, at least for this period written under the careful direction and eye of Benjamin Franklin. Nuance was everything, because it was nuance, that was the almost invisible thread that tied these letters together and if these men were to write these letters for the duration of their lives, for the future of their nation, then they had to learn this for the sake of consistency.

Now who do you think the real recipients of these letters and essays were meant to be? The "declaration" as mentioned above is of course "the right of the people to keep and bear Arms", as it sits nested in the 2nd amendment. "To remove doubts which might be occasioned by the revolution, is a politically correct way to say subdue fear of any future tyrant through ensuring the people are armed. The "ancient law" is often referred to and written about in all the "other" books that explain the history of the 2nd amendment. They are often confused with the inalienable right or a god given right as reference in "We the people". That is all completely nullified to a great extent in the final italicized sentence. The declaration "the right of the people to keep and bear Arms" is not the definition of the 2nd amendment as it sits within the Bill of Rights. To further elaborate on this it states that this is the only place in the constitution where the separation of powers must merge. The government is mandated, without option or discretion to create reality based common sense gun laws for the express purpose of not allowing arms into society in the first place. This is not about deterrence but is purely preventative. This is about PURE REGULATION, because no man can be trusted with too much power once in a society. First and foremost it is the Arms that are on trial, where an individual is someone after the fact of a transgression.

This paragraph was very explicit with the new 2nd amendment. You probably noticed as I originally did the opening words 'To the second'. This at first seems to be a bit of a clever way to point directly to the 2nd amendment. This is however a bit of hiccup here which I later noticed. This essay was dated 1788. In 1788 the Bill of Rights was not yet ratified. In the year 1788 its form would have been 12 articles. It may not even have existed yet, but it most certainly did not exist in its 10 amendment form because that occurred when it was ratified closer to December of 1791. The first two articles were dropped from the twelve causing the 1788 "fourth article" to be renumbered as the **second amendent.** The only other alternative was that this essay had to have been modified after the December 15, 1791. As unlikely as the latter may seem to be it actually appeared to be more likely of the two scenarios. How could I prove that? It's not that I needed these words to be there, but it appeared to be too much of a coincidence. Sometimes when something just feels right it's difficult to let it go. This was not an issue of me trying to make something fit without proof but rather trying to see if I could resolve that there was proof. I did notice that many of the essays were missing dates of publication, including this particular essay.

The federalist papers are a group 85 essays written at about the same time as the Constitutional Convention. They were originally released to the newspapers in New York City. Some of these papers have publication dates, and some others do not. The current consensus regarding the purpose of the Federalist papers were that they were meant to convince the general public to adopt the new constitution. I think it is probably common knowledge in the law community that these papers were a bit poetic, confusing and may have had inconsistencies from time to time. Any inconsistencies would of course have been explained away by professors with varied arguments in much the same way that the 2nd amendment itself has always been discerned. If a constitution is to exist, and it must be followed, then it must be discerned whether it can be truly discerned or not. It is just a cold hard fact because it is not human nature, especially among the wisest of the wise to been tasked by society to undertake these discernments

Now this is "key".

If we take a close look at the "new" 2ⁿᵈ amendment we can now see that it encompasses more aspects of the constitution and the primary purpose of government more so than any other sentence found within it.

It relates to the congress, lawmaking and the people themselves. So what was the real purpose of these essays? They were published anonymously through the pseudonym Philo- Publius? Now Philo means "Friend", and in history there was Roman aristocrat named Publius Valerius Poplicola. who was instrumental in helping to overthrow the monarchy and was considered a friend of the new Republic. The pseudonym is highly symbolic and very appropriate for these papers.

If some of the key founders were actually writing these directly to the public it would appear they are trying to bypass the delegates and their opinions. If these papers went out after decisions were already completed what manner of person would actually read them versus the constitution itself? 85 difficult to read letters versus just reading the constitution itself which is 4500 words in length and takes ½ hour to read. Just how many people were expecting to read these, and exactly how would they go about trying to reverse something if they didn't like what they read? While it's true this document predates the final version of the Bill of Rights, the 12 article version was still very much under construction. It's my understanding that there were many more as it was "loosely" based on the Virginia Constitution.

The collection of these essays were later published in a book called "The Federalist"

Here is a transcription of the Cover..

In the Press,
And speedily will be published,
The FEDERALIST
A Collection of Essays written in favor of the New Constitution.[44]
By a Citizen of New-York,
Corrected by the Author, with Additions and Alterations.[45]
This work will be printed on fine Paper and good Type, in one bandform Volume, duo-decimo, and delivered to subscribers at the

---

[44] Was there an old constitution at this point, or is this perhaps a reference to the newly understood constitution.

[45] The collection of these essays were modified and for good reason

moderate price of one dollar. A few copies will be printed on
Superfine royal writing paper, price 10 schillings.
No money required till delivery.[46]
"Philo-Publius" and the Articles of the Convention"[47]
As agreed upon at Philadelphia, Sept 17th 1787[48].

Now there are many meanings for the word "convention". Two of them could be applied here. It depends on whether or not you choose to speculate on the meaning of the 2nd amendment and read it subjectively, define it by the quotes of the very delegates it had been hidden from, or understand it for its "legitimate meaning" when it is read objectively, or "derived from its text". This is from a quote of James Madison who is purported to be ground zero for the Bill of Rights.

a meeting or formal assembly, as of representatives or delegates, for discussion of and action on particular matters of common concern.

5. a rule, method, or practice established by usage; custom: the convention of showing north at the top of a map.

Here is the first paper published by Alexander Hamilton.

When you read it , read it from the point of view that he is talking the United States after having experienced a misinterpreted 2nd amendment. He now knows that America has just been informed as to its true meaning so he begins to explain things, including the layout of this collection of essays. When he says "UNION" he is referring to the UNION of people and Arms as they exist in the word "Militia".

"E Plurius Enum"

"From Many One"

In a Militia there are many things, People & Arms=E. Plurius Enum = UNION

You may not buy into the latter, and think this is just my interpretation, but later you will see that it is not. It is the direct result of another discovery, and the path to that will be fully explained.

---

[46] Perhaps money, is the collecting back of Arms. "repaying" back to the constitution.

[47] Before the Bill of Rights, there were 12 articles, now think of "the Convention" as being the 2nd amendment itself.

[48] Supremacy Clause.

This is the context he is referring too

|| Federalist No. 1 ||

General Introduction
For the Independent Journal.
Author: Alexander Hamilton
To the People of the State of New York:

AFTER an unequivocal experience of the inefficiency of the subsisting federal government, you are called upon to deliberate on a new Constitution for the United States of America. The subject speaks its own importance; comprehending in its consequences nothing less than the existence of the UNION[49], the safety and welfare of the parts of which it is composed, the fate of an empire in many respects the most interesting in the world. It has been frequently remarked that it seems to have been reserved to the people of this country, by their conduct and example, to decide the important question, whether societies of men are really capable or not of establishing good government from reflection and choice, or whether they are forever destined to depend for their political constitutions on accident and force. If there be any truth in the remark, the crisis at which we are arrived may with propriety be regarded as the era in which that decision is to be made; and a wrong election of the part we shall act may, in this view, deserve to be considered as the general misfortune of mankind.[50]

This idea will add the inducements of philanthropy to those of patriotism[51], to heighten the solicitude which all considerate and good men must feel for the event. Happy will it be if our choice should be directed by a judicious estimate of our true interests, unperplexed and unbiased by considerations not connected with the

---

[49] Union of "People and Arms" I the word Militia.

[50] The wrong election is to ignore the truth of the 2nd amendment and carry on business as usual. The part is the word "Militia" and the election of it is to vote for its own meaning. It is wrong simply because it is a subjective interpretation.

[51] Philanthropy is to think of your neighbours first which of course is your country and a patriotic vision to the United States and honouring the genius of the constitution.

public good[52]. But this is a thing more ardently to be wished than seriously to be expected. The plan offered to our deliberations affects too many particular interests, innovates upon too many local institutions, not to involve in its discussion a variety of objects foreign to its merits, and of views, passions and prejudices little favorable to the discovery of truth[53].

Among the most formidable of the obstacles which the new Constitution will have to encounter may readily be distinguished the obvious interest of a certain class of men in every State to resist all changes which may hazard a diminution of the power[54], emolument, and consequence of the offices they hold under the State establishments; and the perverted ambition of another class of men, who will either hope to aggrandize themselves by the confusions of their country[55], or will flatter themselves with fairer prospects of elevation from the subdivision of the empire into several partial confederacies than from its union under one government.

It is not, however, my design to dwell upon observations of this nature[56]. I am well aware that it would be disingenuous to resolve indiscriminately the opposition of any set of men (merely because their situations might subject them to suspicion) into interested or

---

[52] Don't be swayed by the sales pitch of the NRA. Don't be swayed by "guns don't kill people , people kill people" Recognize that it is impossible to prevent criminality or the mentally ill I a society so why arm them in the first place?

[53] It is acknowledged that the debates around this are extensive and they have all been well thought out in advance. The truth is of course the 2nd amendment which will conflict with many arguments today.

[54] A diminution of power would of course be the people having to give up any arms that were causing chaos and harm to society.

[55] These would be the staunch defenders of the 2nd amendment in its old understanding. The NRA, the gun industry , and those most fearful of a tyrant that will never show his face. These people will probably tote this book as being some grand form of conspiracy and completely false in its findings. It is acknowledge that there will be a fierce pushback because people have grown accustomed to the old 2nd amendment.

[56] Alexander Hamilton does not want to dwell on the arguments against the 2nd amendment in its old meaning but only more in its new. He doesn't want to dwell on it because he doesn't perceive there to be an old meaning.

ambitious views. Candor will oblige us to admit that even such men may be actuated by upright intentions[57]; and it cannot be doubted that much of the opposition which has made its appearance, or may hereafter make its appearance, will spring from sources, blameless at least, if not respectable--the honest errors of minds led astray by preconceived jealousies and fears. So numerous indeed and so powerful are the causes which serve to give a false bias to the judgment, that we, upon many occasions, see wise and good men on the wrong as well as on the right side of questions of the first magnitude to society. This circumstance, if duly attended to, would furnish a lesson of moderation to those who are ever so much persuaded of their being in the right in any controversy. And a further reason for caution, in this respect, might be drawn from the reflection that we are not always sure that those who advocate the truth are influenced by purer principles than their antagonists. Ambition, avarice, personal animosity, party opposition, and many other motives not more laudable than these, are apt to operate as well upon those who support as those who oppose the right side of a question. Were there not even these inducements to moderation, nothing could be more ill-judged than that intolerant spirit which has, at all times, characterized political parties. For in politics, as in religion, it is equally absurd to aim at making proselytes by fire and sword. Heresies in either can rarely be cured by persecution.

And yet, however just these sentiments will be allowed to be, we have already sufficient indications that it will happen in this as in all former cases of great national discussion. A torrent of angry and malignant passions will be let loose. To judge from the conduct of the opposite parties, we shall be led to conclude that they will mutually hope to evince the justness of their opinions, and to increase the number of their converts by the loudness of their declamations and the bitterness of their invectives. An enlightened zeal for the energy and efficiency of government will be stigmatized as the offspring of a temper fond of despotic power and hostile to the principles of liberty.

---

[57] An example of this would be men thinking they are being patriotic with respect to the old 2nd amendment. There is honour in that, and no one can be faulted for it. To say Sandy Hook was a hoax though, is about as far from being Patriotic as one could imagine.

An over-scrupulous jealousy of danger to the rights of the people, which is more commonly the fault of the head than of the heart, will be represented as mere pretense and artifice, the stale bait for popularity at the expense of the public good. It will be forgotten, on the one hand, that jealousy is the usual concomitant of love, and that the noble enthusiasm of liberty is apt to be infected with a spirit of narrow and illiberal distrust. On the other hand, it will be equally forgotten that the vigor of government is essential to the security of liberty; that, in the contemplation of a sound and well-informed judgment, their interest can never be separated; and that a dangerous ambition more often lurks behind the specious mask of zeal for the rights of the people than under the forbidden appearance of zeal for the firmness and efficiency of government. History will teach us that the former has been found a much more certain road to the introduction of despotism than the latter, and that of those men who have overturned the liberties of republics, the greatest number have begun their career by paying an obsequious court to the people; commencing demagogues, and ending tyrants.

In the course of the preceding observations, I have had an eye, my fellow-citizens, to putting you upon your guard against all attempts, from whatever quarter, to influence your decision in a matter of the utmost moment to your welfare,[58] by any impressions other than those which may result from the evidence of truth. You will, no doubt, at the same time, have collected from the general scope of them, that they proceed from a source not unfriendly to the new Constitution. Yes, my countrymen, I own to you that, after having given it an attentive consideration, I am clearly of opinion it is your interest to adopt it. I am convinced that this is the safest course for your liberty, your dignity, and your happiness. I affect not reserves which I do not feel. I will not amuse you with an appearance of deliberation when I have decided. I frankly acknowledge to you my convictions, and I will freely lay before you the reasons on which they are founded. The consciousness of good intentions disdains ambiguity. I shall not, however, multiply professions on this head. My motives must remain in the depository of my own breast. My arguments will be open to all, and may be judged of by all. They shall at least be offered in a spirit which will not disgrace the cause of truth[59].

I propose, in a series of papers, to discuss the following interesting particulars:

THE UTILITY OF THE UNION TO YOUR POLITICAL PROSPERITY THE INSUFFICIENCY OF THE PRESENT CONFEDERATION TO PRESERVE THAT UNION THE NECESSITY OF A GOVERNMENT AT LEAST EQUALLY ENERGETIC WITH THE ONE PROPOSED, TO THE ATTAINMENT OF THIS OBJECT THE CONFORMITY OF THE PROPOSED CONSTITUTION TO THE TRUE PRINCIPLES OF REPUBLICAN GOVERNMENT ITS ANALOGY TO YOUR OWN STATE CONSTITUTION and lastly, THE ADDITIONAL SECURITY WHICH ITS ADOPTION WILL AFFORD TO THE PRESERVATION OF THAT SPECIES OF GOVERNMENT, TO LIBERTY, AND TO PROPERTY.

In the progress of this discussion I shall endeavor to give a satisfactory answer to all the objections which shall have made their appearance, that may seem to have any claim to your attention.

It may perhaps be thought superfluous to offer arguments to prove the utility of the UNION, a point, no doubt, deeply engraved on the hearts of the great body of the people in every State[60], and one, which it may be imagined, has no adversaries. But the fact is, that we already hear it whispered in the private circles of those who oppose the new Constitution, that the thirteen States are of too great extent for any general system, and that we must of necessity resort to separate confederacies of distinct portions of the whole. [1] This doctrine will, in all probability, be gradually propagated, till it has votaries enough to countenance an open avowal of it[61]. For nothing

---

[59] I have adopted the same approach in writing this book as Alexander Hamilton has in writing these letters. Now you can read these documents for what they are. There are still encryptions though, they are mild, but they are there. He speaks of full transparency as I have in the writing of this novel. Where I have discovered the truth of the 2nd , Alexander Hamilton, James Madison and John Jay will be writing about it extensively.

[60] The "State" he speaks of is "state of mind", just as it can be found under "Liberty" in the Merriam-Webster American Dictionary.

[61] This is a man of common sense. He acknowledges that it will take time for the people to both implement and grow used to the new second amendment.

can be more evident, to those who are able to take an enlarged view of the subject, than the alternative of an adoption of the new Constitution or a dismemberment of the Union. It will therefore be of use to begin by examining the advantages of that Union, the certain evils, and the probable dangers, to which every State will be exposed from its dissolution. This shall accordingly constitute the subject of my next address.
    PUBLIUS.

Things will probably have to happen in stages in order to prevent unnecessary and unwanted bloodshed. Time and understanding and a United States of America will be required to undergo such a change for those who wish to call themselves patriot.

Concluding Remarks on the Federalist Papers

Unfortunately I am just one person and the work involved to fully decipher the entire set of Federalist Papers is beyond the scope of this book. I have already "spot deciphered" about 30 percent of these papers in order to establish that they were related to this story. They are. This first volume was written to let the cat out of the bag as well as to establish the utility of my bias for discerning the truth in absence of ideology or nefarious interests.

A Benjamin Franklin Cipher

Out of all the ciphers I've encountered this is the one that convinced me that I was indeed reading ciphers and not imagining things. It propelled me into the surreal. This letter was a buried treasure. It had never been dug up before. It was after this one that I was certain there would be many more. I may not have known the time period in which they existed but it clarified what these frames were up to and how they were going about it.

After scrutinizing and randomly sampling and decoding 25 of the Federalist essays I had resolved the true purpose of that series of essays. The reasoning behind looking through Benjamin Franklin's letters can be found in the section where I discuss the American Philosophical Society.

Using an internet search engine I quickly found the site franklinpapers.org which is a digitized repository of Benjamin Franklin's letters. They are known as "The Papers of Benjamin Franklin" which is sponsored by both the American Philosophical Society and Yale University. There are about 30,000 letters in this archive. The digitized media can be filtered by date or by name. I was also looking for letters that seemed to stand out either due to the title or date. Benjamin Franklin was most certainly aware of the his ciphers and the volume of his work. Rather than forcing someone to seek out a needle in a haystack he appeared to be red flagging his letters in a number of different ways, which later made them much easier to locate.

The last date for his letters were in April of 1790 because that is the month that Benjamin Franklin passed away so I figured the sweet spot in time for his ciphers would coincide with the dates of the Federalist Papers. I began going through the years from 1787 to 1790

It was this letter and James Madison's letter **"the legitimate meaning of the Instrument must be derived from the text itself;"** that I felt were very strong evidence as I carried on through my research. Perhaps like you, I was having a difficult time believing what I was unfolding before me. With just these two letters and knowing what the 2nd amendment really meant I was 100 percent certain that what I was discovering what appeared to be factual. It was the dogma that kept fighting with my mind.

I'm putting this letter ahead of the next section because it is linked to another discovery. With that being said, if you find the next section rather unbelievable then consider this letter here to be a supporting document as evidence to the contrary.

This particular one is a bit involved but in my attempt to keep this book organized I felt this was the appropriate placement for it. For those that are not aware, Benjamin Franklin was both a genius and a polymath. He was extremely prolific in his letter writing, which may lead you to wonder just how I located this particular letter. This letter is actually a ciphered letter that stretches beyond that of symbolism. I have posted its solution towards the end of the book. This letter was found at FranklinPapers.org which is affiliated with Yale University and the American Philosophical Society. There are about 30,000 letters archived here.

TO WILLIAM ALEXANDER (L. c.) October 26 1789.

46 THE WRITINGS OF BENJAMIN FRANKLIN [1789 Philadelphia,
MY DEAR FRIEND,
You may remember, that two or three Years ago, I communicated to you a Claim I had upon the State of Virginia,
on Account of a Purchase it had made of some Types & other
printing Materials belonging to me at the Beginning of the
Troubles ; The Value could not at that Time be ascertained.
Mr. Bache, my Attorney, being unacquainted with it ; & my
Papers and Accounts being lost & destroyed during the
late Confusions. I have now no Means of discovering what
the Quantity was of the Types & what they cost me ; I
only remember that there was a Fount of Law-Character
for which I paid 30^ Sterl? & a large Fount of Greek which
I think was valued at about 40^ Sterl. besides a very considerable Fount of Long-Primer, the Weight of which I
forget, but suppose it might be about 5oo lb which at 1/6 per
lb amounted to 37^ io/ Sterl 8 . There were also some Cases
& other Things of which I cannot speak particularly. You
were so kind as to offer me your Assistance in procuring from
the Government some Satisfaction for this Claim, I now take
the Liberty to request that you would endeavour it as soon as
possible, as I wish to have all my Affairs settled before my
Departure: The Law-Fount & the Greek were probably
of no Use to the Government, & I should be willing to take
them back if they still exist, and are entire. I suppose that

the Value of Goods at that Time will be considered, as well
as the Length of Time during which the Payment has been
delayed. I submit the Whole to the Honour & Equity of
the Government, & shall be thankful for what they will be
pleased to allow me. My best Wishes attend you, being ever
My Dear Friend,
Your's most affectionately
B FRANKLIN.

(Solution to this in Benjamin Franklin Cipher Collection)

SPOILER ALERT – SOLUTIONS SECTION!

TO WILLIAM ALEXANDER (L. c.) October 26 1789.

1773. TO WILLIAM ALEXANDER (L. c.) October 26 1789.
46 THE WRITINGS OF BENJAMIN FRANKLIN [1789 Philadelphia,
MY DEAR FRIEND,
You may remember, that two or three Years ago, I communicated to you a Claim I had upon the State of Virginia, on Account of a Purchase[62] it had made of some Types & other printing Materials belonging to me at the Beginning of the Troubles;[63] The Value could not at that Time be ascertained. [64] Mr. Bache, my Attorney, being unacquainted with it[65] ; & my Papers and Accounts being lost & destroyed during the late Confusions. I have now no Means of discovering what the Quantity was of the Types & what they cost me ; I only remember that there was a Fount of Law-Character[66] for which I paid 30^ Sterl? & a large Fount of Greek [67]which

---

[62] The colonies bought into the claim that guns would be required to defend against tyranny.

[63] The beginning of the troubles is a reference to the slow influx of Arms into society over time.

[64] The value is the public recognition of how important this would be. Does most of America wish for better "gun laws"? Does most of America today really believe there will ever come a point where their government may become so tyrannical that the people will have to raise arms against them? This has never occurred to date.

[65] This is an acknowledgement that the law establishment had no idea about the truth of the 2nd amendment. Mr. Bache did not know of it , simply because it would never have been taught in any school.

[66] 'A well regulated Militia". The small law font is the "r" in regulated. Regulations are in essence laws.

[67] A large Greek font refers to the capital letter in the word Militia. The Greeks had a specific word for Militia which is known as a Phalanx. This term appears to have been thrown around a bit with these men. It is used in a letter between George Washington to John Jay, 10 March 1787 and in an letter between Thomas Jefferson to James Madison, 28 August 1789. You can almost hear their discussions on ciphering and hints.

I think was valued at about 40^ Sterl. besides a very considerable Fount of Long-Primer[68], the Weight of which I forget, but suppose it might be about 5oo lb[69] which at 1/6 per lb[70] amounted to 37^ io/ Sterl 8 . There were also some Cases & other Things of which I cannot speak particularly[71]. You were so kind as to offer me your Assistance in procuring from the Government some Satisfaction for this Claim[72], I now take

---

[68] This is VERY important which you will see later. Remember that Benjamin Franklin didn't have the benefit of a word processor and the ability to do a word or letter count. The Long-Primer is actually the Bill of Rights, but not in its 10 amendment form. It is in its 12 article form because Benjamin Franklin passed away on April 17, 1790 and the current Bill of Rights did not exist until after this time. He obviously would have had no idea about it at the time he was creating this cipher. You are going to learn something astonishing shortly. In the Merriam-Webster Dictionary the definition of Primer is this

1: a small book for teaching children to read
2 : a book or other writing that introduces a subject
Think of it as a "Quick Start Guide".

[69] He says that the long primer must weigh about 500 lbs. As a unit of currency , at this time there are 240 pence per lb , which would equate to 500x240 = 120000

[70] 1/6 of a lb where 1 lb = 240 pence equates to 40 pence PER letter. I have transcribed the 12 article version of the bill of rights in the resource section of this book. If you pull it into a word processor and count the actual letters, excluding spaces the count is EXACTLY 2981 letters. If you multiply that by 40 pence per letter then you arrive at 119240 pence or 496.83 lbs. It appears that Benjamin Franklin's acceptable tolerance for the word "about" is under 1 percent. (99.4 percent). This is a difference of 19 letters out of 3000 (6x500).

[71] I speculate that he is referencing that he cannot speak of the real meaning of the capital "A" and the capital "S" which are cases and things. Only "A" and "M" are capitalized in the 2nd amendment but "people" is not capitalized. He infers that it's all about the Arms and not the people. The "State" is a reference to a state of mind as in a free state or Liberty. Look up "Liberty" in his friend Noah Websters dictionary, or as it is known today the Merriam-Webster Dictionary.

the Liberty to request that you would endeavour it as soon as possible[73], as I wish to have all my Affairs settled before my Departure[74]: The Law-Fount & the Greek were probably of no Use to the Government[75], & I should be willing to take them back if they still exist, and are entire[76].

---

[72] He is asking 'me" aka Alexander William, to notify the government of the USA about this now deciphered letter. This makes the opening statement in the preface of this book both succinct and accurate. There is no arrogance on my part, or illusions of grandeur. Is it surreal to me? Yes, I would say somewhat.

[73] I tried to notify over 30 other people and agencies with respect to this in late December of 2015. My allotted time in the white house switchboard counted down very quickly when I told them that I had solved the riddle of the 2nd amendment. So you see it was just not my idea alone to request an escalation, as I mentioned earlier on. It is now surreal to you the reader if this is not front page news in necessity for this escalation. Faction is irrelevant. If you are American then I ask on behalf the your first four sitting presidents, that this be put into the public view so that all may know the true nature of the Bill of Rights and the 2nd amendment. Patriotism does not get any more real than this. The Constitution was written for "We the people" in a United States of America. If you not American, than be a sport and assist this man in fulfilling his dream for a better future.

It is up to the readers of what I have written to escalate Benjamin Franklin's request a year later. You, the reader are now a part of this narrative of the very book you read if the US government is not yet aware of this book's findings.

[74] His affairs settled is a reference his own time when the 2nd amendment had to be hidden. He wants it recognized that the misinterpretation was only meant for the first 100 years of his nation.

[75] The government has been almost powerless to protect society from Arms for over 224 years now which is due to the subjective interpretation and enciphering of the 2nd Amendment.

[76] Law-font has the hyphen in it. and references 'well-regulated' or the wrong interpretation. The greek was the word "Militia" which is encrypted and is "entire" because it's not broken up. They are of no Use to the government because 'well regulaged' as in 'well lawed is not yet perceived. He wants to take them back which would then expose the truth of the 2nd amendment and then mandate government to protect its people from what must certainly be raging gun violence.

I suppose that the Value of Goods at that Time will be considered[77], as well
> as the Length of Time during which the Payment has been delayed[78]. I submit the Whole to the Honour & Equity of the Government[79], & shall be thankful for what they will be pleased to allow me. My best Wishes attend you, being ever
> My Dear Friend,
> Your's most affectionately
> B FRANKLIN.

It might seem a bit redundant of me to say that Benjamin Franklin was a very clever man. It appears that Benjamin Franklin is well-versed in the origins of names. William Alexander was a real man in history but it's his name that has the most utility in this cipher

William means "resolute protector"   OR protecting the secret of the 2nd amendment.

Alexander means "protector of mankind" OR legitimate purpose of 2nd amendment.

---

[77] The value of the encryption will be perceived in order to get the 2nd into the constitution

[78] The payment is a reference to the true value of the real 2nd amendment after experiencing its harm in society for an extended period of time. It was delayed. This is analogous to "From time to time with the blood of patriots and tryants" as stated by Thomas Jefferson in a letter he wrote to William Stephen Smith Nov, 13 1787 just under two years earlier.

[79] He asks that the entire 2nd amendment be used, the whole of it. If the government is to be of any value to the people or have any honour as a government then the 2nd amendment can only be used in this fashion. To do otherwise, to ignore the whole from this point forward, is to banish the very point of government itself, which would course be dishonourable and be an insult to the labours of the wisest founders who gave the people on this continent a United States in the first place. Like it or not, some men are wiser than others. Faction is simply a cult of ignorance in some situations. There is no truth in consensus. In these particular circumstances, the dogma of the 2nd amendment is currently owned by 320 million people. I am one man and I now write the full hidden truth of the 2nd amendment. That concept is not a theory, however unlikely it might be perceived.

William Alexander is a symbolism for the 2nd amendment. While it can be other things as well, as you can see, but it most certainly is this.

So how did I recognize this as a cipher? First off, I was looking for them. The tone of this letter seemed to taunt the reader to look closer. Benjamin Franklin seemed too aloof, and I'd seen this before already. If someone is being aloof, then in theory, there is a reason for it. It seemed like there was much that he couldn't remember and he seemed overly concerned about what appeared to be an old bill in the twilight of his life. The last time he was associated with the newspaper business was over 20 years earlier. Is it to be supposed that a collection agency had finally managed to track him down? He also seems to talk quite a bit about fonts and their weights.

He couldn't quite remember "this and that" and it was about an old bill in the twilight of his life. There seemed to be too many details in this letter. He was describing fonts? Why? Lots of numbers and weights? Long Primer? He later infers that this old bill he's trying to sort out would be useful to government. Now I only speculate when I say this, but I don't think any human being in the history of man has ever thought that about a government bill. It's almost as if he thinks it's important.

As I was looking at this letter, I did a search on William Alexander and saw that he was also a member of the American Philosophical Society. I was searching for these letters and in just knowing that, it seemed to tie in with a John Adams letter 27th 1784 where he states

> "The Philosophers are speculating upon our Constitutions and I hope will throw out Hints, which will be of Use to our Countrymen".

At this point in time I had not yet resolved if Benjamin Franklin was also writing these ciphered letters. This was the first one I came across in his archive of 30,000 that appeared to be a cipher. In reality though the pool I was drawing from originally started around the time of the constitutional convention to his death in April of 1790. Eventually as the narrative began to grow, so did the start time for these letters. They actually moved back to the time of the Declaration of Independence. I had resolved what these men were up too, but I was also attempting to locate other actors who were in turn writing their own letters for this cause.

After a bit of research on William Alexander I discovered that he had an ancestor of the same name who was known as the Earl of Stirling. The more recent of the two is the 5th Earl of Stirling, while the other was the 1st Earl of

Stirling. I also noticed that one of these men was about 6 years in the grave, while the other was around 119 years in the grave. Both were incapable of reading based on the date stamp of this letter. Now since there were two men of the same name, it would stand to reason one would have a better utility in this cipher than the other.

Now why would Benjamin Franklin write a letter to a dead man and then stick it into the archives of his American Philosophical society. He surely must have known the more recent man had been dead as he was a member of his invite only society. The only logical conclusion I can think of is the symbolism of it. I began to see dots.

Dot 1: Dead eyes can't see.

Dot 2: Letters are usually written to be read.

Dot 3: This letter was archived

Dot 4: The true recipient of this letter would have to be alive to read it.

Dot 5: This letter is dated in the same period of time as the Bill of Rights which in turn has the 2nd amendment which I now know was a a riddle itself. To be more specific though, it was a cipher itself, only its key was suspicion.

I believe that the William Alexander he is making reference too is the 1st Earl of Stirling. It turns out that this man was a Scottish poet in the time of William Shakespeare who had written a poem called "The Doomesday". It references an anarchical society where there is death and destruction. It appears that it the genius Benjamin Franklin was of the opinion that Arms can cause society harm if they are never regulated. Yes, guns can cause harm anywhere they are found be them in Benghazi or on the streets of America.

William Alexander, 5th Earl of Stirling
Born Dec ,4, 1726 New York City, Province of New York
Died January 15, 1783 (aged 56-57) Albany New York

Wikipedia

William Alexander, 1st Earl of Stirling
William Alexander, 1st Earl of Stirling was a Scottish courtier and poet who was involved in the Scottish colonisation of Habitation at Port-Royal, Nova Scotia and Long Island, New York.
Born:1570, Menstrie Castle, Menstrie, United Kingdom

Died: September 12, 1640, London, United Kingdom
Education: University of Glasgow

Wikipedia

To Patrick Henry (unpublished) Oct 8 1785

Philada. Oct. 8. 1785.
Sir,

After congratulating your Excellency, as I do most sincerely, on the continued Respect and Confidence of your Country, manifested by their placing you again in the Chair of Government over them; I beg leave to trouble you with a little Affair that relates to myself.

When I went to France, I left here a Quantity of Printing Letters[80], which my Attorney Mr. Bache[81] tells me were sold to your State for Public Use[82]; but no Agreement was made ascertaining the Value[83], he being unacquainted with it[84]. All the Accounts I had of the original lost, as well as of the Quantity, which was bought in Parcels at different Times and of different Persons, are lost; so that I know not how to make a Charge for them; especially as they were not weigh'd nor any Inventory made of them, nor of the other Printing Utensils delivered with them. As this Transaction pass'd under your former Administration, what I now request is, that your Excellency would require of the Printer who receiv'd them an Account of the Weight of the Types, expressing the different kinds, (because they are different Prices) and also a List of the other Things that accompanied them.

---

[80] The entire second amendment, or just the words "the right of the people to keep and bear arms"

[81] Mr. Bache was Benjamin Franklins son in law, so symbolism of attorney and is future descendents is "affairs of the future"

[82] Sold for public use means he knew by mans nature, they would read the 2nd amendment how they wanted to read it.

[83] I suspect this letter was back dated and archived to help to obscure it beyond the scope of the convention if it was encountered. I believe the Bill of Rights was just plopped down at the convention and the men said absolutely nothing to anyone about the real meaning of the words " the right of the people to keep and bear arms".If men like Patrick Henry stated what they thought it meant, the men of the conspiracy neither agreed or disagreed with any interpretation. It was probably not even mentioned, because to some men, it looked perfect, and to those that knew better, it looked perfect too.

[84] With Mr Bache being symbolic of the future, this would of course be an admission that it was hidden.

[85]When I have obtain'd such an Account fom him, I shall be able to make out mine; and I doubt not your kind Assistance in procuring the Payment[86]. With great Esteem and Respect, I am, Sir, Your Excellency's most obedient and most humble Servant[87]

B. Franklin

His Excelly. Patrick Henry Esqr. &c.

Endorsed: Letter from Dr Franklin

This letter is the "mate" that is referred to in the opening line of the William Alexander cipher as previously illustrated. As you can see it has the same theme of typesets which weaves these two letters together. The utility of this letter is to demonstrate the "false" subjective reading of the 2nd amendment which further adds to the veracity of the objectively read 2nd amendment as being the legitimate interpretation. Mr. Patrick Henry most certainly would have bought into the 2nd amendment as it was known. This is the man that screamed out "Give me liberty or give me death".

---

[85] Basically saying that the 2nd amendment has very little with "the right to keep and bear arms", but with respect to its real meaning, its time to collect back the arms in society. Former Administration is a reference to the Bill of Rights and the period in which it was drafted.

[86] Now that the 2nd amendment is revealed, any man with arms, arms that are deemed unsafe for public consumption, will be relinquished back to the government. There is also respect given to any man who believed in the old version of the 2nd amendment, for they cannot be faulted in its interpretation, as it was meant to be hidden.

[87] The government is obliged to do this as per the constitution, and it's only in this regard that the separation of powers merge. The government is only doing its job in the service of the people, nothing more.

The Bill of Rights

Immediately after discovering the purpose I had a hunch about the Bill of Rights. What I discovered was that the Bill of Rights is actually a "Quick Start Guide" to the 2nd amendments real world administration. Once the 2nd amendment was finally exposed it appears that the framers anticipated a two word question "Now What? How are we supposed to implement this in real world practice?" There is a reason why I placed the Benjamin Franklin cipher immediately prior to this chapter. The "Long Primer: reference is a reference to the Bill of Rights. In the Merriam-Webster dictionary a primer is defined as "a small introductory book on a subject". This reference adds veracity to the Bill of Rights as an implementation guide IN CONUNCTIOIN with how it is currently being used in law. It was crafted just like any of the other letters. This most certainly adds veracity to the claim that the Bill of Rights was predetermined in advance of its "drafting" according to currently known history. As you can see these ciphers are woven together to add veracity from one to the next. Any opinions of coincidence had to be banished from the mind.

Before I get into the details of its usage I would first like to address why I suspected that there might be more to it than meets the eye. I'd call it a bit of a fluke. I used the same approach that I had used in suspecting the 2nd amendment in the first place. I did however have an added advantage in suspecting the Bill of Rights. I knew that the framers were up to something, as opposed to suspecting something was simply off with an amendment, being the second. I knew a trail existed, and was left to be found. Immediately prior to analyzing the Bill of Rights I had just established the true nature and purpose of the Federalist Papers. As I think I have stated, they are essentially a full on user manual written specifically for the 2nd amendment and the true nature of the constitutions usage. At this point in time the actors I had resolved were James Madison, Alexander Hamilton, John Jay and Thomas Jefferson. Sporadic 2nd amendment quotes had led me to the Federalist Papers and in turn the authors of them.

So paying the Bill of Rights a visit was almost an afterthought. The Federalist Papers were very well known in scholastic circles. They are essays, riddled with symbolisms which had a duality in their interpretation. The Bill of Rights is like an essay, and in it lived the 2nd amendment, which has now been resolved to be a cipher. Is it possible that the Bill of Rights also had two different meanings by design? I was not all that familiar with the Bill of Rights at that time. The only three amendments I was most familiar with would be "Freedom of Speech". "The

Right to Bear Arms", and "Claiming the Fifth", which has probably been used in every other court based crime drama in history.

As I read through the Bill of Rights it was the 3rd amendment that seemed to have similarities with the 2nd in that it seemed to period specific to me. The 3rd was pretty much off the charts though in this regard. After looking up the 3rd amendment in Wikipedia, I discovered that the Supreme Court has viewed the 3rd amendment as being the piglet of the Bill of Rights. It has rarely if ever been used. Now why would James Madison put something useless into the Bill of Rights? This is a different creature than the 2nd amendment because we now know that the 2nd amendment to be the a Holy Grail of Arms Control amendment. After marching through the other amendments it was the 10th that then stood out, but in a different way. The Supreme Court has referred to it as being a truism. I think the term truism is simply a politically correct method of calling something pointless. So why would "James Madison" draft a useless and a pointless amendment and then put them into such a highly visible and important document?. There was something going on here, but what was it? Just like any documents I had been studying I was looking for indicators that they were ciphers. Step one was to resolve as to whether or not they were unusual when cross referenced with the norms of reality, and step two was to see if these violations of intelligent thought could be explained when cross referenced with the key to unlocking their truth.

While the Benjamin Franklin's letter was archived, and tucked away in some cabinet hidden from the public view, the Bill of Rights was front and center. There is no other document that the people would be more familiar with. This makes it particularly astonishing and equally unbelievable that it too would be a cipher just as the 2nd amendment had been a riddle. What other document in the entire constitution would be more appropriate than the one the people were most familiar with? This was a document that would never be lost to time. I proceeded to study it more closely inspired by the "oddities" I have just referenced. You may want to sit down for this one. Remember how I've already explained how the ciphers have dual meanings. In the absence of possessing a key, these ciphers would be essentially invisible. For lack of a better expression this document was crafted in such a way its utility would be to kill two birds with one stone. Item 4 in Thomas Jefferson's tutorial on ciphers stated this.

> A perfect cypher, as it appears to me, should possess the following properties.—
> 1. It should be equally adapted to all languages.

2. It should be easily learned & retained in memory.

3. It should be written and read with facility & dispatch.

4. (Which is the most essential property) **it should be absolutely inscrutable to all unacquainted with the particular key or secret for decyphering.** "

It is the word "ALL" in the emboldened text that excludes nobody. No amount of education or high intelligence would be except from being classified as being a part of "All". The ego may not like this but "All" also includes men with egos. It appears to me that step 4 in this ciphering tutorial has been achieved rather successfully because no one has ever suspected the Bill of Rights to be anything other than what it was. A cipher is always associated with a key, and in possessing that, I was completely excluded from "all". The sheer volume of these discoveries is the very proof of the genius that went into these ciphers. I stress this point for both you and myself. I'd pat my own back but my ego is too busy shaking my hand. My ego is an idiot.

I did a cursory study of the 3rd amendment with the key in my other hand its secrets began to bubble to the surface

Here is what Wikipedia has to say about the 3rd amendment.

"The amendment is a response to Quartering Acts passed by the British parliament during the build up to the American Revolutionary War, which had allowed the British Army to lodge soldiers in private residences."

This amendment is supposed to be a "right" then it says at the very end unless it's deemed a law. That doesn't make much sense. Why would James Madison create an amendment to counter a law from foreign nation, and then completely negate it by saying the new government can override it? Isn't the entire Bill of Rights put into place to prevent government overreach? There may have been an extra utility to this amendment which has appeared to work. It may have been put in place as a hint to look closer at the entire Bill of Rights, just as the capitalization of the letters "M", "S" and "A" in the text of the 2nd amendment. Perhaps I'm just reading too much into this, or perhaps I'm not, but it certainly caused me to look much closer at the Bill of Rights while keeping the emphasis capital letters in mind.

I am now going to go through each amendment from top to bottom but I will be skipping the 2nd because this is the amendment that we will be reading the other amendments against. As we move through the Bill of Rights from top to bottom we will be traversing through the 2nd amendment from left to right. Above each amendment I have transcribed the 2nd, and highlighted the approximate association of the each other amendment as we move through them. It is the fact that they line up perfectly that negates any chance of this as being a coincidence.

"A **well** regulated Militia, being necessary to the security of a free State,
the right of the people to keep and bear Arms, shall not be infringed"

First amendment

"Congress shall make no law respecting an establishment of religion, or prohibiting the free exercise thereof; or abridging the freedom of speech, or of the press; or the right of the people peaceably to assemble, and to petition the Government for a redress of grievances."

Interpretation

This amendment addresses the word "well". In reality, before any laws are to be made the effects of lethal Arms must first be reported by the people. They must freely be able to report a violation of their right to the security of a free State. The right for any person to report these infringements on their liberty must not be blocked by government or industry. It should be as sacred as the right to vote. The reference of the people to "peaceable assemble" is in the context of all the people, assembled from sea to shining sea and living in peace, in the absence of gun violence.

"A well regulated **Militia**, being necessary to the security of a free State,
the right of the people to keep and bear Arms, shall not be infringed"

Third Amendment

"No Soldier shall, in time of peace be quartered in any house, without the consent of the Owner, nor in time of war, but in a manner to be prescribed by law"

Interpretation

What we see here are two capital letters. Capitals are used for emphasis to guide us in understanding the "sub" context of the meaning of the word as it relates to the objectively read 2nd amendment. In the 2nd amendment capitals have been used as red flags to add to the veracity of its legitimate meaning. Two of them "Militia" and "State" highlight the literary encryptions. "Arms" is capitalized because it is the very check and balance is to be associated with. Now just like a Militia which is composed of people and Arms so too is a soldier, however a soldier is under the command of federal control and would have no restrictions as to the Arms that he is allowed to possess. In this context he is of course well-regulated.

Now the Owner is a reference to the government because it is the government that essentially owns the Soldier and the military grade arms that he is allowed. A house is a symbolism for a container and the reference to "quartered" is in regards to the four clauses of the 2nd Amendment. This is used to drive the point home that the 2nd amendment is a gun control amendment. The "consent" of the Owner is a directly related to the laws that he must provide , being gun control laws. If the soldier is to enter society , or the public domain, bringing with him Arms, as long as those Arms meet the criteria as dictated by the 2nd clause of the 2nd amendment then and only then will he be allowed to carry those particular Arms into society. The 3rd Amendment is a piglet no more, as observed by the Supreme Court, as its true utility is now exposed further rendering the subjectively read 2nd amendment to a fallacy. If I may say so, it brings home the bacon in this previously unperceived context.

> "A well regulated Militia, being **necessary to the security of a free State,**
> the right of the people to keep and bear Arms, shall not be infringed"

Fourth Amendment

> "The right of the people to be secure in their persons, houses, papers, and effects, against unreasonable searches and seizures, shall not be violated, and no Warrants shall issue, but upon probable cause, supported by Oath or affirmation, and particularly describing the place to be searched, and the persons or things to be seized"

Interpretation

The third amendment describes what a secure society should look like. Lethal or military grade weaponry is only allowed to the soldier, unless it's deemed safe in the public domain. What is happening at this point is a gun has been fired. Something has occurred in the public domain with Arms and it must be quickly resolved. We know that a gun has been fired because of the extra bit of unnecessary information which is "papers, and effects". Smooth bore muskets required a wad of paper to be rammed into their barrels as part of the loading process. Once fired though, there are effects. The effects are noise, smoke, smell and of course the potential for a crime scene or lethal accident. Papers and effects[88].

The unreasonable searches and seizures are related to the person who is empowered with a gun. If the gun is empowering a person enough to conduct this attack then it is unreasonable for this gun to be in public. The warrants that shall issue are related to the output of the 2nd amendment. "but upon probable cause" is related to arms that should not be in public. These arms were the probable cause of this violation of liberty.

The place to be searched is a reference to the public domain. The things to be seized are the guns because they must now be put on trial. The things are a reference to Arms. Oath or affirmation is a direct reference back to freedom of speech. Anyone witnessing the offense must be allowed to talk

---

[88] This is the cryptic phrase I alluded to in the section on "How to read this book".

"A well regulated Militia, **being necessary to the security of a free State,** the right of the people to keep and bear Arms, shall not be infringed"

Fifth Amendment

"No person shall be held to answer for a capital, or otherwise infamous crime, unless on a presentment or indictment of a Grand Jury, except in cases arising in the land or naval forces, or in the Militia, when in actual service in time of War or public danger; nor shall any person be subject for the same offence to be twice put in jeopardy of life or limb; nor shall be compelled in any criminal case to be a witness against himself, nor be deprived of life, liberty, or property, without due process of law; nor shall private property be taken for public use, without just compensation"

Interpretation

Now with respect to this particular interpretation I would like to claim the fifth[89].

Note the distinction of Military, naval or conscription clause where people are allowed to be armed in this circumstance, because they would be well-regulated and lawfully armed under the jurisdiction of the government. This is important.

The encryption here is that we are just looking at Arms in the public domain. It is the Arms themselves that are on trial now. If the arms themselves empowered a person to such an extent, regardless of mental health or otherwise to have taken part in a massacre then no person in the general public should ever be subject to the same offence (of the weapon) again. The safety of the population comes first. For a person to be a witness against himself with respect to arms I believe is a reference to suicide. The due process of well regulated Arms laws are needed to ensure that people will not be deprived of life, liberty or property. A private is a rank in the military, and part of his gear, or property would be a firearm. This has used a similar encryption as the 3rd, but instead of "soldier", a soldiers rank is used which in this case is "private".

---

[89] With this being a one time in a human history kind of opportunity, I succumbed to my own human nature, and will henceforth have to deal with both the guilt and shame of it"

"Just compensation" is a reference to the arms that are "awarded" to the public after being resolved through the "just" laws, as mandated by the 2nd amendment. The "just compensation", If one is to compensate then one is to award so in this context award is the output variable "Arms" in the all too familiar clause "the right of the people to keep and bear Arms". This means that the ONLY arms a "private" may take into the public domain, while he/she is not in service are those that don't violate the 2nd clause of the 2nd amendment.

"A well regulated Militia, **being necessary to the security of a free State,
the right of the people to keep and bear Arms**, shall not be infringed"

Sixth Amendment

"In all criminal prosecutions, the accused shall enjoy the right to a speedy and public trial, by an impartial jury of the State and district wherein the crime shall have been committed, which district shall have been previously ascertained by law, and to be informed of the nature and cause of the accusation; to be confronted with the witnesses against him; to have compulsory process for obtaining witnesses in his favor, and to have the Assistance of Counsel for his defence."

Interpretation

This amendment stipulates that the arms laws of the 2nd amendment must be maintained and administered quickly. The constitutional directive of the 2nd amendment has the word "shall" in it. The constitution also uses the word the same word "shall" that is found in the directive for a president to start the process of nominating a Supreme Court Justice if a vacancy comes up. There are to be no loopholes perceived here. The inalienable right of the liberty as associated with "We the People" is the very function of the constitution.

Trials must be speedy to resolve whether the arms promoted the chance of success for the criminal activity, or a violated in any way the liberty of public. It must be speedy to insure that new or existing laws can be modified so that this "loophole" is plugged. The offence may only have been an anomaly so the current Arms laws may not require any modifications. It should be noted though, that there should always be a test of the 2nds current laws to make sure there are no arms laws loopholes, as new arms related criminal cases occur. The "accused" is the classification of grouping of Arms or Arms related devices.

"A well regulated Militia, **being necessary to the security of a free State,**
the right of the people to keep and bear Arms, shall not be infringed"

Seventh Amendment

'In Suits at common law, where the value in **controversy shall exceed twenty dollars,** the right of trial by jury shall be preserved, and no fact tried by a jury, shall be otherwise re-examined in any Court of the United States, than according to the rules of the common law.'

Interpretation

This particular amendment seems to have many other references with respect to the 2nd amendment.

Twenty dollars is just a symbolism. Its main purpose is to allow for anomaly / and or limits of severity. Remember the primary purpose of the 2nd amendment is all about protecting the liberties of all the people with respect to arms allowed into society. This is an acknowledgement that guns are tools which can be used for hunting, but they should not be an effective tool for hunting humans.

Once it's deemed that the violation has passed this threshold then more arms laws are required. The arms are on trial here, not the individual. Once specific weapon or group are deemed a danger, they can't be retried anywhere else in the country in the hopes of their reintroduction. Arms are not about self defence, because they are far more deadly as offensive devices.

I think I have already mentioned that these ciphers are stitched together with themes and references. There is a footnote in Federalist Papers that I believe ties directly to this particular amendment.

In Federalist Paper 12

The Utility of the Union In Respect to Revenue

by Alexander Hamilton

His footnote says.

"'1. If my memory be **right** they amount to **twenty** per cent."

(I have highlighted the words that stitch this particular Federalist essay directly to the seventh amendment once read through the 2nd amendment).

Remember the "right" with 20 in it, which of course is this one.

The context of revenue in this essay is regarding "duties" collected on Imports of items (arms), the duty collected is a percent. Though it looks at it from the opposite side of things it is still a reference to limiting arms through arms laws. Higher duties equates to a higher restrictions, or more comprehensive laws. The collection of revenue can also be symbolic in terms of increasing the liberty of the public domain.

"A well regulated Militia, being necessary to the security of a free State,
the right of the people to keep and bear Arms, shall not be infringed"

Eighth Amendment

Excessive bail shall not be required, nor excessive fines imposed, nor cruel and unusual punishments inflicted.

Interpretation

The trial is now over, however there are still some guns in society that are deemed "safe". These would generally be used for hunting. Excessive bail not being required is directly proportionate to the lethality of the weapon. If the weapons are not that lethal, and some accident happens then the bail, in theory would not be all that excessive. Excessive fines are related to liberty "necessary to the security of a free State". It's a delicate balance. This is where the rubber meets the pavement and if there is any nefarious exploitation for reasons of industry, it would be here.

Cruel and unusual punishment relates to using fire arms outside the purview of hunting against ones fellow man. It may also be a reference to slaughter animals for fun as opposed as a food source. It is a warning not to abuse the privilege of having a gun in society. If violations in this regard increase in numbers, then those guns will be removed, never to be put on trial again. The guns are always on trial.

"A well regulated Militia, being necessary to the security of a free State,
the right of the people to keep and bear Arms, shall not be infringed"

Ninth Amendment

The enumeration in the Constitution, of certain rights, shall not be construed to deny or disparage others retained by the people

Interpretation

This is a direct reference to the enumeration of powers in the constitution.

Congress must be allowed to create arms laws, to protect the rights of ALL the people. This is the only place where separation of powers must merge. It is the right of the people to have the government enabled to protect them from any introduction of dangerous arms into society. While the separation of powers specifies what each branch can and cannot do, the 2nd amendment is completely exempt from any boundaries that have been specified. Congress MUST make arms laws.

The most important thing that the ninth amendment is saying is that the Bill of Rights is still perfectly intact as is. The encoded second meaning should in no way disparage the meanings of the other rights as they have been known. The 2nd amendment is of course exempt from this because it is the entire point of this. The ninth is clarifying that the other 9 amendments are still intact.

"A well regulated Militia, being necessary to the security of a free State,
the right of the people to keep and bear Arms, shall not be infringed"

Tenth Amendment

The powers not delegated to the United States by the Constitution, nor prohibited by it to the states, are reserved to the states respectively, or to the people.

Interpretation

Now let's take a closer look at this "truism amendment" and read it through the lens of the 2nd amendment.

The powers not delegated to the United States by the Constitution (less lethal arms), nor prohibited by it to the states (less lethal arms), are reserved to the states respectively (in society), or to the people (as in the output variables of the 2nd amendment).

The "United States" is the government head".
Powers = Arms
Constitution = 2nd amendment (as does "it").
states = reference to the feeling and environment in the public domain, as per 2 amendment. It's also written with a lowercase 's', telling us that these are the same type of 'states".
Lethal Arms would be the ones that are strictly in the domain of the Federal head in a fully well- regulated environment with officers, training etc.
Any reference to arms in this ciphered amendment is always a reference to non lethal arms, even though it may appear to be steering us away from them. The message is further reinforced that it's all about non lethal arms in society. The arms are on trial from societies point of view only.
The context of ALL the arms in this amendment as ciphered will always be in the non-lethal arms and will be associated to the state in society or the people in it, or not the government head.

The powers not delegated to the United States by the Constitution

(less lethal arms),

nor prohibited by it to the states

(less lethal arms) (to the security of a free state)

are reserved to the states respectively

(less lethal arms are only allowed in a peaceful state of society, the peace must be respected because it is the golden rule, the ONLY measurement)

or to the people

(which are the people that are living in this free state, people are allowed only non lethal arms. The context of "or" = 'in other words").

Make no mistake about it that this was a bit of a bear to figure out. It would make no sense that one of these amendments would not be associated with the 2nd amendment. This rule could be applied to all the other ciphers. If they wrote one cipher for the future, they would have written 1000. Inconsistency has no place in reality if the nature of the experiment is first established as fact. The authors of the letters were on a mission and did not deviate from it

Concluding Comments

This is a quick start guide on how the 2nd amendment is to be administered irrespective of any currently elected factions of ideology. The framers knew it would not be enough to just have the 2nd amendment revealed one day. By putting the together a guide like this is to remove any subjectivity and "lesser opinions" of those who would seek nefarious loopholes. It's an overview on how the 2nd amendment is to be used in real world practice.

Perhaps one of the most important words in the 2nd amendment is the word "well". What's interesting is that now that this code has been exposed, it MUST be treated as an instruction manual of sorts. The first 10 amendments of the Bill of Rights have in themselves, just been amended with twice the information that was previously perceived. The secondary information of the Bill of Rights now reflect the rules and guidelines pertaining specifically to the 2nd amendment on the day it was to be revealed. That day has just arrived and as we all know, yesterday is not a place that can be lived in, but only learned from. People must be allowed to report a "gun violation" through the freedom of speech. If there are cover-ups in this regard the cover up would be in violation of the 2nd amendment. It is a right of ALL the people. The word "well" should always defer to the people's right to being protected from gun violence because this is the entire point of the 2nd amendment. The sincere promise of "high treason" should be coming into play here with the same exuberance that NRA had used in its previous defence of this amendment. It is of course possible that in the name of being patriot, they may continue to be this amendments staunchest advocate. Time will tell. This is a HOLY GRAIL of arms control amendment, put in place to protect the People. It has been paid for by over 1,000,000 American lives and trillions of dollars in arms related violence costs. Apparently it costs about 228 billion dollars a year for gun violence related costs. The old 2nd amendment never existed and was always a figment of the imagination which is the same place where the fear lived that supported it. It is now based on common sense prudence. No man can be trusted with too much power, so there must be a check and balance against him.

The real checks and balances have been working perfectly until recently because they had been currently being ignored by those that feel their opinions are worth more than the men that wrote the constitution. I refer to "shall nominate", and it will be interesting to see if the "shall" as found in "shall not be infringed" will be ignored as well. That would be a shame in this new light of the labors the framers took for the future of their nation. It was their promise of the American dream and it was never meant to be a nightmare.

Yes the 2nd amendment is an inalienable right, but one that has yet to be experienced by the people. The inalienable right to self defence never existed under the United States Constitution. Remember that the preamble of the constitution specifically defines the inalienable rights, being Life, Liberty and the Pursuit of Happiness. Previously the 2nd amendment existed only in the Pursuit of Happiness. Liberty is defined in the 2nd amendment in the words, "security of a free State". If the inalienable rights of the constitution are not allowed to live in harmony, then the constitution itself is under attack.

Does this mean you cannot defend yourself? Of course you can defend yourself, but just not with arms that are deemed harmful to society. Fear is nothing more than a bad habit. Courage is the confrontation of fear in order to accommodate a greater good. Courage in the defense of the constitution is the very heartbeat of Patriotism. Prudence should always be applied to reality and not emotion alone.

5-The Privately Held Hoards

The context of this chapter's title was borrowed from Thomas on June 12, 1823 to Justice William Johnson. The very hoards that he is referring to in his letter are ones that I will now be presenting to you which are grouped more or less by the framers that wrote them. While this would perhaps of made a good title for the book itself it wouldn't be totally accurate because the hoards are at least 4 times larger than what this physical book can hold. I had the luxury of hand picking them and if such a thing can be said, I picked the ones that I thought would be most appropriate. The framers built redundancy into their letters to describe the narratives because they could not have known if which ones would either survive the passage of time or would be available to us for scrutiny. By the time I located this letter I had already established the primary authors of these letters and this one numbered about 145 in the order, located about 7 months into the research. With the knowledge of this amount of letters it was not to difficult to discern the references that Thomas Jefferson was alluding to, including the nature of the word "private". In the deciphering of these letters they will be laid open and "broken up" with their secondary meanings mined out of them.

> "History may distort truth, and will distort it for a time, by the superior efforts at justification of those who are conscious of needing it most. Nor will the opening scenes of our present government be seen in their true aspect, until the letters of the day, now held in **private hoards**, shall be broken up and laid open to public view.

These private letters are all woven together with common themes. As you start reading them you will start to get familiar with them and in doing that the next letter will become a bit easier to first recognize and then read. If you are researching this yourself from documents online it is very likely that you will discover other letters that also belong to private hoards. It is not too likely that an answer book for these is supplied so the veracity of any "solution" is supported by other letters which use some of the same themes. I have revisited some letters after discovering new patterns in others. If you are certain that a particular letter is indeed a cipher then you can use the information it provides you in its construction. An example of this is the use of the word "quarters". There are four clauses in the 2nd amendment and if it "fits" the context of the 2nd amendment then it is highly likely that you have discovered a cipher. From that point the mining starts. There are sometimes historical references made but from the point of view of the framers, some of which I had to research because I was unfamiliar with events. If there is a date, it is sometimes associated with a particular event which can be tied in some way back to the cipher itself, supporting it, or adding more information to what it is telling you. There are also words used, perhaps the slang of the day which in turn may be able to be resolved or not.

There are many ways to communicate information through language where the easiest is perhaps the slogan. Short and concise and usually appeals to emotion while filling a perceived need."The right of the people to keep and bear Arms" is perhaps the most fitting of examples. These ciphers on the other hand are about as far from a slogan as you can get and in that light not so easily consumed. They will get easier to read but what kept me going was of course the importance of this subject matter in supporting the second amendment. It was also quite a bit of fun because in seeing how these letters were crafted it is an intimate insight into the ingenuity of their authors. These letters were written for a future time which has finally arrived and it was important to these men that you of course understand these letters. It was also important to these men that they have a story to tell and while it may seem like work to read them, it was most certainly work to write them.

I cannot know where you are at in your belief of what has been revealed so far. I can say that in my own research I didn't want to be wasting my time on some wild goose chase. It took time to sway me and it was a struggle trying to figure out just what it was that I appeared to be finding. I had to establish that these hoards existed. I didn't have the benefit of that Thomas Jefferson quote above. I did however have the benefit of some letters that were undeniably ciphers that pointed to the legitimate meaning of the 2nd amendment. The Benjamin Franklin letter of Oct 26, 1789 to William Alexander was one of the earliest and undeniably the most powerful. If you have not read that one, then I urge you too. It proves these hoards exist with math, and math cannot be denied. Once you have that established, then ask yourself just one question.

Why would the framers write only ONE SINGULAR letter for the future of their nation with respect to this truth? Seems a bit lazy doesn't it? No, these men were patriotic to their brainchild, and their letters spanned 84 years and I have located thus far, over 400.

What should drive the point home is the section on the United States Seal. The only text will you have to deal with in this case are the words are a few words of Latin. These are like crossword puzzles, and like crossword puzzles some may stump you and others may not. Some have stumped me, which is partly why some are incomplete in their answers. For the most part though, my primary purpose was to establish these letters as being ciphers. Do what I did, even if you can't complete them, do just that alone, and you will have your proof. It's possible that certain contexts may have been lost to over time and perhaps a trained historian would be more likely to pick up on some symbolism that I did not see. I do not have a degree in history or law and what I have learned thus far has been on the fly. My passion stems from recognizing the importance of my initial discovery, but liking history has been helpful as well.

Benjamin Franklin-Sets the Board-Chess Theme Ciphers

When Benjamin Franklin was in Paris he suddenly decided to reanimate an essay of his that he had written decades earlier. At one point in time, our time, I thought this was the first "hoarded letter" because it was my hypothesis that the 2nd amendment had evolved from George Mason's Virginian declaration of rights which was completely about a month prior to the Declaration of Independence. My hypothesis got blown out of the water when much to my astonishment I discovered another cipher and then many more that began by at last 1752. The following cipher was written just in advance of the Constitutional Convention which helps to establish the new dynamic that it was in fact orchestrated. The war was well underway and in the absence of a federal head Benjamin Franklin saw that the time was ripe. He started to ramp up his ciphers and also began to recruit those that could help him, and being near the end of his own life the younger the better.

As you now read this you are living in the final phase of the experiment. The span of time in which these documents were written covers about 82 years. It is not an easy thing to keep a secret. These men managed to pull it off though perhaps too effectively. These letters are part of the Benjamin Franklin series but thought I would group them under the Morals of Chess letters in light of the "Chevalier" cipher letters. A Chevalier is French for a "knight" which is of course a piece on a chess board.

"The Morals of Chess", [before 28 June 1779]

Sir,
Playing at Chess, is the most ancient and the most universal game known among men; for its original is beyond the memory of history, and it has, for numberless ages, been the amusement of all the civilized nations of Asia, the Persians, the Indians, and the Chinese. Europe has had it above 1000 years; the Spaniards have spread it over their part of America, and it begins lately to make its appearance in these northern states. It is so interesting in itself, as not to need the view of gain to induce engaging in it; and thence it is never played for money. Those, therefore, who have leisure for such diversions, cannot find one that is more *innocent;* and the following piece, written with a view to correct (among a few young friends) some little improprieties in the practice of it, shows at the same time,

that it may, in its effects on the mind, be not merely *innocent*, but *advantageous*, to the vanquished as well as to the victor.

The MORALS OF CHESS.

The game of Chess is not merely an idle amusement. Several very valuable qualities of the mind, useful in the course of human life, are to be acquired or strengthened by it, so as to become habits, ready on all occasions. For life is a kind of chess, in which we have often points to gain, and competitors or adversaries to contend with, and in which there is a vast variety of good and ill events, that are, in some degree, the effects of prudence or the want of it. By playing at chess, then, we may learn:

1. *Foresight*, which looks a little into futurity, and considers the consequences that may attend an action: for it is continually occurring to the player, "If I move this piece, what will be the advantages[9] of my new situation? What use can my adversary make of it to annoy me? What other moves can I make to support it, and to defend myself from his attacks?

2. *Circumspection*, which surveys the whole chess-board, or scene of action, the relations of the several pieces and situations, the dangers they are respectively exposed to, the several possibilities of their aiding each other; the probabilities that the adversary may make this or that move, and attack this or the other piece; and what different means can be used to avoid his stroke, or turn its consequences against him.

3. *Caution*, not to make our moves too hastily. This habit is best acquired by observing strictly the laws of the game, such as, *if you touch a piece, you must move it somewhere; if you set it down, you must let it stand*. And it is therefore best that these rules should be observed, as the game thereby becomes more the image of human life, and particularly of war; in which, if you have incautiously put yourself into a bad and dangerous position, you cannot obtain your enemy's leave to withdraw your troops, and place them more securely; but you must abide all the consequences of your rashness.

And, *lastly*, we learn by chess the habit of *not being discouraged*[1] by *present* bad appearances in the state of our affairs, the habit of *hoping for a favourable change*, and that of *persevering in the search of resources*. The game is so full of events, there is such a variety of turns in it, the fortune of it is so subject to sudden vicissitudes, and one so frequently, after long contemplation, discovers the means of extricating one's self from a supposed insurmountable difficulty, that one is encouraged to continue the contest to the last, in hopes of victory by our own skill, or, at least, of giving a *stale mate*,[2] by the negligence of our adversary. And whoever considers, what in chess he often sees instances of, that particular pieces of[3] success are apt to produce *presumption*, and its consequent, inattention, by which more is afterwards lost than was gained by the preceding advantage; while misfortunes produce more care and attention, by which the loss may be recovered, will learn not to be too much discouraged by the present success of his adversary, nor to despair of final good fortune, upon every little check he receives in the pursuit of it.

That we may, therefore, be induced more frequently to chuse this beneficial amusement, in preference to others which are not attended with the same advantages, every circumstance, that may increase the pleasure of it, should be regarded; and every action or word that is unfair, disrespectful, or that in any way may give uneasiness, should be avoided, as contrary to the immediate intention of both the players,[4] which is to pass the time agreeably.

Therefore, 1st. If it is agreed to play according to the strict rules, then those rules are to be exactly observed by both parties; and should not be insisted on for one side, while deviated from by the other: for this is not equitable.

2. If it is agreed not to observe the rules exactly, but one party demands indulgencies, he should then be as willing to allow them to the other.

3. No false move should ever be made to extricate yourself out of a difficulty, or to gain an advantage. There can be no pleasure in playing with a person once detected in such unfair practice.

4. If your adversary is long in playing, you ought not to hurry him, or express any uneasiness at his delay. You should not sing, nor whistle, nor look at your watch, nor take up a book to read, nor make a tapping with your feet on the floor, or with your fingers on the table, nor do anything that may disturb his attention. For all these things displease. And they do not show your skill in playing, but your craftiness or your rudeness.

5. You ought not to endeavour to amuse and deceive your adversary, by pretending to have made bad moves, and saying you have now lost the game, in order to make him secure and careless, and inattentive to your schemes; for this is fraud, and deceit, not skill in the game.

6. You must not, when you have gained a victory, use any triumphing or insulting expression, nor show too much pleasure; but endeavour to console your adversary, and make him less dissatisfied with himself by every kind and civil expression, that may be used with truth, such as, You understand the game better than I, but you are a little inattentive; or, You play too fast; or, You had the best of the game but something happened to divert your thoughts, and that turned it in my favour.

7. If you are a spectator, while others play, observe the most perfect silence. For if you give advice, you offend both parties; him, against whom you give it, because it may cause the loss of his game; him, in whose favour you give it, because, though it be good, and he follows it, he loses the pleasure he might have had, if you had permitted him to think till it occurred to himself. Even after a move or moves, you must not, by replacing the pieces, shew how it might have been played better: for that displeases, and may occasion disputes or doubts about their true situation. All talking to the players, lessens or diverts their attention, and is therefore unpleasing; nor should you give the least hint to either party, by any kind of noise or motion.— If you do, you are unworthy to be a spectator.— If you have a mind to exercise or show your judgments, do it in playing your own game when you have an opportunity, not in criticising or meddling with, or counselling, the play of others.

Lastly. If the game is not to be played rigorously, according to the rules above mentioned, then moderate your desire of victory over your adversary, and be pleased with one over yourself. Snatch not eagerly at every advantage offered by his unskilfulness or inattention; but point out to him kindly that by such a move he places or leaves a piece in danger and unsupported; that by another he will put his king in a dangerous situation, &c. By this generous civility (so opposite to the unfairness above forbidden) you may indeed happen to lose the game to your opponent, but you will win what is better, his esteem, his respect, and his affection; together with the silent approbation and good will of impartial spectators.

To Joseph Reed Passy, Mar 19. 1780.

[ls: New-York Historical Society; copy: Library of Congress]

Passy, Mar 19. 1780.
Sir

I beg leave to introduce to your Excellency's Acquaintance and Civilities, Monsr le Chevalier De Chastellux; Major General in the French Troops, now about to embark for America, whom I have long known & esteem'd highly in his several Characters of a Soldier[90], a Gentleman, & a Man of Letters[91]. His excellent Book on Publick Happiness shews him the Friend to Mankind[92,] and as such intitles him wherever he goes[93], to their Respect and good Offices. He is particularly a Friend to our Cause[94] & I am sure your Excellency will have great Pleasure in his Conversation.

With great Esteem & Respect

His Ex. Jos. Read Eq. Prest. of Penna

Notations in different hands: Dr. Franklin Passy. May 19. 1780 / Introducing Marquis De Chastellux

To Joseph Reed, March 19. 1780.

[copy: Library of Congress Passy]

Sir,

The Chevalier D'Oyré Captain in the Royal Corps of Engineers[95], being about to embark with The Troops for America[96], and as possibly the Operations of War[97] may lead or Permit[98] him to visit

---

[90] Reference to Militia again.

[91] The letters form the world "Militia".

[92] Friend of Mankind aka "Alexander" same theme used. This is also the true nature of the 2nd amendment.

[93] Good for any time or place.

[94] He is the cure for the anticipated gun violence. A friend of life and liberty.

[95] Another reference to the word "Militia" only that it has been "engineered" or crafted.

[96] and the troops are "people and arms" as hidden within the word, which is for the future of America , after having embarked on its journey through time.

[97] The "operations of War" would be the well regulating of military force, which includes arms.

Philadelphia, I beg leave to recommend him to your Excellency's Civilities as a Gentleman of Excellent Character in this Country, and a friend of our Cause. With the highest Esteem and Respect, I have the honour to be, Your Excellency's most obedient and most humble servant.

His Excelly. Joseph Reed Esq. President of the state of Penn.

---

[98] Permit is to give the Right to Government to regulate Arms. At this time Philadelphia was the capital of the USA and Joseph Reed was the current president.

Om the Chevalier - (unpublished) Paris this 30 June 1785

The
I have just learned that you are on the point of going to Philadelphia I beg you to want to remember you that I have had the honor to write to you several times to ask you to pay me a sum of 36 l.t.[99] For Petits Boulets and Petit Bombes that Mr. Feutry has come to pray to me to do what I have done execute in the forges of Lorainne. When these things arrived, I handed them over to Mr. Feutry, who told me that you were in charge of this commission, and that he would present the memorial to you. Since that time I have not seen Mr. Feutry, I have written to you at Differenttes end without having Received from Reponsse[100]. I have even been at Passy without ever having the honor of speaking to you, and I have decided not to bother you for such a trifle. When I saw yesterday Mr. Cadet, who told me to go out at the moment, Farewell to whom I Contai This little girl annecdotte. He told me that I should have taken the party to write to you again, and that he was sure that if these objects had been ordered from your share, you would pay them[101]. It was in the seventeenth of 1777 that I caused these Bombs and Boullets to be made[102], of which the experiment ought to have been made[103], and consequently, if the experiment had been completed[104], it was to be ordered a certain quantity.

---

[99] There are exactly 36 letters "l.t." in "the right of the people to keep and bear Arms" which is costing society a heavy price.

[100] There is no response because nothing is known about these words "the right the people to keep and bear Arms".

[101] There is confusion here, because "the right of the people to keep and bear Arms" has never existed.

[102] Simply different types of Arms, which emphasises that "Arms" can be populated by anything. It's a generic.

[103] This is entire experiment that Benjamin Franklin had devised, the chess game, in which he hypothesised that a knight "Chevalier" would show up. Yes, this is cool.

[104] If 2nd amendment was finally discovered then what must be ordered is the quantity and type of Arms in Society with respect to the words "A well regulated Militia".

Pardon Monsieur, to speak so long to you for a Pareille Bagatelle.

I am with a Deep Respect Mr. Your very humble and obeis. Servant

Knight
Ancient Iron Quay of the Megisserie
House of the Bar

I'd first like to look at how this sentence ends. As a cipher it can be connected to the Morals of Chess. Benjamin Franklin is explaining how the Knight is to make his move. Megisserie means "a process or method". Benjamin Franklin is saying that the knight must use the 2nd amendment as a key in the process of unlocking the ciphers. The key would be ancient in the eyes of the those for whom it was crafted for, being of course the future. The key is for you the reader. The Bar may be a reference to the Laws as a result of regulating as directed by the 2nd amendment.

There is a similar letter to this one written to Patrick Henry in that the theme is a tone that words "the right of the people to keep and bear Arms" never existed. This is a full on cipher which can be tied directly to the "William Alexander Ciphers". This cipher is just an earlier version of it. The utility of using the same themes with different actors was obviously observed by Benjamin Franklin. One theme in the absence of its reoccurrence could be attributed to coincidence, where the re-usage of a same theme would shore up the associated letters collectively as being ciphers.

From - Chevalier (unpublished) Paris on 16 May 1784

"Sir,
Monsieur feutry machiniste came to my house in 1777 to ask me to make him make in different font machines like Bombe and Boullets[105] we examined attentively together the models that he brought and on the observations that I made him it me Pray to make new ones telling me that I would be Well Paid of my advances by you Monsieur I have therefore executed all that he asked to me. As soon as these Pieces have been arrived, and I have brought them by the Diligence, I have restored them to them. He thanked me very much and told me that he would pay me at the first moment. But I have not seen him again. I have passed several times at Passy to have the honor of seeing you, but always you were embarrassed or went out.

I should have thought I was wanting to the Respect which is yours. If I had refused to Mr. Feutry to employ these articles, always telling me that it was for your Count and promising me to pay them.

I pray you, Monsieur, to honor me with a word of Re- penses, if I have to rely on the payment of these articles, of which the details of my debars are the other. I would not write to you yet if I had not left the Commerce for a year, and if I had not to pay my Registers.

I am with Respect Monsieur Your very humble and obedient servant

Knight
Mr. De M Square House [Archan] d
Quay of the megisserie at L'Ecritoire.
From 11th September 1777
Delivered for The Count of Mr. The Doctor franklin by order of Mr. feutry machinist[106]

---

[105] Bombs and Bullets and font machines is a reference to the device we now know to be the 2nd amendment which is composed of fonts.

[106] Perhaps "Feurty machinist" is also symbolic of someone in the "future" who can rebuild the 2nd amendment by reorganizing it? It words would have to be read in order.

Two Bombs and 2 Boullets Punched with holes from Part to Part. . . 18 d.
Port of models by the Courier and the cost of the Caisse[107]. . . 6
For the rearrangement of the said models[108], and to have
Dittes 4 Pieces of fontte by the Diligence[109]. . . 6
Total of my Debentures 30 d.
Addressed: A Monsieur / Monsieur franklin / In his house of Passy / A Passy
641200 = 041-u606.html

---

[107] The 'A' in arms is uppercase. The cost of the "Arms" is much more than that of the 'people". Its about putting the Arms on trial not the people.

[108] People and Arms must be rearranged in their view with respect to Militia in order to read the 2nd.

[109] The word "well" Be diligent in its usage and there will be less harm to society.

To the Chevalier — (unpublished) June-July, 1785

That I have receiv'd his Letter, and one he wrote me formerly on the Subject of Bombs and Bullets said to have been order'd for me by Mr. Feutry in 1777. As I remember nothing of any such Transaction, and Mr. Feutry is a Man of Veracity, I am inclin'd to think M Chevalier is mistaken as to his naming me as the Person who was to pay for those Bombs. But if Mr. Chevalier can now or any any time hereafter produce to me any Note of Mr. Feutry's Writing expressing that those Things were made for me, I will immediately order Payment. Mr. Feutry has liv'd long in Paris since that Date, and I suppose may be still in or near it, and I wonder that Mr. Ch. should be so long without recovering his Money from the Person who employ'd him.

Feutry, Aimé-Ambroise-Joseph Tue, Aug 12, 1777

When Benjamin Franklin lived in Passy, an area of Paris he lived in a home with the Chaumont Family. A friend of theirs was Feutry, Aimé-Ambroise-Joseph according to his background that can be found at Franklinpapers.org. This man was a French poet , and being a French poet, he wrote in French. It appears that either Benjamin Franklin enlisted his talents, OR he contrived these letters himself. I suspect it was probably the latter. Suspicion being the enemy, Benjamin Franklin simply utilized the existence and nature of this man to contrive these ciphers. There appear to be about 30 of them and I've spot checked a few and present them to you here now.

So after seeing the reference to Feutry I then jumped back into Benjamin Franklin's archives and found some of his letters. I first discovered that this man was described as being a poet. These letters were all written in French so I had to first get them translated and used a google translate for that. If there was a rhyme it may have been lost, but the meaning still appears to be there. The year 1777 was also important.

Feutry, Aimé-Ambroise-Joseph Tue, Aug 12, 1777

(translated from French).

Fable imitated from the English, from Doctor Percival A young nobleman living in his lands, and an old Philosopher, his neighbor and his friend.
I can hardly believe Mr.
During the sea gusts,

Can never from the bitter flow
Calm irritated fury.
The fact, my good neighbor, seems to me important;
I should like to see the experience.[110]
The wind blows violently;
I had watched this moment:
We are near the great pond,
Let us seize this circumstance.[111]
I had an abundance of oil,[112]
And we can get to work on the spot.[113]
I appreciate your impatience.
Picard, take the nacelle, and win the other side.
Hurry up ... the wind becomes stronger;
For the test it is perfectly ...
Holà, Picard, it's quite far,
Fix yourself there ... very well ... but you have to be careful[114]
To gently pour both bottles[115]
And on this side, to make us see better
Of the operation the effect and the power.
Come on, you can spread the oil, ...
Good ... see you as she runs,
Extends, and covers, around the boat,
A large area of water?
Ah! my friend! Already I see her appeased:
What an astonishing prodigy! For what reason?

---

[110] Think of your neighbour first.

[111] There is much gun violence which is the storm

[112] Highly motivated to scrutinize the 2nd amendment and try to loosen up its secrets.

[113] Oil loosens up things and the spot is the word "Militia" which will separate from it the words "People and Arms".

[114] "Very well" is a clue as to where to look in the 2nd amendment. It drives home the veracity of this cipher.

[115] Bottles contain things. In one is the word "people" and in the other is the word "Arms". Pour them over the word Militia carefully to extract them. Do this carefully and avoid talking about what Militias are for otherwise you will be lost. The 2nd amendment was always about what a Militia actually is and its parts.

To understand it is very easy;[116]
It is that (as Pierzon says,
In his notte, article sinking)
The wind then, in spite of its whirlwind,
And its efforts to open a passage
Gliding over the liquor abandoned to the waves,
Can not lift them and restores them.
So-I hear ... the thing is admirable.
Yes, my dear count, and, moreover, applicable
To the frightful storms of a too restless heart[117]
Pour into it virtues the anointing aid
He will soon enjoy tranquility.[118]
Sending to Mr. Franklin
You! Whose sweet eloquence[119]
Produces the same effects, to our surprised looks,
And which by a gentle and powerful influence
Touches, moves, persuades, and calms the spirits,
Accepts this tribute of my gratitude.
On the public vessel of so many united states,[120]
O Franklin! Worthy choice of their high prudence![121]
For their happiness, at the helm admitted,[122]
You guide his course by braving the tempest;[123]
Go, glory awaits you, and from your enemies,[124]

---

[116] Watching the 2nd amendment transform into something that has never before been seen.

[117] The restless heart I believe is a reference to fear, and the "count" would be a reference to all the Arms that are in society due to misreading the 2nd amendment.

[118] Security of a free State aka Butterflies and Bunny Rabbits.

[119] The observation of how perfect the 2nd amendment is, and infers its of Benjamin Franklins construction.

[120] Symbolic for the 2nd amendment

[121] It's prudent to not let lethal arms into society in the first place

[122] It must be "well regulated to the security of a free State"

[123] The fears of men or those that wish to hold onto the old debate.

[124] The proof of a reduction in gun violence is now available, which is the glory.

Your heart, your soul, and your learned writings,
Have already made the superb conquest.[125]
628308 = 024-414a001.html

From Feutry Paris, April 21, 1777. in the evening

ALS: American Philosophical Society

"Sir,
To give a pea for a big bean, as one old Belgian proverb says (and I am of this good Nation) is my story with you. I have had the honor of addressing to you a portion of my feeble works, and you are gratifying me with your scientific works! I dare again, Sir, to send you The Trifle Jointe, whose warning alone and the introduction, must or can be read. I await, in flanders, my **choice of moral stories**, in four parts, and my **memoirs of Lacour d'Auguste (Octavian Caesar**) to put them at your feet. Deign, sir, to give me the day, the precise moment, when I shall be able to have the happiness of seeing you, of admiring you, of hearing and instructing you. If I osois, I would say here, **Barbarus hìc ego sum, quia non intelligor illis**[126]. I am with as much esteem, attachment, respect and veneration as your very humble and obedient Servant

Feutry.
House of Mr. de Cormainville Marshal of Camps, in the armies of the King. Barriere ste. Anne, at the new france.

Feutry: Verse for Franklin's Portrait April 27, 1777.

Ds: American Philosophical Society
Passy, April 27, 1777.
Towards to put under Franklin's Portrait of Mr. etc.

Honor of the New World and Humanity,
This wise and true sage guides and enlightens them;

---

[125] The 2nd amendment has finally been revealed along with the genius behind it.

[126] Latin : "Here I am, because it is not understood what"

Like another Mentor, he hides from the vulgar eye,
In the form of a Mortal, a Divinity.
By his very sincere and very humble admirer

Feutry
Rating: Verses

The 2nd amendment was meant for the new world, which is the future one when its truth is finally revealed. The wisdom of the 2nd amendment is the only the only reality based solution to gun violence. The "vulgar" eye is in related to the false outlook on the 2nd amendment. The other mentor is probably a reference to Jesus, which is of course an exaggeration but the utility of the 2nd amendment does transcend time and place and can be used for the public good of all mankind.

This also ties in a bit with the symbolisms of the United States Seal, but only hints at it.

From Aimé (or Amé) -Ambroise-Joseph Feutry

(unpublished)

> Your name alone, of Tyrants, will become terror,
> O Franklin! You have a double excellence:
> You owe the one to the virtues, and the other to the birth,
> Since it was already in the depths of your heart.
> Feutry
> On the 22nd of March, in the evening.
> Endorsed: verses

This little poem is interesting and appears to say it all. Here we have in a rather concise poem a narrative about tyrants. This relates to the 2nd amendment being a direct threat to tyrants, or those that would be empowered by weaponry. A direct reference to Franklin also infers that it was of his construction. The virtues of the 2nd amendment are that it will protect the people and the birth is a reference that its truth will one day be born to the public view. I suppose the NRA could be thought of as being a modern day type of tyrant in this regard and the degree of terror will be demonstrated by the magnitude of their pushback with respect to this book. If there is no pushback from this organization then I suspect they will find this research refreshing and will promptly update their views on the true nature of patriotism. They will continue with their staunch defence of this constitutional right for all of the people. They will promote the safe usage of hunting rifles and be meticulous in preventing or pointing out any violations of their usage. Further to this the "Double excellence" is a reference to "People and Arms" within the word "Militia" now being seen as variables which can be tied to "People and Arms" at the end of the sentence.

From Aimé (Amé) -Ambroise-Joseph Feutry Paris, this 8th of July, 1781

Als: American Philosophical Society

"Sir,
Here I was resuscitated, at the strictest of terms, for I had been thrown over my head, believing myself dead. An abundant sweat, a favorable crisis have restored me to life. Judge[127] of my condition, Sir, I had an internal, inflammatory and putrid fever, accompanied by redoublements and transports[128]. I was 30 Days in bed. I begin to walk in the room and take a little air at the window[129]; But my weakness is so excessive[130] that my guard must give me the arm to go from one end of the room to the other[131]. I believe, sir, that there are more than legitimate excuses for dispensing me with having the honor of going to court[132]. I am afraid my convalescence will be as long as my illness[133]. Fortunately, my devout wife, who had left two days before I fell ill, for our retreat in Chatillon-sur-Loing, where I shall certainly go and find her as soon as I can, absolutely ignored the state[134] in which I Been reduced, and will always ignore it[135]. I have the honor to address to you my Memoirs of the Court of Augustus, 2nd edition; I dare believe this work worthy of your looks and placed in your library.

---

[127] Reference to regulations and law.

[128] The right to keep and bear Arms. Redoublement is reading more into the 2nd amendment that exists. There are are also two words that are part of the encryption, being "Militia" and "State".

[129] He needs to catch his breath because of his fear. He's tense.

[130] The weakness he refers to is fear.

[131] He needs Arms to guard himself. Going from one end of the room to the other, is to read the 2nd amendment in its entirety.

[132] Court related to "well regulated" and Arms on Trial.

[133] As long as the illness of his fear lasts, he will be trapped in thinking he needs Arms. One fuels the other.

[134] The state she may have ignored, is "State" as related to a colony. She viewed her husband's illness as being psychosomatic.

[135] He is adamant in his interpretation of the 2nd amendment.

I dare more, Sir, to recommend the bearer[136], my copyist[137]. His job is not lucrative with me[138]. This man is poor but full of probity. I recommend it to you, The race is a little long. Excuse my franchise Belgium.

I am respectfully your very humble and very obedient servant

Feutry
Home of M Bussiere,
Opposite St-Yves, St. James Street.
See what the literary year, No. 16, page 42, has just said of my work.

    Some may argue that I've been reading too much into this. Well, my starting point was that this document was located in Benjamin Franklins archive and he did not suddenly forget about the ciphers that he was writing. This letter falls within a time zone when he was crafting these letters, as were the other members of the cabal. He, and the others were now heavily involved in seeding these letters for the future. With that being said, count the indicators, and symbolisms that I have thus far observed. Often times the, cabal will reference other literary works to further shed light on the public good. "Judge", "arms", "illness", "ignore it", "guard", start to add up fast because all these terms are easily associated with the 2nd amendment as we now know it. It is likely that this letter was completely contrived and archived as man have been. Now if it was not crafted by Benjamin Franklin and was in fact written by Feutry then this man is privy to the ciphers and was recruited by Benjamin Franklin to help with this mission. This individual would have been trusted, and viewed as a boon to these ciphers. Now Feutry was a poet, and a master of symbolism. If other letters can be established to be ciphers, and of his writing, then it would be clear that this man was recruited and one of a very small select group of men that knew of the truth of the 2nd amendment. Mason Loch Weems, was also an author and a bit of poet, who was most certainly recruited to help out with this story, only he was probably recruited by Thomas Jefferson about 30 years after the death of Benjamin Franklin. I'm sure it was agreed too in the early meetings of this cabal

---

    [136] Reference to someone who reads only the right to bear Arms.

    [137] Copying the "operative clause" of the 2nd amendment.

    [138] Of course reading the 2nd amendment this way is not lucrative to the security of a free state "of mind".

to recruit others to help out, but only if it was certain that they would be fully vested in this cause for the future liberty of the United States of America.

Benjamin Franklin-Cipher Collection

It appears that Benjamin Franklin was the man that drafted/crafted the 2nd amendment because the earliest ciphers that reference come from a time when James Madison was only one year of age. The year was 1752. He was a wordsmith with exceptional talent and experience. The letters that I've located will be illustrated for the first time as being ciphers. He was a scientist and also studied human nature most of his life. Much of this is demonstrated with his psychological witticisms that make up the bulk of his publication known as Poor Richards Almanac which spanned 26 years. The first publication in this series was written when he was only 26 years of age. It should be obvious now that the primary encryption of the 2nd amendment was psychological. It was a literary sleight of hand which he talks about in

A new dynamic in history has been exposed that has never before been known. A secret of the constitution has been exposed along with the cabal that was associated with it. There was much energy and thought put into hiding things and as I stated earlier suspicion was both the enemy and a friend.

For the most part it appears that Benjamin Franklin was self taught and well read. As you have seen he founded the American Philosophical Society and had no issue with attracting other intellectuals to share ideas, knowledge and research to be better understand the world in order to make it a better place.

We hear George Washington reference a "dangerous experiment". You will be shown his other letters and the nature of his symbolisms. Now that we know what these men were up too, I don't think it unreasonable to assume that they were cross checking each others letters in the interest of preserving and 2nd amendment for the future with symbolisms. It would have been a very difficult thing to balance and a slip up, could no

There are two David Hartleys being father and son, with whom Benjamin Franklin was acquainted with. The father was early philosopher and studied Psychology and had passed away in 1756. There appears to have been quite a bit of correspondence between Dr. Franklin and the younger David Hartley. David Hartley Senior was the author of a book called 'Observations of Man, His Frame, His Duty and His Expectations". This particular book talks about how man learns to learn, and how his cognitive processes work. This of course would be a way to describe the motivations of men.

Some men think of themselves first and then society, and others think of society first and expect to reap the benefits that such thought will reap and cultivate. Some men think in black and white, and some men think in the gray. This is very pertinent to this book, because it first off illustrates that Benjamin Franklin must have been acquainted with this book. It's a psychology book.

The founding fathers studied many past civilizations and forms of governments which of course were composed of man. They did this because before them of course was an opportunity to design a society which was going to be run by men. To study the benefits and failings of past civilizations and pick out the best aspects of them would of course be a logical thing to do for those that were willing to put thought and energy into their decisions. Benjamin Franklin was also reputed to have had a keen interest in the opposite sex. A book on human psychology would have been of mandatory reading for a man like Benjamin Franklin. Benjamin Franklin was attempting to draft a constitution with others. that had to handle mans motives, regardless of what they are so that

Originally in my research I was trying to resolve the narrative of the 2nd amendment. As the letters and actors were revealed themselves so did the timeline in which they were written as a collective. The timeline started to expand and while this book covers a timeline of James Madison's death, it only does so because at that point in my research I had no clue that letters were being written for the future. I had no concept or suspicion of that particular narrative. I was simply, as stated before trying to figure out just how and why the 2nd amendment was lost. I had nothing to go on, but the truth of it, and the name of its original author. These two facts were the only two facts that I could validate with historical text.

I then arrived at the narrative of the letters. I had encountered many letters, all of which were obviously encrypted in some fashion. All the letters had of course been in plain sight and never before resolved to this level. It was when I released that nobody would actually sign the Bill of Rights if they really knew what the 2nd amendment meant that the letters made sense. Once the 2nd amendment had been successfully hidden in the constitution then of course it would have to be revealed or all would have been for nothing. It was an issue of great National security though that it must one day be revealed. A multitude of letters must be seeded and preserved for the future to defend the truth of the 2nd amendment. Not only must its truth be known, but so too must its full story be told, and to do that, there must be supporting evidence from the founding fathers and their recruits.

The utility of having many founding fathers writing letters as a collective for the future could not have gone unnoticed. Not only could more letters be written, which is essential but also they would collectively have the full backing of some of the most cherished and key framers of the United States Constitution. If these letters were all to be written for the future, then Benjamin Franklin must also have seen the utility of recording all the names of these men in the membership records of the American Philosophical Society. He is saying to the future, "Here we are, and this is when we started our work, read our letters carefully". I think there is logic in this theory and it has been validated in every case but one. Every one of these men has indeed written letters, but can the sweet spot, the timeline be reasonably expected to move back to 1780? Now if this can be done, and Benjamin Franklin was the true architect of the 2nd amendment and indeed the "dangerous experiment", then why would he wait for others to join in on these letters? There is no harm in writing encrypted letters before constitution actually exists, he is simply starting the seeds, and there is utility in this because he wants the future to know the full story behind his experiment. He wants full transparency in the narrative. Perhaps Benjamin Franklin talked this over with a few of the other founders before the enrolment process began. The date of enrolment though signifies in my mind anyway, a starting point to these letters, and it wouldn't' have surprised me in the slightest if Benjamin Franklin was the first to write them. He would have probably used his own letters as an example to the others, in what I like to call the Benjamin Franklin School of Ciphering for Security of Liberty.

I have located over 250 ciphers written by Benjamin Franklin and these are for the most part the initial ones that I found. I cannot fit them all into this book, and based on the importance of the subject matter my primary goal was to ensure that I had "enough" to prove the legitimate meaning of the 2nd amendment. Some of his more interesting letters can be found in the final Chapters. These are the United States Seal, The Lightning Experiment, and the Whale Tale.

From Alexander Small March 15th 1777

ALS: American Philosophical Society
St Philips Minorca March 15th 1777
Dear Friend

The most upright Intentions cannot command Success[139]. The Shallow Ken of Man cannot penetrate into futurity[140]; and cannot therefore ascertain what is, or is not most beneficial to Societies. What we have here to do, is to act the most consistently with our Judgment of Circumstances[141]. I know you have done this[142].

Britain is most certainly hurting herself by an enormous Increase of her Debt; and is perhaps a just Scourge in your Country, for the excessive Luxury and Dissipation you were running into. This Scourge will restore you to your Senses; and will Send every Man to live Soberly and dilligently under his Vine[143]. Had not this scourge been inflicted, your growing Luxury and Effeminacy would have rendered you an easy Prey to some future enterprising Genius[144]. Your Children will not soon forget what has now happened, which may the longer preserve a Love of Liberty among them. On the whole I do not know whether I should condole with you, or congratulate. Friendship, at any rate demands my trying whether this can come to your

---

[139] "Militia" is the encryption. Militias stand upright. It cannot command success because its hidden in the

2A

[140] The 2A was encrypted because men were less willing to think about the damage Arms

could cause in society, hence their "shallow ken".

[141] The circumstances are.. "we cannot use the true 2A in our time, so let us fashion it so that it can be used in the future. Let us insert it into a constitution which we already knew we are going to need so that its true protection would be available to the future , in spite of the "shallow ken of man".

[142] The 2nd amendment was carefully crafted.

[143] A recognition of men having too much power and finally deciding to live under the constitution or the "vine". Later symbolisms are the tree of liberty, branches of government in order to restrict power. Power = Arms and Power = Money. Liberty is lost when the few have power over the many.

[144] A tryant

hands[145]. I have delayed writing for some time, in hopes I might have your Direction. As this has not happened, I have directed my Letter so as to carry it among your Philosophical friends[146]. I dare say the Ami des Hommes, and his friends live in friendship with you. An Account of your and Family's Health, will give great pleasure to Dear Sir Your Affectionate and faithful friend

Alexr Small

P:S: When I settled in this Island, I soon found the want of duely Ventilating our Hospitals. This set me on recollecting what I had learned from you and having drawn it up in the best Manner I could, I sent a Copy of it to our Friend Sr. J: Pringle. I have not heard from him since. If this reaches your hands, I will send you a Copy of it, that you may yourself put the finishing hand to it, if greater Concerns give you Leisure. What can be a greater Concern than to give Relief to the Sick? You remember Cicero's expression; Homines nulla in re propius ad Deos accedunt, quam Salutem Hominibus dando. Vale! et Sit Sana Mens in Sano Corpore! This will be now probably delivered to you by a worthy friend of Mine, and Fellow Labourer here, Mr. MacNeille.

Addressed: A Monsieur / Monsieur Benjamin Franklin / L:L:D: et de l' A:R:S: Etranger / a Paris

Notation: Small Alexander March 15. 1777.

So I started to look through letters dating back to 1780, and I already had my suspicions regarding the symbolism of "gout". I then found this letter.

To Alexander Small July 22, 1780.

Reprinted from William Temple Franklin, *The Private Correspondence of Benjamin Franklin, LL.D., F.R.S., &c* ... (2nd ed.; 2 vols., London, 1817), 1, 65-6.

Passy, July 22, 1780.

You see, my Dear Sir, that I was not afraid my masters would take it amiss if I ran to see an old friend though in the service of their enemy. They are reasonable enough to allow that differing politics

---

[145] Candid friend to truth theme

[146] This letter is to be left for future eyes to be discovered. I guess I'm now a philosopher in the reading of it. The interpretations I'm now making have just been validated in a very surreal way across 239 years.

should not prevent the intercommunication of philosophers who study and converse for the benefit of mankind[147]. But you have doubts about coming to dine with me. I suppose you will not venture it; your refusal will not indeed do so much honour to the generosity and good nature of your government, as to your sagacity[148]. You know your people, and I do not expect you. I think too that in friendship I ought not to make you more visits as I intended: but I send my grandson to pay his duty to his physician[149].

You enquired about my gout, and I forgot to acquaint you, that I had treated it a little cavalierly[150] in its two last accesses[151]. Finding one night that my foot gave me more pain after it was covered warm in bed, I put it out of bed naked[152]; and perceiving it easier[153], I let it remain longer than I at first designed, and at length fell asleep leaving it there till morning. The pain did not return, and I grew well[154]. Next winter having a second attack, I repeated the experiment; not with such immediate success in dismissing the gout, but constantly with the effect of rendering it less painful, so that it permitted me to sleep every night[155]. I should mention, that it was my

---

[147] He is setting up the letter to converse about philosophy

[148] He is telling us to mine out the symbolisms in this letter.

[149] This is interesting. 'grandson" is his distant future of America. He uses this symbolism often. The physician is a reference is to that of an author, who has treated the 2nd amendment with a treatment of discernment, subsequently prescribing its new meaning as a cure for the ailment. .

[150] Points at "Militia"

[151] Access the two parts of Militia, People and Arms.

[152] Naked is reference to dressing up "Militia", talking about what it's for, how it was used. He is saying to remove all that conjecture and look at it for what it is. Uncover it completely, for there was a "cover up" going on and see it just for "people and Arms".

[153] Once something is no longer covered up, then it would of course be easier to perceive. This is pretty explicit once the symbolism is both recognized to exist and resolved.

[154] So after accessing the two words, which would expose the 2nd amendment, the pain went away.

[155] Symbolism is that nothing is going to happen overnight if you remove guns, but it would get better.

son who gave me the first intimation of this practice[156]. He being in the old opinion that the gout was to be drawn out by transpiration[157]. And having heard me say that perspiration was carried on more copiously when the body was naked than when clothed, he put his foot out of bed to increase that discharge, and found ease by it, which he thought a confirmation of the doctrine. But this method requires to be confirmed by more experiments, before one can conscientiously recommend it. I give it you, however, in exchange for your receipt of tartar emetic, because the commerce of philosophy as well as other commerce, is best promoted by taking care to make returns[158].

I am ever, Yours most affectionately

So what do we have here? This letter appears to be innocent enough and it seems to be Benjamin Franklin talking to a friend about his gout. We seem to have a conversation between a liberally minded genius and polymath telling another Philosopher about an experiment he has devised. Yes, after much thought and deep contemplations Benjamin Franklin appears to have devised an experiment that he thought was so important that he would put pen to paper and share it with another cerebral. The experiment was that "If you hang your foot off the side of your bed in the cool air, then you may find relief from your gout.". This doesn't sound like a particularly sophisticated experiment too me in the hopes of discovering something new and of benefit to mankind. I would suspect, that over the years, there is a possibility that other men, even ones of simpler minds, may have actually made such strides before. Now what I say next, you may not like,

---

[156] Now his son gave him the idea to do this, because his son is symbolic of Americas future, and as such would have a more experienced view of the constitution.

[157] Drawn out is symbolic of weaponry and transpiration is the evaporation of water from plant leaves.

[158] Commerce is an exchange where philosophy relates to understanding the best way to stop gun violence is to not let arms into society in the first place, (curing gout and not just being left with your arms) and the other commerce is exchanging the knowledge that the real checks and balances of the constitution would ever allow a tyrant to reveal himself to such an extent that Arms would be required. The returns are the returns of Arms, but only once these two symbolisms of commerce have been experienced and understood. This is of course the purpose of this letter.

but the message should still be clear. Benjamin Franklin was not trying to convey some feet of genius here in the common language, but only used the feet of a genius to hide its true meaning. Something smelled a bit off in this 236 year old letter with the only key that could have allowed it to be perceived, the 2nd amendment of the United States Bill of Rights. One of those rights had to have existed before all the others, and it is this one that would be my best guess. I see other symbolisms here but I feel that I've revealed enough to attribute it to the "dangerous experiment".

Just as I was wrapping up this section on Alexander Small, I went back and did a search in Benjamin Franklin's letters for any more correspondence that related to Alexander Small. I discovered that THREE letters all lined up with exactly the same date, all either To or from Alexander Small. The one I have just shown you is the middle letter and its date is "normal". The other two are written to Benjamin Franklin but the dates are a bit unusual. While they all are July 22 1780, one of them has 'Wednesday Noon[After July 22, 1780' and the other has '[before July 22, 1780'.

One other thing, "Alexander" is a name that means "protector of mankind". Alexander Small was a Scottish physician and a philosopher. I think Benjamin Franklin borrowed this man's good name and used it as a device to categorize his letters. He has done this before with a William Alexander, and it appears that Thomas Jefferson did this with Justice William Johnson. Now William Alexander had written Benjamin Franklin some letters that were actually some very well thought out ciphers. To further elaborate on the veracity of this discovery, at that time, William Alexander was deceased and in the grave. I think it requires no debate to further claim that dead men can't write letters. Now "William Alexander" would translate to "Protector " AND "protector of mankind" because William means "protector. When applied to the 2nd amendment it makes sense. The nature of the 2nd amendment was that its secret had to be protected and that its utility was that was to protect mankind from the dangers of firearms. You can almost see the grin on Benjamin Franklins face when he devised this, and he certainly wasn't going to get any complaint from William Alexander.

So let's see if we can establish the true context of these letters. The date, July 22 is the date that George Washington took command of the Continental Army in 1777. I believe that Thomas Jefferson's quote "the tree of liberty must be refreshed from time to time with the blood of patriots and tyrants" is reflected within these three letters. That particular letter was to William Stephen Smith on Nov. 13, 1787.

The early part of the Day represents the beginning of America. The middle of the day represents when the 2nd amendment was misunderstood and the later part represents when it is finally understood. With respect to Thomas Jeffersons quote above , time to time is a span of time, with the span being the middle letter and the other two letters pertaining to either side of it.

Keeping this in mind we will first put these letters in a chronological order.

There is the [Before] letter, and the [Afternoon] letter , so we will put the non designated letter in the middle, which would be when Arms are causing the most harm.

From Alexander Small [before July 22, 1780]

als: American Philosophical Society
Hotel de York Paris [before July 22, 1780]
Dear Sir
Being thus far in my way to England, and being informed that you live out of Town, I take this Opportunity of enquiring of your Welfare, and beg to know whether Capt Nairn, Brother to Mr Nairn in Cornhill, gave you a paper on Ventilation, and the History of it. I hope to receive a favourable Answer to these particulars, and ever remain Dear Sir Your Faithful humble Servant
Alexr Small
Addressed: A Monsieure / Monsieure le Docteure / franquelain a pacie
Notation: Alex Smal Paris.

So here we have talk of Ventilation which is the cure for arms. Remember the symbolism here is that you are not feeling well and your feet hurt so all you have left is your Arms. So we don't have talk of gout here, however we do have talk of two brothers a Captain Nairn and his brother (who is related) is Cornhill. Corns of course are an ailment of the feet. A nairn is a Scottish county. He also mentions the history of Ventilation so this probably refers to historical Arms laws. I must admit that Benjamin Franklin has a pretty good sense of humour. Hopefully he isn't defeating you with his symbolism here. Guns of course ventilate and paper is also rammed down the barrel to load them. The "particulars" is a symbolism for musket balls flying all over the place and the favourable answer is the 2nd amendment. "In my way to England" is a reference to "the right to keep and bear Arms" in the sense that it is felt to be needed to get in the way of King George or a tyrant. Living out of town, is the truth of the 2nd amendment, because "A well regulated militia, being necessary to the security of a free State" has never lived in the 2nd amendment while it's been misconstrued.

From Alexander Small [after July 22, 1780]

> ALS: American Philosophical Society
> Wednesday Noon [after July 22, 1780]
> Dear Sir
> When I had the pleasure of seeing You I did not know that we were to quit our present Habitation before five O'Clock. I therefore trouble with this, to desire that you will by him send Your Commands for England, and the paper I left with you.
> Let your Evening and Morning Contemplation be the Inscription on the Peace of Munster. As much depends on *You,* in Proportion to *your neglect* of the Means, in that proportion will the *Deaths* the *delay* occasions be laid to *your* Charge. Blessed are the Peace Makers, said the preacher of Peace and Good will to Men. Let your Speedy appearance in London give Joy to thousands; and to none, more than to Dear Sir Your Faithful and Affectionate Servant
> Alexr Small
> *Addressed:* To Dr Franklin / Passey
> *Notation:* Small.

From Alexander Small [before July 20, 1781]

> An Observation of Dr. Franklin's deserves a Place here; especially as it is not generally attended to[159]. The common opinion is indeed against it. The Banks of Rivers which have a quick motion & run on a clean sandy bottom, are very agreeable & healthy situations: but the sides of rivers which have ouzy bottoms, or marshy banks, or which are in the neighbourhood of extensive marshes, are to be avoided. When necessity or any particular advantage obliges people to build near such bad neighbours, the South side, says the Doctor, is the most eligible; because the warm southerly winds, which promote a tendency to putrefaction, & are the most frequent, blow the noxious vapours from the buildings, whereas the northerly winds, which blow but seldom, compared with the former, & which generally blow

---

[159] This is a red flag. It says "Hello, I'm a cipher, look closer". Its also in the same series associated with Alexander Small

strongly, check Putrefaction, & speedily carry off the noxious vapours.

Benjamin Franklin has been observing the harm Arms are causing society and sees the need for a 2nd amendment. What is not attended to are gun laws. The Banks of Rivers help to regulate the river quickly. The "running in an orderly fashion" symbolism are the troops being kept in line and under guidance. It is when the troops leave the rivers guidance that things go bad. Things are no longer healthy. The bad neighbours is a reference to "the right of the people to keep and bear Arms", which is a neighbour to "necessary to the security of a free State" (free flowing river aka military weaponry only under guidance of government). The "south" is also symbolic of "Virginia" where men like Patrick Henry who was most certainly a windy man would have been for guns. It was Patrick Henry who screamed out "Give me Liberty or Give me Death". Putrefaction = Death. The north winds are a reference to Philadelphia would be much more effective in preventing death because it is here where the real 2nd amendment was born. The noxious vapours are related of course the vapours of gun powder, and if there are less guns, then of course there will be much less vapour.

Now if one were to try and read this letter "normally", one might wonder just what in the be jesus is the point of this letter? This is a letter of advice from a genius, but is this the kind of knowledge that would have any benefit as it is passed down through the ages. The most ridiculous thing about this, if read normally is that a southerly wind will reach a house whether it's on the north or south side and marshland doesn't particularly care which way the wind blows when it decides to choose a location. The date has pertinence too. I'm not exactly sure what the reference is too.

Wind and Ventilation seem to be attributed to Alexander Small. While it may be true that in reality that Alexander Small was interested in ventilation, Benjamin Franklin saw the utility in this and encrypted it into this three letter cipher explaining the three states of the 2nd amendment.

From David Hartley July 27 1784 (up)

Rue Canmartin July 27 1784
My Dear friend
I have thought it a long while that my Confinement has prevented my seeing you. I was in hopes to have had the pleasure of seeing you to day, but I was indiscreet in going out the night before last, which has encreased the pain and swelling of my foot. My foot is again rather better than it was yesterday, but I am afraid to venture out to day. I hope still to see you on Thursday. I received no letters by the messenger of last night from the Secretary of State, but I understand that the report of the privy council and other documents respecting American trade are laid before Parliament. I presume therefore that that Subject will soon be taken into Consideration. Yours most affectionately
D H
To Dr Franklin &c &c &c

Here we have one of many letters from David Hartley. I believe there is some symbolism in here. Right at the start of the letter there appears to be a directive to think about this letter. This letter appears to have been written on the same day as the one above from John Adams. Now if someone is at home, in bed with bad feet, what is it that they have left? All they would have left, is their arms. Perhaps it is the arms, that are causing the distress, and not the feet? Perhaps, it is scary to venture outside if there are so many arms allowed in society? It seems each time he talks with Benjamin Franklin that his

From David Hartley Aug 4 1784 (up)

Rue Caumartin Wednesday Morning Aug 4 1784
My Dear friend
I have not received any letters from England—but I hear that a continuation of the American bill is passed. That is all the news that I hear—My leg has been very bad again: I now write in bed. I have been confined for these last four days almost entirely to my bed and mattrass. The pain now begins again to abate. Your ever affectionate
D H
To Dr Franklin &c &c &c
Addressed: To Dr Franklin / &c &c &c / Passy
Endorsed: D Hartley Esqr Aug. 4. 84 to BF.

This man sure likes to talk about his leg. You will also learn that Benjamin Franklin knew that the "Bill of Rights" would be used by at last 1780. I have seen "4" used before so the days are symbolic of the 4 clauses of the 2nd amendment.

Alexander Small (up) Philad Sept. 28. 1787

Dear Sir,

I received your kind Letter of June 6. 86. and I answered it, tho' long after the Receipt. I do not perceive by your second Favour of July 87. that my Answer had then come to hand, but hope it may since that time.

I have not lost any of the Principles of Public Oeconomy you once knew me possess'd of; but to get the bad Customs of a Country chang'd[160], and new ones[161], though better, introduc'd, it is necessary first to remove the Prejudices of the People[162], enlighten their Ignorance,[163] and convince them that their Interest will be promoted by the propos'd Changes[164]; and this is not the Work of a Day[165]. Our Legislators are all Landholders; and they are not yet persuaded that all Taxes are finally paid by the Land. Besides, our Country is so sparsely settled, the Habitations particularly in the Back Counties, being perhaps 5 or 6 Miles distant from each other, that the Time and Labour of the Collector in going from House to house, and being oblig'd to call often before he can receive the Tax, amounts to more than the Tax[166] is worth; and therefore we have been forc'd into the Mode of indirect Taxes, i.e. Duties on Importation of Goods and Excises.

---

[160] The right to bear Arms

[161] The right of the people to be protected from bad Arms in their society

[162] Those that are biased towards their own self defence first.

[163] No experience yet of a new constitution with respect to its real checks and balances.

[164] The "new" 2nd amendment.

[165] Many many letters will have to be written and it will also take a great deal of time.

[166] At this time the people are Armed due to the war of Independence. Taxes are a symbolism for collecting the Arms to put in the domain of government control to protect the people.

216

I have made no Attempt to introduce the Form of Prayer here[167], which you and good Mrs. Baldwin do me the Honour to approve. The Things of **this**[168] World take up too much of my Time, of which indeed I have too little left to undertake any thing like a Reformation in Matters of Religion[169]. When we can sow good Seed[170] we should however do it, and wait, when we can do no better, with Patience Nature's[171] Time for their Sprouting. Some lie many Years in the Ground[172], and at length certain favourable Seasons or Circumstances[173] bring them forth with vigorous Shoots and plentiful Productions.

Had I been at home as you wish soon after the Peace, I might possibly have mitigated some of the Severities against the Royalists, believing as I do that Fear and Error, rather than Malice occasion'd their Desertion of their Country's Cause, and Adoption of the King's. The public Resentment against them is now so far abated, that none who ask Leave to return are refus'd, and many of them now live among us much at their Ease. As to the Restoration of confiscated Estates, it is an Operation that none of our Politicians have as yet ventur'd to propose. They are a sort of People that love to fortify themselves in their Projects by Precedent[174]. Perhaps they wait to see your Government restore the forfeited Estates in Scotland to the

---

[167] To introduce a prayer is to let it be known, so it is to be a secret. The secret is of course the 2nd amendment.

[168] The world is the United States in the 1790s.

[169] Reforming the matters of religion is a reference to getting people to think of each others' welfare as well even though they aren't in spite of being religious.

[170] Sewing good seed are the letters.

[171] It is the nature of mans experience of the "broken" constitution. It is hoped that one day man will be able to resolve the true meaning of liberty as its promised in a United States of America.

[172] 224 plus years to be exact.

[173] San Bernandino inspired me to pay the 2nd amendment a visit, and being liberally minded I did the research and discovered the plentiful productions of the letters.

[174] They would be hard pressed to give up their Arms because they feel they must be fortified against government.

Scotch, those in Ireland to the Irish, and those in England to the Welsh!¹⁷⁵

I am glad that the distressed Exiles who remain with you have receiv'd or are likely to receive some Compensation for their Losses, for I commiserate their Situation. It was clearly incumbent on the King to indemnify those he had seduc'd by his Proclamations: But it seems not so clearly consistent with the Wisdom of Parliament to resolve doing it for him.¹⁷⁶ If some mad King hereafter should think fit in a Freak to make War upon his Subjects in Scotland, or upon those of England by the Help of Scotland and Ireland, (as the Stewarts did) may he not encourage Followers by the Precedent of these Parliamentary Gratuities, and thus set his Subjects to cutting one another's Throats, first with the Hope of Sharing in Confiscations, and then with that of Compensation in case of Disappointment? The Council of Brutes in the old Fable were aware of this. Lest that Fable may perhaps not have fallen in your Way, I enclose a Copy of it.

Your Commercial Treaty with France seems to show a growing Improvement in the Sentiments of both Nations in the Oeconomical Science. All Europe might be a great deal happier with a little more Understanding. We in America have lately had a Convention for framing a new federal Constitution. Enclos'd I send you the Result of their Deliberations. Whether it will be generally acceptable and carried into Execution is yet to be seen; but present Appearances are in its favour.

I am always glad to hear from you and of your Welfare. I remember with Pleasure the happy Days we have spent together. Adieu, and believe me ever, my dear Friend, Yours most affectionately

    B Franklin
    Mr Small

---

[175] Sarcasm here where every other country is taking over the property of its inhabitants.

[176] It would take more than a crazy ruler to take over all the peoples property and liberty, which is a way of saying Arms are not needed, no fortifications are required.

This letter was also written at the same time as the Federalist Papers and uses much the same symbolisms here. This is just Benjamin Franklin putting his own spin on it. This is also more proof of their collaboration and purpose of mind.

Mystery Letter- Pre 2nd Convention

I came across this letter written which appears to be written anonymously. Benjamin Franklin would often send in anonymous letters under different pseudonym.

I believe it was written by Benjamin Franklin due to its content, and Benjamin Franklins MO.

"The Pennsylvania Gazette. In 1729, **Benjamin Franklin** bought a **newspaper**, the Pennsylvania Gazette. **Franklin** not only printed the paper, but often contributed pieces to the paper under aliases. His **newspaper** soon became the most successful in the colonies."

www.ushistory.org/**franklin**/info/

This letter talks about the dangers of militias coexisting in society.

Philadelphia Independent Gazetteer, 30 April 1788

Benjamin Franklin m.o.

of a letter from Franklin county, 24th April, 1788.

"The necessary arrangements," as they are termed here[177], have taken place in these counties; committees of observation[178] and correspondence are appointed in every township, who correspond with the militia officers and leading men in every county in the state; the counties of Cumberland, Dauphine, and Franklin, appear to take the lead, and have been long since repairing and cleaning their arms, and every young fellow who is able to do it, is providing himself with a rifle or musket, and amunition: They have also nominated a commanding officer, it is said to be General——, and say that they can turn out, at ten days warning, TWENTY THOUSAND expert woodsmen, completely armed; this is I believe very true, as all the counties, this side the Susquehanna, are nearly unanimous, and near three fourths of the other counties. They say the strength of their opponents are in the city, and give out that it will be in vain for them to make any resistance; they mean to make * * * and are promised assistance from a neighbouring state, who, I find, are as

---

[177] termed as " A well regulated militia, being necessary.." as termed in the 2nd amendment (4th article at this point in time).

[178]

warmly opposed as this state to the system. The lawyers, &c. when they precipitated with such fraud and deception the new system upon us, it seems to me, did not recollect, that the militia had arms; however, it will be an awful lesson to tyrants, if they should feel the resentment of an enraged people; I can assure Mr. Wilson that the people are now as determined to secure their liberties as he is anxious for power and offices. And let the worst come to the worst, the opposition have the constitution of the state, the established law of the land, on their side; this yet remains good and firm, any doings, or acts of a faction, or illegal mob convention, to the contrary notwithstanding. A civil war is dreadful, but a little blood spilt now, will perhaps prevent much more hereafter. However, another general convention being called, will prevent anything like it happening; the people appear anxious for farther powers being granted to Congress; and are generally agreed, that those offered by the minority of the convention of this state would be quite sufficient, and all their rights and privileges would be then secured by the proposed bill of rights, consequently unity and harmony would follow: on the other hand, if the votaries of power and offices do not agree to peaceable measures, by having another general convention called, I dread the consequences to themselves.

"N. B. I hear no more of the attempt to execute the order of Council to disarm the militia, I believe the sub---lieutenants in most of the counties refused to deliver up the arms, it was well enough, for the people were determined not to part with them. It is hinted that since the western members went down, they cancelled the order."

Cite as: The Documentary History of the Ratification of the Constitution Digital Edition, ed. JohnP.Kaminski, Gaspare J. Saladino, Richard Leffler, Charles H. Schoenleber and Margaret A.Hogan.Charlottesville:University of VirginiaPress,2009.

Canonic URL: http://rotunda.upress.virginia.edu/founders/RNCN--03---17---02---0065

[accessed 27 Dec 2011]

What's interesting about this letter is that Benjamin Franklin was connecting his ciphers through a narrative which must be discerned. You see there are two sides to the narrative of the 2nd amendment, one which we have been familiar with for over 200 years and the other which has been revealed by this research. The letters are not linked directly by date only a date range. It is the surface contexts of the letters that fit each other like a glove. I only found this letter after looking for it based on the Oct 26, 1789. These letters are ordered chronological. I'd recommend reading the latter letter first and then jump back to this one. It is the latter that references this letter where this does not reference the latter.

(see letter dated Oct 26 1789 – related to this letter).

To Patrick Henry (unpublished) Oct 8 1785

Philada. Oct. 8. 1785.

Sir,

After congratulating your Excellency, as I do most sincerely, on the continued Respect and Confidence of your Country, manifested by their placing you again in the Chair of Government over them; I beg leave to trouble you with a little Affair that relates to myself.

When I went to France, I left here a Quantity of Printing Letters, which my Attorney Mr. Bache tells me were sold to your State for Public Use[179]; but no Agreement was made ascertaining the Value, he being unacquainted with it. All the Accounts I had of the original lost, as well as of the Quantity, which was bought in Parcels at different Times and of different Persons, are lost; so that I know not how to make a Charge for them; especially as they were not weigh'd nor any Inventory made of them, nor of the other Printing Utensils delivered with them. As this Transaction pass'd under your former Administration, what I now request is, that your Excellency would require of the Printer who receiv'd them an Account of the Weight of the Types, expressing the different kinds, (because they are different Prices) and also a List of the other Things that accompanied them. When I have obtain'd such an Account fom him, I shall be able to

---

[179] 'the right to keep and bear Arms" was sold to Patrick Henry's state of mind. He was fearful of tyrants found comfort in being Armed for the contingency of a tyrant. He failed to recognize that a tyrant is anyone that enforce their will on others. To allow arms in the public domain is to empower tyrants.

make out mine; and I doubt not your kind Assistance in procuring the Payment. With great Esteem and Respect, I am, Sir, Your Excellency's most obedient and most humble Servant
  B. Franklin
  His Excelly. Patrick Henry Esqr. &c.
  Endorsed: Letter from Dr Franklin

Patrick Henry was the governor of Virginia, an anti-federalist, lawyer, businessman, slave owner and an orator. He is also the man who was quoted as saying *"The great object is that every man be armed"*. There would have been very little effort to get this man to buy into the 2nd amendment when it is subjectively read. That quote was before the 2nd amendment even existed. Yes he thought Arms were needed, but he most certainly did not know what the 2nd amendment really meant. Benjamin Franklin is stating as much with this cipher.

I started looking for the Patrick Henry letter after reading the William Alexander from below. In this letter a letter is referenced from 2-3 years earlier regarding a claim on the State of Virginia. Even thought the recipients were different these letters were both talking about printing and fonts and its date fell into the sweet spot as referenced. Compound this with the fact that Patrick Henry was the Governor of Virginia then this must be the referenced letter. This letter is a cipher, so it stands to reason that the Patrick Henry letter of similar construction is also a cipher. It's interesting how Benjamin Franklin is seeding his library with these letters and subtly cross referencing them to help ensure secrecy. These letters were put here to be hunted out by future historians, and would of course only be recognized with the key of the 2nd amendment.

To Richard Henry Lee, April 12th, 1785.

(unpublished) Passy

Sir,
M. de Chaumont, who will have the Honor of presenting this Line to your Excellency, is a young Gentleman of excellent Character, whose Father was one of our most early Friends in this Country, which he manifested by crediting us with a thousand Barrels of Gun powder, and other military Stores in 1776 before we had provided any apparent Means of Payment. He has, as I understand, some Demands to make on Congress, **the Nature of which I am unacquainted with**, but my Regard for the Family makes me wish that they may obtain a speedy Consideration, and such favorable Issue as they may appear to merit. To this End I beg Leave to recommend him to your Countenance and Protection, and am with great Respect, &c.
(signed) B. FRANKLIN

Jacques-Donatien Le Ray de Chaumont is considered a french father of the American revolution who later settled in America. He is a similar type of man to Oliver Pollack who you will be acquainted with in the following letter. Both letters appear to be an encryptions. M. de Chaumont was very sympathetic to the American cause and also provided Benjamin Franklin with a mansion to stay in. It's my opinion that M. de Chaumont didn't know the secret of the 2nd amendment but it is the symbolism of the man's nature that is being utilized here. He is after all a friend of the New Nation, and in light of this riddle being solved, he is a friend of the new 2nd amendment and the new culture that will evolve from it. Richard Henry Lee would not have come from this same camp however, because he represents "old school".

This is evidenced by Richard Henry Lees quote.

"A militia when properly formed are in fact the people themselves... and include all men capable of bearing arms. . . To preserve liberty it is essential that the whole body of people always possess arms."

The term "line" I believe references the 2nd amendment itself. Richard Henry Lee is a reference to the type of man that would read "a right of the people to keep and bear Arms", like it, and then call it common sense. He would then use the rest of the 2nd amendnt to validate what he liked most about it. He would even see hyphens where none existed, and perhaps perceive it as a booboo, chuckle, prop himself up a bit in his own head, and then move on. Benjamin Franklin however is completely "unacquainted" with this interpretation, because he knows what it actually says. He knows the true purpose and utility of this people's right. "Countenance and Protection" is a reference to finally understanding and usage and true utility of the "new" 2nd amendment.

I have also observed that this letter is 5 weeks apart with the Patrick Henry letter, which can be DIRECTLY linked to an encrypted William Alexander letter, which in turn is DIRECTLY linked to the 2nd amendment and the Bill of Rights. That letter is dated Oct 26, 1789 and has the same symbolisms as found in the Patrick Henry letter. These are the letters that talked of fonts and typesets, which of course hid their true meaning. They were hidden through the fact that it would be no surprise to see a well known printer talking about fonts and typesets. At first glance there is nothing really suspicious here.

Patrick Henry and Richard Henry Lee are demonstrative of those in society that would have been very passionate about gun ownership. This bias has of course evolved over time, because beyond fear, avarice has now found a place to champion the same cause. Patrick Henry was the man said "Give me Liberty or give me Death", which demonstrates a nuance of self, over society". When someone uses the word "me" it is a pretty good tell of where their headspace is at.

It is interesting how Benjamin Franklin has woven threads through letters separated by years, all for the express purpose that one day they would be read and understood in a future time. This is happening right now, as you read this. Benjamin Franklin is simply seeding the archives and has just uses two men as symbolisms. They symbolise the "pro-gun anti federalist, fear of tyrant, government is bad" camp. Does this sound a bit familiar, because this is nothing more than the raw nature of man, as it was observed by a genius about 230 years ago. Nothing has really changed, because mans nature does not really change, and the constitution was written for all of mankind, in spite of his nature. This is Benjamin Franklins long game, as he states in his essay "Morals of Chess", which he re-animated and enhanced in 1779.

To John Jay (unpublished)

Passy, April 12th. 1785.

Dear Sir,

Mr. de Chaumont, Son of my Landlord, who goes to America on some Business of his Father's, will have the Honor of delivering this Line to you. He is a young Gentleman of excellent Character, and the Family have been Friends of America from the Beginning of our Dispute. I take the Liberty, therefore, of recommending him, earnestly, to your Civilities and Counsels. With sincere and great Esteem, I have the Honor to be, &c.

(signed) B. FRANKLIN

To Mr Secy Jay

This letter is "almost" identical to the one written above. I actually thought that I had copied it twice at one point. It's written to John Jay, who we know was one of the key players in both hiding and exposing the 2nd amendment. The letter itself looks a bit suspicious, but what really drives the point home is its similarity with the one above, as written to Richard Henry Lee. The letters were written on the exact same day, so that they could be contrasted. The letter to Richard Henry Lee talks of gunpowder and Arms being released into the public domain where this one does not. They both talk of a "line". The line is a symbolism for the 2nd amendment, and as we now know, it can be read both objectively and subjectively. The "family" is a reference to the family of America, because that is who the line was always meant to serve. The contrived letter to Patrick Henry and Richard Henry Lee both talk of being "unacquainted" with something. That is the EXACT word that is used, "unacquainted". This is driving home the point that Benjamin Franklin has no idea about a "right to keep and bear Arms" as being any part of the 2nd amendment when it is read independent of the line itself. The symbolism of "father" may be a reference to a "founding father" or creator of the line itself. The term "honor" is a reference to a "justice", which brings us immediately into the realm of constitutional interpretation.

Now it gets interesting.

The family is the family of liberally thinking men who are more concerned about the entire future of America and in such thinking are her friends. Now the son of this family, are the descendants of it, or the future. Think of a liberally minded man in the future who has a full understanding of the "line". Thomas Jefferson called this person the "candid friend to truth". The son is me. Now if Benjamin Franklin and Thomas Jefferson think I'm a young gentleman of excellent character and the rest of the universe has a different viewpoint on this research, so be it. If it helps any, I am a son of America, albeit a distant one. My gggg grandfather was born Ebenezer Smith, Vermont, 1796.

From William Alexander (unpublished) Jan 22 1786

William Alexander[180]

>Richmond 22 Jany 1786
>
>My Dear Sir,
>
>I heard with great joy your safe arrival with your two Grand sons[181] and Williams[182] where I hope you now enjoy amidst your Charming Family those Pleasures you have so well earnd and of which you have so true a relish.[183] I thought it idle to trouble[184] you with letters even to thank you for those you gave me when I left Europe[185]. You cannot doubt the warmth of my Attachment[186]. It will last whilst I last that is all I shall say.
>
>**I write the present at the request of my friend Oliver Pollock Esquire now a residenter in your State**[187]. He sufferd deeply in the late revolution, and has the more merit as it was by voluntary

---

[180] This man is deceased at this time. It's a device that Benjamin Franklin has used they symbolism of this man's name as part of the cipher.

[181] Reference to future understanding of the 2nd amendment where two things are now understood, people and Arms as they reside in a Militia.

[182] William means "resolute protector" as a name so "Williams" is plural and references the grandsons who the words "people and Arms" as they live in a Militia. This of course exposes the real meaning of the 2nd amendment.

[183] The Charming Family is all the USA, which has "earned" the 2nd amendment because of what it has cost.

[184] Not knowing the 2nd amendment, being it in limbo or idle, would of course be trouble.

[185] The letters are idle because they have been in waiting, and they go both ways. They were written for love of nation. The letters have always been waiting to be found.

[186] The real meaning of the 2nd Amendment, but can't say more because it's a secret.

[187] Oliver Pollock was very much liberally minded and he is symbolic of a man fighting for true liberty in his country. He thought of others first, just as the people of America must be united in thinking of their own neighbours and not themselves and fears regarding the 2nd amendment.

services from a Place and in a Country where he was Exempted from any other obligation than affection for the Cause[188]. He has large Claims on this State as well as on the United States[189]. The first he has now got setled and I believe the last in some measure[190]. If you can be of use to Him you will serve a deserving Man, and this I say with the more Confidence as his itch and affairs have passd through my hands[191].

It will give you pleasure to know that I am well and doing well[192]. Permit me to assure Mr. and Mrs. Bache and my two younger friends of my affection. **Can I be usefull to any of them?[193] My situation enables me to do litle services of many kinds in this Country[194]**. Consider me as a second self in what Concerns you and yours[195]. Being most fervently Dear Sir Your most obedient humble servant
W Alexander
His Excellency B: Franklin Esqr Philadelphia
Addressed: His Excellency Ben: Franklin Esqre

---

[188] The cause is to stop the oppression of gun violence that is ravaging America.

[189] Note the inferred differentiation? The first state refers to a state of tranquility, liberty, where the latter is all being united in its attainment.

[190] The first "State" is settled in the actual wording of the 2nd Amendment, where the last is a reference to the entire 2nd amendment as a "measure" or tool to create this "State" in the United States Constitution.

[191] This man is symbolic of the person that will be researching the letters. The "itch" is my "passion" in this in recognition of its profound importance. Of course Benjamin Franklin's affairs have now become my own because he passed them to me as if they were a baton passed through time.

[192] "well and doing well" is a reference that the 2nd amendment is in fact fine and is not outdated

[193] He hopes that once the 2nd amendment as been discovered, it will be of use for the future. Benjamin Franklin of course can only suspect what will happen over time.

[194] His situation of course is that he'd like to discuss it more, but unfortunately he has passed over 200 years ago.

[195] Benjamin Franklin is referring to this letter as him in the future, talking directly to America. A second self self, reanimated or he knows who he is talking too

Endorsed: W Alexander

After a bit of research I have discovered that Oliver Pollack was a wealthy merchant. He was very liberally minded and spent his fortune to help fight the British. He sold his flour for half price at one point to help out Louisiana. The start

Can he be useful, where "he" is a reference to the utility of the 2nd amendment and its narrative. Second only a reference to the second meaning of the second amendment and not its reference as the 2nd amendment because at this point in time, Bejamin Franklin would have only known it as the fourth article. Mr. and Mrs. Bache are Benjamin Franklins' future daughter and husband. The dead William Alexander says "consider me a second self", which is telling us that he, is really Benjamin Franklin.

From William Alexander (unpublished) 10 June 1786

Richmond 10 June 1786

Dear Sir

I would not have troubled you with business were it not for account and by the desire of an Old Servant of Yours Nicolas La Fargue. He gave me a power of attorney[196], a *Depot* for The hands of Mr. Holcker as french Consul for 8 Loan office Certificates 7400 dollars—also a Loan office Certificate 27 April 1779—500[dollars] Upon Enquiring the State of these Matters[197] I left the depot untouchd, as it could not be Sold[198] but at Immense loss and untill lately no step was taken to liquidate These funds the Loan office Certificate I have got Committed   Certificate for the *Intt to 1st Janry 1783.* You have inclosed the depot, and the Certificate for $500 and one for the Intt 9- and dollars—which I request you will deliver to La Fargue upon his returning you my obligation with an acknowledgment on the Back of it, that my trust is discharged. I Charge him no postage or Expences.[199]

I could wish my Friend Billy[200] woud not forget his old acquaintances[201]. It woud give me real pleasure to hear of Your and his welfare by Him[202]. I repeat that If he [has] nothing to do I will be Glad to see him here[203]. The   Indolence that prevails here leaves

---

[196] The power of attorney is a 2nd amendment having the power to regulate Arms. Its been left for the future, but hidden and one day both discovered and delivered.

[197] Again, a reference to "State" it's the liberty for all that really matters.

[198] The 2nd amendment would never be endorsed.

[199] Perhaps a clue that this letter was never mailed at all, but only archived for the future.

[200] Bill of rights reference

[201] The nature of the men were that they were wise and liberally minded. It is this nature that must be aquainted with the Bill of Rights when discerning it or the constitution itself.

[202] Again, we have "friend" I am the friend of Billy or the Bill of rights in that I discovered it can provide welfare for all. I am the "Him" because the welfare came by "Me".

[203] He's glad that I'm deciphering the letter if there is in fact no gun violence in the future? The "here" is in the reading of the letter itself.

wonderfull means of advantage to Such as have Energy of Mind[204]. I have some hopes of Seeing you ere long[205], and with respects to Your amiable family[206] I remain with the highest Esteem Dear Sir Your most obedient humble servant

    W: Alexander

    His Excelly Bn Franklin President of the State of Pensylvania Philadelphia

Endorsed: Mr Alexander

From William Alexander (UP) 30 May 1784

(The narrative encrypted)

    Richmond Virginia 30 May 1784[207]
    My Dear Sir[208]

I cannot let my first ship go without dropping you a few lines— Jona. woud inform you of my arrival of the severity of the Winter, and of my Journey to Philadelphia which was necessary for settling a plan for conducting my money transactions which I did to my Satisfaction. I had the pleasure of Seeing your amiable Daughter Grand Children and Mr. Bache, and received every mark of kindness[209] from all of

---

[204] The truth of 2nd amendment has been in limbo for a very long time. The energy of mind will be required to understand this and the narrative. Perhaps it's an acknowledgement that it would take a bit of work to uncover what was hidden. An energy more in subduing bias, than anything else.

[205] This I believe is an inferred apology of sorts, because it was always hoped that it would take the minimum amount of time would pass. The variables and circumstances of the future could never be truly known though, but were most certainly anticipated.

[206] Amiable in that everyone would see the logic in the 2nd amendment and be friendly to this right for all the people as it was always meant to be.

[207] At this time Benjamin Franklin was in Europe and didn't get back until 1785.

[208] While this letter is assumed to be sent to Benjamin Franklin, it is sent to "Sir" , who of course is someone in the future. I'm going to assume that its just a lucky guess, 50/50, since I'm a man that discovered it. I will now revert back to being constitutionally correct.

[209] 'receiving a mark of kindness would be like being wished "well".

them—Your Town pleases me much, not merely on account of the regularity[210] of the streets, but the seeming energy of the Inhabitants[211], in a word The Congress may Set[212] where it pleases but Philadelphia is, and always will be the Capital of America[213]—**with regard to my business I have met with all the obstructions I expected and some that I coud not forsee**[214], particularly there is a want of order and economy in business in this State[215], that exceeds all Imagination[216]—a Man must literaly[217] do what Poor Richard Advises[218], to have anything done he must go, judge what follows from this[219] for a .Operson whose business must Lye equally on the four great rivers, and over an Extent of 50 leagues on each of these rivers[220], with a very little time I hope however to have my machine

---

[210] Reference to regulated.

[211] Inhabits are the people in "militia" which of course is the word.

[212] Congress is doing the regulating and the set of words is people and Arms.

[213] The Capital of America is an "A", which can be found in the 2nd amendment in only one place.. "Arms".

[214] Where it is called "business here" , George Washington referred to it as a "dangerous experiment", and

[215] Economy and Business is the 2nd amendment being used. There will be a back and forth of "Arms" over time in order to maintain the security of a free State.

[216] He doesn't know the future circumstances of Arms and People

[217] I went to find some advice in Poor Richards Almanac ..and found a phrase where "Lye" occurred.

[218] This was Benjamin Franklins pseudonym when he wrote "Poor Richards Almanac in 1733".

[219] 243: He that would live in peace and at ease, must not speak all he knows, nor judge all he sees. (this is a reference to liberty, it is a secure state of mind). Judge all he sees, is simply the other side of the debate where ones imagination and paranoia is going wild.

[220] "**533**: the rivers and bad governments, the lightest tings swim at the top" The government is bad simply because the 2nd amendment is misinterpreted. The 4 great rivers are the 4 parts of the 2nd amendment, each separated by a comma. Give them equal weight, and go deeper to find their meaning.

mounted[221], to go with tolerable regularity of Some Advantage, what can be done for a little time will be merely to keep afloat[222], without dammage to the Con[223] this I think we shall do in all events.

I have on mature deliberation fixed myself here for the present[224], it is pretty Centrical, the seat of Government and of the weekly post, but I am obliged to Contrive posts for my own

---

[221] In this Almanac I located this... "A lie stands on one leg, the truth stands on two" Something standing is a Militia, but the truth..is a reference that Militia viewed as its two constituent parts, people and Arms. The machine of course is the 2nd amendment, mounted into the constitution at a future time. IT APPEARS THAT BENJAMIN FRANKLIN IS THE TRUE AUTHOR OF THE 2ND AMENDMENT.

[222] To keep afloat is a reference the lightest things swim at the top for government, which is the lie or untruth. It is simply what the 2nd amendment appears to be at the surface. A little time turned out to be 224 years.

[223] There is no damage to the constitution simply because the words speak for themselves. There is no interpretation required. He also hopes that his machine will be used, and tolerated so that its advantage of protecting all the people will be maintained to the countries advantage.

[224] A reference to the 2nd amendment having been constructed in a suitable fashion to service initially the requirements of getting a constitution signed. The deliberation was probably conducted by the "think tank" of the actors involved.

business[225], and when I begin vigourously[226], must keep 7 or 8 horses running Constantly backward and forward[227].

The difficulties I have to encounter give me time to Lay my plan in such a way as will require less mending than if we had been hurried at first.[228]

I have been very well received by the Governor[229] and have got acquainted and even **Connected with all the Ingenious Men in this state**[230], who make any figure, Except Mr. Jefferson and two or three more yet absent—**In a word**[231] If my Constitution will stand this

---

[225] The business is the work and labour involved to create carefully constructed letters for the future. The constitution itself would be a piece of cake, compared to the labour involved in this. (Perhaps that is debatable, but at least it would be non political. I only know steam is venting from my ears with a fury as I try to decipher this letter, so thought to construct it in the first place? Good grief.)

[226] Write lots of letters. Stack the cards for the future. Some letters may be lost. This is an issue of National security. It is the final legacy of these men to make the Constitution whole. The future will be completely out of their control, once they have passed. In writing the perfect constitution for the people to fight oppression, the people themselves must not be allowed to enter a state of tyranny. Men who can force their will on others at a whim, including a murder and massacre, simply because of the advantage of being armed.

[227] Symbolic of writing letters , many letters which have dual meanings and dual audiences. They must be perfectly balance to both hide from Benjamin Franklins time, and illuminate to ours.

[228] He is starting this work BEFORE the constitutional conventions. It is an orchestration with actors and confidents to help him out. It seems very likely that the Federalist papers were created well in advance of their dates. Can it that be proved? Does it really matter? It's merely a curiosity at this point in time.

[229] The governor of Virginia at this time was Patrick Henry. 'the right of the people to keep and bear Arms, shall not be infringed" would have been very well received by this fierce anti federalist.

[230] The state is a reference to the 2 states of understanding, Patrick Henry in one group, and the primary actors in the other.

[231] 'Militia'

Climate[232], I can live here agreeably[233] But unless necessity were to oblige me[234], woud not think of bringing out my Family—were Philadelphia my residence I certainly woud. At present I consider myself as in another world[235], and wish to forget every thing in the old one, but my Friends and my Business.

    I have met with Many very Ingenious and Worthy Men in whose Society[236] I coud pass my life with pleasure—Amongst the old race Col Geo: Mason and Mr. With surprised me, And there are young Men getting Forward who will yield to their predecessors in Nothing—Mr. Madison[237], must soon have a considerable weight in this state, or in any state in which he is Employed[238]—

    Your old Colleague Arthur Lee is sent to treat with the Indians, He is at present neither in Congress nor assembly— [239]

    I beg to be remembered to your Grandson and secretary and all our Friends with You—I hope my boy[240] gives you and Him

---

[232] The climate of the 2nd amendment being read subjectively because 'people and Arms" are hidden in one word, a word, which is of course "Militia" and 'the right to keep and bear Arms' had so much appeal.

[233] They don't want an uprising if the truth of the 2nd amendment is revealed prematurely to the required public experience of the constitutions checks and balances against tyranny.

[234] Necessity is the current state of the United States with respect to gun violence , small arms in society, the police, and of course a congress that refuses to do anything regarding gun regulation. With this amendment , if they ignore it , they could be held to treason. I of course speculate with the respect to this, for I am not educated in either law or the constitution. I'm simply adding my own two cents here.

[235] The true utility will be left in another world, a world in the future.

[236] Direct reference to the American Philosophical Society, and in the context of this letter they all took part in this plan.

[237] James Madison of course wrote the 2nd amendment.

[238] James Madison is employed of course to present the 2nd amendment which will have two different states of understanding, be it subjective for the time being or objective for the future.

[239] To understand the nature of this man, see letter addressed to him dated April 3 1778.

[240] Apparently Benjamin Franklin referred to George Washington as

Satisfaction—I was pleased with His letter to Williams about the Baloons, I sent it to Dr. Foulke and it helped to make one, which he had begun upon my Information—I think the Dr will Succeed in his Business which is still more material. He and his Family did every thing possible to render my stay in Philadelphia agreeable[241]. You have got a New Colleague of whom fame Speaks highly—You will learn that we are limiting our Foreign trade to a few points in the Bay—This will soon make Norfolk a great Mart and will I think be of general Service and of advantage to us[242]. Let me know my Dear Sir if I can be usefull to you or yours in this Country and believe me unalterably My Dear Sir Your most devoted humble Servant

    W: Alexander

    Dr B. Franklin M.P. of the United States at Passy

Now how do I know that this particular letter is a cipher? I have already located another one, which was written to a William Alexander.

There are 2 William Alexander's in history that are pertinent to the story of the 2nd amendment. One of them was a soldier, who died during the war of independence and the other was his ancestor and a Scottish Poet. He was a philosopher of sorts. There is also a William Alexander recorded as a member in the American Philosophical Society. Now besides a bloodline, there was something else both of these men had in common at the date this letter was written. They were both dead. The latter Alexander Hamilton, the soldier, passed on January 15, 1783, one year and 3 months before the date on this letter. So what is going on here? It is actually encrypted with symbolism in this letter and in another to Benjamin Franklin,

First off this letter is from a "Philospher", so now we know its true intent when we tie it back to a letter John Adams wrote to the Hague July 27th 1784. In that letter he states

> "The **Philosophers** are speculating upon our Constitutions and I hope will throw out **Hints**, which will be of Use to our Countrymen."

Hints for countrymen? Constitution in the plural? Philosophers? Why not be explicit? Perhaps the plural constitution is a reference to 2 different

---

[241] The family of course is the group of men that

[242] I really don't' have a clue what this means, theres only so much I can decipher. I am trying though. I'm compelled too.

interpretations of the 2nd amendment and its hidden story. Just as the 2nd amendments true utility has been revealed, would it not also be extremely useful to explain the full story behind it, both in its usage and its validation? Its why I write this book, I have laboured to collect the dots that when connected draws a line just under 224 years long.

Poor Richards Almanac

https://archive.org/stream/poorrichardsalma00franrich/poorrichardsalma00franrich_djvu.txt

From Benjamin Franklin to Arthur Lee, 3 April 1778

To Arthur Lee
AL (draft):6 American Philosophical Society
Passy, April 3: 1778
Sir

It is true I have omitted answering some of your Letters.7 I do not like to answer angry Letters. I hate Disputes. I am old, cannot have long to live, have much to do and no time for Altercation. If I have often receiv'd and borne your Magisterial Snubbings and Rebukes without Reply, ascribe it to the right Causes, my Concern for the Honour and Success of our Mission, which would be hurt by our Quarrelling,8 my Love of Peace, my Respect for your good Qualities, and my Pity of your Sick Mind, which is forever Tormenting itself, with its Jealousies, Suspicions and Fancies that others mean you ill, wrong you, or fail in Respect for you. If you do not cure your self of this Temper it will end in Insanity, of which it is the Symptomatick Forerunner, as I have seen in several Instances. God preserve you from so terrible an Evil: and for his sake pray suffer me to live in quiet. I have the honour to be very respectfully, Sir, Your most humble Servant

Hon. A. Lee Esq.

I'd like to point out an observation about this letter. I've just found this, as I was trying to get some more information on the Arthur Lee, to accompany the previous letter May 30 1784. It is the tone of this letter. On one hand Benjamin Franklin states he doesn't like to Altercations and then in the same letter he seems to be rather frank in expressing what he thinks of this man. This letter also highlights his frustration with men like this, since they clash with his own love of peace. Peace of course, is supposed to be the output of the 2nd amendment. Is it possible that Benjamin Franklin is backdating letters to be archived, or are these letters just showing a consistency in his views? With respect to backdating letters, I have also noticed the usage of 500lbs in one cipher, and then in another I have been unable to resolve 500 dollars, where it was expressed twice. If these are the same reference, then it would be true that Benjamin Franklin is backdating letters. The 500 symbolism can be found only in the ciphered William Alexander letters.

From William Alexander (unpublished)

Richmond 28 April 1786
Dear Sir
Your letter gave me great pleasure, As it Informd me You were then in Good health. So long as You continue well, You have Sufficient Materials in yourself to assure your happiness. I wish you had said a few words about my Friend Temple in whose Success I am much Interested. Here is a Country where much may be done with some ready Money. If nothing Solid occurs for Him and He Chuses to spend a few Months in this Country, **I will give Him what lights I can, and in every event His time will not be Entirely lost. His expence here will be Nothing. If He buys and brings down Good horses** He may pay his Expences to Richmond with Them. **The stage is a fix'd thing as to time and Expence both which he Can compute to a penny.**

I wrote immediatly to Petersbg concerning Mr. Flagg whom I coud easily provide for as a Clerk, If he be Inteligent and industrious, but Hitherto I have heard nothing about Him. There is a young Man of the Same name, who is a kind of Painter and I fear will have but moderate Success. The Present goes by a friend of Mine from Gothenburg Mr. I: Jacobson He passes through your Town in his way to Newyork. I beg to recommend Him to your Civ[ilities] and with my respects to Mr. and Mrs. Bache and your Family, I beg to assure you that I shall Ever be Dear Sir Your devoted humble Servant

W: Alexander

I have heard lately from my Br and the Girls in London. They are all well and happy

His Excellency B: Franklin Esquire

Addressed: His Excellency / Benjamin Franklin / Governor of the State / Pensilvania

Endorsed: Mr Alexander

I have looked more closely at this letter simply because it was written by William Alexander. I say this because it was the name itself that was of utility. William Alexander could not have possibly written this letter because he was resting in his grave for just over three years at this time. It appears to tie into the one that written earlier in May 30, 1784. Good Horses may be a symbolism of "good" letters, or the letters that are written for the future too expose the 2nd amendment. In the May 30th letter Alexander Hamilton had stated "

> **"Contrive posts for my own business, and when I begin vigourously, must keep 7 or 8 horses running Constantly backward and forward."**

Backword and Forward relate to "hidden" and "explicit" where goal was a perfect balance of "suspicion". Good letters are "forward" or for the future. The "few months" may refer to early USA. The 'stage is fixed" is a reference to the 2nd amendment being set up, the letters being written and just waiting to be discovered at a future time. "Time and expence" is a reference that it will take time for the 2nd to be discovered, and until it is, there will be expense to society due to the harm its misunderstanding will cause.

Remember, this man has died in January 15, 1783. These particular letters require scrutiny.

From William Alexander (unpublished) 30 July 1783

> Paris 30 July 1783
> Dear Sir
> Our friend W—, has taken his measures and has already agreed with most of his people at 6, 12, 18 Months and 2 Years by equal payments—He hopes he will meet no difficulty with the others but thinks that the Extension of his protection to a Year (it Expires the 6 Septr) woud secure his Object by preventing any troublesome Man from laying by the Catch undue Advantage to the prejudice of his more liberal minded neighbours. I beg You will think of this, And If You approve—I suggest it to the Minister—Explaing to Him that Nothing less than full payment is proposed to every body—that W—s expects to pay much sooner than the time he takes—but as this depends on American remittances, he Chuses Not to run the hazard of Another Stop. I have been in town only Since last night, so that I coud not pay You my respects at Passy, being obliged to Return

home to day. I beg my best wishes to Your Son and am with the warmest Attachment Dear Sir Your most obliged humble servant
    W Alexander

From A— B— (unpublished) June 3 1786

Philada June 3 1786
Respected Sir

As my whole address to You is particularly intend'd for the Benefit of our fellow Creatures shall on that Account omit Apologizing for the Abruptness of its Intrusion and as it is Yet a matter to be brought to proof by some person of Abilities shall be as brief as possible lest I shoud give you Trouble in an affair which from Reasons (I cant foresee) be of no Avail.

I Can hardly say according Sir to the different Acceptations of the World whether I am really unfortunate or not. In One View (I mean the Scriptural one) I am Undoubtedly happy being under the Almighty's Chastisement. In the Other the World in General thinks me Unfortunate and in short Norwithstanding my Every exertion both in my Own Business as well as other I have been Oblig'd to fall into I find Myself Disappointed and very poor.

It was sir during my Attempts to reinstate myself that I made One or Two Valuable discoveries which I Imagine woud prove of service to the Interest of this Country but for want of Friends and means to make a proper Establishment have been forcd to relinquish the Whole. Among Others as the following may have a Tendency to help the Unfortunate in the time of most severe distress have thought propr to transmit it to Your Improving Judgment as probably a something may arrise from the hint which may be serviceable to ManKind and prevent the feelings of Humanity being hurt so frequent as of Late days. My Thoughts being Affect by the repeated unhappy Consequences attending the Wreck of Vessels I Roughly Constructed a Boat in Minature which I overlaid with Cork, her Ballast room or near of the whole I neatly filld with the same Article, then by means of a peice of Lead answering to the place of a Keelsom kep her upright and sunk her a proportionable part with Water. I then according to weight placd on and about a number of figures to Occupy the place of Mariners &c the Whole being now placd in a Vessel of Water I found to my intire satisfaction it would not either sink or remain in any other position (notwithstanding the most Violent agitation) than its proper one its filling with water and occasioning a small difference in her Draught and being of small Consequences. The use of the Above is too Obvious for Me to Comment on whoud it answer, and have therefore taken the Liberty to offer it to Your superior Judgment as if it is found Improbable it May be of much service to the Unforunate. I have the Honor to subscribe myself to be with Respect Sir your Most Obedient and Verry Humble Servant

A B

PS If an Interview be though Necessary a Line in Miss Dunlop and Cla will be sure to be seen and propr Attention paid.

Addressed: To / Hond Benjmn Franklin / Philada

Endorsed: Anonyme

From David Hartley Rue Caumartin Wednesday Morning Aug 4 1784

My Dear friend

I have not received any letters from England—but I hear that a continuation of the American bill is passed. That is all the news that I hear—My leg has been very bad again: I now write in bed. I have been confined for these last four days almost entirely to my bed and mattrass. The pain now begins again to abate. Your ever affectionate

D H

To Dr Franklin &c &c &c

Addressed: To Dr Franklin / &c &c &c / Passy

Endorsed: D Hartley Esqr Aug. 4. 84 to BF.

Here we have a very short letter to Benjamin Franklin that does not have one question in it. The context is American Bills, sore legs, writing from bed. All of a sudden with what appears to be mid sentence this mans leg suddenly appears to be getting better.

Symbolism. There is just arms in society and they are causing the people anguish. The letter is being written to America regarding the bill, or 2nd amendment and he is reporting the arms troubles in his area. The pain starts to abate because the bad arms are being removed from society. Confined last four days may be symbolic of the 4th article in the Bill of Rights, pre ratification.

Remember this equates to the 2ⁿᵈ amendment once ratified. Benjamin Franklin of course could not have any knowledge of the ratified Bill of Rights because he passed away in 1790. He is confined with just himself and his working arms, just as people and arms are confined within the term "Militia".

From David Hartley (unpublished) Rue Canmartin July 27 1784

My Dear friend
I have thought it a long while that my Confinement has prevented my seeing you. I was in hopes to have had the pleasure of seeing you to day, but I was indiscreet in going out the night before last, which has encreased the pain and swelling of my foot. My foot is again rather better than it was yesterday, but I am afraid to venture out to day. I hope still to see you on Thursday. I received no letters by the messenger of last night from the Secretary of State, but I understand that the report of the privy council and other documents respecting American trade are laid before Parliament. I presume therefore that that Subject will soon be taken into Consideration. Yours most affectionately
D H
To Dr Franklin &c &c &c

The symbolism here, similar to the last. Mr. David Hartley could be talking to the future. He is the word 'Militia" still confined which implies the 2ⁿᵈ amendment is still hidden. Indiscreet in going out the night before last was that he was always hidden in the past, as he was meant to be. The reference to seeing you on Thursday can also be read as You seeing me in the future. He is assuming that the future is having gun violence issues and that there are discussions about how to handle it. The subject is of course the 2ⁿᵈ amendment, which today has been brought to the fore front in discussions.

To John Adams (unpublished) Aug. 6. 1784.

Passy, Aug. 6. 1784.
Sir,
Mr. Bingham sent me last Night from Paris, your Excellency's Letter of the 27th past, inclosing a Copy of one from Mr. Jefferson. I **had before sent you a Copy of one from the same to me, which I hope you receiv'd. I enclose herewith Copies of a Letter from Mr. Thomson, some new Instructions, and one of the Commissions; the other two are in the same Words, except that instead of the Words**

[*the United Netherlands*] **there is, in one, *France,* and in the other, *Sweden.*** These came by M. de la Luzerne, but it was not before Wednesday last that I receiv'd them. You will see that a good deal of Business is cut out for us, Treaties to be made with I think twenty Powers, in two Years, so that we are not likely to eat the Bread of Idleness; and that we may not surfeit by eating too much, our Masters have diminish'd our Allowance. I commend their Oeconomy, and shall imitate it by diminishing my Expence. Our too liberal Entertainment of our Countrymen here has been reported at home by our Guests to our Disadvantage, and has given Offence. They must be contented for the future, as I am, with plain Beef and Pudding. The Readers of Connecticut Newspapers ought not to be troubled with any more Accounts of our Extravagance. For my own part, if I could sit down to Dinner on a Piece of their excellent Salt Pork and Pumpkin, I would not give a Farthing for all the Luxuries of Paris.

I am glad to hear that your Family are safely arrived at London, and that you propose to bring them here with you. Your Life will be more comfortable.

I thank you much for the Translation of Abbé Mably's Letters. The French Edition is not yet publish'd here. I have as yet only had time to run over the Translator's Preface, which seems well written. I imagine Mr. Sowdon to be a Presbyterian Minister, as I formerly corresponded with one of that Name in Holland, who I suppose might be his Father. I have not seen the Piece you mention of a B—n Academician. I should not object to his Enjoyment of the Discovery he has made that *Despotism* is the best possible Form of Government, by his living under it as long as he pleases: For I admire the Decision of his Prince in a similar Case, the Dispute among his Clergy concerning the Duration of Hell Torments. With great Respect I have the honour to be, Sir, Your Excellency's most obedient and most humble Servant

B. Franklin
His Excellency John Adams, Esqr
Endorsed: Dr Franklin Aug. 6. 1784

To Noah Webster, Jr. (unpublished)

Philada. Decr. 26th 1789.
Dear Sir,
I received some Time since your Dissertations on the English Language. (The Book was not accompanied by any Letter or Message, informing me to whom I am obliged for it; but I suppose it is to yourself.) It is an excellent Work, and will be greatly useful in turning the Thoughts of our Countrymen to correct Writing[243]. Please to accept my Thanks for it, as well as for the great Honor you have done me, in its Dedication. I ought to have made this Acknowledgment sooner, but much Indisposition prevented me.[244]

I cannot but applaud your Zeal for preserving the Purity of our Language, both in its Expressions and Pronunciation, **and in correcting the popular Errors, several of our States are continually falling into with respect to both**. Give me leave to mention some of them, tho' possibly they may already have occurr'd to you. I wish

---

[243] If a man can write correctly, then it falls in line that he will also be able to read correctly as well. The countrymen are those of the future. To "turn" their thoughts is to have them actually read the 2nd amendment with a better understanding of language and its usage. Thoughts can be turned if the meaning of "State" is put into the context the second amendment. In the Merriam-Webster Dictionary it appears that Noah Webster saw his way clear to define Liberty as "the quality or state of being free". Overlay that with "necessary to the security of a free State" and we can now actually start to read the 2nd amendment. We can use not only a dictionary, but one that appears to have been influenced by the very man that wrote the 2nd amendment. This letter establishes a relationship between the founder of the dictionary and the man who I believe actually crafted the 2nd amendment to begin with. This might be the final "hoarded" letter of Benjamin Franklins. He passed about 4 ½ months later, and from that time to this, his letters had been waiting.

[244] The Indisposition is that the 2nd had to be hidden. He could not let the cat of the bag with an explicit Acknowledgement. Note the use of capitals. They are clues. "Thoughts", "Countryman", "Writing". He is asking his future countrymen to think about the writing of the 2nd amendment. Noah Webster's "Work" is to be "Dedicated" to help out.

however that in some future Publication of your's, you would set a discountenancing Mark upon them. The first I remember is the Word *improved*. When I left New England in the Year 23, this Word had never been used among us, as far as I know, but in the Sense of *ameliorated* or *made better,* except once in a very old Book of Dr. Mather's entitled *Remarkable Providences.* As that eminent Man wrote a very obscure Hand, I remember that when I read that Word in his Book, used instead of the Word *employed,* I conjectured that it was an Error of the Printer, who had mistaken a too short *l* in the Writing for an *r,* and a *y* with too short a Tail for a *v,* whereby *imployed* was converted into *improved*; but when I returned to Boston in 1733, I found this Change had obtained Favor, and was then become common; for I met with it often in perusing the Newspapers, where it frequently made an Appearance rather ridiculous: Such, for Instance, as the Advertisement of a Country= House to be sold, which had been many Years *improved* as a Tavern; **and in the Character of a deceased Country-Gentleman**, that he had been, for more than 30 Years, *improved* as a **Justice-of-Peace**. This Use of the Word *improve* is peculiar **to New-England**, and not to be met with among any other Speakers of English, either on this or the other Side of the Water.

During my late Absence in France I find that several other new Words have been introduced into our parliamentary Language; for Example, I find a Verb formed from the Substantive *Notice, I should not have* NOTICED *this, were it not that the Gentleman* &c. Also another Verb, from the Substantive, *Advocate, The Gentleman who* ADVOCATES, or *who has* ADVOCATED *that Motion,* &c. Another from the Substantive *Progress,* the most awkward and abominable of the three, *The Committee having* PROGRESSED *resolved to adjourn.* The Word *opposed,* tho' not a new Word, I find used in a new Manner, as, *The Gentlemen who are* OPPOSED *to this Measure, to which I have also myself always been* OPPOSED. If you should happen to be of my Opinion with respect to these Innovations you will use your Authority in reprobating them.

The Latin Language, long the Vehicle used in distributing Knowledge among the different Nations of Europe, is daily more and more neglected; and one of the modern Tongues, viz the French, seems in Point of Universality to have supplied its Place; it is spoken in all the Courts of Europe, and most of the Literati, those even who do not speak it, have acquired Knowledge enough of it, to enable them easily to read the Books that are written in it. This gives a considerable Advantage to that Nation; it enables its Authors to inculcate and spread thro' other Nations such Sentiments and Opinions on important Points as are most conducive to its Interests, or which may contribute to its Reputation, by promoting the common Interests of Mankind. It is perhaps owing to its being written in French, that Voltaire's Treatise on Toleration, has had so sudden and so great an Effect on the Bigotry of Europe, as almost entirely to disarm it. The general Use of the French Language has likewise a very advantageous Effect on the Profits of the Bookselling Branch of Commerce, it being well known that the more Copies can be sold that are struck off from one Composition of Types, the Profits encrease in a much greater Proportion than they do in making a greater Number of Pieces in any other kind of Manufacture. And at present there is no Capital Town in Europe without a French Bookseller's Shop corresponding with Paris. Our English bids fair to obtain the second Place. The great Body of excellent printed Sermons in our Language, and the Freedom of our Writings on political Subjects, have induced a Number of Divines of different Sects and Nations, as well as Gentlemen concerned in public Affairs, to study it, so far at least as to read it. And if we were to endeavour the facilitating its Progress, the Study of our Tongue might become much more general. Those who have employed some Part of their Time in learning a new Language must have frequently observed, that while their Acquaintance with it was imperfect, Difficulties, small in themselves, operated as great ones in obstructing their Progress. A Book, for Example, ill printed, or a Pronunciation, in speaking, not well articulated, would render a Sentence unintelligible, which from a clear Print, or a distinct Speaker, would have been immediately comprehended. If therefore we would have the Benefit of seeing our Language more generally known among Mankind, we should endeavour to remove all the Difficulties, however small, that discourage the learning it. But I am sorry to observe, that, of late Years, those Difficulties, instead of being diminished, have been augmented. In examining the English Books that were printed between the Restoration and the Recession of George the 2d, **we**

may observe, that all Substantives were begun with a Capital, in which we imitated our Mother Tongue, the German. This was more particularly useful to those who were not well acquainted with the English, there being such a prodigious Number of our Words, that are both Verbs and Substantives, and spelt in the same Manner, tho' often accented differently in Pronunciation. This Method has, by the Fancy of Printers, of late Years, been laid aside; from an Idea, that suppressing the Capitals shews the Character to greater Advantage; those Letters, prominent above the Line, disturbing its even, regular Appearance. The Effect of this Change is so considerable that a learned Man of France, who used to read over Books, tho' not perfectly acquainted with our Language, in Conversation with me on the Subject of our Authors, attributed the greater Obscurity he found in our modern Books, compared with those of the Period abovementioned, to a Change of Style, for the worse, in our Writers; of which Mistake I convinced him by marking for him each Substantive with a Capital, in a Paragraph, which he then easily understood, tho' before he could not comprehend it. This shews the Inconvenience of that pretended Improvement. [*different hand:* division]

From the same Fondness for an even and uniform Appearance of Characters in the Line the Printers have of late banished also the Italic Types, in which Words of Importance to be attended to in the Sense of the Sentence, and Words on which an Emphasis should be put in Reading, used to be printed. And lately another Fancy has induced some Printers to use the short round s instead of the long one, which formerly served well to distinguish a Word readily by its varied Appearance. Certainly the omitting this prominent Letter makes the Line appear more even; but renders it less immediately legible; as the paring all Men's Noses might smoothe and level their Faces, but would render their Physiognomies less distinguishable. Add to all these Improvements backward, another modern Fancy, that *grey* Printing is more beautiful than *black*; hence the English new Books are printed in so dim a Character as to be read with Difficulty by old Eyes, unless in a very strong Light and with good Glasses. Whoever compares a Volume of the Gentleman's Magazine printed between the Year 1731 and 1740 with one of those printed in the last 10 Years, will be convinced of the much greater Degree of

Perspicuity given by black Ink than by grey. Lord Chesterfield pleasantly remarked this Difference to Faulkener, the Printer of the Dublin Journal, who was vainly making Encomiums on his own Paper, as the most complete of any in the World, "but, Mr. Faulkener," says My Lord, "don't you think it might be still farther improved, by using Paper and Ink not quite so near of a Colour." For all these Reasons I cannot but wish that our American Printers would in their Editions avoid these fancied Improvements, and thereby render their Works more agreable to Foreigners in Europe, to the great Advantage of our Bookselling Commerce.

Farther to be more sensible of the Advantage of clear and distinct Printing, let us consider the Assistance it affords in Reading well aloud to an Auditory. In so doing the Eye generally slides forward three or four Words before the Voice. If the Sight clearly distinguishes what the coming Words are, it gives time to order the Modulation of the Voice to express them properly. But if they are obscurely printed, or disguised by omitting the Capitals and long s's, or otherwise, the Reader is apt to modulate wrong, and finding he has done so, he is obliged to go back and begin the Sentence again; which lessens the Pleasure of the Hearers. This leads me to mention an old Error in our Mode of Printing. We are sensible that when a Question is met with in Reading, there is a proper Variation to be used in the Management of the Voice. We have therefore a Point, called an Interrogation, affix'd to the Question in order to distinguish it. But this is absurdly placed at its End, so that the Reader does not discover it, 'till he finds he has wrongly modulated his Voice and is therefore obliged to begin again the Sentence. To prevent this the Spanish Printers, more sensibly, place an Interrogation at the Beginning as well as at the End of a Question. We have another Error of the same kind in printing Plays, where Something often occurs that is marked as spoken *aside*. But the Word *aside* is placed at the End of the Speech when it ought to precede it, as a Direction to the Reader that he may govern his Voice accordingly. The Practice of our Ladies in meeting five or six together to form little busy Parties, when each is employed in some useful Work; while one reads to them, is so commendable in itself, that it deserves the Attention of Authors and Printers to make it as pleasing as possible, both to the Reader and Hearers.

> After these general Observations permit me to make one that I imagine may regard your Interest. It is that your Spelling-Book is miserably printed here, so as in many Places to be scarcely legible, and on wretched Paper. If this is not attended to, and the new one Lately advertised as coming out should be preferable in those Respects, it may hurt the future Sale of your's.
>
> I congratulate you on your Marriage of which the Newspapers inform me. My best Wishes attend you, being, with sincere Esteem Sir, Your most obedient and most humble Servant
>
> B Franklin
>
> *Addressed:* Noah Webster Junr Esqr / Hartford / [*Crossed out:* Boston] Favd by Capt. Rich
>
> *Notation:* Recd and forwarded by Your affectionate Father Wm. Greenleaf Boston April 11 '90 Honord by Mr Slover
>
> *Endorsed:* Dr Franklin. Philad. December 26. 1789

In 1791 Noah Webster published a book titled "Little Readers Assistant". Please note the date. Within that book, there is a chapter called "The literature of Politics". I was not however able to read the entire chapter but found this in its preview. With respect to the entire narrative that this book has revealed, suffice to say I found this a good read.

> "This chapter therefore unfolds something like a mobius strip, with both themes—Literature and Politics—continually uppermost. If this sounds like complicated travelling , it may be easier to envision the company of Benjamin Franklin, whose many literary innovations were inspired by a desire to create a new polity for new times. **Indeed, Franklin did not just travel the mobius strip of literary politics** and political literature, **he was one of its chief engineers in the English colonies."**
>
> Polity : form of government.
>
> Mobius strip: A strip of paper that is joined at both ends after it has been twisted.

This is the very nature of the ciphers, because there are two sides to them and they were written because of politics of the day. This explicitly says that Benjamin Franklin was at the very least a chief engineer of these letters. This also proves that Noah Webster was employed to help these men with their plan through the utility of his very dictionary. Remember he defines the word

Liberty = the quality or state of being free:

This seems to line up rather conveniently with the second clause of 2nd amendment

"being necessary to the security of a free State" thus removing it from any inference of "colony" and transforming it into a feeling of "Butterflies and Bunny rabbits".

Philadelphia Independent Gazetteer, 30 April 1788

Extract of a letter from Franklin county, 24th April, 1788.

"The necessary arrangements," as they are termed here, have taken place in these counties; committees of observation and correspondence are appointed in every township, who correspond with the militia officers and leading men in every county in the state; the counties of Cumberland, Dauphine, and Franklin, appear to take the lead, and have been long since repairing and cleaning their arms, and every young fellow who is able to do it, is providing himself with a **rifle**[245] or musket, and amunition: They have also nominated a commanding officer, it is said to be General——, and say that they can turn out, at ten days warning, TWENTY THOUSAND expert woodsmen, completely armed; this is I believe very true, as all the counties, this side the Susquehanna, are nearly unanimous, and near three fourths of the other counties. They say the strength of their opponents are in the city, and give out that it will be in vain for them to make any resistance; they mean to make * * *and are promised assistance from a neighbouring state, who, I find, are as warmly opposed as this state to the system. The **lawyers**, &c. when they precipitated with such fraud and deception the new system upon us[246], it seems to me, did not recollect[247], that the militia had arms[248]; however[249], it will be an awful lesson to tyrants[250], if they

---

[245] "rifle" was highlighted where musket was not. These are both subsets of "Arms" but one, the rifle, is being viewed and more lethal, hence the distinction. It's an example of comparing one class of arms against another because the 2nd amendment puts the arms on trial.

[246] Double meaning. The fraud is the 2nd amendment in the constitution(system of government). Cherry picking the constitution by reading only what they wanted to read.

[247] Recollect the Arms from the people (militia). Note the usage of the comma which really isn't required. It's an interesting nuance that adds veracity to the new context of this letter once filtered through the secret of the 2nd amendment. the lawyers did not "recollect" is a reference to "not well-regulating" from a point of law.

[248] Of course a Militia has Arms because a militia is just people and arms, but it is the nature of the arms that the people possess that is of utmost importance because those arms are "necessary to the security of a free state".

should feel the resentment of an enraged people[251]; I can assure Mr. Wilson that the people are now as **determined** to secure their liberties as he is **anxious** for power and offices; and let the worst come to the worst, the opposition have the constitution of the state[252], the established law of the land[253], on their side[254]; this yet remains good and firm, any doings, **or acts of a faction[255], or illegal mob convention[256], to the contrary notwithstanding. A civil war** is dreadful[257], but a little blood spilt now[258], will perhaps prevent much more hereafter. However, another general convention being called, will prevent any thing like it happening; the people appear anxious for farther powers being granted to Congress[259]; and are generally agreed, that those offered by the minority of the convention of this state would be quite sufficient, and all their rights and privileges

---

[249] Now when the 2nd amendment is finally exposed.

[250] The people will learn that they themselves are the tyrants if they oppose the 2nd amendments new meaning. The lesson is in learning the full story of the 2nd amendment, and it's awful because in thinking of themselves first over 1,000,000 Americans have died from gun violence.

[251] The resentment comes from those who want and demand common sense gun laws and are at their wits end regarding gun violence and the rhetoric of the old 2nd amendment. The tables will have completely turned and now favour liberty for all instead of a perceived liberty for just the few.

[252] Constitution of the state is "necessary to the security of a free state" once constituted in the mind legitimately as well as the constitution itself.

[253] This is a cipher, so chronology is not important because it transcends time. The 2nd amendment is ratified and has all the protections of the Supremacy Clause.

[254] Gun Control advocates now have the constitution on their side.

[255] The faction of gun advocates.

[256] It would be illegal to ignore the constitution.

[257] Civil war over this would be silly. People can still hunt.

[258] There probably be some blood spilt over this in the transition as Arms are collected, but in the long run, it's a small price to pay for the benefit that will be realized.

[259] People are now so fed up with gun violence that they want congress to be empowered to regulate gun laws. The 2nd amendment now grants powers to do this, in fact, they have no choice. This is a peoples right.

would be then secured by the proposed bill of rights[260], consequently unity and harmony would follow: on the other hand, if the votaries of power and offices do not agree to peaceable measures[261], by having another general convention called, I dread the consequences to themselves.[262]

"N. B. I hear no more of the attempt to execute the order of Council to disarm the militia, I believe the **sub-lieutenants** in most of the counties refused to deliver up the arms, it was well enough, for the people were determined not to part with them. It is hinted that since the western members went down, they cancelled the order."

This letter is particularly interesting because we don't know who it was authored by. There is at least one other letter that I have located that is anonymous as well but has been attributed to belonging to Benjamin Franklin. It's not that logic that I used to attribute this letter to him though but only the logic that he was doing this sort of thing. It's my believe that Benjamin Franklin realised that it would be too dangerous to attribute such a letter as this to himself, because it was known that he was in middle of helping to draft the constitution. If you will allow me to say it, he was a 'key player' in it. God bless a captive audience. This letter is most obviously about Militias and even taking back the Arms. It is very explicit with almost a casual tone to it because it doesn't at all come across as being argumentative. This is a cipher. There are two things are talked about here, one being that if there are to be Arms in public then they would be used under the direction of a general and lieutenants on a mission of war. The name of the general is not named, because no name is required. It is the word general that brings into the condition of the people having arms would be under the command of the government, or a general. The three "***",s are left blank which most certainly make war. It doesn't take a genius to see what this infers, so why hide it? Benjamin Franklin is not hiding this because they are

---

[260] The 2nd amendment.

[261] Those that do not want to give up their arms regardless of reason.

[262] Why another convention? Some on the far right may argue that another convention is needed to redesign the constitution. It is not a good idea to even go there, because now every level of intelligence and wisdom would have a vote in a constitution which was very well thought out. No longer would the constitution be guiding human nature, but every motive of human nature would be designing it and voting only in the context of self interest as opposed to the interest of "We the People" in spite of themselves.

simply place holders for any war, which would give purpose to the people being armed in the first place. It infers that this is the only situation when lethal arms would be allowed, because this is essentially conscription.

Now the very first sentence starts off with "the necessary arrangements", which are emphasised twice once with quotes, and "as they are termed here". is the opening sentence of the cipher. We know that in the 2nd amendment can be interpreted two ways and the second clause has the word necessary in it, which can be arranged to be read in two different was, one subjectively and one objectively. There is also talk of lawyers which seems a bit odd, but not when applied to the 2nd amendment. It is also explained that the sub-lieutenants had refused to give up their Arms after the war had ended. On the threshold of a new government being formed, and not yet fully established and perhaps endorsed by the people and the states it was, to say the least, awkward to take back the arms. In the footnotes I have drilled down to the nature of the cipher. It is because this appears to be a full on cipher that I believe it was written by Benjamin Franklin. It is after all from Franklin County. We also know that a very small group of people have known about the 2nd amendments true secret. I don't believe there are many letters that talk about actually taking back the arms. If the framers talked about this, or argued for it, then it might seem suspicious as to why they would suddenly endorse the 2nd amendment as it's subjectively read because it is fully unregulated. I believe I mentioned before that I found it suspicious that there was no argument from the "liberal" viewpoint on society and its safety. It's almost as if no liberals existed in the late 18th century with respect to the 2nd amendment and this seemed to me to be an impossibility which begged the question, "Why did they submit so easily?" We now know that it was not them that submitted, but it was the people that submitted to their own fear and want of power and control and then in their minds re-authored the 2nd amendment. That is of course unfair to put it so candidly but it was most certainly part of the equation. The other part is that it was a riddle to begin with. This is perhaps one of the constitutions best examples of "fine print" to which would enable it to care for the people, as it should.

Benjamin Franklins last Speech Sept 17, 1787

Mr. President

I confess that there are several parts of this constitution which I do not at present approve, but I am not sure I shall never approve them[263]: For having lived long, I have experienced many instances of being obliged by better information[264], or fuller consideration, to change opinions even on important subjects, which I once thought right[265], but found to be otherwise. It is therefore that the older I grow, the more apt I am to doubt my own judgment[266], and to pay more respect to the judgment of others[267]. Most men indeed as well as most sects in Religion, think themselves in possession of all truth, and that wherever others differ from them it is so far error[268]. Steele a Protestant in a Dedication tells the Pope, that the only difference between our Churches in their opinions of the certainty of their doctrines is, the Church of Rome is infallible and the Church of England is never in the wrong. But though many private persons think almost as highly of their own infallibility as of that of their sect, few express it so naturally as a certain french lady, who in a dispute with her sister, said "I don't know how it happens, Sister but I meet

---

[263] He is alluding to something was hidden and wiil one day be revealed. He is at the end of his life and he knows it. How can he approve of a constitution in death unless in life he knows it's exactly how he wanted it to be? He is talking to the future. This is a ciphered letter.

[264] After the people have lived long with the constitution, they will be obliged by the new 2nd because it is a right of all the people. It is a "better" version of the old. He then goes on to admit that in live we all change our minds about things after much reflection. Experience is the teacher.

[265] Thinking the right to bear Arms was the right, but now the truth is found, is now otherwise.

[266] The more older we grow in life, where as I this case is America for the past 224 years.

[267] The others he speaks of is the wisdom of the framers who wrote the 2nd and the Federalist Papers.

[268] Some people are very stubborn in their beliefs and have hard time to let them go.

with no body but myself, that's always in the right[269] — *Il n'y a que moi qui a toujours raison.*"

In these sentiments, Sir, I agree to this Constitution with all its faults, if they are such; because I think a general Government necessary for us, and there is no form of Government but what may be a blessing to the people if well administered, and believe farther that this is likely to be well administered for a course of years, and can only end in Despotism, as other forms have done before it, when the people shall become so corrupted as to need despotic Government, being incapable of any other[270]. I doubt too whether any other Convention we can obtain, may be able to make a better Constitution. For when you assemble a number of men to have the advantage of their joint wisdom, you inevitably assemble with those men, all their prejudices, their passions, their errors of opinion, their local interests, and their selfish views[271]. From such an assembly can a perfect production be expected? It therefore astonishes me, Sir, to find this system approaching so near to perfection as it does; and I think it will astonish our enemies, who are waiting with confidence to hear that our councils are confounded like those of the Builders of Babel; and that our States are on the point of separation, only to meet hereafter for the purpose of cutting one another's throats. Thus I consent, Sir, to this Constitution because I expect no better, and because I am not sure, that it is not the best. The opinions I have had of its errors, I sacrifice to the public good. I have never whispered a syllable of them abroad. Within these walls they were born, and here they shall die. If every one of us in returning to our Constituents were to report the objections he has had to it, and

---

[269] I have taken liberty myself in the "The Narratives we build section" to possibly shed some light on this.

[270] If there is faction and a gulf in the middle class, then the people themselves are shirking responsibility. They put faith in human nature and then empower it by voting for deregulation. Vote with greed and liberty is lost.

[271] This is exactly why the convention was orchestrated in advance. This is also why this letter was written. It was too clarify just why the convention was orchestrated in advance for the time when it was to be discovered. He is saying that some opinions matter more than others, if a perfect constitution is to be constructed, so don't allow those lesser opinions a voice in it.

endeavor to gain partizans in support of them, we might prevent its being generally received, and thereby lose all the salutary effects & great advantages resulting naturally in our favor among foreign Nations as well as among ourselves, from our real or apparent unanimity. Much of the strength & efficiency of any Government in procuring and securing happiness to the people, depends, on opinion, on the general opinion of the goodness of the Government, as well as of the wisdom and integrity of its Governors. I hope therefore that for our own sakes as a part of the people, and for the sake of posterity, we shall act heartily and unanimously in recommending this Constitution (if approved by Congress & confirmed by the Conventions) wherever our influence may extend, and turn our future thoughts & endeavors to the means of having it well administred.[272]

On the whole[273], Sir, I can not help expressing a wish that every member of the Convention who may still have objections to it, would with me, on this occasion doubt a little of his own infallibility, and to make manifest our unanimity, put his name to this instrument[274].

Then the Motion was made for adding the last **Formula[275]**, viz Done in Convention by the unanimous Consent &ca. which was agreed to and added accordingly[276].

---

[272] He is confident that if the constitution is obeyed and adhered to then a nation will be protected. Voter suppression has helped Trump become elected. The enemies of the USA have helped Trump to get elected. Stealing Obamas Justice appointment have helped to get Trump elected because some voters on the right voted for him to protect their 2nd amendment through his unsanctioned appointment. Congress was in violation of the constitution. Even a Supreme Court Justice.

[273] All of the constitution or the "Militia" as an encryption , where one of its parts are the people in the convention. The convention being the 2nd amendment.

[274] Just as the Constitution is both a formula and an instrument to protect liberty so too is the 2nd amendment to protect life, without which liberty could never exist.

[275] The formula is a reference to the success of hiding the legitimate meaning of the 2nd amendment, as in successfully added.

Addressed: D. Carrol Esqr.

Endorsed: D Carrol Draft of Franklin's last Speech in the Convention for forming the Constitution of the United States, September, 1787.

George Washington

William Milnor to George Washington, 29 November 1774

From William Milnor
Philada Novr 29th 1774
Honorable Sir

Your favour of the 17th Inst. came to hand on fryday last,[1] I have made the strictest search, after a Sash[277] and have sent the only one, that is to be had in this City, I am sorry to inform you, 'tis not intirely New tho' not much changed. I have bought it Conditionly[278] if not approved of, to be returnd by the first post & taken again, I had no Alternitive, as no Other Could be had. The Epaulette is inclosed with the pamphlets—the Gorget is Making, & will Come by the Next post—after the strictest inquiry, I could find no Other Treatise on Military Discipline, but the one I have sent you[2]—I have enclosed you a Vile pamphlet said to be wrote by Dr Cooper of New York, & likewise another small pamphlet called Strictures on the former, said to be wrote by General Lee of this City[3]—here I must beg youl excuse my presumeing to exceed your Orders, as 'tis with an intintion to amuse. for if you have patience to read the first, I think you will be deverted with the last.

I have Applyed to two Gunsmiths, One palmer tells me he Can make one hundred by May next, And Nicholson says he can make the like Number by March, they both agree in the priece at £3.15.

---

[276] There is now a second reference to adding which on its surface may appear redundant. The point here is that it was 'agreed too" and now would live in the constitution. It was amended legally even though the other delegates refused to read the fine print.

[277] A sash is worn by officers, and once there are officers, then the soldiers are well-regulated.

[278] Conditionally is a reference that "well regulated <> well-regulated". It is not going to last.

this Currcy.₄ Palmer says Mr Cadvalder had agreed With him for 100 at that price, a Jersy Musquet was brought to palmer for a patern, Mr Shreive Hatter of Allexandira has one of that sort, which you may see, & if you Conclude to have any, please to inform me by the first post, as the Gunsmiths I blieve will soon be preengaged, & there is not one Musquet to be bought in this City at present, if you should chose any Alteration, from that Musquet please to let us know₅—Mr Fleecen assures me the Drums Coulers &c. shall be ready to come with the first Vessels & you may be assured I shall forward them with the Utmost speed.₆ I am Dear sir with the greatest respect, Your Most Obedt humble Sert

    William Milnor

Cipher?

Society of Free Quakers. William Milnor Died Feb 5, 1807 at the age of 70.

At Foundersonline, the government website there is a footnote assigned to the favor of Fryday last.

It states "The letter has not been found."

The reason that no letter was found is because there was none written. This is a cipher. The reference to a letter is a reference to a letter in the alphabet. Note that the word 'letter' is not even used but rather "instant" is. The reference is to both letters and spaces. We already know that all the ciphers we have located are directly related to the 2nd amendment. So let us test this and see if we can discover the earliest letter to date. It won't take long, so let's go out on a limb regarding this and use our fingers and toes.

A well regulated Militia? "A well regulated " = 17 letters and spaces. At that instant, the word "Militia" can then be found. "Militia, once understood is the key to the 2nd amendment and is very well understood. E Plurious Enum. (see seal section).

I have located a letter in the book Colonial Families of Philadelphia which was authored by John W. Jordan, LL.D (1840-1920). It is dated January of 1776. I started to snoop around a bit more to see if I could find out any more information regarding John Milner. If the top letter is a cipher as it appears to be then based on the rest of my research one way for the ciphers to be linked together is through a recipient or senders name. So this is the letter that I located.

In his book John W. Jordan gives us a bit of background on John Milner, the man.

> Though a birthright member of the Society of Friends, and affiliated with Philadelphia Monthly meeting , where his marriage took place in 1760, his patriotism led him to violate the ultra peace principles in that Society, by becoming a member of the Associators of Philadelphia , the first armed force organized for the defence of liberties and rights of the Colonies, under the direction of the Committee of Safety, and we find him enrolled as a member of Captain Cowperthwaite's company, First Battalion, Philadelphia Militia , in 1776.
>
> From a correspondence in the possession of his descendants in Philadelphia it appears that William Milnor was personally associated with George Washington., and enjoyed his confidence and friendship. From one of these letters bearing date January, 1776 it appears that William Milnor had previously to that date applied for a captain's commission in the Continental Service, but later withdrew it.

John W. Jordan as a historian was seeking only the truth of history and since he could not validate his observation, he does state "appears". He sees a bit of mystery here which has yet to be clarified.

What we see here is a Militia man given rank but not under the direction of the Continental Service, or to be more specific, the full timers. This is the capacity in which this man possessed his Arms. He was not 'well-regulated" in a professional capacity. In "the cipher" below it states the same thing because it references his rejection to this, but in a cipher. The cipher acknowledges in what manner this man was bearing Arms. We then see the word "appears" again but now in the context of just when John Milner had applied to be in the Continental Service as referenced in the cipher. A cipher has free reign with reality and fiction. There is no numbered day in the ciphered letter? Why is this? I believe it is only the Year that has pertinence in the cipher. Without a day, the year stands out. "January" represents the starting boundary for a year. If one was to use the rules of chronology one would normally go back to Dec 20th and if the starting point is January of 1776, then we would be looking at Dec 20th of 1775. The letter starts out with "Your kind favour and being a cipher with no day designation and then seeing a "kind favour" with no year designation, I decided it seemed logical to simply merge the two to arrive at Dec 20 1776. Once I did this, then a historical event of pertinence suddenly appeared. There was a reason the 'day number' was left out. Yes, I know. Keep in mind I had already been going over these ciphers for over a year at this point and was becoming very familiar with how these men were thinking. Had this been the first letter I encountered, these particular observations would have escaped me. Once a cipher has been resolved as a cipher, then everything must be looked at.

John Milner to George Washington January 1776

"Your kind favor of 20th December came safe to the hand and gave me relief. I am happy in assurances that I have not displeased you in my conduct so far I am unhappy however, because I cannot get into the Army – I had thrown a petition for a Captaincy and had the greatest prospect of Success, Mr. Franklin, in consequence of your letter had made the way clear for me ***"

There follows some explanation in reference to the objections of his family and the necessity of continuing his business or suffer such loss as would place his family in danger of want, he continues

"Their reasonings, together with the entreaties of my dear partner, prevailed on me to withdaw my petition. I never found any prospect of fatigue an annoyance to any undertaking, when a probability of a good genteel substance for my little flock offered in view; and this business would be a very agreeable one to me if these unhappy disturbances were to end. But I cannot conclude this letter until I have assured your Excellency that I shall remain a poor, unhappy wretch, as long as I am chained, and cannot take an active part in my Country's cause. Whether a true patriotic concern for my Country, or secret thirst after honor, or both combined, is the spring by which my spirits are actuated. I have the vanity to believe the former is the chief motive, and that only the experience is wanted to make me a soldier."

So what happened on Dec 20th 1776? A historical event occurred known as the battle of Trenton Falls. I don't believe the letter to be a cipher, but is linked to the one above. This is only a partial transcript from the letter. At this point in time the troops were waiting out the winter. This of course means for two months the troops are now hanging around with their arms in society. George Washington reflects on this and states it in the paragraph below.

George Washington to John Hancock, 20 Dec 1776

> Camp above Trenton Falls Decr 20th 1776.
> Sir
> It may be said, that this is an application for powers, that are too dangerous to be intrusted. I can only add, that desperate diseases, require desperate remedies, and with truth declare, that **I have no lust after power but wish with as much fervency as any man upon this wide extended Continent for an Opportunity of turning the Sword into a ploughshare**; But my feelings as an Officer and a man, have been such, as to force me to say, that no person ever had a greater choice of difficulties to contend with than I have. **It is needless to add, that short inlistments, and a mistaken dependance upon Militia, have been the Origin of all our misfortunes, and the great accumulation of our Debt.**

He could not be any clearer in his viewpoint here. He is being very explicit when he states flat out, that "**any man upon this wide extended Continent for an Opportunity of turning the Sword into a ploughshare**". He speaks of the public domain of course. This is the "kind favor" that we can apply to the cipher above. I think George Washington would have easily been able to connect the dots as to the first name of Mr. Franklin, being of course Benjamin.

George Washington to James Madison, 30 November 1785

To James Madison
Mount Vernon Novr 30th 1785.
My dear Sir,

Receive my thanks for your obliging communications of the 11th—I hear with much pleasure that the assembly are engaged, seriously, in the consideration of the revised Laws. A short & simple code, in my opinion, tho' I have the sentiments of some of the Gentlemen of the long robe against me, would be productive of happy consequences, and redound to the honor of this or any Country which shall adopt such.

I hope the resolutions which were published for the consideration of the House, respecting the reference to Congress for the regulation of a Commercial system will have passed. **The proposition in my opinion is so self evident that I confess I am at a loss to discover wherein lyes the weight of the objection to the measure.**[279] We are either a United people, or we are not[280]. If the former, let us, in all

---

[279] George Washington likes the 2nd amendment because its perfectly constructed and reality based to protect the people from the variability of lethal weaponry.

[280] It is his opinion that there should be no middle ground on this. He and the others could not have known the future nature of propaganda, and the vast moneys involved. What I say next is only a continuation of the raw truth that he already knows. Now there is money involved but it is on both sides of the equation. Does the Arms industry have more of a right to make 43 billion dollars a year or do the people have more of a right to save 228 billion dollars a year in gun violence related costs? If the gun industry pushes back on these findings, then they will have shown their hand. They will be telling all of America that they have defined their own "happiness" in the pursuit of happiness as being money alone and that their greed is more important to the life and liberty of all of America. It would be a blatant attempt to hijack the constitution. Pretty cut and dry. Any noise from this point forward can be classified as propaganda. "United", full stop, as per George Washington. With no disrespect meant to Charlton Heston, I'm going to assume that these two man have had a little chat. One of them now understands that he had acted up on the wrong side of history. He didn't know though because he thought he was being patriotic in his beliefs. Now things are a bit different though, which is the point I'm trying to make. Things

matters of general concern act as a nation, which have national objects to promote, and a National character to support—If we are not, let us no longer act a farce by pretending to it. for whilst we are playing a dble game, or playing a game between the two we never shall be consistent or respectable—but may be the dupes of some powers and, most assuredly, the contempt of all. In any case it **behoves us to provide good Militia Laws**[281], and **look well to the execution of them**—but, if we mean by our conduct that the States shall act independently of each other it becomes **indispensably necessary**—for therein will consist our strength and respectabity in the Union.

It is much to be wished that public faith may be held inviolate—Painful is it even in thought that attempts should be made to weaken the bands of it. It is a dangerous experiment—once slacken the reins and the power is lost—and it is questionable with me whether the advocates of the measure foresee all the consequences of it[282]. It is an old adage that honesty is the best policy—this applies to public as well as private life—to States as well as individuals. I hope the Port and assize **Bills no longer sleep but are awakened to a happy establishment**. The first with some alterations, would in my judgment be productive of great good to this Country—without it, the Trade thereof I conceive will ever labor & languish—with respect to the Second if it institutes a speedier administration of Justice it is equally desirable.

It gives me great pleasure to hear that our assembly were in a way of adopting a mode for establishing the Cut betwn Elizabeth river & Pasquotank which was likely to meet the approbation of the State of No. Carolina—It appears to me that no Country in the Universe is better calculated to derive benefits from inland Navigation than this

---

have flipped, for the better, and forever. To die for fear is not a cause worth dying for. Fear can easily be dispelled with courage and with that Liberty for all can be had.

[281] This should be pretty self explanatory. Japan has about 12 homicides a year due to their good Militia laws. USA has closer to 13,000 because none have existed. Not a coincidence. Japan and USA exist on the same spinning ball where guns exist.

[282]

is—and certain I am, that the conveniences to the Citizens individually, and the sources of wealth to the Country generally, which will be opened thereby will be found to exceed the most sanguine imagination—The Mind can scarcely take in at one view all the benefits which will result therefrom—The saving in draught Cattle, preservation of Roads &ca &ca will be felt most interestingly—This business only wants a beginning—Rappahanock—Shannondoah—Roanoke—and the branches of York River will soon perceive the advantages which water transportation (in ways hardly thought of at first) have over that of Land and will extend Navigation to almost every Mans door.

From the complexion of the debates in the Pensylvania it should seem as if that Legislature intended their assent to the proposition from the States of Virginia & Maryland (respecting a road to the Yohiogany[)] should be conditional of permission given to open a Communication between the Chesapeak & Delaware by way of the rivers Elk & Christeen—which I am sure will never be obtained if the Baltimore interest can give it effectual opposition. 1

The Directors of the Potomack Company have sent to the Delegates of this County to be laid before the Assembly a Petition (which sets forth the reasons) for relief in the depth of the Canals which it may be found necessary to open at the great & little Falls of the River—As public œconomy and private interest equally prompt the measure and no possible disadvantage that we can see will attend granting the prayer of it, we flatter ourselves no opposition will be given to it.

To save trouble—to expedite the business, and to secure uniformity without delay, or an intercourse between the Assemblies on so trivial a matter we have taken the liberty of sending the draught of a Bill to Members of both Assemblies which if approved will be found exactly similar. 2 With the highest esteem and regard I am Dr Sir Yr Obedt & Affecte Hble Ser.

Go: Washington

This can be viewed almost as being a welcome letter to James Madison with respect to him joining the American Philosophical Society. You will see that his membership record is dated 1785. There are important symbolisms here which I will be pointing out in footnotes. According to membership records of the American Philosophical society James Madison was the last man in the group to gain membership. The "assembly" I believe is a reference to Benjamin Franklin, Thomas Jefferson, John Adams, Alexander Hamilton, John Jay and of course James Madison.

Note that the word "Laws" is capitalized in his letter. George Washington is referencing the "2nd amendment" directly with the phrase "a short and simple code". It is one sentence, it is short, and it is simple to understand once it is read objectively, otherwise, it is difficult to discern and would be often debated. In reality though, I think the actual short and simple code is the word "Militia". It is very short and it is very simple because a Militia is just people and Arms. It is simple because it can be decoded with a dictionary. Once that has been accomplished then the entire 2nd amendment can then be looked at different because "people and Arms" can now be seen as variables. He sees the 2nd amendment as something that is perfect for any nation to control their arms, in the interest of keeping society safe, any society safe. Its flexible and its timeless and it demands ongoing maintenance protect any societies liberty. He makes reference to a double game which is a reference to the 2nd amendment having two distinct purposes. The first of which is to get the constitution signed. The 2nd part of course is go ensure that the people are protected from arms in society. He states this in the phrase.. "it behoves us to provide Militia Laws", and he capitalizes both Militia and Laws. He doesn't want there to be any mistake as to what he is making a reference too. Then he says "look well" to their execution of them. Sort of sounds like "A well regulated Militia", doesn't it? He then frames the next sentence with a the term "becomes indespensably necessary" as a reference to counter the states from acting independently from each other with respect to militia laws. Now let's take a quick look at the 2nd amendment again.. "A well regulated Militia, being necessary to the security of a free State".

The word "Union" is a used as a cipher for "people" and "arms" which are the constituent parts of any Militia irrespective of time or place. This symbolism is used extensively throughout the Federalist papers. Knowing this is the key to reading the 2nd amendment with 100 percent objectivity. "E Plurius Enum" has also been used as a cipher in this regard which you will see later.

The experiment points directly to Benjamin Franklin because he is a known scientist. It appears that George Washington may be telling us that this was Benjamin Franklin's idea.

George Washington Farewell Address 1796

The unity of government which constitutes you one people is also now dear to you. It is justly so; for it is a main pillar in the edifice of your real independence, the support of your tranquility at home, your peace abroad, of your safety, of your prosperity, of that very liberty which you so highly prize.

But as it is easy to foresee[283] that, from different causes and from different quarters[284], much pains will be taken[285], many artifices employed, to weaken in your minds the conviction of this truth; as this is the point in your political fortress against which the batteries of internal and external enemies will be most constantly and actively (though often covertly and insidiously) directed, it is of infinite moment that you should properly estimate the immense value of your national Union to your collective and individual happiness; that you should cherish a cordial, habitual, and immovable attachment to it; accustoming yourselves to think and speak of it as of the **palladium** of your political safety and prosperity; watching for its preservation with jealous anxiety;

discountenancing whatever may suggest even a suspicion that it can in any event be abandoned; and indignantly frowning upon the first dawning of every attempt to alienate any portion of our country from the rest, or to enfeeble the sacred ties which now link together the various parts. For this you have every inducement of sympathy

.....

"These considerations speak a persuasive language to every reflecting and virtuous mind and exhibit the continuance of the Union as a primary object of patriotic desire[286]. Is there a doubt whether a common government can embrace so large a sphere? **Let experience solve it[287].** To listen to mere speculation in such a case

---

[283] There will be harm in society proportionate to the lethality of arms and side effects of their introduction.

[284] One quarter of the 2nd amendment is just reading "the right of the people to keep and bear Arms.

[285] Reference to harm in society if dangerous arms allowed in.

[286] The Union of people and guns to make the object Militia. Virtuous mind is thinking of all of society by not allowing guns into society in the first place.

[287] Guns kill people. Deterrents do not stop arms violence.

were criminal[288]. We are authorized to hope that **a proper organization of the whole**[289], with **the auxiliary agency of governments** for **the respective subdivisions, will afford a happy issue to the experiment**[290]. It is well worth a fair and full experiment. With such powerful and obvious motives to union affecting all parts of our country[291], while experience shall not have demonstrated its impracticability, **there will always be reason to distrust the patriotism of those who in any quarter may endeavor to weaken its bands**[292]."

I would like to thank President Barack Obama in using this excerpt from George Washington's farewell speech on January 10, 2017. I don't think for a moment that I've found all the letters, the ciphers that these men had laboured to create. In the absence of an internet search I smelled a cipher coming through my television.

After looking at the transcript of President Barack Obama's farewell speech it was the word "truth" that I had heard him quote from George Washington's farewell address. Words like "truth" and "legitimate" are often used in these ciphers because they infer that there is a current fallacy. There is also a greek theme that has often been used to weave these letters all together.

In one Benjamin Franklin Cipher the word "Large Greek Font" is used. This is the "M" in the word militia because there is a greek word for militia which is "Phalanx". In conjunction with this there is also a small law font with is the letter "r" which is lower case in the word regulated. Palladium is a greek word for guarding. In that particular letter the recipient was a dead man by the name of William Alexander.

---

[288] Speculation = 'Only a good guy with a gun can stop a bad guy with a gun"

[289] Organize the whole word "Militia" into two parts "People and Arms"

[290] The issue by government is of course the output of the 2nd amendment being safe arms only. This is of

Course the entire point of the expereiment.

[291] Guns for self defence while "people and arms" are hidden is not a proof that removing the arms will not work in reality.

[292] There are of course 4 quarters, or clauses within the second amendment and patriotism is false in one of those quarters. This quarter is "the right to keep and bear Arms". To weaken the bands is only quote this one quarter and not use every quarter to make a whole. Read the entire second amendment with equal weight.

William means "resolute protector" (also used by Thomas Jefferson in letter june 12 1823 to William Johnson).

Alexander means "protector of mankind" (the symbolism is about the government protecting society through the 2nd amendment)

George Washington to John Jay, 10 March 1787

To John Jay
Mount Vernon Mar: 10th 1787
Dear Sir,

I am indebted to you for two letters: The first, introductory of Mr Anstey needed no apology—nor will any be necessary on future occasions.₁ **The other, of the 7th of Jany is on a very interesting subject, deserving very particular attention.**

How far the revision of the fœderal system, and giving more adequate powers to Congress may be productive of an efficient government, I will not, under my present view of the matter, presume to decide. That many inconveniencies result from the present form, none can deny. Those enumerated in your letter are so obvious, & sensibly felt that no logick can controvert, nor is it probable that any change of conduct will remove them. And that all attempts to alter or amend it will be like the propping of a house which is ready to fall, and which no shoars can support (as many seem to think) may also be true.

But, is the public mind matured for such an important change as the one you have suggested? What would be the consequences of a premature attempt?

My opinion is, that this Country have yet to *feel,* and *see* a little more, before it can be accomplished. **A thirst for power, and the bantling**—I had like to have said monster—sovereignty, which have taken such fast hold of the States individually, **will, when joined by the many whose personal consequence in the line of State politics will in a manner be annihilated, form a strong phalanx against it**; and when to these the few who can hold posts of honor or profit in the National government are compared with the many who will see but little prospect of being noticed, and the discontents of others who may look for appointments the opposition would be altogether irresistable till the mass as well as the **more discerning part of the Community shall see the Necessity.**

Among men of reflection few will be found I believe, who are not *beginning*[293] to think that our system is better in theory than

---

[293] How can one begin to evaluate a system that has not yet been put into practice? This is why "beginning" has been highlighted. Reflection cannot occur

practice—and that, notwithstanding the boasted virtue of America it is more than probable we shall exhibit the last melancholy proof that Mankind are not competent to their own government without the means of coercion in the Sovereign.

Yet, I would try what the wisdom of the proposed Convention will suggest; and what can be effected by their Councils. It may be the last peaceable mode of essaying the practicability of the pres[en]t form, without a greater lapse of time than the exigency of our Affairs will admit. In strict propriety a Convention so holden may not be legal—Congress however may give it a colouring by recommendation, which would fit it more to the taste, without proceeding to a definition of powers. This, however Constitutionally it might be done, would not, in my opinion, be expedient; for delicacy on the one hand, and Jealousy on the other would produce a mere nihil.

My name is in the delegation to this Convention[294]**; but it was put there contrary to my desire, and remains there contrary to my request. Several reasons at the time of this appointment and which yet exist combined to make my attendance inconvenient, perhaps improper tho. a good deal urged to it**[295]—With sentiments of great regard & friendship I have the honor to be—Dr Sir Yr Most Obedt and Affecte Hble Servt

---

until the very thing that requires reflection actually exists. This paragraph directly relates to chaos caused by arms in society, and the current tug of war that is witnessed today as the government tries to create arms laws, but is obstructed by the perceived meaning of the 2nd amendment. This is not a reflection on America, but a reflection on man and his ability to govern himself. It stresses the importance of any government, being mandated to protect its people from arms.

[294] The convention is the method used to encrypt the word Militia. The symbolism of George Washington has a duality where the first is he represents the birth of the United States as its first President, but secondly he is of course a soldier and is part of a Militia. He has been delegated or assigned to this word.

[295] He also doesn't like this for obvious reasons now, and he never wanted this for the future of his nation harmed. "Yet exist" is a reference to the future and the term "tho. A good deal urged to it" simply parrots the the letter written to James Madison in 1785 when he says.. It is a dangerous experiment —once slacken the reins and the power is lost—and it is questionable with me whether the advocates of the measure foresee all the consequences of it

Go: Washington

P.S. Since writing this letter I have seen the resolution of Congress recommendatory of the Convention proposed to be held in Philadel[phi]a the 2d Monday in May.

What we see here is the use of the word 'phalanx' which when referenced in Noah Webster's Merriam-Webster dictionary it returns

Phalanx : a body of heavily armed infantry in ancient Greece formed in close deep ranks and files;

Benjamin Franklin also indirectly used this word in one of his ciphers a few years later in a letter dated Oct 26 1789 to William Alexander. Benjamin Franklin references two fonts where one is the 'large greek' font and the other a 'small law font'. Now this is a rather uncanny coincidence or a very specific riddle. Two letters, directly related the definition of two words, and further clarified by whether or not they are capitalized. It also signifies that a capitalized "Militia" in mid sentence was by design.

'A well regulated Militia, being necessary to the security of a free State, the right of the people to keep and bear Arms, shall not be infringed'.

Phalanx, Militia, spears, muskets can only be related in one way, people and Arms. The concept is very simple here, once it is understood. It's arms that are allowed in the individuals hands. George Washington, Benjamin Franklin, John Jay, John Adams, James Madison, Thomas Jefferson and Alexander Hamilton were all working in unison to create the letters, such as the one I reference right now. It is not like their issue of National Security was suddenly forgotten during the balance of their lives once their pact was established. These letters were all written for you, right now because the simple fact that you live in their future and the old 2nd amendment has been rendered fallacy.

George Washington says to use a strong phalanx, which he does to hide the word militia. He also does this for another reason. A phalanx is an ancient Greek militia armed with spears and pikes. He describes the entire population of a state as consisting of those people that enjoy power through arms and refers to them as children and even monsters. He also points out that some of the states would endorse this as well through their own politics. He says that the greater population of the people will both experience **annihilated**

George Washington to Alexander Hamilton, 18 Oct 1787

Mount Vernon Octr 18th 1787.
Dear Sir,
Your favor without date came to my hand by the last Post.1 It is with unfeigned concern I perceive that a political dispute has arisen between Governor Clinton and yourself. For both of you I have the highest esteem and regard. But as you say it is insinuated by some of your political adversaries, and may obtain credit, "that you palmed yourself upon me, and was dismissed from my family"; and call upon me to do you justice by a recital of the facts. I do therefore, explicitly declare, that both charges are entirely unfounded. With respect to the first, I have no cause to believe that you took a single step to accomplish, or had the most distant ⟨ide⟩a of receiving, an appointment in my ⟨fam⟩ily 'till you were envited thereto. And ⟨with⟩ respect to the second, that your quitting ⟨it was⟩ altogether the effect of your own ⟨choic⟩e.

When the situation of this Country ⟨calls⟩ loudly for unanimity & vigor[296], it is to be lamented that Gentlemen of talents and character should disagree in their sentiments for promoting the public weal, but unfortunately, this ever has been, and more than probable, ever will be the case, in the affairs of man.

Having scarcely been from home since my return from Philadelphia, I can give but little information with respect to the general reception of the New Constitution[297] in this State[298]. In Alexandria however[299], and some of the adjacent Counties, it has been embraced with an enthusiastic warmth of which I had no conception[300]. I expect notwithstanding, violent opposition will be

---

[296] He asks the everyone gets behind the new meaning of the 2nd amendment.

[297] He cannot know the reception of the new constitution but suspects it will be now be welcomed by all. He knows it's the nature of man.

[298] State of Chaos

[299] Alexandria means Defender of men, which makes sense with respect to the 2nd amendment as related to geography because was ultimately written as a check and balance to defend the nations life and liberty.

[300] He anticipates that that relief of a solution will be in the favour of most.

given to it by some characters of weight & influence[301], in the State[302].

Mrs Washington unites with me in best wishes for Mrs Hamilton and yourself. I am—Dear Sir Yr Most Obedt & Affecte Hble Servt

---

[301] Weight and influence is more a reference to those that will making the most noise in society, "some" is simply a reference to "few" at the far end of the spectrum.

[302] A state of fear and paranoia.

Alexander Hamilton to George Washington, 30 Oct 1787

From Alexander Hamilton
October 30. 1787
Dr Sir

I am much obliged to Your Excellency for the explicit manner in which you contradict the insinuations mentioned in my last letter—The only use I shall make of your answer will be to put it into the hands of a few friends.1

The constitution proposed has in this state warm friends and warm enemies[303]. The first impressions every where are in its favour; but the artillery of its opponents makes some impression[304]. The event cannot yet be foreseen[305]. The inclosed is the first number of a series of papers to be written in its defence[306].

I send you also at the request of the Baron De Steuben[307] a printed pamplet containing the grounds of an application[308] lately made to Congress. He tells me there is some referrence to you[309], the object of which he does not himself seem clearly to understand[310]—But imagines it may be in your power to be of service to him[311].2

There are public considerations that induce me to be somewhat anxious for his success. He is fortified with materials which in Europe could not fail to establish the belief of the contract he alleges—The documents of service he possesses are of a nature to convey an

---

[303] The first "warm" is happiness where the second "warm" is anger.

[304] People are of course currently armed which makes things a bit awkward.

[305] Tell me about it.

[306] These are the full papers known as the Federalist Papers. Conclusive proof in this letter as to their real nature and purpose.

[307] This man trained or regulated the forces of George Washington.

[308] Bill of Rights.

[309] The reference is George Washington as the leader of the nation and as a soldier.

[310] The object is the word 'Militia', which he doesn't understand because it is an encryption.

[311] George Washington as a symbolism of the United States ,will now be able to protect the people with common sense gun laws. He "imagines" is related still to his misunderstanding of the object, but feels it is a good thing.

exalted idea of them—The compensations he has received though considerable, if compared with those which have been received by American officers, will according to European ideas be very scanty in application to a stranger who is acknowleged to have rendered essential services. Our reputation abroad is not at present too high— To dismiss an old soldier empty and hungry—to seek the bounty of those on whose justice he has no claims & to complain of unkind returns and violated engagements will certainly not tend to raise it. I confess too there is something in my feelings which would incline me in this case to go farther than might be strictly necessary rather than drive a man at the Baron's time of life, who has been a faithful servant, to extremities. And this is unavoidable if he does not succeed in his present attempt.

What he asks would, all calculations made, terminate in this—an allowance of his Five hundred and Eighty guineas a year. He only wishes a recognition of the contract—He knows that until affairs mend no money can be produced. I do not know how far it may be in your power to do him any good; but I shall be mistaken, if the considerations I have mentioned do not appear to Your Excellency to have some weight.[3] I remain with the great Respect and esteem Yr Excellys Obed. serv.

A. Hamilton

Alexander Hamilton to George Washington, Nov 10, 1787

To Alexander Hamilton
Mount Vernon Novr 10th 1787.
Dear Sir,

I thank you for the Pamphlet, and for the Gazette contained in your letter of the 30th Ult. For the remaining numbers of **Publius**, I shall acknowledge myself obliged, as I am persuaded the subject will be well handled by the Author[312].[1]

The new Constitution[313] has, as the public prints will have informed you, been handed to the people of this state[314] by an unanimous vote of the Assembly[315]; but it is not to be inferred from hence[316] that its opponents are silenced; on the contrary, there are many, and some powerful ones—Some of whom, it is said by overshooting the mark[317], have lessened their weight[318]: be this as it may, their assiduity stands unrivalled[319], whilst the friends to the Constitution content themselves with barely avowing their

---

[312] This is curious, because we know that Alexander Hamilton was author in these papers. It might be author who finally publishes these findings as they must be, in order for all the people to understand. He is persuaded, is a similar symbolism to Thomas Jefferson's, 'Candid friend to truth" It is his belief that person reading these ciphers was compelled to with only a nations true liberty in mind.

[313] As we now see it in the future.

[314] In a state of violence and loss of liberty.

[315] People and Arms are the "assembly" into the word "Militia" which is now exposed and understood

[316] From hence, is the future of course, and there will be a pushback on this rather stunning revelation.

[317] It is anticipated that by the time this revelation comes to light that strongest gun rights opponents will be in a time when there is much overshooting. George Washington is saying that if it has gotten to this point , it is far too much, and this final legacy is the only solution to gun violence.

[318] Basically the argument that "guns don't kill people" is starting to wear thin when proportioned against the carnage and growing faction in society.

[319] Persistence in their belief that having arms is a god given right and should trump the needs of a society. This cannot be demonstrated any more than those that believe that Sandy Hook was faked.

approbation of it[320]. Thus stands the matter with us, at present[321]; yet, my opinion is, that the Major voice is favourable[322].

Application has been made to me by Mr Secretary Thompson (by order of Congress) for a copy of the report, of a Committee, which was appointed to confer with the Baron de Steuben, on his first arrival in this Country—forwarded to me by Mr President Laurens. This I have accordingly sent. It throws no other light on the Subject than such as are to be derived from the disinterested conduct of the Baron. No terms are made by him "nor will he accept of any thing but with general approbation"—I have however, in my letter enclosing this report to the Secretary, taken occasion, to express an unequivocal wish, that Congress would reward the Baron for his Services, sacrafices and merits, to his entire satisfaction. It is the only way in which I could bring my sentiments before that honble body, as it has been an established principle with me, to ask nothing from it.2 With very great esteem & regard I am—Dear Sir Yr Most Obedt Servt

Go: Washington

Can you see why I picked out this letter when I first read it? At the time I read this letter, I had already resolved the true nature of the Federalist Papers which were authored under the pseudonym Publius. The authors were Alexander Hamilton, James Madison and John Jay.

---

[320] The people that claim to believe in the constitution show their disproval of it by twisting it.

[321] The present is now, the moment this has been revealed to all.

[322] This is a reference that the majority of the people at this point in time, would have to be in favour of common sense gun laws.

George Washington To Henry Lee, Jr. Sep 22 1788

(Private)

Dear Sir, Mount Vernon Septr 22d 1788

Your letter of the 13th instant was of so friendly & confidential a complexion, as to merit my early attention and cordial acknowledgments.

I am glad Congress[323] have at last decided upon an Ordinance[324] for carrying the New[325] government into execution. In My Mind, the place for the meeting of the new Congress was not an object of such very important consequence[326]: but I greatly fear that the question entailed upon that body, respecting their permanent residence[327], will be pregnant with difficulty & danger[328]. God grant that true patriotism[329] & a spirit of moderation[330] may exclude a narrow locality[331] and all ideas unfriendly to the Union[332] from every quarter[333].

Your observations on the solemnity of the crisis & its application to myself, bring before me subjects of the most momentous & interesting nature. In our endeavours to establish a new general government, the contest, nationally considered, seems not to have

---

[323] Senators are men with power, or people with Arms. Congress is then all the people who own firearms.

[324] Decided on less lethal arms because of the new 2nd amendment.

[325] "New" is capitalized for emphasis. New as in one that is now going to govern and execute "well regulated Militia"

[326] The people with less lethal arms, as created by common sense gun laws isn't a big deal anymore.

[327] The fear comes from the small group that are keeping the lethal arms in their residence.

[328] This is of course dangerous to all of society.

[329] True love of counry.

[330] Guns are ok, but not lethal ones, think of nation first.

[331] The narrow locality is the one clause and those who read only "the right of the people to keep and bear Arms"

[332] Union of people and Arms as the encryption. 2A in its true form.

[333] There are four quarters in the 2nd amendment and the one that would be unfriendly to the its true meaning is the quarter that contains the words "the right of the people to keep and bear Arms".

been so much for glory, as existence. It was for a long time doubtful whether we were to survive as an independent Republic, or decline from our fœderal dignity into insignificant & wretched fragments of Empire. The adoption of the Constitution so extensively, & with so liberal an acquiescence on the part of the Minorities in general, promised the former: until, lately, the Circular letter of New York carried, in my apprehension, an unfavorable, if not an insidious tendency to a contrary policy. I will hope for the best, but before you mentioned it, I could not help fearing it would serve as a Standard to which the disaffected might resort. It is now evidently the part of all honest men, who are friends to the New Constitution, to endeavor to give it a chance to disclose its merits and defects, by carrying it fairly into effect, in the first instance. **For it is to be apprehended, that by an attempt, to obtain amendments before the experiment has been candidly made**[334] "more is meant than meets the ear"—that an intention is concealed to accomplish slily, what could not have been done openly—to undo all that has been done. If the fact so exists, that a kind of combination is forming to stifle the government in embrio; it is a happy circumstance that the design has become suspected. Preparation should be the sure attendant upon forewarning. Probably, prudence, wisdom, & patriotism were never more essentially necessary than at the present moment[335]: and so far as it can be done in an irreproachable direct manner, no effort ought to be left unessayed to procure the election of the best possible characters to the new Congress[336]. On their harmony, deliberation & decision every thing will depend. I heartily wish Mr Madison was in our Assembly: as I think, with you, it is of unspeakable importance Virginia should set out in her fœderal measures under right auspices.

---

[334] This letter is of course related to the "dangerous" experiment.

[335] There should be no sudden moves and everyone should understand what is going on first.

[336] It's difficult to tell the people who to elect to congress. The danger is that some may obstruct or twist the constitution to rob liberty from the land. Since the government is to be constituted of the people, choose wisely. This choice includes the choice to vote. No votes shall be suppressed.

The principal topic of your letter is, to me, a point of great delicacy indeed: insomuch that I can scarcely, without some impropriety, touch upon it. In the first place, the event to which you allude may never happen[337]—amongst other reasons—because, if the partiality of my fellow Citizens conceive it to be a mean by which the sinews of the new government would be strengthened, it will of consequence be obnoxious to those who are in opposition to it; many of whom, unquestionably, will be placed among the Electors. This consideration alone would supercede the expediency of announcing any definitive, and irrevocable resolution. You are among the small number of those, who know my invincible attachment to domestic life, and that my sincerest wish is to continue in the enjoyment of it, solely, until my final hour. But the world would be neither so well instructed, or so candidly disposed as to believe me to be uninfluenced by sinester motives; in case any circumstance should render a deviation from the line of conduct I had prescribed myself indispensable. Should the contingency you suggest take place, and (for argument sake alone let me say) should my unfeigned reluctance to accept the Office be overcome by a deference for the reasons and opinions of my friends; might I not, after the Declarations I have made (and Heaven knows they were made in the sincerity of my heart) in the judgment of the impartial World and of Posterity, be chargable with levity and inconsistency; if not with rashness & ambition? Nay farther, would there not even be some apparent foundation for the two former charges? Now justice to myself and tranquility of conscience require that I should act a part[338], if not above imputation, at least, capable of vindication[339]. Nor will you conceive me to be too solicitous for reputation. Though I

---

[337] Henry Lee jr represents the future. The event which may never happen is a tyrant showing his face in government, providing the constitution is obeyed.

[338] He is part of the cabal, in fact, this very letter is a result of his acting.

[339] It should not be viewed as a conspiracy that the 2nd was hidden. It should be reflected upon that it had to be done in light of 18th century circumstances. The constitution was yet to be experienced, the government was brand new and small, the people had Arms now due to the war. Most importantly however the 2nd amendment is based solely on reality based gun laws. The guns are always on trial, not just the people, so that the people will be protected from the guns.

prize, as I ought, the good opinion of my fellow Citizens; yet, if I know myself I would not seek or retain popularity at the expence of one social duty or moral virtue. While doing what my conscience informed me was right, as it respected My God, my Country & myself, I could despice all the party clamour and unjust censure, which must be expected from some, whose personal enmity might be occasioned by their hostility to the governmt. I am conscious, that I fear alone to give any real occasion for obloquy—and that I do not dread to meet with unmerited reproach—And certain I am, whensoever I shall be convinced the good of my Country requires my reputation to be put in risque, regard for my own fame will not come in competition with an object of so much magnitude[340]. If I declined the task it would be upon quite another principle. Notwithstanding my advanced season of life, my encreasing fondness for Agricultural amusements, and my growing love of retirement augment and confirm my decided predeliction for the character of a private Citizen: Yet it would be no one of these motives, nor the hazard to which my former reputation might be exposed, or the terror of encountering new fatigues & troubles that would deter me from an acceptance—but a belief that some other person, who had less pretence & less inclination to be excused, could execute all the duties full as satisfactorily as myself. To say more would be indiscreet; as a disclosure of a refusal beforehand, might incur the application of the Fable, in which the Fox is represented as undervaluing the Grapes he could not reach[341]. You will perceive, my dear Sir, by what is here observed (and which you will be pleased to consider in the light of a confidential communication) that my inclinations will dispose & decide me to remain as I am; unless a clear & insurmountable conviction should be impressed on my mind, that some very disagreeable consequences must in all human probability result from the indulgence of my wishes.1

---

[340] George Washington's reputation for telling the truth vers the Object , aka 2nd amendment and in its new meaning be rejected and with it George Washington.

[341]

If you return by land[342], I shall expect without failure the pleasure of your Company[343]. I am much indebted to you for your obliging offer of forwarding such articles as I might want from New York[344]; though I shall not have occasion at this moment to avail myself of your goodness[345]. Mrs Washington offers her best Compliments to Mrs Lee, with ardent wishes for the reestablishment of her health; which joined with my own, will conclude me, with great regard and esteem Dear Sir Yr most Obedt & Affecte Sert

Go: Washington

ALS, Vi; LB, DLC:GW.

1. In his correspondence with friends, GW continued to argue with himself in much these same terms until he was elected president in the spring of 1789.

---

[342] Return is symbolic of being born to the land.

[343] A Company is the business of going through the letters and publishing them.

[344] This is a direct reference to the Federalist papers which are now deciphered.

[345] George Washington cannot accept them due to the moment in time in which he exists. He is symbolic of America but in younger days. The moment he speaks of is the in the future. He is talking to me. Surreal.

John Adams

John Adams contributed to my research in one very important way. He instructed me to look for letters written by Philosophers. He also inferred that there were ciphered letters written for the future. In discovering the 2nd amendment for what it was one of the first things that comes to mind was a feeling that a terrible thing has happened in history. One can't help but wonder how long this secret had to have been hidden for or if by some tragic accident it had been lost. We now know that it had to be lost, but not forever. John Adams has told us in his one of his letters a specific range of time. The time he had used was 100 years, and in this way the man has told us how long the secret should be hidden for. Since he was part of the cabal for this plan, I don't think it would be a stretch to assume this was the general consensus on the matter. If it can be said, I believe these men were "comfortable" with their secret being kept for at least 100 years in order for that not to be another revolution because of the revelation. In their minds it would have been enough time for the people to experience the real checks and balances of the constitution.

There is something else about John Adams that I discovered with respect to the tone of his letters. History reports that he was pretty flamboyant in his insults, truly a master in his artistry of disparagement. If his passion was his powder, then the insult itself would be of the highest calibre. If he was to take a shot, he did not even require a line of sight, because it was the retort that would ring the ears and shatter any dignity cowering between them.

John Adams has said this in a letter.

He belonged to the American Philosophical society which can be looked up in at its website. These were invite-only memberships. He was a federalist. With suspicion being the enemy would it not be better that there be no knowledge of a cabal? I don't see it likely that it would have been widely advertised that these men were part of society. What these men were working on transcends the politics of their day. It was a pact to the grave for the service not of themselves, but of the future of their nation. These were a class of men that would have also done something about global warming had they seen the writing on the wall for it. This was just how they rolled, and their opinions mattered more than most, which has proven itself in the constitution as written. It has to be respected though, as does the English language it was written in. The opposing factions to their cause were far more concerned with their new found kingdoms, being their own State Rights. It is only the Federal head that is more concerned with "We the People" than the individual states themselves are more concerned with "We the people" but only in the context of their state, or a "Me the People" viewpoint.

This particular letter is rather interesting. On July of 1783 Benjamin Franklin has written a cipher that proves that the 2nd amendment had been fully formed. Remember that this letter is taken in conjunction with all the others. The 2nd amendment was obviously hidden, and if it was hidden, then at some time it had to have been formed. If the narrative is known, then it is just a matter of searching back in time until the occurrence of these letters simply stops. Only James Madison had not yet been invited to join American Philosophical Society in 1783. This letter has many purposes. The first purpose was for John Adams to convey his contempt towards Benjamin Franklin. With this letter, and some of his others he is distancing himself from the group. The primary benefit to this would of course be to remove suspicion. It was simply an orchestration. The other benefit, perhaps much greater would be for some of these men would appear to live on one side of the political spectrum, and others would not. They were essentially setting up encampments, in both political parties so that it would be far easier to orchestrate the constitutional debates. Remember that they knew a constitution was needed, the perfect constitution and in it must reside the 2nd amendment to protect the people despite their fears to preserve both life and liberty. The other purpose of this letter, is perhaps to tell us that Benjamin Franklin was the author of the 2nd amendment and that it was his experiment. There are symbolisms here that we can now resolve in knowing what the 2nd amendment really means.

John Adams to James Warren, 13 April 1783

To James Warren
Confidential.
Paris April 13th. 1783.
Dear Sir,
I have in some late Letters opened to You in Confidence the Dangers, which our most important Interests have been in, as well as the Opposition and Jealousy and Slanders, which your Ministers have met with, from the vain, ambitious and despotic Character of one Minister, I mean the C. de Vergennes— But You will form but an imperfect Idea after all of the Difficulties We have had to encounter, without taking into Consideration another Character equally selfish

and interested—equally vain and ambitious—more jealous and envious, and more false & deceitful, I mean Dr. Franklin.

It is a Saying of Algernoon Sidney concerning Sir Walter Rawleigh, that "his Morals were not sufficiently exact for a great Man"[2]—And the Observation can never be applied with more propriety than to Dr. Franklin.— His whole Life has been one continued Insult to good Manners and to Decency. His Son, and Grandson, as he calls him with characteristic Modesty; the Effrontery with which he has forced these his offspring up in the World, not less than his Speech of Polly Baker[346], are Outrages to Morality & Decorum, which would never have been forgiven in any other American— These things however are not the worst of his Faults— They shew however the Character of the Man; in what Contempt he holds the Opinions of the World, and with what Haughtiness he is capable of persevering through Life in a gross & odious System of Falsehood and Imposture.[3]

A sacred regard to Truth is among the first and most essential Virtues of a public Man— How many Kings have involved themselves and their Kingdoms in Misfortunes, by a Laxness in this particular? How much Mischief has been done in all Ages by Ministers of State, who have indulged themselves in a Duplicity and Finesse, or in other Words, in an Hipocrisy and Falsehood, which some are even abandoned enough to recommend and prescribe to Politicians, but which never yet did any thing but Harm and Mischief.— I am sorry to say, but strict and impartial Justice obliges me to say, that from five complete Years of Experience of Dr. Franklin, which I have now had in Europe, I can have no Dependence on his Word. I never know when he speaks the Truth, and when not. If he talked as much as other Men, and deviated from the Truth as often in proportion as he does now, he would have been the Scorn of the Universe long ago— But his perpetual Taciturnity has saved him.

It would be Folly to deny, that he has had a great Genius, and that he has written several things in Philosophy and in Politicks, profoundly[347]— But his Philosophy and his Politicks have been

---

[346] This speech was a fictitious work of Benjamin Franklin written years earlier. The general theme is that some laws are simply not fair or reflect reality.

[347]

infinitely exaggerated, by the studied Arts of Empiricism[348], until his Reputation has become one of the grossest Impostures[349], that has ever been practised upon Mankind since the Days of Mahomet.[350]

A Reputation so imposing in a Man of Artifice and Duplicity[351], of Ambition and Vanity, of Jealousy and Envy, is as real a Tyranny as that of the Grand Seignior. It is in vain to talk of Laws of Justice, of Right, of Truth, of Liberty[352], against the Authority of such a Reputation. It produces all the Servility of Adulation—all the Fear, all the Expectation & Dependence in common Minds, that is produced by the imposing Pomp of a Court and of Imperial Splendour. He has been very sensible of this, & has taken Advantage of it[353].

As if he had been conscious of the Laziness, Inactivity and real Insignificance of his advanced Age, he has considered every American Minister, who has come to Europe, as his natural Enemy. He has been afraid that some one would serve his Country, acquire a Reputation, and begin to be thought of by Congress to replace him.—

Sensible that his Character has not been so much respected in America as in Europe, he has sought an Alliance to support him with Mr de Sartine[4] and the C. de Vergennes and their "Autours" Satellites. It is impossible to prove, but from what I know of him, I have no doubt, that he is the Man, who, by means of the Emissaries or Satellites just alluded to, made to those Ministers all the malicious Insinuations against Mr. Lee & Mr. Izard, which, altho' absolutely false and groundless, have made as much Noise in the World, & had

---

[348] People who read the 2nd amendment have read what they wanted to read.

[349] One day the 2nd amendment would be viewed to be false.

[350] This is quite a statement to make. It seems pretty extreme, when he says something was practiced on mankind. The 2nd amendment was of course practiced on Mankind for over 200 years.

[351] He was sneaky in making the 2nd amendment because it has two meanings.

[352] The real meaning of the 2nd amendment had to be hidden.

[353] He has used human nature to his advantage to encrypt the 2nd amendment by using "the right of the people to keep and bear Arms". Servitude of Adulation and fear in the common minds, is a reference to politics of fear. People would see the utility of Arms as a contingency to protect from a tyrant for all time.

almost the same Effects, as if they had been true—5 From the same detestable Source came the Insinuations and Prejudices against me, and the shameless abandoned Attack upon me, the History of which You know better than I.— Hence too the Prejudices against Mr. Dana, Mr. Jay & every other. These are my Opinions, tho' I cannot prove them, otherwise than by what I have seen and heard myself, what results from a long Series of Letters & Transactions, and what I know of the Characters of the Men. The C. has had his Head filled with so many Prejudices against others, and in favor of him, and has found him so convenient a Minister,—ready always to comply with every Desire,—never asking any thing but when ordered and obliged to ask for Money—never proposing any thing—never advising any thing, that he has adopted all his Passions, Prejudices & Jealousies, and has supported him, as if his own Office depended upon him— He and his Office of Interpreters have filled all the Gazettes of Europe with the most senseless Flattery of him, and by means of the Police set every Spectacle, Society, and even private Club and Circle[354] to clapping him with such Applause[355], as they give to Opera Girls.— This being the unfortunate Situation of foreign Affairs[356], what is to be done?

Franklin has, as he gives out, asked Leave to resign— He does not mean to obtain it[357], but to save the Shame of being recalled[358]. **I wish with all my Soul he was out of public Service, and in Retirement, repenting of his past Life, and preparing, as he ought to be, for another World[359]**. But as the Peace is made, and he is old, and it will

---

[354] Armed with a club and attacking with the arch of a circle.

[355] Applause is a reference to the sound of hitting , and the Opera girls reference means simply a lot of it. The "foreign" affairs are the affairs of the future, which of course are unknown, but are anticipated.

[356] The foreign affairs are the affairs of the unknown future. What is to be done? Letters, encryptions and concealments.to give the future a legacy.

[357] Benjamin cannot help his current period.

[358] The shame is the futures understanding that guns can kill people and that human nature is the true enemy to liberty. Men must never be given too much power because they are not immune to their own failings.

[359] Symbolism of Franklin feeling bad about what they had to put their future nation through. Preparing for the other world again, is a reference to the future.

make a horrid Wonder in the World to remove him, and it would be impossible to publish the whole Truth in Justification of it to the People of America as well as of Europe, perhaps it may be as well to let him alone.— But at least Congress should firmly and steadily support their other Ministers against his insidious Manœuvres— They should add no more Feathers to his Cap. This will however be difficult. He will watch Opportunities, and French Influence will forever aid him, and both will be eternally attacking openly and secretly every other Minister—so that I am persuaded he will remain as long as he lives, the Demon of Discord among our Ministers, and the Curse and Scourge of our foreign Affairs.

France has suffered as much as America, by the unskilful & dishonest Conduct of our foreign Affairs. They have had no Confidence in any but him— And he either knew nothing or cared nothing about Affairs— They have not only not confided in any other, but they have persecuted every other— By which Means France has not derived half the Advantage from the Alliance in the War, nor will She hold half the Benefit after the Peace, which She might have done, if She had vouchsafed to hearken to the Advice of those, who would have given it honestly and wisely.

To enter into the contemptible detail of all the unworthy Artifices[360], the Follies and Impositions[361], that have been the Fruit of these Characters[362]; the "petit Commerce" of— &c— &c—the Arts in Holland, Spain, Russia, Sweeden, Denmark and all the rest of Europe, to prevent the progress of our Cause, and defeat our Negociations; to straiten in the Article of Money, and distress Us in the War; to keep Us humble, tame and dependent; to strip Us of the Fishery and Western Lands; the Millions of Affronts, Neglects, Contempts, or, in one French Word, "Desagremens," which have been put upon the Servants of Congress, would fill Volumes.

The preparing is the letters hes writing for the future to set things straight with respect to the 2nd amendment.

[360] Reference to looking closely at the 2nd amendment. The unworthy artifices are "a right of the people to keep and bear Arms"

[361] Follies and impositions, are a reference to the damage of the 2nd amendment

[362] The fruit , is a reference to people reading what they want to read.

The Moral and the Politick of all is—"See with your own Eyes—judge with your own Understanding—repeal every shackling Instruction to your Ministers—support them inflexibly against all foreign Influence, and all little spiteful Intrigues.["]³⁶³

For my own part, I have been made a Sacrifice to such Intrigues in so gross a manner, that unless I am restored and supported, I am unalterably determined to retire— So resolves your / invariable Friend

It has been discerned by historians that John Adams was not overly fond of Benjamin Franklin. It should be apparent why in the following letter however the actual context for it has never been known until now. In light of the new dynamic I suspect, that was a game of good founder bad founder going on in the continental conventions and well into the years when these men held office.. Any future scholars would not perceive a cabal or at least not one with John Adams in it. This would be important because the secret had to be kept while these men played shuffleboard in the great beyond. Remember it was imperative that the people must experience the checks and balances of the constitution first. Both in and outside of the constitutional convention a cabal broken up would have the benefit of orchestrating faction to fulfill the ultimate purpose of creating the perfect constitution. Broken up into political factions these men could further orchestrate a demonstrated usage of the constitution for future generations. Remember that this constitution was a brand new thing, and it might be wise to take it for a test drive and iron out the kinks. There is a letter that Benjamin Rush had written to John Adams about a dream that he had about John Adams and Thomas Jefferson reconciling later in life. The letter, written in 1809, has been viewed as a prophetic dream, even by John Adams, but it was not. After taking a brief glance at this letter, it is another cipher that explains the hidden narratives in history that are now being exposed by this research. These men were never enemies, political or otherwise because they were on a much higher mission and were part of the cabal which formed by at least 1780.

John Adams To Benjamin Franklin July 19. 1784

(unpublished) The Hague

---

³⁶³ Direct reference to the 2ⁿᵈ amendment again once understood. It's the moral thing to understand it. The shackling is congress defending its old meaning. The spiteful intrigues are wide and varied but are based in avarice and the politics of fear.

Sir

I have the Honour of your Letters of the 27 of June and 4 July, and should advise your Excellency to present the C. de Mercy, a Copy of the Instruction as you propose.

By the Length of Time, We have been left without Information respecting foreign Affairs, and by other Circumstances, there are greater Divisions among our Countrymen, respecting these as well as their Finances, than are Salutary. It is now near two Years that I have led the Life of a Spider after having led that of a Toad under an Harrow for four years before. But I Swear I will not lead one nor the other much longer. I cant recollect that I have had a Letter from Congress, Since the Peace.

I read somewhere, when I was young "This Expectation makes the Blessing dear / Heaven were not Heaven, if We knew what it were." But this Expectation must not be disappointed continually. Mr. Hartley will wait too, I apprehend, as long as We, and for my Part I humbly propose that **We should banish all Thoughts of Politicks, and begin a Course of Experiments in Physicks or mechanicks, of telescopical or miscroscopical observations:** Bertholon and Spalanzani, and Needham have so entertained me of late, that I think to devote myself to similar Researches. With great Respect, I have the Honour to be, Sir your Excellencys most obedient humble servant

John Adams

His Excellency Dr Franklin

When read, since the declaration of independence he states that he has lead the life of a toad, which is an animal that sits and watches and waits. The life of a spider is a little bit more industrious constantly building their webs, hoping one day to catch something. I believe the symbolism here is that they are hoping to catch the attention of someone in the future with their letters. He also makes a reference to his countrymen and how things are not as peaceful perhaps as they would have wished.

The expectations reference I believe has to do with the people's expectations of true liberty. I sense that you may think I am reaching a bit with my interpretation on this, but keep in mind, I am seeking letters like this, letters with symbolisms. The next letter will tie in nicely with what I am reading here. There is a reference to a Mr. Hartley, whos actual name was David Hartley. History will show that here is a father and a son, the father was an English philosopher of psychology, the other was a friend of Benjamin Franklin and the mans son. Now David Hartley the professor had passed away in 1757, which was about 27 years previous to the date on this letter. There is something else interesting about this philosopher, he had written a book called "Observations on Man, his Frame, his Duty, and his Expectations". So here we have two sentences, back to back one with a Mr. Hartley in it, the other with a comment about expectations, in quotes. Is this a coincidence? I think Mr. John Adams was trying to tell us, yes you the reader, being in the future that it is the older Mr. Hartley that is referenced. Then he goes on to infer that Mr. Hartley is alive and waiting. Waiting for what? Alive how?

There have often been references to the "grand or great experiment" with respect to the United States form of government.. In the symbolisms we can now derive what is being said. It appears that there will be experiments created here. Now of course symbolisms would involve taking a very close look at the text and letters of these men. Nothing is going to be explicit. There is a reference to telescopes and microscopes. Telescopes are of course instruments that are used to look at things that are far off with varied and unknown distances, such as the future. Pierre Bertholon de Saint-Lazare was a physicist who experimented with electricity. Lazzaro Spallanzani was an Italian priest who was also a Biologist and physiologist. John Turberville Needham was a Catholic priest who was also a biologist.

John Adams (up) The Hague July 27th 1784

Sir

I embrace the opportunity, by Mr: Bingham to enclose to your Excellency, Copy of a Letter from Mr. Jefferson, by which it appears that **we are joined in some affairs** which will give me the Occasion to visit Paris once more, and reside there for some little time at least.

As Mr. Jefferson will not probably arrive before the latter End of August, and nothing can be done before he comes, I shall wait at the Hague for my Wife and Daughter, who are happily arrived in London, and endeavour to go with them, in Time to meet your Excellency and Mr: Jefferson upon his arrival at Paris.

The Philosophers are speculating upon our Constitutions and I hope will throw out Hints, which will be of Use to our Countrymen. The Science of Government as it is founded upon the genuine Principles of Society, is many Centuries behind that of most other

Sciences, that of the fine Arts, as well as that of Trades and Manufactures. As it is the first in Importance it is to be hoped it may overtake the rest[364], and that Mankind may find their Account in it[365]. The Berlin Academecian has set an Example, which if liberally[366] followed, may produce great Effects, **for I dont believe that many will find with him upon Examination that Despotism or even Monarchy is the best possible form of Government.**

They have sent me from Amsterdam, Copies of a Translation, of the Abby de Nably's Letters, made by an English Episcopal Clergyman at Amsterdam, whom I don't know. I enclose one to your Excellency and have the Honour to be, with great Respect &c

Dr: Franklin.

When I found this letter I rather liked it. It helped me to seek out others letters. I already knew that the key actor's involved were from the American Philosophical society. It is the highlighted sentence regarding hints. For emphasis John Adams was nice enough to capitalize. Philosophers-Constitutions-Hints-Use-Countrymen. Hints are pieces of the new narrative that we derive from

---

[364] As invention and industry march forward it is hoped that government will catch up with these to ensure that they are not harmful to society. This is the very basis for the 2nd amendment, since it directs government itself to continually study arms in the public domain and any harmful effects they may have. If some are deemed to be harmful, beyond the point of anomaly, then they must be removed and left in the domain of the military itself.

[365] This "philosophy" is not only important for America, but for all of mankind. Everyone deserves liberty.

[366] The best way that this can be achieved is through a liberal approach. The old rhetoric of the 2nd amendment was much more oppressive to the population at large. It was both a monarchal and despotic view for it was basically saying "every man for himself". The truth of the 2nd amendment, as finally illuminated in this book, is all about thinking of your neighbours first, and all of society. It is a much more liberal approach to arms violence in society. Why arm the criminals, mentally ill with instruments of destruction in the first place and thus punishing all of society with loss of liberty. "Life, liberty and the pursuit of happiness, where life is the foundation for liberty , and liberty is the foundation for a pursuit of happiness. While the last may never be achieved because of the individual himself, the other two have been increasingly stripped from American society for over 200 years.

the ciphered letters once they have been deciphered.. He tells us to look for letters associated with the Philosophers and that the nature of the letters has to do with the constitution. It mustn't be assumed that this letter was written to point to discovering the nature of the 2nd amendment. John Adams has written this letter for the future at a point in time where a researcher is now seeking out the ciphered letters. He knows that the reader of this letter is already aware of the ciphered letters, so he's helping us to resolve how to locate them. He is not trying to tell anyone that there are ciphered letters, but if we know they exist, then the context of this makes far more sense. We know what these men were up too, and so did they. It had to be impossible to understand the full nature of this letter in the absence of a key to it. "Of **Hints, which will be of Use to our Countrymen**", would be an understatement because the collection of letters is the very power of them to expose the unknown narrative and prove beyond doubt the legitimate meaning of the 2nd amendment..

John Adams to Benjamin Rush, 4 April 1790

New York April 4. 1790

Dear Sir

The Tories as you observe in your friendly Letter of 24 Feb. are more attached to each other; they are also, We must candidly confess, more of real Politicians. They make to themselves more merit with the People, for the smallest services, than the Whigs are able to do for the greatest. The Arts the Tr[umpetts] the Puffs, are their old Instruments and they know how to employ them. The History of our Revolution will be one continued Lye from one End to the other. The Essence of the whole will be *that Dr Franklins electrical Rod, Smote the Earth and out Spring General Washington. That Franklin electrified him with his Rod—and thence forward these two conducted all the Policy Negotiations Legislation and War.* These underscored Lines contain the whole Fable Plot and Catastrophy. if this Letter should be preserved, and read an hundred Years hence the Reader will say "the Envy of this J.A. could not bear to think of the Truth"! He ventured to Scribble to Rush, as envious as himself, Blasphemy that he dared not speak, when he lived. But ["]Barkers at the Sun and Moon are always Silly Curs." But this my Friend, to be Serious, is the Fate of all Ages and Nations. And there is no Resource in human nature for a Cure. Brederode did more in the Duch Revolution than William 1st. Prince of Orange. Yet Brederode is forgotten and William the Saviour, Deliverer and Founder.—Limited Monarchy is founded in Nature. No Nation can adore more than one Man at a time. It is an happy Circumstance that the object of our Devotion is so well deserving of it. that he has Virtue so exquisite and Wisdom so consummate. There is no Citizen of America will say, that there is in the World so fit a Man for the head of the Nation. From my Soul I think there is not. and the Question should not be who has done or suffered most, or who has been the most essential and Indispensible Cause of the Revolution, but who is best qualified to govern Us? **Nations are not to sacrifice their Future Happiness to Ideas of Historical Justice. They must consult their Own Weaknesses, Prejudices, Passions, Senses and Imaginations as well as their Reason**. "La Raison n'a jamais fait grande chose." As the K. of Prussia says in his Histoire de mon tems.

The more Extracts you Send me from your Journals, the more will you oblige me—I beg especially a Copy of my Character. I know very well it must be a partial Panegyrick. I will Send you my Criticisms upon it. You know I have no affectation of Modesty. My Comfort is that such vain folly as Cicero, Neckar Sir William Temple & I are never dangerous.

If I Said in 1777 that We should never be qualified for Republican Government till We were ambitious to be poor" I meant to express an Impossibility. I meant then and now Say that No Nation under Heaven ever was, now is, or ever will be qualified for a *Republican Government*, unless you mean by these Words, *Equal Laws* resulting from a Ballance of three Powers the Monarchical, Aristocratical & Democratical. I meant more and I now repeat more explicitly, that **Americans are peculiarly unfit for any <, Start deletion, *but the*, End,> Republic but the Aristo-Democratical-Monarchy; because they are more *Avaricious* than any other Nation** that ever existed the Carthaginians and Dutch not excepted. The Alieni Appetens Sui profusus reigns in this nation as a Body more than any other I have ever Seen.

When I went to Europe in 1778 I was full of Patriotic Projects like yours of collecting Improvements in Arts Agriculture, Manufacture Commerce Litterature & Science. But I Soon found my Error.—I found that my offices demanded every moment of my time and the Assistance of two or three Clerks—and that all this was not enough. I was obliged to make it a Rule never to go out of my *Road* for any Curiosity of any kind. J.J. Rousseau understood it very well when he Said that Ambassadors "doivent tout leur tems á cet Objet Unique, ils sont trop honnêtes gens pour voler leur Argent.[, Start insertion,", End,] Emile Tom. 4. p. 361. if he meant this as a Sarcasm, he was in the Wrong. I never knew one who attempted or affected Philosophy, that was good for any Thing in the Diplomatique Line—and I know that every Hour that I might have employed that Way would have been a Robbery upon the Duties of my Public Character.

Your Family pictures are charming; and the tender Piety you express for your Mother, is felt by me in all its force, as I have a Mother living in her Eighty Second Year, to whom I owe more than I can ever pay. This Mother and a Father who died 30 years ago, two of the best People I ever knew formed the Character, which you have drawn. alass! that it is no better! I said before that Vanity is not dangerous. a Man who has bad designs is Seldom or never vain. It is such modest Rascals as Caesar, who play tricks with Mankind, read his Commentaries. What consummate caution to conceal his Vanity! Contemptu famæ, fama augebatur. This Tyrants and Villains always knew.

   Adieu Mon Ami

   John Adams

   Pray can you recollect a Feast at Point no Point in the Fall of 1775 and the Company that returned with you and me in a Boat and our Conversation. I want a List of the Names of that Party who returned in the Same Boat with Us to Philadelphia.

I used this letter in the preface because I thought it would be useful to add validity to my claim that letters were written for future.

At times in my research I was certain these men must have wondered just how long it would take for their letters to be "discovered" in their true context. I new the letters were written for the future simply because of their tone and the narrative that was forming. What I found particularly important was that John Adams explicitly says that this letter was written for the future in that he infers it would take 100 years to be found. To assume that it would take 100 years just for the letter to be dusted off and "read" has no foundation in logic. This letter was written by the 2nd sitting president of the United States and I'm pretty sure that scholars would have studied it many times before the threshold of 100 years was ever met. When he says "read", he really means deciphered so that the truth of it is known and that actually took a little over 224 years. I don't think he viewed this as a maximum threshold of time but rather a minimum one. He probably figured this was a safe amount of time to have passed. There is an irony in this because while a context was required to understand this letter, its previous context was misleading. Some historians have taken this letter as an inference that John Adams was highly jealous of both George Washington and Benjamin Franklin. It's a logical conclusion if you your understanding of the 2nd amendment is purely subjective but not in its new context once objectively read.

The highlights in this letter are of my doing. The italicized parts of the letter were created by John Adams. The italicized parts are the "underscored lines" that John Adams refers too.

At times in my research I was certain these men must have wondered just how long it would take for their ciphers to be "discovered" and their context exposed. I was able to recognized letters as being ciphers because of their tone and my current understanding of the evolving new narrative from previous ciphers. What I found particularly important was that John Adams explicitly says that this letter was written for the future in that he infers it would take 100 years to be found. To assume that it would take 100 years just for the letter to be dusted off and "read" has no foundation in logic. This letter was written by the 2nd sitting president of the United States and. It would not have sat in a box for 100 years and then magically been discovered in the sense of parchment and ink. When he says "read", his reference must be with respect to the cipher of it. This letter cannot be looked at in a vacuum because John Adams was part of the cabal and in that light, he knew of these letters, was writing these letters and didn't suddenly forget about such an important mission in the writing of this letter. My point being is that if he knew the plan, why would he write a letter that would look like a cipher and yet not be a cipher? Why would he confuse the issue for a future historian or researcher? In a matter of National Security and Constitutional legacy, he would not have done this, because he would have been highly sensitive to it. It is up to us to first resolve that his is a cipher letter and then figure it out. If we can't then we can't but to can't doesn't make this an isn't. With that being said I have not deciphered this entire letter yet, because I have not yet resolved all of its symbolisms. There is no rule book in this. There is nothing to say that a cipher may be nested in just a few paragraphs of a letter, but it has been my experience that pretty much all the letter is a cipher.

    I would like to reiterate on the importance of his 100 year time frame that John Adams is referring too. He uses an actual stretch of time starting from the ratification of the Bill of Rights because is a cipher. Part of why I felt horrified when I discovered what the 2nd amendment actually says is the tremendous loss of life due to gun violence since the day it was written. Perhaps no so much per capita in the late 18th century, but as Samuel Colts profits started to come in I would suspect the per capita started to go up. The Wild West was born and then we move into the days of Tommy Guns and the advent of gangsters. I think its important to understand that a MINIMUM span of time had to pass before the 2nd amendment was revealed.   December 16th 1791 would have been too soon.

    I don't think he viewed this as a maximum threshold of time but rather a minimum one . He probably figured this was a safe amount of time to have passed. I have seen this letter There is an irony in this because while a context was required to understand this letter, its previous context was misleading. Some historians have taken this letter as a inference that John Adams was highly jealous of both George Washington and Benjamin Franklin. It's a logical conclusion if you have been reading the 2nd amendment subjectively, but it is not if you have been reading it objectively.

This letter has previously been interpreted to demonstrate John Adams disdain towards both George Washington and Benjamin Franklin.

Nothing could be further from the truth. John Adams is using two founding fathers as symbolisms only. The symbolism here is that George Washington represents a soldier, and the lightning rod is a reference to gun fire, or arms. A citizen in essence becomes a soldier once he is armed except that he is not regulated by government or men of rank, only whim. The "essence of the whole" is an instruction to join "people and Arms" and you will get something that appears or has the essence of the word "Militia".

Policy negotiations, legislation and war all surround the 2nd amendment and how it is to be used and where the arms should be allowed to exist, and for what. The nature of the war itself was arming its citizenry and empowering them, and from that chaos was born when those men were not directed and well-regulated. The "two" are symbolic of the constituent parts of a Militia, being "people" and 'arms"

He then refers to plot and catastrophy where the plot is the 2nd amendment being written and secreted into the constitution. The catastrophy is that its protections would have to be held back from society simply because society still had to get used to the brand new constitution . The "envy" relates to his envy of the society in the future, that would one day know the truth of "to keep and bear arms". He was horrified that he could not share its truth in his time. "Blasphemy that he dared not speak, when he lived". "Barkers at the sun and moon are silly curs" relates to the politics of fear and people thinking that they needed guns to protect themselves from their fears, or the new constitution and the government it would produce. These are also the loudest people in society. Now does this sound somewhat familiar?

Now, as I've mentioned before, when I was doing my research and at the point I realized what these men were up too. I often wondered how long they thought it would take America to discover the truth regarding the 2nd amendment. In one sentence John Adams validated both what I had thought these men were up too, and at the same time perhaps he answered my own question, even if he was just conjecturing on it. He says..

> "if this Letter should be preserved, and read an hundred Years hence",

This letter was meant for you the reader, in a future time of John Adams, and not the recipient of the letter. The recipient is more information for us to understand that Mr. Edmund Randolph was perhaps an ally and a confident in the constitutional conventions, and perhaps helped to direct the others to a Bill of Rights. There could have been a game of "good founding father – bad founding father" being orchestrated. The audience of course, were the one that didn't even realize they were a part of the play. The audience were men who went by the names of Patrick Henry, George Mason, Richard Henry Lee, and of course others. Getting the 2nd amendment into the constitution was so important that the liberally minded intellectuals of the day used every device and alliance they could muster to attain its goal. The goal was singular in purpose which was to create a constitution with checks and balances to ward off oppression, both from a tyrant, and perhaps something much worse, anarchy.

It should also be noted, that Benjamin Rush was known to be a philosopher.

To John Adams from Benjamin Rush, 13 April 1790

Philadelphia April 13. 1790
Dear Sir

Your last letter is a treasure.—Every sentence in it is full of instruction. I have often contemplated that passion in mankind to concentrate all their homage and admiration in One Man, in all the revolutions which advance knowledge or happiness.—Cicero Observed it, and deplored it in the fame and power of Pompey. I have thought at last that I had discovered in this weakness in human nature, the high destiny of the soul even in its ruins.—Does it not prove that it was created originally to concentre all its love and adoration in One Supreme Being, and that all its Obligations are due to that Being only? Is it not the counter passion of the love of fame, which is only a misplaced desire after immortal life & happiness? Are not all our follies & vices the counterfits of virtues? Are not the love of pleasure of power—of wealth—of activity—& of rest,—nothing but passions and propensities which have corresponding Objects held out to them by revelation, but which are at present under a false direction?—A belief that this is the case has Often afforded me great pleasure, for as I Observe folly & vice to be universal, and as I believe the creator of human souls has in infinite wisdom made no means without an end,—and made nothing in vain, so I have derived, from contemplating the weak & corrupt passions and desires that have been mentioned, a satisfactory argument in favor of the tendency, and Ultimate termination of all human beings in complete and eternal happiness in every respect suited to their present tempers but under a new, and different direction.—

Had the King of Prussia never said nor wrote another sentence than the one you have quoted from him upon human reason, he would have deserve the high rank he holds among philosophers and kings—Mr Boyle has expressed the same idea, but with much less force. "We are governed, says this great man by our prejudices, and not by our reason."—What did Reason do in the council or the field in the late American War? Were not most of the wise measures of Congress the effects of passion—accident or necessity, & were not all the successful movements or engagements of our army little else than lucky blunders? Most of the valuable discoveries in philosophy have been the effects of accident. This is eminently the case in medicine. We owe more to Quacks, who never reason, for useful & powerful articles in the Materia Medica, than to the learning of MDs:—I love to establish the truth of these propositions, inasmuch as they lead tot he belief of a general & particular providence, and at the same time show the weakness and folly of human nature. Man is indeed fallen! He discovers it every day in domestic in social, & in political life. Science—Civilization & government have in vain been employed to cure the defects of his nature. Christianity is alone equal to this business. Did its mild & gentle Spirit prevail in our Country it would do more towards rendering our liberty perpetual, than the purest republic that my imagination, or the strongest monarchy that yours, could devise. Let us not despair. The peaceable manner in which our Constitutions has been changed in the United States & in Pennsylvania make it probably than man is becoming a more rational creature in America than in other parts of the World.—

I made no note of the company or conversation to which you allude in your letter, but as nearly as I can recollect, the company in the boat consisted of yourself—Owen Biddle—David Rittenhouse—Michl. Hellegas—Chas. Humphries—and myself. The most interesting subject discussed was a proposal to write a letter to Lord North discovering to him (as a friend to Government) that there was a design among the rebels to burn some of the Arsenals in Great Britain, & to urge his Lordship to take measures to prevent it. This deception was to be practised only to shew the risk of engaging in a war with America, & that Great Britain at 3,000 miles from her was not invulnerable. The proposition was made in a joke, but Mr Hellegas was so much pleased with it, that he thought it merited serious Attention.

Now Attend to some more of your speeches in the first years of the revolution.

Upon my asking Mr J: Adams what he thought of sending Mr. Dickinson to Europe as a minister—he said, "Mr D: is the most unfit man in the world to be sent abroad.—He is such a friend to monarchy, that he would prostrate himself at the feet of every throne he saw. I would prefer Dr. Wetherspoon to him."—Octobr: 1776

When Genl. Sullivan brought Lord Howe's proposition to Congress for a Conference, in Sepr. 1776, Mr Adams said privately to me "that he wished the first ball that had been fired on the 27th of Augst: had gone thro' his head." On the floor of Congress, he called the General "a decoy duck." The issue of the Conference shewed Mr A: to be right in his principles & predictions.—Upon perceiving a disposition in Congress to appoint a Committee to confer with Lord Howe, he said to me at his lodgings "that mankind were made for slavery, & that they must answer the end of their creation sooner or later."

I intended to have conclude this letter by transcribing your character from my notebook—but upon reading it over, I find so many things said in favor of your principles & conduct in the years 1775 & 1776, that I should be suspected of flattery should I send you a copy of it. I shall give you a specimen of the manner in which I have observed in drawing characters by sending you that of your colleague Robt; Treat Paine's—whose name follows yours in the notebook.

"Robt Treat Paine - He was educate a Clergyman, and Afterwards became a lawyer. He was facetious in his manner both in public and in private. He had a certain Obliquity of Understanding which prevented his seeing things in the same light that they struck other people. He opposed every thing, and hence he got the name of the Objection maker in Congress. He was thought by his colleagues to be cool to independance. He was a useful member of Congress, especially upon Committees where he was punctual & faithful."

In my notebook I have recorded a conversation that passed between Mr Jefferson & myself on the 17th of March of which you were the principal subject. We both deplored your Attachment to monarchy, and both agreed that you had changed your principles since the year 1776. The proofs of this change were derived from your letter to Mr Hooper which was afterwards published in this city— upon a form of Government for North Carolina.—

What say you to a visit to Philada: Next spring?—You have many friends in this city—as well as in the state. Do bring Mrs. Adams along with you. After You have been feasted by our fashionable people, I will claim a family evening from you, & while Mrs Adams is engaged with Mrs Rush in enumerating the years in which they were both neglected by their husbands during the war, I will read extracts from my note book to you, & afterwards receive more materials for it from your conversation. Take care what you say, or write to me. I wish I could whisper the same caution to some other gentlemen high in power & office in New York. Some of them will find themselves, (if they survive me) turned inside outwards.—I have never deceived my Country in a single instance,—nor shall I deceive posterity. In my present retirement I daily hear of Acts & speeches in New York which mark worse than British degrees of Corruption. My only consolation is, our people will not follow their rulers. They are as yet unprepared for sophisticated Government. There will be a change I believe in the representation of several of the states next year. This is matter of opinion only for I am now only a spectator of public measures, & shall probably be so indifferent as to a change in our State (if it should be proposed) as not to give a vote at our next election.—

Adieu—yours sincerely,

Benjn. Rush

P.S. On the 20th of July 1776 I met Mr Adams in 4th Street near the Indian Queen, and received from him Congratulations on being appointed a member of Congress. I spoke in high terms of one of my Colleagues, and said I believed him to be an honest man. "That said Mr Adams is saying a great deal of a public Character, for political integrity is the rarest Virtue in the whole World." In a subsequent conversation at his lodgings he said "that public & private integrity did not always go together, and illustrated the position in the character of Mr [Shewell] of Boston who in private life, was strictly just but in public life, wholly unprincipled."—

I have had occasion a thousand times in political life to see these remarks confirmed.

This letter has been written by adjournments.—If the subjects of it are discordant, you must ascribe it to that circumstance.—

John Adams to George Washington, 31 October 1791

United States October the 31st: 1791.

Sir,

The Senate of the United States have received with the highest satisfaction the assurance of public prosperity contained in your Speech to both Houses: the multiplied blessings of providence have not escaped our notice or failed to excite our gratitude.

The benefits which flow from a restoration of public and private confidence[367] are conspicuous and important and the pleasure with which we contemplate them is heightened by your assurance of those further communications[368] which shall confirm their existance and indicate their source[369].

Whilst we rejoice in the success of those military operations which have been directed against the hostile indians[370], we lament with you the necessity that has produced them[371], and we participate the hope[372] that the present prospect of a general peace, on terms of moderation and justice[373], may be wrought into complete and permanent effect[374], and that the measures[375] of government may equally embrace the security[376] of our frontiers[377] and the general

---

[367] Restoration or final legacy of the constitution to demonstrate it was always meant to protect life and liberty through directing any government to create common sense gun laws.

[368] The future communications are the ciphers to be read in the future.

[369] the 2nd amendment will be validated by the ciphers the ciphers validated by the 2nd amendment.

[370] While not politically correct, I believe this is a symbolism regarding mans primitive side.

[371] The necessity to hide the 2nd amendment, which is of course directly related to the "military operation"

[372] Hope that the 2nd amendment be discovered.

[373] Some arms are ok, just not the lethal ones. Moderation, but justice of all of society first.

[374] That the 2nd finally be used as it was always meant and bring peace to the nation within its borders through an dramatic reduction in gun violence

[375] Government putting guns on trial after measuring their harm in society.

[376] 'being necessary to the security of a free state in the future.

interests of humanity; our solicitude to obtain, will ensure our zealous attention, to an object so warmly espoused by the principles of benevolence[378], and so highly interesting to the honor and welfare of the nation.

The several subjects which you have particularly recommended and those which remain of former Sessions will engage our early consideration; we are encouraged to prosecute them with celerity and steadiness by the belief, that they will interest no passion, but that for the general welfare[379], by the assurance of concert[380] and by a view of the arduous and important arrangements which have been already accomplished[381].

We observe, Sir, the constancy and activity of your zeal for the public good[382]. The example will animate our efforts to promote the happiness of our Country.

By order of the Senate
John Adams
Vice President of the United States, and President of the Senate

This letter was written 6 weeks before the Bill of Rights was ratified.

John Adams to Benjamin Rush, 19 March 1812

Quincy March 19. 1812
Dear Sir
The greatest part of the History in your last Letter was well known to me, and I could write you Six Sheets for your three, full of

---

[377] The frontiers he refers to are those of the future when the 2nd amendment is finally exposed.

[378] The object is of course the 2nd amendment because it cares only for the people. The proponents of common sense gun laws and the founding fathers are on EXACTLY the same page.

[379] The 2nd amendment is a right specifically targeting the general welfare of the people to the security of a free state of mind or peace in society.

[380] The constitutional convention was orchestrated.

[381] The arrangements are the federalist papers, the knowledge of the orchestration and the 2nd amendment

[382] George Washington is symbolically the father of America and his zeal for the public good is the astonishing labor and planning the cabal went through.

Anecdotes, of a Similar complexion. I wanted no Satisfaction. If I had, your Letter would have given it.

The great Character, was a Character of Convention. His first Appointment was a magnanimous Sacrifice of the North to the South: to the base Jealousy, Sordid Envy, and ignorant Prejudices of the Southern and middle States, against New England. I know what I Say, and I will not tremble like your old Friend at the danger of "giving offence."

Mr Widgery, previous to his return home, from our Legislature waited on our Governor Sullivan, pour prendre Congé. The Governor had heard from Some Tatler of a light Speech concerning him Self, and recd his Visitor coldly. W. felt it and discovered Some Sensibility of it, S. irritated, Said "I Set little Value <, Start deletion,of, End,> on these visits of Ceremony from "Men who Set So little Value upon me, in other Companies." W. raised his head, and with great dignity Said "Sir!" "Who made You Governor"? An Explanation ensued and a Reconciliation.

I mentioned a Character of Convention. There was a time when Northern, Middle and Southern Statesmen, and northern Middle and Southern Officers of The Army, expressly agreed to blow the Trumpets of Panegyrick in concert; to cover and dissemble all Faults and Errors; to represent every defeat as a Victory, and every Retreat as an Advancement; to make that Character popular and fashionable, with all Parties in all places and with all Persons, as a Centre of Union, as the Central Stone in the Geometrical Arch.

There you have the Revelation of the whole Mystery. Something of the same kind has occurred in France and has produced a Napoleon and his Empire. **And, my Friend, Something hereafter may produce Similar Conventions to cry up a Burr, a Hamilton**[383], an Arnold or a Cæsar, Julius or Borgia. And on Such foundations have been created Mahomet Zingis Tamerlane Kouli, Alexander and all the

---

[383] Alexander Hamilton was shot and killed in a duel with Aaron Burr July 12 1804. It's purported that Hamilton did not fire back. He must have known he was possibly martyring himself for the 2nd amendment. The convention is the interpretation of the 2nd amendment as its not understood will continue to cause gun violence and grief for society "cry up".

other great Conquerors this w[, Start insertion,o, End,]rld has produced.

Pray have you not often heard The Honourable Timothy Pickering Speak of The Great Character? I have. And at various Periods of time from 1791 when I lived in Mrs Keppele's house at the Corner of Arch Street and fourth Street, to 1797 after I was chosen President.

I lament, my dear Friend, that you were not in Congress in 1774 and 1775. A thousand Things happened there in those Years that no Man now living knows but myself. Mr Gerry, Mr Lovel was not there. Gerry not till 1776. Lovel not til 1777.

1774 was the most important and the most difficult Year of all. We were about one third Tories, one third timid and one third true Blue. We had a Code of Fundamental Laws to prepare for a whole Continent of incongruous Colonies. It was done; and the Declaration of Independence in 1776, was no more than a repetition of the Principles, the Rights and Wrongs asserted and adopted in 1774.

Ought not your Philosophical Society to institute an Inquiry into the Truth of the terrible Accounts of Earthquakes at the Southward and Westward. I Suspect Something very wicked at the bottom of most of those Stories that falsis terroribus implent our good Ladies and innocent Children.

Monticello owes a Letter to mare Mont Maromont, or Merry Mount, or Mount Wollaston, for by all these Names the Place has been called.

If You have educated or Suffered to be brought up your Family in Idolatry you ought to read to them that Chapter in the Old Testament which contains Moses's tremendous Curses against Idolatry.

If I were to write this Letter over again I could make it methodical and correct the grammar, without Sending it to Petersburg.

I am as ever Yours
John Adams

From John Adams March 8 1823

"I have received your letter of the 26th of last month and I thank you for your infinitesimal miniature of President Washington. I cannot see it even with the help of a Solar microscope and should not be able to distinguish the features on the figure clearly enough to know whether it is a fair representation of the hero, but the young eyes of my family and friends say that it is as good a likeness of him as they have seen from any pencil or chisel. I am always pleased to see correct representations of that great man. The more they are multiplied and the wider they are scattered and diffused the better, but I totally despise the miserable catchpenny tricks by which he is represented in situations whence he never stood and as the **author of measures in which he had nothing to do**, and which he did **not even approve**. This is a kind of rapine of fame confounding all distinctions between right and wrong, truth and falsehood, virtue and vice, subversive in short of all political morality."

John Adams

This following letter links up with the letter George Washington wrote to James Madison in 1785. Lets now compare these two letters found there to be some rather revealing quotes in that letter

"It is a **dangerous experiment**—once slacken the reins and the power is lost—and it is questionable with me whether the advocates of the **measure** foresee all the **consequences** of it."

The measures bring us back to the 2nd amendment. Now I think we are constantly being told that George Washington had nothing to do with these measures because he is often symbolized as being a man of truth, and as a man of truth, and a soldier he is misrepresented in the old understanding of the word "militia" in the 2nd amendment. So even 38 years later, we can see John Adams reiterating these themes in letters for the future. I found this letter up for auction. I think it's going for 20,000 dollars at the moment.

Thomas Jefferson

Essay On Exercise August 19 1785.

"Encourage all your virtuous dispositions, and exercise them whenever an opportunity arises, being assured that they will gain strength by exercise as a limb of the body does, and that exercise will make them habitual...[384]Give about two of them [hours] every day to exercise; for health must not be sacrificed to learning. A strong body makes the mind strong. As to the species of exercise, I advise the gun. While this gives a moderate exercise to the body, it gives boldness, enterprize, and independance to the mind. Games played with the ball and others of that nature, are too violent for the body and stamp no character on the mind. Let your gun therefore be the constant companion of your walks. Never think of taking a book with you. The object of walking is to relax the mind. You should therefore not permit yourself even to think while you walk. But divert your attention by the objects surrounding you. Walking is the best possible exercise. Habituate yourself to walk very far. The Europeans value themselves on having subdued the horse to the uses of man. But I doubt whether we have not lost more than we have gained by the use of this animal. No one has occasioned so much the degeneracy of the human body. An Indian goes on foot nearly as far in a day, for a long journey, as an enfeebled white does on his horse, and he will tire the best horses. There is no habit you will value so much as that of walking far without fatigue. I would advise you to take your exercise in the afternoon. Not because it is the best time for exercise for certainly it is not: but because it is the best time to spare from your studies; and habit will soon reconcile it to health, and render it nearly as useful as if you gave to that the more precious hours of the day. A little walk of half an hour in the morning when you first rise is adviseable also. It shakes off sleep, and produces other good effects in the animal oeconomy."

This letter appears to be about exercise and carrying a gun. At first glance it seems to be an endorsement of open carry. It is not. This isn't just my opinion

---

[384] The missing information is found in the next letter and explained. This information which was taken away had no utility in the "Essays" version which appear to have a bias that guns are good.

because Thomas Jefferson would not have suddenly changed his mind for a brief instant it time, and violate a pact he had joined into as early as the Declaration of Independence.

At the very start of this essay he is asking the reader to think hard with your better angels. He then moves into symbolism with the words "will gain strength by exercise AS a limb of the body does". He moves us now to the analogy of exercise. He says "a strong body", makes the mind strong. The body of course is now being exercised and is only an analogy to virtuous dispositions, or lines of thinking. He is trying to tell the leader to use this bias in their thinking. Now he talks about the exercise and he advices the gun. He is saying to think about the gun but with virtuous dispositions around it. He says to "never" think of taking a book with you, which is code for "the truth of the 2nd amendment cannot be found in any book", so it must be resolved through much thinking, but in the context of all of society, and not just self. "The object of walking is to relax the mind", is a wish that the old fears that motivate for want of the 2nd amendment can be dispelled by pondering its true nature. To not "think" is to not let your old habits of thinking take over your mind. He wants you to "retrain" your mind, or unlearn your previous passions and replace them with new ones. The introduction of animals is a symbolism of animal nature.. Animals are unable to "reason" at the same level of men. Sleep is the tendency to revert to non-virtuous disposition. Good effects in the animal economy, is the limitation of non-virtuous thinking, in spite of mans tendency to think of self first. In practicing thinking about others first, one will essentially become less selfish. He wants us to grow our minds in this direction, and with no pun meant, this is the very heart of the 2nd amendment. It is also acknowledged that this will be a struggle for all men, simply because of human nature. This is not an essay about exercise, it just initially looks like it. We just revealed the truth of it with the key of the 2nd amendment, and it took 20 minutes.

The discovery of this letter and its analysis and decryption occurred before the following one, which is the actual source. While there is a duplication here, it is the fact the one you have just read in its current form exists further demonstrates the true nature of the letter itself.

This is the full letter from which the above essay was chopped out of. I have included both so that you can see how a previous historian(s) was lead astray. In the absence of knowing what the 2nd amendment really was you can see why the previous letter was written as it was. The irony of this should be pretty glaring, and the utility of keeping both these documents in their own forms are an EXACT

PROOF of what Thomas Jefferson is talking about. The above letter has been contrived by its authors to be an alternative fact. If I'm to quote this letter the author above did not take the advice of Thomas Jefferson when he says

> "And never suppose, that in any possible situation, or under any circumstances, it is best for you to do a dishonorable thing, however slightly so it may appear to you. Whenever you are to do a thing, though it can never be known but to yourself, ask yourself how you would act were all the world looking at you, and act accordingly."

I struggle to find an angle to see this interesting facet of the dynamic at play here in order to resolve the right angle to call this "neat" without offending the author of the essay. It is not my intent because no man is immune from his own human nature. The struggle will never end, but to survive with each other, there are better avenues to take.

Peter Carr was Thomas Jefferson's nephew. There is a good chance he would have met him often and it would have been quite easy to tell him his thoughts in person, because it is far easier to converse directly than by a letter. What is the rush to tell his nephew this information? This is a hoarded letter, and the symbolism is that the young nephew represents the future of Thomas Jefferson, through lineage. The future of America, is who this letter is directed at. Thomas Jefferson can only convey his advice to the future through a letter because of that nuisance of a thing known as life span. Is his nephew in dire need of this advice, or are we? Exactly. Once the truth of the 2nd amendment is revealed to the future, he knows that many will find it upsetting because a narrative that they have come to rely on just vanished. There will of course be a period of instability and confusion as a nation slowly moves from one train of thought to another. It's my hope that it can at least be acknowledged that the previous train of thought has been running out of control for some time. Thomas Jefferson simply asks that you stop fueling it with falsehoods and abandon it and get onboard the new truth of the 2nd amendment. His advice goes beyond that because he gives us advice in how to think. He is not an alternative fact kind of man, and is very familiar with the source of it. I have written a section on "The Narratives we Build" to help elaborate on this. I have also dug just a little bit deeper. I went to the starting place where we are all on the same page, regardless of faction and have tried to reason out the causes of the divergence. In a way, this book is the very proof of those divergences because this book was derived from truth.

> DEAR PETER, – I received, by Mr. Mazzei, your letter of April the 20th. I am much mortified to hear that you have lost so much time;

and that when you arrived in Williamsburg, you were not at all advanced from what you were when you left Monticello. Time now begins to be precious to you. Every day you lose, will retard a day your entrance on that public stage whereon you may begin to be useful to yourself. However, the way to repair the loss is to improve the future time. I trust, that with your dispositions, even the acquisition of science is a pleasing employment. I can assure you, that the possession of it is, what (next to an honest heart) will above all things render you dear to your friends, and give you fame and promotion in your own country. When your mind shall be well improved with science, nothing will be necessary to place you in the highest points of view, but to pursue the interests of your country, the interests of your friends, and your own interests also, with the purest integrity, the most chaste honor. The defect of these virtues can never be made up by all the other acquirements of body and mind. Make these then your first object. Give up money, give up fame, give up science, give the earth itself and all it contains, rather than do an immoral act. And never suppose, that in any possible situation, or under any circumstances, it is best for you to do a dishonorable thing, however slightly so it may appear to you. Whenever you are to do a thing, though it can never be known but to yourself, ask yourself how you would act were all the world looking at you, and act accordingly.

Encourage all your virtuous dispositions, and exercise them whenever an opportunity arises; being assured that they will gain strength by exercise, as a limb of the body does, and that exercise will make them habitual. *From the practice of the purest virtue, you may be assured you will derive the most sublime comforts in every moment of life, and in the moment of death. If ever you find yourself environed with difficulties and perplexing circumstances, out of which you are at a loss how to extricate yourself, do what is right, and be assured that that will extricate you the best out of the worst situations. Though you cannot see, when you take one step, what will be the next, yet follow truth, justice, and plain dealing, and never fear their leading you out of the labyrinth, in the easiest manner possible. The knot which you thought a Gordian one[385], will untie itself before you. Nothing is so mistaken as the supposition, that a person is to extricate himself from a difficulty, by intrigue, by chicanery, by dissimulation, by trimming, by an untruth, by an injustice[386]. This increases the difficulties ten fold; and those who pursue these methods, get themselves so involved at length, that they can turn no way but their infamy becomes more exposed. It is of great importance to set a resolution, not to be shaken, never to tell an untruth. There is no vice so mean, so pitiful, so contemptible; and he who permits himself to tell a lie once, finds it much easier to do it a second and third time, till at length it becomes habitual; he tells lies without attending to it, and truths without the world's believing him. This falsehood of the tongue leads to that of the heart, and in time depraves all its good dispositions[387].*

An honest heart being the first blessing, a knowing head is the second. It is time for you now to begin to be choice in your reading; to begin to pursue a regular course in it; and not to suffer yourself to be turned to the right or left by reading any thing out of that course. I have long ago digested a plan for you, suited to the circumstances in which you will be placed. This I will detail to you, from time to time, as you advance. For the present, I advise you to begin a course of antient history, reading every thing in the original and not in translations. First read Goldsmith's history of Greece. This will give you a digested view of that field. Then take up antient history in the detail, reading the following books, in the following order: Herodotus, Thucydides, Xenophontis Hellenica, Xenophontis Anabasis, Arrian, Quintus Curtius, Diodorus Siculus, Justin. This shall form the first stage of your historical reading, and is all I need mention to you now. The next, will be of Roman history (*). From that, we will come down to modern history. In Greek and Latin poetry, you have read or will read at school, Virgil, Terence, Horace, Anacreon, Theocritus, Homer, Euripides, Sophocles. Read also Milton's Paradise Lost, Shakspeare,

---

[385] He is telling you that the 2nd amendment, once confusing can in fact untied from its fallacy, if you read it correctly.

[386] Exploitation of the 2nd amendment. I talk about this in "The Narratives we Build" section".

[387] Sound familiar? The danger of alternative facts.

Ossian, Pope's and Swift's works, in order to form your style in your own language. In morality, read Epictetus, Xenophontis Memorabilia, Plato's Socratic dialogues, Cicero's philosophies, Antoninus, and Seneca. In order to assure a certain progress in this reading, consider what hours you have free from the school and the exercises of the school. Give about two of them, every day, to exercise; for health must not be sacrificed to learning. A strong body makes the mind strong. As to the species of exercise, I advise the gun. While this gives a moderate exercise to the body, it gives boldness, enterprise, and independence to the mind. Games played with the ball, and others of that nature, are too violent for the body, and stamp no character on the mind. Let your gun therefore be the constant companion of your walks. Never think of taking a book with you. The object of walking is to relax the mind. You should therefore not permit yourself even to think while you walk; but divert your attention by the objects surrounding you. Walking is the best possible exercise. Habituate yourself to walk very far. The Europeans value themselves on having subdued the horse to the uses of man; but I doubt whether we have not lost more than we have gained, by the use of this animal. No one has occasioned so much, the degeneracy of the human body. An Indian goes on foot nearly as far in a day, for a long journey, as an enfeebled white does on his horse; and he will tire the best horses. There is no habit you will value so much as that of walking far without fatigue. I would advise you to take your exercise in the afternoon: not because it is the best time for exercise, for certainly it is not; but because it is the best time to spare from your studies; and habit will soon reconcile it to health, and render it nearly as useful as if you gave to that the more precious hours of the day. A little walk of half an hour, in the morning, when you first rise, is advisable also. It shakes off sleep, and produces other good effects in the animal economy. Rise at a fixed and an early hour, and go to bed at a fixed and early hour also. Sitting up late at night is injurious to the health, and not useful to the mind. Having ascribed proper hours to exercise, divide what remain, (I mean of your vacant hours) into three portions. Give the principal to History, the other two, which should be shorter, to Philosophy and Poetry. Write to me once every month or two, and let me know the progress you make. Tell me in what manner you employ every hour in the day. The plan I have proposed for you is adapted to your present situation only. When that is changed, I shall propose a corresponding change of plan. I have ordered the following books to be sent to you from London, to the care of Mr. Madison. Herodotus, Thucydides, Xenophon's Hellenics, Anabasis and Memorabilia, Cicero's works, Baretti's Spanish and English Dictionary, Martin's Philosophical Grammar, and Martin's Philosophia Britannica. I will send you the following from hence. Bezout's Mathematics, De la Lande's Astronomy, Muschenbrock's Physics, Quintus Curtius, Justin, a Spanish Grammar, and some Spanish books. You will observe that Martin, Bezout, De la Lande, and Muschenbrock are not in the preceding plan. They are not to be opened till you go to the University. You are now, I expect, learning French. You must push this; because the books which will be put into your hands when you advance into Mathematics, Natural philosophy, Natural history, &c. will be mostly French, these sciences being better treated by the French than the English writers. Our future connection with Spain renders that the most necessary of the modern languages, after the French. When you become a public man, you may have occasion for it, and the circumstance of your possessing that language, may give you a preference over other candidates. I have nothing further to add for the present, but husband well your time, cherish your instructors, strive to make every body your friend; and be assured that nothing will be so pleasing, as your success, to, Dear Peter,

    Your's affectionately,

    (*) Livy, Sullust, Caesar, Cicero's epistles, Suetonius, Tacitus, Gibbon.

Thomas Jefferson to Noah Webster, Jr., 4 December 1790

Philadelphia Dec. 4. 1790.
Sir

Your favor of Oct. 4. [i.e. 14] came to my hands on the 20th. of November. Application was made a day or two after to Mr. Dobson for the copies of your essays, which were recieved, and one of them lodged in the office. For that intended for myself be pleased to accept my thanks. I return you the order on Mr. Allen, that on Dobson having been made use of instead of it. **I submit to your consideration whether it might not be adviseable to record a second time your right to the Grammatical institutes in order to bring the lodging of the copy in my office within the 6. months made a condition by the law?** I have not at this moment an opportunity of turning to the law to see if that may be done: but I suppose it possible that the failure to fulfill the legal condition on the first record might excite objections against the validity of that.

In mentioning me in your essays, and canvassing my opinions, you have done what **every man has a right** to do, and it is for the good of society that **that right should be freely exercised. No republic is more real than that of letters,** and I am the last in principles, as I am the least in pretensions to any dictatorship in it. Had I other dispositions, the philosophical and dispassionate spirit with which you have expressed your own opinions in opposition to mine, would still have commanded my approbation. **A desire of being set right in your opinion**, which I respect too much not to entertain that desire, induces me to hazard to you the following observations. It had become an universal and **almost uncontroverted position in the several states**, that the purposes of society do not require a surrender of **all our rights** to our ordinary governors: that there are **certain portions of right not necessary** to enable them to carry on an effective government, and which experience has nevertheless proved they will be constantly incroaching on, if submitted to them. That there are also certain fences which experience has proved peculiarly efficacious against wrong, and rarely obstructive of right, which yet the governing powers have ever shewn a disposition to weaken and remove. Of the first kind for instance is freedom of religion: of the second, trial by jury, Habeas corpus laws, free presses. These were the settled opinions of all the states, of that of Virginia, of which I was writing, as well as of the others. The others had in consequence delineated these unceded portions of right, and these fences against wrong, which they meant to exempt from the power of their governors, in instruments called declarations of rights and constitutions: and as they did this by Conventions which they appointed for the express purpose of reserving these rights, and of delegating others1 to their ordinary legislative, executive and judiciary bodies, none of the reserved rights can be touched without resorting to the people to appoint another convention for the express purpose of permitting it. Where the constitutions then have been so formed by Conventions named for this express purpose they are fixed and unalterable but by a Convention or other body to be specially authorised. And they have been so **formed by I believe all the states except Virginia. That state concurs in all these opinions, but has run into the wonderful error that her constitution,** tho made by the ordinary legislature, cannot yet be altered by the ordinary legislature. I had therefore no occasion to prove to them the expediency of a constitution alterable only by a special convention. Accordingly I have not in my notes advocated that opinion, tho it was and is mine, as it was and is theirs. I take that position as admitted by them: and only proceed to adduce arguments to prove that they were mistaken in supposing their constitution could not be altered by the common legislature. Among other arguments I urge that the Convention which formed the constitution had been chosen merely for ordinary legislation, that they had no higher power than every subsequent legislature was to have, that all their acts are consequently repealable by subsequent legislatures, that their own practice at a subsequent session proved they were of this opinion themselves, that the opinion and practice of several subsequent legislatures had been the same, and so conclude 'that their constitution is alterable by the common legislature.' Yet these arguments urged to prove that their constitution is alterable, you cite as if urged to prove that it ought not to be alterable, and you combat them on that ground. An argument which is good to prove one thing, may become ridiculous when exhibited as intended to prove another thing. I will beg the favor of you to look over again the passage in my Notes, and am persuaded you will be sensible that you have misapprehended the object of my arguments, and therefore have

combated them on a ground for which they were not intended. My only object in this is the rectification of your own opinion of me, which I repeat that I respect too much to neglect. I have certainly no view of entering into the contest whether it be expedient to delegate unlimited power to our ordinary governors? My opinion is against that expediency. But my occupations do not permit me to undertake to vindicate all my opinions, nor have they importance enough to merit it. It cannot however but weaken my confidence in them when I find them opposed to yours, there being no one who respects the latter more than Sir Your most obedt. & most humble servt,
 Th: Jefferson

The American dictionary is the Merriam-Webster Dictionary. Noah Webster is the original founder

"Life, Liberty and the Pursuit of Happiness."

Liberty: "the quality or state of being free"

Security :"the state of being protected or safe from harm"

"being necessary to the security of a free State"

The ONLY purpose of this letter is to tell us that Noah Webster is going to be defining what the 2nd amendment really means in his dictionary.

To Thomas Jefferson from Noah Webster, Jr., 12 Dec 1790

Hartford Decr 12th 1790
Sir
By the last mail I had the honor of recieving yours of the 4th current. I am much obliged by the polite manner in which you express your sentiments of my opinions, and by your frendly suggestion respecting a second recording of my Institute. On examining the date of my first record, I find the six months not yet elapsed—the date is June 22—so that by forwarding a copy with this, it will reach you before the expiration of 6 months, viz. the 22d Instant. As soon as you recieve it, Sir, I will thank you for a certificate dated prior to the 22d. A more correct copy may afterwards be lodged in your office in exchange for this.

There seems, Sir, to be some misapprehension between us, respecting the opinions advanced in your Notes and my Essays. You suppose I have mistaken your arguments respecting the Constitution of Virginia or at least the design of them—On reviewing your arguments and my answer, I do not find the ground of the supposition. I must have understood your design as now explained, for I begin my remarks on your argument, with a passage of yours in which you express the same opinion as is contained in your letter. You repeat in your letter the opinion advanced in the Notes, that "there are some fundamental rights which a state ought not to place in the power of an ordinary legislature." It is this opinion which I have combated in my Essays. However it is not material—if I have mistaken your design, I hope I have not given any false coloring to your argument.

I will not trouble you with a controversy on a political question, to which I am wholly incompetent. A respect for your talents would prevent me, were there no other consideration. My opinion on the great question between us is simply this—That a state is a corporation whose power is always equal, but cannot be exercised but by delegation—That the will of the state exists no where but in the resolves of its delegates, because the opinions of the members of the corporation can be no where else combined—That the will of the state however, thus declared by the decrees of its delegates, is the only rule of action for the state—That this will is always equal to itself and of equally binding force whether denominated constitution, law, statute or ordinance—That the members of the corporation cannot express the will of the corporation, without a meeting for the purpose, and as this is impossible, no instructions of individual members can be binding upon the delegation; consequently no specific powers can be delegated, nor specific rights reserved by the state; for the will of the state exists only in the will of the delegation—That both policy and right require that the delegation should at all times possess the whole power of the state for the purpose of preventing all possible wrong and obtaining all possible good—That every right claimed by a citizen of a free government is liable to vary with circumstances; except what rest wholly on the moral law; that therefore every right, created by political law, should be always subject to be modified by the power that created it, viz. the will of the state, which is always the will of the delegation.—That in short, the election and organization of the body which is to express the will of the state, is the only power which the people and a convention can exercise, and the only power which an ordinary legislature can not.

Are my ideas too speculative? Perhaps so, but I have lived the most of my life in a state where they are mostly realized. The constitution of Connecticut is however a very bad one; not because the legislature cannot reform it; but because they dare not. An idea of some constitutional powers, paramount to their own, in the government, together with habit; prevents a reformation of the worst evils that can befal a government: a union of the legislativ with the judicial powers and a want of a supreme executiv[388]. A bold stroke will be necessary to cut up the evil[389]—and a bold stroke will, ere many years[390], be made for the purpose.

Excuse, Sir, the length of this letter, and give yourself no trouble in replying. Your office has a demand upon your attention which no individual has a right to interfere with.

Enclosed is a Copy of the "Little Readers Assistant" which I beg leave to lodge in your office, in compliance with the **copy right**[391] act

---

[388] Eventually the executive will me in charge of regulating arms

[389] Hiding the 2nd amendment.

[390] It will be in limbo for a long time , but misunderstood or er

[391] Right being the 2nd amendment, and the definitions are compliant with its truth.

of **Congress** having lately recorded the title **for securing the property**. As a school book, it is getting into use, and tho it may **never be so generally used**[392] as the **Institute, yet it may diffuse some useful truths**[393]; **which is my primary object in all my publications**[394]. The farmers catechizm at the end[395], I design to improve in a future impression. I am, Sir, with perfect respect your most obliged and hum Servant

Webster Noah Published the "Little Readers Assistant in 1791 which is really just a dictionary.

---

[392] Not generally = not Militia, one man army but a general in that he is self regulating.

[393] He is referring to definitions which can be directly attributed to the 2nd amendment. "Liberty" The "primary" object is a reference to the "first definition found. After two hundred years the order may have been changed, but for Liberty = "1. the quality or state of being free" ",to the security of a free state" This is no coincidence. Noah Webster was enlisted to help out with the correct interpretation of the 2nd Amendment. "1. Arms: to furnish or equip with weapons. It is a generic. 1: People "to supply or fill with people." This fits perfectly because it is more in line with being a variable populated with a subset. It is not ALL the people. Regulate 1 to govern or direct according to rule"well : 1: in a skillful or expert manner

[394] The object is the hidden truth of the second amendment , and all his publications are a reference to his ciphered letters which have been hidden in plain sight, as this one is.

[395] A farmer plants things, and in the dictionary at the end of **Catechism** something resembling a catechism especially in being a rote response or **formulaic statement.** The 2nd amendment in its entirety is essentially a formula with variables.

To William Stephen Smith Paris, Nov. 13, 1787

DEAR SIR,

-- I am now to acknoledge the receipt of your favors of October the 4th, 8th, & 26th. In the last you apologise for your letters of introduction to Americans coming here. It is so far from needing apology on your part, that it calls for thanks on mine. I endeavor to shew civilities to all the Americans who come here, & will give me opportunities of doing it: and it is a matter of comfort to know from a good quarter what they are, & how far I may go in my attentions to them. Can you send me Woodmason's bills for the two copying presses for the M. de la Fayette, & the M. de Chastellux? **The latter makes one article in a considerable account, of old standing, and which I cannot present for want of this article.** -- I do not know whether it is to yourself or Mr. Adams I am to give my thanks **for the copy of the new constitution**. I beg leave through you to place them where due. It will be yet three weeks before I shall receive them from America. **There are very good articles in it: & very bad**. I do not know which preponderate. What we have lately read in the history of Holland, in the chapter on the Stadtholder, would have sufficed to set me against a chief magistrate eligible for a long duration, if I had ever been disposed towards one: & what we have always read of the elections of Polish kings should have forever excluded the idea of one continuable for life. Wonderful is the effect of impudent & persevering lying. The British ministry have so long hired their gazetteers to repeat and model into every form lies about our being in anarchy, that the world has at length believed them, the English nation has believed them, the ministers themselves have come to believe them, & what is more wonderful, we have believed them ourselves. Yet where does this anarchy exist? Where did it ever exist, except in the single instance of Massachusetts? And can history produce an instance of rebellion so honourably conducted? I say nothing of it's motives. They were founded in ignorance[396], not wickedness. God forbid we should ever be 20 years without such a rebellion. **The people cannot be all, & always, well informed. The part which is wrong will be discontented in proportion to the importance**

---

[396] The people that want arms for themselves aren't fully aware of the damage it will do to society at large back in the late 18th century.

of the facts they misconceive[397]. **If they remain quiet under such misconceptions it is a lethargy, the forerunner of death to the public liberty**[398]. We have had 13. states independent 11. years. There has been one rebellion. That comes to one rebellion in a century & a half for each state. What country before ever existed a century & half without a rebellion? & **what country can preserve it's liberties if their rulers are not warned from time to time that their people preserve the spirit of resistance?**[399] **Let them take arms.**[400] The remedy is to set them **right** as to facts, pardon & pacify them.[401] What signify a few lives lost in a century or two?[402] **The tree of liberty must be refreshed from time to time with the blood of patriots & tyrants.**[403] It

---

[397] 2nd amendment will become more and more confusing as the effects of "gun violence" are experienced in society. He wants a rebellion from the people themselves, simply because they no longer want arms violence. He has "admitted" that there is a "part" that will be wrong, and that there is something that is "misconceived". Why is he not actually saying explicitly what that part is?

[398] He is explicit though that it has to do with "death". He even makes a reference as to "it" being the forerunner to death? We now know the true utility of the 2nd amendment, and what his real reference is. Public Liberty, is simply a reference to ALL of society, not the individual. It is the public peace where gun violence is only an anomaly, and not something that is reported like the daily weather.

[399] The "spirit" has no substance, it is the thing imagined. It is fear, and it is in every man. It is in this same sentence that Liberties are tied to the entire country, and not the individual. What is key here is the word "WARNED" It is used in the context of "his time" WARNING "our time". It is the founding fathers "warning" or "telling" the "rulers" or government of a future period.

[400] Collect the dangerous Arms from the public domain. The misconception is now over as to the true utility of the 2nd amendment.

[401] The "right" in the bill of rights. The facts are its true utility, in fact this very book. He wants everyone to be united, and all sides of the political spectrum to remain calm, and to forgive those that were most adamant about protecting the 2nd amendment as it was known.

[402] 2.25 five centuries to be more specific.

[403] He states only two times. The first is the anticipated ratification of the Bill of Rights and "activation" of a 2nd amendment as "bought" by the other delegates who were fast to read. The next time was Dec 2, 2015 when the 2nd

is it's natural manure. Our Convention has been too much impressed by the insurrection of Massachusetts: and in the spur of the moment they are setting up a kite[404] to keep the hen-yard in order. I hope in God this article will be rectified before the new constitution is accepted. – You ask me if any thing transpires here on the subject of S. America? Not a word. I know that there are combustible materials there, and that they wait the torch only. But this country probably will join the extinguishers. – The want of facts worth communicating to you has occasioned me to give a little loose to dissertation. We must be contented to amuse,[405] when we cannot inform.[406]

(Sent from Thomas Jefferson)

This is "tree of liberty" letter that I have quoted many times as an example of two different interpretations within the cipher. There is more to it, which further validates its reference directly to the 2nd amendment and much of the narrative as to why it had to be encrypted. There are more encryptions in here which I'm certain are consistent with the narrative.

Thomas Jefferson was doing his part with the ciphers at the same time the Federalist papers were being written by Alexander Hamilton, James Madison and John Jay. It is proof that he was joined with the others in their efforts to provide evidence and further validate what they were really up too and why. Now after reading the footnotes regarding this letter, I would ask that you ponder this. William Stephen Smith was a New York state representative, a Federalist and the husband of John Adams daughter. This man, as a federalist, would have been in favor of the "convention' of the 2nd amendment as it is now known to you. He would have been an ideal confident because of his politics and being married

---

amendment was finally read objectively in the public domain. The patriots are gun violence victims, and tyrants simply the perpetrators of gun violence because there was no check and balance against their power. Their blood now numbers over 1,000,000 during these two times. It will still continue to flow on mass until this book reaches the masses which of course must include SCOTUS so they can align their rulings with the constitution. Hence, "must be refreshed".

[404] Kite reference again threading these ciphers together over 80 years.

[405] 'amuse' as in he cannot be explicit because this is a cipher, but in the process of deciphering, as I'm doing now ,we (the future) can now be informed.

[406] The further elaborates on "contented" by saying that he absolutely CANNOT be explicit, simply because this very letter must also exist in his own time.

into the family of John Adams. It is even possible that he never received this letter, since just illustrating a man's qualities and circumstance would have its own utility to the cipher. This "device" has been used many times before, especially by Benjamin Franklin, who was of course the dean of the "Ciphering Institute". . In any event, the letter was preserved, and archived.

Thomas Jefferson to John Payne Todd, 15 August 1816

Monticello Aug. 15. 16.

You have given me, my dear Payne, a very handsome keep-sake which has amused me much, and not the less by the puzzle it has afforded me, to find out the method of rectifying it. I at length discovered it, and that it was only necessary to loosen a little a single screw to throw it out of geer, and to throw it in again after setting the index. it was exactly 10° wrong. it is indeed a very convenient travelling thermometer.

You must now accept a keep-sake from me, which may suit you as a sportsman, better than myself who have ceased to be one. I send by the stage, to be lodged for you at Orange C. H. a box containing a pair of Turkish pistols. they were originally with wheel-locks[407], which not being convenient[408], I had locks of the modern form substituted[409], but so that they can be changed for the former in a moment. they are 20. inch barrels so well made that I never missed a squirrel 30. yards with them. I fixed one in a wooden holster to hang in the loop of the pommel of my saddle to be handily taken out & in, having used it daily while I had a horse who would stand fire. [410]I had other holsters also made for both[411] to hang them at the side of my carriage for road use; & with locks & staples to secure them from being handled by curious people[412]. one of the

---

[407] Note the use of the hyphen, which is synonymous with "well-reguated' as it was used from the Virginia Declaration of Rights.

[408] The use of the hyphen was not "convenient" in the 2nd amendment because 'well-regulated' has NOTHING to do with the 2nd amendment. Once the hyphen is removed then "well regulated" in the form of statutes has a much better utility.

[409] The 2nd amendment is more "modern" than the Virginia Declaration of Rights with respect to the chronology of its publication.

[410] Out and In is the well regulation of Arms in society. If they are causing harm then they must be brought back in from their out location.

[411] Both is a reference to "Arms and People" as variables. They are "both" hidden in the word Militia.

[412] Holsters are what the secret was hidden in such as the word "Militia" and "State", and they were hidden so as to not make people curious or suspicious.

wheel locks is a little out of order[413], and will require a skilful gunsmith[414] to put to rights[415] it is now cocked[416], and I could not find out how to discharge it[417].

the key is with them[418]; and they wind up to the right, or with the sun[419]. in the hope they will afford you sport[420] in your daily rides, I pray you to accept the assurance of my friendship & respect and to present the same to the president and mrs Madison.

TH: Jefferson

This letter has the exact same utility as James Madison's letter that I've labeled "The well regulated fallacy", which can be found further along. Where James Madison explains it in a round-about way, Thomas Jefferson enciphers it in this letter. John Todd Payne was the step son of James Madison who went by the name Payne Todd as well. The name John is derived from "Gracious", "Todd" means fox as in sly as a fox and Payne is phonetically the same as 'pain'. Note the usage of a hyphen in the first sentence which was has been read into the meaning the words "well regulated" as found in the 2nd amendment by the other delegates and historians alike. The reason why the 'keep-sake' is handsome is

---

[413] Again a reference to the 'wheel-locks" now being "out of order". The hyphen doesn't exist in "well regulated" so of course it would have NOTHING to do with "well-ordered" or "well-regulated". Also, the 2nd amendment is now much more useful and accurate. The "wiggle" room in this adjustment, or subjective reading of it is no longer causing "Payne", aka "Pain". It is now read objectively and is a far more useful thing. It has been fixed.

[414] I am the skilful gunsmith that he speaks of, who ironically has a last name Smith. I'm not one who usually

[415] Put its legitimate meaning back into the Bill of Rights.

[416] At this point in time, it's ready to figure out, being the puzzle.

[417] It's a hint, to look closer at this. In reality why would a man tell another that he couldn't figure out how to fire a gun? Now why would an older man tell a younger man such thing when ones dignity is held in jeopardy? If this letter is not a cipher then perhaps this is the most astonishing discovery I have ever made because at this time, Thomas Jefferson was 72, and John Payne was 25 years of age.

[418] The 2nd amendment is a "key".

[419] They key will shed light as the sun does on the history and truth.

[420] Sport in that you must play with the key to make it work with the letters or solve it.

because it is a clue as to the true nature of the 2nd amendment, and it's a puzzle because it requires solving. Also note the unusual way in which this this letter was started. There is no "Sir" or "Dear John Payne", which is generally a no brainer where letter writing is concerned. As a cipher, we can translate what Thomas Jefferson is saying which is "The pain you are causing my nation can be resolved with this puzzle". In the next sentence we then see the word "necessary" being used because once the screw is loosened the attachment of 'well-regulated Militia' to the word "State" is now removed within the necessary clause. The 2nd amendment has now become a measuring device, an instrument or in other words, a thermometer. The clause "being necessary to the security of a free State" must always read in the context of "bunny rabbits and butterflies". Society must be at peace and the travelling thermometer can be used throughout time to maintain the peace because the guns themselves will now be on trial. History is not required to derive the meaning of the 2nd amendment.

It appears that Thomas Jefferson has linked his cipher to one of Benjamin Franklins where he talks of his "kite" experiment. It is similar because both of these ciphers use primitive guns which are also symbolic of an "older, more primitive" 2nd amendment which can be improved upon, or fixed. The gun used from Benjamin Franklin's cipher 64 YEARS EALIER referenced a "matchlock" where this references a "wheel lock", but precursors to the then modern day flintlock.

John Payne Todd to Thomas Jefferson, 31 August 1816

From John Payne Todd
Mont Pelier Augt 31st 16.
My Dear Sir,
A week after the valuable letter you honored [me]1 with, I received your highly prized present, a pr of Turkish Pistols of curious workmanship[421] which shall be preserved with all that devotedness of respect and affection I feel for you[422]—Until the present moment I had hoped to have paid you my respects and thanked you in person

---

[421] Workmanship is the word "Militia" with the words people and Arms within it.

[422] It's persevered, because it's both hidden and cannot be removed. Its locked in.

but learning from Mr Rush of your intended visit to Bedford I am induced to pospone this pleasure; in the mean time I beg you to be assured of my wishes for a continuance of your health [and]2 of my very affectionate tho' respectful attachment[423].

    J. Payne Todd.

---

[423] Its hoped that it will be discovered for a continuance health because the 2nd is a mandate to create reality based Arms control laws.

Thomas Jefferson Inaugural Address, Wednesday, March 4, 1801

As astonishing as this may sound the inaugural address of Thomas Jefferson was meant more for you the reader, than it was meant for the people at the dawn of the 19th century. He and the others of the cabal knew that this transcript would be an important historical document and be preserved for the future. It appears that other inaugural addresses had encryptions as well, including those of George Washington.

First Inaugural Address Given at the Capitol Building, Washington, DC Wednesday, March 4, 1801

Friends and Fellow Citizens: Called upon to undertake the duties of the first executive office of our country, I avail myself of the presence of that portion of my fellow citizens which is here assembled to express my grateful thanks for the favor with which they have been pleased to look toward me[424], to declare a sincere consciousness that the task is above my talents, and that I approach it with those anxious and awful presentiments which the greatness of the charge and the weakness of my powers so justly inspire[425].

A rising nation, spread over a wide and fruitful land, traversing all the seas with the rich productions of their industry, engaged in commerce with nations who feel power and forget right, advancing rapidly to destinies beyond the reach of mortal eye -- when I contemplate these transcendent objects, and see the honor, the happiness, and the hopes of this beloved country committed to the issue, and the auspices of this day[426], I shrink from the

---

[424] The portion of citizens appears to be any American that is reading this right now. I say this because of what he says next. It would be pleasing because we are discovering the truth of something that has caused the nation so much heart ache and troubles, and loss of liberty.

[425] He knows of the harm the 2nd amendment will have caused, but also states that he could do nothing about it in his day. He was not empowered to use the 2nd amendment because it still would have been much to soon to reveal it with in his time.

[426] This day is a reference to right now. It is the "day" when the 2nd amendment is truly needed. He does not know the exact circumstances and extent of the troubles but he has hope that all will sort itself out. The

contemplation, and humble myself before the magnitude of the undertaking. Utterly, indeed, should I despair did not the presence of many whom I here see remind me that in the other high authorities provided by our Constitution I shall find resources of wisdom, of virtue, and of zeal on which to rely under all difficulties[427].

To you, then, gentlemen, who are charged with the sovereign functions of legislation, and to those associated with you, I look with encouragement for that guidance and support which may enable us to steer with safety the vessel in which we are all embarked amidst the conflicting elements of a troubled world[428]. During the contest of opinion through which we have passed the animation of discussions and of exertions has sometimes worn an aspect which might impose on strangers unused to think freely and to speak and to write what they think;[429] but this being now decided by the voice of the nation, announced according to the rules of the Constitution, all will, of course, arrange themselves under the will of the law, and unite in common efforts for the common good[430]. All, too, will bear in mind this sacred principle,[431] that though the will of the majority is in all cases to prevail, that will to be rightful[432] must be reasonable; that the minority possess their equal rights, which equal law must protect, and to violate would be oppression.

---

transcendant Objects are "people and arms" in the 2nd amendment which are finally recognized objectively within the word "Militia"

[427] He is asking that the congress, the senate and the judiciary to be virtuous , and work together to set things right for all the people and stabilize this new knowledge. He knows that this will probably irritate more than a few of the citizens.

[428] The vessel is the 2nd amendment again, and the troubled world, are the rumblings of anarchy , disunion and chaos.

[429] He recognizes that there will be many dissenters

[430] The common good is the very essence of the 2nd amendment. Its rhetoric is think of your neighbours first, as opposed to every man for himself.

[431] Note the words here use bear, sacred and principle.

[432] Rightful, equal law, minority..the 2nd amendment is all about the rights for everybody, the rights of everybody not to be oppressed by any man, who with arms would be able to violate. Note the term "would be". He is saying that lethal arms must be allowed to be introduced into society in the first place.

Let us, then, fellow citizens, unite with one heart and one mind[433]. Let us restore to social intercourse that harmony and affection without which liberty and even life itself are but dreary things[434]. And let us reflect that, having banished from our land that religious intolerance under which mankind so long bled and suffered, we have yet gained little if we countenance a political intolerance as despotic, as wicked, and capable of as bitter and bloody persecutions. During the throes and convulsions of the ancient world, during the agonizing spasms of infuriated man, seeking through blood and slaughter his long-lost liberty, it was not wonderful that the agitation of the billows should reach even this distant and peaceful shore; that this should be more felt and feared by some and less by others, and should divide opinions as to measures of safety. But every difference of opinion is not a difference of principle. We have called by different names brethren of the same principle. We are all Republicans, we are all Federalists. If there be any among us who would wish to dissolve this Union or to change its republican form, let them stand undisturbed as monuments of the safety with which error of opinion may be tolerated where reason is left free to combat it.

I know, indeed, that some honest men fear that a republican government can not be strong, that this Government is not strong enough; but would the honest patriot, in the full tide of successful experiment, abandon a government which has so far kept us free and firm on the theoretic and visionary fear that this Government, the world's best hope, may by possibility want energy to preserve itself?[435] I trust not. I believe this, on the contrary, the strongest

---

[433] Lets all get onto the same page.

[434] Implement 2nd amendments and begin healing the nation and restoring liberty for all.

[435] This is interesting. The United States constitution is still very new, and the country is still very young in 1801. Thomas Jefferson obviously knew that it would have been premature to illuminate the truth of the 2nd amendment because the people needed time to experience the checks and balances of the constitution. He references the experiment. He is saying to all current Americans to remain patriotic to your country, and though he doesn't know it, Americans have now

Government on earth. I believe it the only one where every man, at the call of the law, would fly to the standard of the law, and would meet invasions of the public order as his own personal concern.

Sometimes it is said that man can not be trusted with the government of himself. Can he, then, be trusted with the government of others? Or have we found angels in the forms of kings to govern him? Let history answer this question. Let us, then, with courage and confidence pursue our own Federal and Republican principles, our attachment to union and representative government. Kindly separated by nature and a wide ocean from the exterminating havoc of one quarter of the globe; too high-minded to endure the degradations of the others; possessing a chosen country, with room enough for our descendants to the thousandth and thousandth generation; entertaining a due sense of our equal right to the use of our own faculties, to the acquisitions of our own industry, to honor and confidence from our fellow citizens, resulting not from birth, but from our actions and their sense of them; enlightened by a benign religion, professed, indeed, and practiced in various forms, yet all of them inculcating honesty, truth, temperance, gratitude, and the love of man; acknowledging and adoring an overruling Providence, which by all its dispensations proves that it delights in the happiness of man here and his greater happiness hereafter – with all these blessings, what more is necessary to make us a happy and a prosperous people?

Still one thing more, fellow citizens – a wise and frugal Government, which shall restrain men from injuring one another[436], shall leave them otherwise free to regulate their own pursuits of industry and improvement, and shall not take from the mouth of labor the bread it has earned[437]. This is the sum of good government, and this is necessary to close the circle of our felicities. About to enter, fellow-citizens, on the exercise of duties which comprehend everything dear and valuable to you, it is proper you should understand what I deem the essential principles of our

---

had over 200 years to experience those checks and balances of the constitutions.

[436] Keep out the dangerous arms.

[437] Everyman is entitled to the liberty to work and have a living wage.

Government, and consequently those which ought to shape its Administration

I will compress them within the narrowest compass they will bear, stating[438] the general principle, but not all its limitations. Equal and exact justice to all men, of whatever state or persuasion[439], religious or political; peace, commerce, and honest friendship with all nations, entangling alliances with none; the support of the State governments in all their rights, as the most competent administrations for our domestic concerns and the surest bulwarks against antirepublican tendencies; the preservation of the General Government in its whole constitutional vigor, as the sheet anchor of our peace at home[440] and safety abroad; a jealous care of the right of election by the people -- a mild and safe corrective of abuses which are lopped by the sword of revolution where peaceable remedies are unprovided; absolute acquiescence in the decisions of the majority, the vital principle of republics, from which is no appeal but to force, the vital principle and immediate parent of despotism; a well disciplined militia, our best reliance in peace and for the first moments of war, till regulars may relieve them; the supremacy of the civil over the military authority; economy in the public expense, that labor may be lightly burthened; the honest payment of our debts and sacred preservation of the public faith; encouragement of agriculture, and of commerce as its handmaid; the diffusion of information and arraignment of all abuses at the bar of the public reason; freedom of religion; freedom of the press, and freedom of person under the protection of the habeas corpus, and trial by juries impartially selected.

These principles form the bright constellation which has gone before us and guided our steps through an age of revolution and reformation. The wisdom of our sages and blood of our heroes have

---

[438] Curious grouping of words here isn't it? Ironically I thought of the 2nd amendment as a compass to guide USA back to a place of real liberty. The "narrowest compass" that TJ refers to here is the 2nd amendment. There is NO wiggle room in its direction, because its very difficult to wiggle in a confined space.

[439] Being either side of the gun debate issue.

[440] Federal government is in charge of the military and arms within the nation to protect the people.

been devoted to their attainment. They should be the creed of our political faith, the text of civic instruction, the touchstone by which to try the services of those we trust; and should we wander from them in moments of error or of alarm, let us hasten to retrace our steps and to regain the road which alone leads to peace, liberty, and safety. I repair, then, fellow-citizens, to the post you have assigned me.

With experience enough in subordinate offices to have seen the difficulties of this the greatest of all, I have learnt to expect that it will rarely fall to the lot of imperfect man to retire from this station with the reputation and the favor which bring him into it. Without pretensions to that high confidence you reposed in our first and greatest revolutionary character, whose preeminent services had entitled him to the first place in his country's love and destined for him the fairest page in the volume of faithful history, I ask so much confidence only as may give firmness and effect to the legal administration of your affairs.

I shall often go wrong through defect of judgment. When right, I shall often be thought wrong by those whose positions will not command a view of the whole ground. I ask your indulgence for my own errors, which will never be intentional, and your support against the errors of others, who may condemn what they would not if seen in all its parts. The approbation implied by your suffrage is a great consolation to me for the past, and my future solicitude will be to retain the good opinion of those who have bestowed it in advance, to conciliate that of others by doing them all the good in my power, and to be instrumental to the happiness and freedom of all.

Relying, then, on the patronage of your good will, I advance with obedience to the work, ready to retire from it whenever you become sensible how much better choice it is in your power to make[441]. And may that Infinite Power which rules the destinies of the universe lead our councils to what is best[442], and give them a favorable issue[443] for your peace and prosperity.

---

[441] America is now empowered, in fact mandated, to protect the people from arms.

[442] Think of your fellow man first as god would like you to do.

443 A favourable issue is of course arms that are not lethal to society in order to keep peace.

To Dr. Benjamin Rush Monticello, September 23, 1800

DEAR SIR,

-- I have to acknowledge the receipt of your favor of Aug. 22, and to congratulate you on the healthiness of your city. Still Baltimore, Norfolk & Providence admonish us that we are not clear of our new scourge. When great evils happen, I am in the habit of looking out for what good may arise from them as consolations to us, and Providence has in fact so established the order of things, as that most evils are the means of producing some good[444]. The yellow fever will discourage the growth of great cities in our nation[445], & I view great cities as pestilential to the morals[446], the health and the liberties of man[447]. True, they nourish some of the elegant arts, but the useful ones can thrive elsewhere, and less perfection in the others, with more health, virtue & freedom, would be my choice.

I agree with you entirely, in condemning the mania[448] of giving names to objects of any kind after persons still living[449]. Death alone can seal the title of any man to this honor[450], by putting it out of his power to forfeit it. There is one other mode of recording merit, which I have often thought might be introduced, so as to gratify the living by praising the dead. In giving, for instance, a commission of chief justice to Bushrod Washington, it should be in consideration of his integrity, and science in the laws[451], and of the services rendered to

---

[444] The 2A in its hidden form is of course an evil, but in time after the people have been demonstrated the folly of gun violence it will then become a good.

[445] "Yellow belly", or fearfull existed in the late 18th century so this could be symbolism for fear.

[446] Great cities are a symbolism for the masses, under the influence of the 2A. People want their Arms for protection

[447] .Health and lost liberty are the results of gun violence.

[448] It is the desire to classify any type of weaponry as being Arms.

[449] This appears to be calling all weapons "Arms" after which is a normalization of varying types irrespective of their lethality by those still living, in spite of the death they had just caused in society.

[450] "title" in terms of ownership which is his Arms.

[451] The 2nd amendment is an equation (science) which mandates creating laws

our country by his illustrious relation, &c. A commission to a descendant of Dr. Franklin[452], besides being in consideration of the proper qualifications of the person, should add that of the great services rendered by his illustrious ancestor, Bn Fr, by the advancement of science, by inventions useful to man[453], &c. I am not sure that we ought to change all our names. And during the regal government, sometimes, indeed, they were given through adulation; but often also as the reward of the merit of the times, sometimes for services rendered the colony. Perhaps, too, a name when given, should be deemed a sacred property[454].

I promised you a letter on Christianity, which I have not forgotten. On the contrary, it is because I have reflected on it, that I find much more time necessary for it than I can at present dispose of. I have a view of the subject which ought to displease neither the rational Christian nor Deists, and would reconcile many to a character they have too hastily rejected. I do not know that it would reconcile the _genus irritabile vatum_ who are all in arms against me. Their hostility is on too interesting ground to be softened. The delusion into which the **X. Y. Z.** plot shewed it possible to push the people; the successful experiment made under the prevalence of that delusion on the clause of the constitution, which, while it secured the freedom of the press, covered also the freedom of religion, had given to the clergy a very favorite hope of obtaining an establishment of a particular form of Christianity thro' the U. S.; and as every sect believes its own form the true one, every one perhaps hoped for his own, but especially the Episcopalians& Congregationalists. The returning good sense of our country threatens abortion to their hopes, & they believe that any portion of power confided to me, will be exerted in opposition to their schemes. And they believe rightly;

---

[452] Descendant of Benjamin Franklin is a symbolism for the future people when the 2nd Amendment will be known.

[453] This might be a symbolism for the person in the future that discovers the nature of the 2nd amendment.

[454] I'm certain there is something going on in here. I'm still trying to figure out the "names" theme. Dr. Benjamin Franklins inventions that are useful to man I believe relates to his invention of the 2nd amendment. This one letter could tell us he is the original author.

for I have sworn upon the altar of god, eternal hostility against every form of tyranny over the mind of man. But this is all they have to fear from me: & enough too in their opinion, & this is the cause of their printing lying pamphlets against me, forging conversations for me with Mazzei, Bishop Madison,& c., which are absolute falsehoods without a circumstance of truth to rest on; falsehoods, too, of which I acquit Mazzei & Bishop Madison, for they are men of truth.

But enough of this: it is more than I have before committed to paper on the subject of all the lies that has been preached and printed against me. I have not seen the work of Sonnoni which you mention, but I have seen another work on Africa, (Parke's,) which I fear will throw cold water on the hopes of the friends of freedom. You will hear an account of an attempt at insurrection in this state. I am looking with anxiety to see what will be it's effect on our state. We are truly to be pitied. I fear we have little chance to see you at the Federal city or in Virginia, and as little at Philadelphia. It would be a great treat to receive you here. But nothing but sickness could effect that; so I do not wish it. For I wish you health and happiness, and think of you with affection.

Adieu.

Thomas Jefferson

This letter points to Thomas Jefferson's active participation in the American Philosophical Society. He also is in full understanding of the Federalist Papers and their direct association with the 2nd Amendment. He endorses them whole heartedly. I have also encountered another importance piece of literature written by a friend of his Colonel John Taylor who wrote "Construction Construed and Constitution Vindicated". This work also validates this new narrative of history through the word play of its author.

Thomas Jefferson to James Madison 20 Dec. 1787

Papers 12:440

I will now add what I do not like. First the omission of a bill of rights providing clearly and without the aid of sophisms for freedom of religion, freedom of the press, protection against standing armies, restriction against monopolies, the eternal and unremitting force of the habeas corpus laws, and trials by jury in all matters of fact triable by the laws of the land and not by the law of Nations. To say, as Mr. Wilson does that a bill of rights was not necessary because all is reserved in the case of the general government which is not given, while in the particular ones all is given which is not reserved might do for the Audience to whom it was addressed, **but is surely gratis dictum, opposed by strong inferences from the body of the instrument, as well as from the omission of the clause of our present confederation which had declared that in express terms**. It was a hard conclusion to say because there has been no uniformity among the states as to the cases triable by jury, because some have been so incautious as to abandon this mode of trial, therefore the more prudent states shall be reduced to the same level of calamity. It would have been much more just and wise to have concluded the other way that as most of the states had judiciously preserved this **palladium**, those who had wandered should be brought back to it, **and to have established general right instead of general wrong**. Let me add that a bill of rights is what the people are entitled to against every government on earth, **general or particular**, and what no just government should refuse, or rest on inference.

There are a few symbolisms here. I believe "general or particular" alludes to the dual purpose of the Bill of Rights. "general" appears to be a direct reference to the world "Militia". Particular references each of the first 10 amendments and validates that nothing has changed in the revelation of them having a secondary meaning. Both are allowed to live harmoniously and both are there to benefit and validate the rights of all the people.

Letter to James Madison November 18, 1788

DEAR SIR,

My last to you was of the 31st. of July: since which I have received yours of July 24. Aug. 10. And 23. The first part of this long silence in me was occasioned by a knoledge that you were absent from N. York; the latter part, by a want of opportunity, which has been longer than usual: Mr. Shippen being just arrived here, and to set out tomorrow for London, I avail myself of that channel of conveiance. Mr. Carrington was so kind as to send me the 2d. vol. of the Amer. phil. transactions, the federalist, and some other interesting pamphlets; and I am to thank you for another copy of the federalist and the report of the instructions to the ministers for negotiating peace. The latter unluckily omitted exactly the passage I wanted, which was what related to the navigation of the Missisipi. With respect to the Federalist, the three authors had been named to me. I read it with care, pleasure and improvement, and was satisfied there was nothing in it by one of those hands, and not a great deal by a second. **It does the highest honor to the third, as being, in my opinion, the best commentary on the principles of government which ever was written.**[455] In some parts it is discoverable that the author means only to say what may be best said in defence of opinions in which he did not concur.[456] But in general it establishes firmly the plan of government. I confess it has rectified me in several points. As to the bill of rights however I still think it should be added, and I am glad to see that three states have at length considered the perpetual re-eligibility of the president as an article which should be amended.[457] I should deprecate with you indeed the meeting of a

---

[455]

[456]

[457] This is a reference to the 3 branches of government. "re-eligibility" of president as an article is a reference to the 4th article of the original Bill of Rights. The president should be in charge of all things military, he should be allowed to protect the people from both from foreign armies, and internal ones, and there is

new convention. I hope they will adopt the mode of amendment by Congress and the Assemblies, in which case I should not fear any dangerous innovation in the plan. But the minorities are too respectable not to be entitled to some sacrifice of opinion in the majority. Especially when a great proportion of them would be contented with a bill of rights.—Here things internally are going on well[458]. The Notables, now in session, have indeed past one vote which augurs ill to the rights of the people. But if they do not obtain now so much as they have a right to, they will in the long run.[459] The misfortune is that they are not yet ripe for receiving the blessings to which they are entitled.[460] I doubt, for instance, whether the body of the nation, if they could be consulted, would accept of a Habeas corpus law, if offered them by the king. If the Etats generaux, when they assemble, do not aim at too much, they may begin a good constitution. There are three articles which they may easily obtain. 1. their own meeting periodically. 2. the exclusive right of taxation. 3. the right of registering laws and proposing amendments to them as exercised now by the parliaments. This last would be readily approved by the court on account of their hostility against the parliaments, and would lead immediately to the origination of laws. The 2d. has been already solemnly avowed by the king: and it is well understood there would be no opposition to the first. If they push at much more, all may fail. I shall not enter futher into public details,

---

no better way to protect the liberty of all than to not lethal arms to the public in the first place.

[458] He as stating that people who believe they are entitled to arms, should also think of that sort of effect on the entire population. In essence the chaos and obstruction to life and liberty that gun violence can cause to all.

[459] In the long run, is a reference to the future. One day it will be discovered and finally this right will be revealed to all.

[460] The "misfortune" is of course an understatement in this authors opinion, but how could Thomas Jefferson have realized that it would take over 200 years this truth to be revealed. The misfortune is measured today as 88 gun deaths a day in America, and trending. Not yet ripe, is a reference to the newness of the nation, the newness of this constitution which will take the people time to evaluate. The argument that people would need to be armed to protect against a tyrant is a mute point in light of the true checks and balances of the constitution.

because my letter to Mr. Jay will give them. That contains a request of permission to return to America the next spring, for the summer only. The reasons therein urged, drawn from my private affairs are very cogent. But there is another more cogent on my mind, tho' of a nature not to be explained in a public letter. It is the necessity of attending my daughters myself to their own country, and depositing them safely in the hands of those with whom I can safely leave them. I have deferred this request as long as circumstances would permit, and am in hopes it will meet with no difficulty. I have had too many proofs of your friendship not to rely on your patronage of it, as, in all probability, nothing can suffer by a short absence. But the immediate permission is what I am anxious about; as by going in April and returning in October I shall be sure of pleasant and short passages out and in. I must intreat your attention, my friend, to this matter, and that the answers may be sent me thro' several channels. Mr. Limozin at Havre, sent you by mistake a package belonging to somebody else. I do not know what it contained, but he has written to you on the subject, and prayed me to do the same. He is likely to suffer if it be not returned.

Supposing that the funding their foreign debt will be among the first operations of the new government, I send you two estimates, the one by myself, the other by a gentleman infinitely better acquainted with the subject, shewing what fund will suffice to discharge the principal and interest as it shall become due, aided by occasional loans, which the same fund will repay. I inclose them to you, because collating them together, and with your own ideas, you will be able to devise something better than either. But something must be done. This government will expect, I fancy, a very satisfactory provision for the paiment of their debt , from the first session of the new Congress. Perhaps in this matter, as well as the arrangement of your foreign affairs, I may be able, when on the spot with you, to give some information and suggest some hints, which may render my visit to my native country not altogether useless. I consider as no small advantage the resuming the tone of mind of my constituents, which is lost by long absence, and can only be recovered by mixing with them: and shall particularly hope for much profit and pleasure, by contriving to pass as much time as possible with you. Should you have a trip to Virginia in contemplation for that year, I hope you will time it so as that we may be there together. I will camp you at Monticello where, if illy entertained otherwise, you shall not want that of books. In firm hope of a happy meeting with you in the spring or early in summer I conclude with assurances of the sincere esteem & attachment with which I am, Dear sir, Your affectionate friend & servt,

    TH: JEFFERSON

    P.S. The inclosed letters are extremely interesting to me, and recommended to your friendly and particular care.

From Thomas Jefferson to John Taylor, 26 November 1798

To John Taylor
November 26. 98.
Dear Sir
We formerly had a debtor & creditor account of letters on farming; but the high price of tobo. which is likely to continue for some short time, has tempted me to go entirely into that culture and in the mean time my farming schemes are in abeyance, and my farming fields at nurse against the time of my resuming them. but I owe you a political letter. **yet the** infidelities of the post office **and the circumstances of the times are against my writing fully & freely**[461]**, whilst my own dispositions are as much against writing mysteries, innuendos & half confidences.** I know not which mortifies me most, that I should fear to write what I think, **or my country bear such a state of things**[462]. yet Lyon's judges, and a jury of all nations, are objects of rational fear. we agree in all the essential ideas of your letter. **we agree particularly in the necessity of some reform, and of some better security**[463]**, for civil liberty**[464]**. but perhaps we do not see the existing circumstances in the same point of view. there are many considerations dehors of the state which will occur to you without enumeration**[465]**. I should not apprehend them if all was sound within.** but there is a most respectable part of our state who have been enveloped in the X.Y.Z. delusion[466], and who destroy our unanimity for the present moment[467]. this disease of the imagination will pass over[468], because the patients are essentially republican. indeed the

---

[461] He can't be explicit simply because there can be no suspicion.

[462] This is a someone curious use of words, especially in light of the previous sentence.

[463] "the security of free State".

[464] Merriam-Webster : liberty: "the quality or state of being free"

[465] Enumerated powers of government in the constitution

[466] The delusion is the separation of powers with respect to the federal government not being allowed to create arms regulations. The delusion is the 2nd amendment when read subjectively.

[467] The "present moment" lasted 224 years.

[468] People want to have arms because they are fearful of what might happen irrespective of what is happening throughout society.

Doctor⁴⁶⁹ is now on his way to cure it, in the guise of a taxgatherer⁴⁷⁰. but give time for the medicine to work, & for the repetition of stronger doses which must be administered. the principle of the present majority is excessive expence; money enough to fill all their maws, or it will not be worth the risk of their supporting. they cannot borrow a dollar in Europe, nor above 2. or 3. millions in America. this is not the fourth of the expences of this year, unprovided for. paper money would be perillous even to the paper-men. nothing then but excessive taxation can get us along. and this will carry reason & reflection to every man's door⁴⁷¹, and particularly in the hour of election⁴⁷². I wish it were possible to obtain a single amendment to our constitution; I would be willing to depend on that alone for the reduction of the administration of our government to the genuine principles of it's constitution; I mean an additional article taking from the federal government the power of borrowing. I now deny their power of making paper money or any thing else a legal tender. I know that to pay all proper expences within the year would, in case of war, be hard on us. but not so hard as ten wars instead of one. for wars would be reduced in that proportion. besides that the state governments would be free to lend their credit in borrowing quotas.1—for the present I should be for resolving the alien & sedition laws to be against the constitution & merely void, and for addressing the other states to obtain similar declarations: and I would not do any thing at this moment2 which should commit us further, but reserve ourselves to shape our future measures or no

---

⁴⁶⁹ Dr. Benjamin Franklin. This appears to be an acknowledgement that Benjamin Franklin was the true architect of the 2ⁿᵈ amendment. Remember his quote? "In this world there can nothing that can be said to be certain , but death and taxes".

⁴⁷⁰ The doctor is a symbolism, for he is treating the victims of gun violence. He is the tax gatherer in the sense of how society is being taxed due to gun violence. The medicine is the increasing scrutiny on the 2ⁿᵈ amendment because of arms violence.

⁴⁷¹ The reason is "why the 2ⁿᵈ amendment was hidden", and the reflection societies experience of it.

⁴⁷² The hour of "election" is right now, 224 years later, now that we know the 2ⁿᵈ amendment was the constitution.

measures, by the events which may happen. it is a singular phaenomenon, that while our state governments are the very best in the world without exception or comparison, our general government has, in the rapid course of 9. or 10. years, become more arbitrary, and has swallowed more of the public liberty than even that of England. I inclose you a column cut out of a London paper to shew you that the English tho charmed with our making their enemies our enemies, yet they blush and weep over our sedition law.—but I inclose you something more important. it is a petition for a reformation in the manner of appointing our juries, and a remedy against the jury of all nations, which is handing about here for signature and will be presented to your house. I know it will require but little ingenuity to make objections to the details of it's execution. but do not be discouraged by small difficulties make it as perfect as you can at a first assay, and depend on amending it's defects as they develope themselves in practice. I hope it will meet with your approbation & patronage. it is the only thing which can yield us a little present protection against the dominion of a faction, while circumstances are maturing for bringing & keeping the government in real unison with the spirit of their constituents. I am aware that the act of Congress has directed that juries shall be appointed by lot or otherwise as the laws now [at the date of the act]3 in force in the several states provide. the New England states have always had them elected by their selectmen, who are elected by the people. several or most of the other states have a large number appointed [I do not know how] to attend, out of whom 12. for each cause are taken by lot. this provision of Congress will render it necessary for our Senators or Delegates to apply for an amendatory law, accomodated to that prayed for in the petition. in the mean time I would pass the law as if the amendatory one existed, in reliance that, our select jurors attending, the federal judge will under a sense of right, direct the juries to be taken from among them. if he does not, or if Congress [refuses?] the amendatory law, it will serve as eye water for their constituents. health, happiness, safety, & esteem to yourself and my ever honored & antient friend mr Pendleton. Adieu.

    PrC (DLC); faint; at foot of first page: "Mr. Taylor." Enclosure: Petition to the General Assembly of Virginia, [2 or 3 Nov. 1798]. Other enclosure not identified, but see note below.

Infidelities of the post office: TJ had George Jefferson see that this letter was delivered safely to Taylor (George Jefferson to TJ, 3 Dec. 1798).

Ideas of your letter: see Taylor to TJ, 25 June 1798. The column cut out of a London paper enclosed by TJ has not been found, but on 3 Nov. 1798 the Philadelphia Aurora noted that the London Morning Chronicle had praised the strong position taken by the United States in its dispute with France but chided Congress for wishing "to shackle the liberty of the press." Such a position was to be expected in Russia or France, but it was scandalous and "fatal to liberty" for a representative government "to infringe a grand principle in order to reach a few base incendiaries."

Act of congress: see TJ to Madison, 26 Oct. 1798.

1. Sentence interlined.

2. Preceding three words interlined in place of "[for the present?]."

3. This and following set of brackets supplied by TJ.

In this letter Thomas Jefferson tells his friend outright that he will be writing in cipher when he says he won't be writing it freely because of the infidelities of the post office and circumstances of the times.

Thomas Jefferson Letter to John Taylor May 28, 1816

Thomas Jefferson
Monticello
May 28, 1816
Full Document
Academic Standards

DEAR SIR, On my return from a long journey and considerable absence from home, I found here the copy of your "Enquiry into the principles of our government," which you had been so kind as to send me; and for which I pray you to accept my thanks. The difficulties of getting new works in our situation, inland and without a single bookstore, are such as had prevented my obtaining a copy before; and letters which had accumulated during my absence, and were calling for answers, have not yet permitted me to give to the whole a thorough reading; yet certain that you and I could not think differently on the fundamentals of rightful government, I was impatient, and availed myself of the intervals of repose from the writing table, to obtain a cursory idea of the body of the work.

I see in it much matter for profound reflection; much which should confirm our adhesion, in practice, to the good principles of our constitution, and fix our attention on what is yet to be made good. The sixth section on the good moral principles of our government, I found so interesting and replete with sound principles, as to postpone my letter-writing to its thorough perusal and consideration. Besides much other good matter, it settles unanswerably the right of instructing representatives, and their duty to obey. The system of banking we have both equally and ever reprobated. I contemplate it as a blot left in all our constitutions, which, if not covered, will end in their destruction, which is already hit by the gamblers in corruption, and is sweeping away in its progress the fortunes and morals of our citizens. Funding I consider as limited, rightfully, to a redemption of the debt within the lives of a majority of the generation contracting it; every generation coming equally, by the laws of the Creator of the world, to the free possession of the earth he made for their subsistence, unincumbered by their predecessors, who, like them, were but tenants for life. You have successfully and completely pulverized Mr. Adams' system of orders, and his opening the mantle of republicanism to every government of laws, whether consistent or not with natural right. Indeed, it must be acknowledged, that the term republic is of very vague application in every language. Witness the self-styled republics of Holland, Switzerland, Genoa, Venice, Poland. Were I to assign to this term a precise and definite idea, I would say, purely and simply, it means a government by its citizens in mass, acting directly and personally, according to rules established by the majority; and that every other government is more or less republican, in proportion as it has in its composition more or less of this ingredient of the direct action of the citizens. Such a government is evidently restrained to very narrow limits of space and population. I doubt if it would be practicable beyond the extent of a New England township. The first shade from this pure element, which, like that of pure vital air, cannot sustain life of itself, would be where the powers of the government, being divided, should be exercised each by representatives chosen either pro hac vice, or for such short terms as should render secure the duty of expressing the will of their constituents. This I should consider as the nearest approach to a pure republic, which is practicable on a large scale of country or population. And we have examples of it in some of our States constitutions, which, if not poisoned by priest-craft, would prove its excellence over all mixtures with other elements; and, with only equal doses of poison, would still be the best. Other shades of republicanism may be found in other forms of government, where the executive, judiciary and legislative functions, and the different branches of the latter, are chosen by the people more or less directly, for longer terms of years or for life, or made hereditary; or where there are mixtures of authorities, some dependent on, and others independent of the people. The further the departure from direct and constant control by the citizens, the less has the government of the ingredient of republicanism; evidently none where the authorities are hereditary, as in France, Venice, &c., or self-chosen, as in Holland; and little, where for life, in proportion as the life continues in being after the act of election.

The purest republican feature in the government of our own State, is the House of Representatives. The Senate is equally so the first year, less the second, and so on. The Executive still less, because not chosen by the people directly. The Judiciary seriously anti-republican, because for life; and the national arm wielded, as you observe, by military leaders irresponsible but to themselves. Add to this the vicious constitution of our county courts (to whom the justice, the executive administration, the taxation, police, the military appointments of the county, and nearly all our daily concerns are confided), self-appointed, self-continued, holding their authorities for life, and with an impossibility of breaking in on the perpetual succession of any faction once possessed of the bench. They are in truth, the executive, the judiciary, and the military of their respective counties, and the sum of the counties makes the State. And add, also, that one half of our brethren who fight and pay taxes, are excluded, like Helots, from the rights of representation, as if society were instituted for the soil, and not for the men inhabiting it; or one half of these could dispose of the rights and the will of the other half, without their consent.

"What constitutes a State?
Not high-raised battlements, or labor'd mound,

Thick wall, or moated gate;
Not cities proud, with spires and turrets crown'd;
No: men, high minded men;
Men, who their duties know;
But know their rights; and knowing, dare maintain.
These constitute a State."

In the General Government, the House of Representatives is mainly republican; the Senate scarcely so at all, as not elected by the people directly, and so long secured even against those who do elect them; the Executive more republican than the Senate, from its shorter term, its election by the people, in practice, (for they vote for A only on an assurance that he will vote for B,) and because, in practice also, a principle of rotation seems to be in a course of establishment; the judiciary independent of the nation, their coercion by impeachment being found nugatory.

Much, then, the control of the people over the organs of their government be the measure of its republicanism, and I confess I know no other measure, it must be agreed that our governments have much less of republicanism than ought to have been expected; in other words, that the people have less regular control over their agents, than their rights and their interests require. And this I ascribe, not to any want of republican dispositions in those who formed these constitutions, but to a submission of true principle to European authorities, to speculators on government, whose fears of the people have been inspired by the populace of their own great cities, and were unjustly entertained against the independent, the happy, and therefore orderly citizens of the United States. Much I apprehend that the golden moment is past for reforming these heresies. The functionaries of public power rarely strengthen in their dispositions to abridge it, and an unorganized call for timely amendment is not likely to prevail against an organized opposition to it. **We are always told that things are going on well; why change them? "Chi sta bene, non si muove," said the Italian, "let him who stands well, stand still." This is true; and I verily believe they would go on well with us under an absolute monarch, while our present character remains, of order, industry and love of peace, and restrained, as he would be, by the proper spirit of the people. But it is while it remains such, we should provide against the consequences** of its deterioration. And let us rest in the hope that it will yet be done, and spare ourselves the pain of evils which may never happen.

On this view of the import of the term republic, instead of saying, as has been said, "that it may mean anything or nothing," we may say with truth and meaning, that governments are more or less republican as they have more or less of the element of popular election and control in their composition; and believing, as I do, that the mass of the citizens is the safest depository of their own rights, and especially, that the evils flowing from the duperies of the people, are less injurious than those from the egoism of their agents, I am a friend to that composition of government which has in it the most of this ingredient. And I sincerely believe, with you, that banking establishments are more dangerous than standing armies; and that the principle of spending money to be paid by posterity, under the name of funding, is but swindling futurity on a large scale.

I salute you with constant friendship and respect.

Thomas Jefferson is telling John Taylor that a "State" is not a physical place such as Virginia, or its governing bodies which are symbolised by the spires and turrets, which of course a king would have. He talks about high minded men and knowing and things of the mind. The state he speaks of is liberty, as already shown by Noah Webster. He talks of preserving the tranquility of mind and he ties it to "rights" which of course is tied nicely to the second amendment. It is the only place in the entire Bill of Rights where the word "State" can be found. Note too that it is the only word that is capitalized throughout the entire sentence, just as it is also capitalized in the 2nd amendment. This little poem has a purpose of great importance and was constructed for only one reason. Within just a few short years of this letter, John Taylor goes on to write a book called "Construction Construed, Constitution Validated". That book in turn, uses symbolisms to address the truth of the 2nd amendment, and the narrative. Would Thomas Jefferson really have written a little poem for just one man in a letter? Perhaps, but in knowing the full narrative and the dangerous experiment, I believe this is yet another letter meant for the future. It explains the word State. It also links us to John Taylor, who may have already started his book construction construed at this point in time, probably at the bequest of Thomas Jefferson. The purpose of this letter pulls John Taylor into the narrative, and asks the reader to investigate him as well. "A well regulated Militia, being necessary to the security of a free State,"

Canons of Conduct Feb 2 1817

Paul Clay son of friend Charles Clay

Thomas Jefferson often took the opportunity to advise his children, grandchildren and others on matters of personal conduct. Over the years he developed a list of axioms for personal behavior. Some seem to have been of his own invention; others derived from classical or literary sources.

Jefferson's most extensive list is the one he sent to Cornelia Jefferson Randolph, his granddaughter, while she was visiting her older sister and brother-in-law.[1]

a dozen Canons of conduct in life

1. never put off to tomorrow what you can do to-day.
2. never trouble another with what you can do yourself
3. never spend your money before you have it
4. never buy a thing you do not want, because it is cheap, it will be dear to you.
5. take care of your cents: Dollars will take care of themselves!
6. pride costs us more than hunger, thirst and cold.
7. we never repent of having eat[en] too little.
8. nothing is troublesome that one does willingly.
9. how much pain have cost us the evils which have never happen d!
10. take things always by their smooth handle.
11. think as you please, & so let others, & you will have no disputes.
12. when angry, count 10. before you speak; if very angry, 100.

Jefferson sent a slightly shorter version of the above list to Paul Clay, the son of his friend Charles Clay, in 1817,[2] and a still more refined version in 1825 to John Spear Smith, on behalf of his son Thomas Jefferson Smith.[3] In his 1825 letter, Jefferson listed a "decalogue of canons for observation in practical life."

Decalogue of Canons for Observation February 25 1825

to Thomas Jefferson Smith

1 Never put off till tomorrow what you can do to-day.

2 Never trouble another for what you can do yourself.

3 Never spend your money before you have it.

4 Never buy what you do not want, because it is cheap; it will be dear to you.

5 Pride costs us more than hunger, thirst and cold.

6 We never repent of having eaten too little.

7 Nothing is troublesome that we do willingly.

8 How much pain have cost us the evils which have never happened!

9 Take things always by their smooth handle.

10 When angry, count ten, before you speak; if very angry, an hundred

I came across these writings of Thomas Jefferson at www.Monticello.org.

Thomas Jefferson has also used the expression "Canons of Conduct" in a letter to James Madison dated August 28, 1789 which. I bring this up here because it further shows how these men were weaving their ciphers together across time. One day 28 years later it appears that Thomas Jefferson decided to craft out another cipher.

Thomas Jefferson wrote two versions of these letters, one with 12 items and then the subsequent one with 10 items. This mimics the progression of the Bill of Rights from 12 articles to its final ratified version of 10 amendments. So we have what appears to be a link with math and chronology. The next symbolism is of course the word "Canons" which is a pretty explicit term for Arms. Then everything is attributed to conduct and how we should behave ourselves. He talks of how to become a better person. This is not the first time he has put this out there. Another one of his letters talks of exercising the mind and thinking of guns. This is another set of ciphers directly related to the 2nd amendment and asks that all think of neighbours first over self. The other symbolism is that these letters were written for children, which is symbolic for the future of the nation, or symbolic of growing out of old ways of thinking. It's a choice. Now if someone was to argue that these two essays were simply written just for children then why would Thomas Jefferson be so compelled to write a second version a year later and remove two items? Remember that these were for children. Is it to be assumed that it was keeping him up at night thinking about the deep errors of his ways by having two extra lines? Did he think that they would be so life changing that they could doom a child to misguided life so these offensive lines must be removed? Then after he does this he doesn't give the new Canons to the first set of children but rather to a new set of children. No, I'm pretty certain these are ciphers, because I'm equally certain that Thomas Jefferson was highly intelligent. Any other conclusion on these letters would disparage that fact.

LETTER CLVII.—TO JOHN ADAMS, January 22, 1821

TO JOHN ADAMS.
Monticello, January 22, 1821.

I was quite rejoiced, dear Sir, to see that you had health and spirits enough to take part in the late convention of your State, for revising its constitution, and to bear your share in its debates and labors. **The amendments of which we have as yet heard[473], prove the advance of liberalism in the intervening period[474]; and encourage a hope that the human mind will some day get back to the freedom it enjoyed two thousand years ago[475]**. This country, which has given to the world the example of physical liberty[476], owes to it that of moral emancipation also[477], for as yet it is but nominal with us. The inquisition of public opinion overwhelms, in practice, the freedom asserted by the laws in theory[478].

Our anxieties in this quarter are all concentrated in the question, what does the Holy Alliance in and out of Congress mean to do with us on the Missouri question? And this, by the bye, is but the name of the case, it is only the John Doe or Richard Roe of the ejectment. The real question, as seen in the States afflicted with this unfortunate population, is, Are our slaves to be presented with freedom and a dagger? For if Congress has the power to regulate the conditions of the inhabitants of the States, within the States, it will be but another exercise of that power, to declare that all shall be free. Are we then to see again Athenian and Lacedæmonian confederacies? To wage another Peloponnesian war to settle the ascendancy between them?

---

[473] The amendments 2nd meanings are not yet known, which collectively are a primer for the 2nd amendment.

[474] Once known the 2nd amendment will be recognized as being more liberal.

[475] Two thousand years ago the arms were not as dangerous as they were in 1790. It is hoped that the mind will recognize this and the 2nd amendment fully utilized once understood.

[476] Physical liberty is the liberty of owning firearms

[477] Being set free from the damage of the 2nd by taking a real view on it , a more moral once otherwise mental liberty will only be nominal.

[478] The people have a theory that they think they need arms for the contingency of a tyrant. The laws related to the peoples view on "well regulated" meaning "well-regulated".

Or is this the tocsin of merely a servile war? **That remains to be seen: but not, I hope, by you or me.** Surely, they will parley awhile, and give us time to get out of the way. What a Bedlamite is man? But let us turn from our own uneasiness to the miseries of our southern friends. Bolivar and Morillo, it seems, have come to a parley, with dispositions at length to stop **the useless effusion of human blood in that quarter**[479]. I feared from the beginning[480], **that these people were not yet sufficiently enlightened**[481] **for self-government**[482]; and that after wading through blood and slaughter, they would end in military tyrannies, more or less numerous[483]. Yet as they wished to try the experiment[484], I wished them success in it: they have now tried it, and will possibly find that their safest road will be an accommodation with the mother country, which shall hold them together by the single link of the same chief magistrate, leaving to him power enough to keep them in peace with one another, and to themselves the essential power of self-government and self-improvement[485], until they shall be **sufficiently trained by education and habits of freedom, to walk safely by themselves.** Representative government, native functionaries, a qualified negative on their laws, **with a previous security by compact for freedom of commerce**[486],

---

[479] The 2nd amendment has four parts, and the quarter relates to one part, "the right of the people to keep and bear Arms".

[480] The beginning being "A well regulated Militia".

[481] These people are those in the Militia and enlightened means having their Arms removed due to the laws.

[482] Note the "hyphen". This is a clue, that these men knew how to use hyphens, and it cleverly points to 'well regulated which of course has none in it.

[483] The 2nd amendment has always be said to be for a tyrant, and yet we have a reference to multiples. This is simply a reference to those that are empowered by dangerous Arms in society. Today more or less numerous amounts to 90 tyrants a day now.

[484] Same experiment that George Washington had referred to as the "dangerous experiment".

[485] a nice sprinkling of hyphens.proving once again that the framers were knowledgeable on when to and when not to use them.

[486] The compact is the 2nd amendment and the commerce is the back and forth of Arms as dictated by the laws.

freedom of the press[487], habeas corpus[488], and trial by jury, would make a good beginning. This last would be the school in which their people might begin to learn the exercise of civic duties as well as rights. For freedom of religion they are not yet prepared. The scales of bigotry have not sufficiently fallen from their eyes, to accept it for themselves individually, much less to trust others with it. But that will come in time, as well as a general ripeness to break entirely from the parent stem[489]. **You see, my dear Sir, how easily we prescribe for others[490] a cure for their difficulties, while we cannot cure our own.[491] We must leave both[492], I believe, to Heaven[493], and wrap ourselves up in the mantle of resignation, and of that friendship of which I tender to you the most sincere assurances.**

Th: Jefferson.

---

[487] Freedom of press relates to publishing this book

[488] The federal government is now has full jurisdiction of the 2nd amendment, not state courts. The supremacy clause should kick in because of State Constitutions that currently have a "2nd amendment rights".

[489] Parent stem is the constitution, but what will break from it is the false 2nd amendment.

[490] The others are not other countries, but some other countrymen in the future of the United States.

[491] Frustration that the protections of the 2nd amendment had to be hidden.

[492] Both relates to making sure the 2nd is hidden for their time and beyond until people can finally understand the real checks and balances of the constitution AND to the future beyond that when its hoped to be discovered.

[493] Its beyond their control in this life.

To Justice William Johnson Monticello, June 12, 1823

DEAR SIR,
-- Our correspondence is of that accommodating character, which admits of suspension at the convenience of either party, without inconvenience to the other. Hence this tardy acknowledgment of your favor of April the 11th. I learn from that with great pleasure, that you have resolved on continuing your history of parties. Our opponents are far ahead of us in preparations for placing their cause favorably before posterity. Yet I hope even from some of them the escape of precious truths, in angry explosions or effusions of vanity, which will betray the genuine monarchism of their principles. They do not themselves believe what they endeavor to inculcate, that we were an opposition party, not on principle, but merely seeking for office. The fact is, that at the formation of our government, many had formed their political opinions on European writings and practices, believing the experience of old countries, and especially of England, abusive as it was, to be a safer guide than mere theory. The doctrines of Europe were, that men in numerous associations cannot be restrained within the limits of order and justice, but by forces physical and moral, wielded over them by authorities independent of their will. Hence their organization of kings, hereditary nobles, and priests. Still further to constrain the brute force of the people, they deem it necessary to keep them down by hard labor, poverty and ignorance, and to take from them, as from bees, so much of their earnings, as that unremitting labor shall be necessary to obtain a sufficient surplus barely to sustain a scanty and miserable life. And these earnings they apply to maintain their privileged orders in splendor and idleness, to fascinate the eyes of the people, and excite in them an humble adoration and submission, as to an order of superior beings. **Although few among us had gone all these lengths of opinion, yet many had advanced, some more, some less, on the way**[494]**. And in the convention which formed our government, they endeavored to draw the cords of power as tight as they could obtain them, to lessen the dependence of the general functionaries on their constituents, to subject to them those of the States, and to weaken their means of maintaining the steady equilibrium which the**

---

[494] A reference to the the letters that were written.

majority of the convention had deemed salutary for both branches, general and local. To recover, therefore, in practice the powers which the nation had refused[495], and to warp to their own wishes those actually given[496], was the steady object of the federal party[497]. Ours, on the contrary, was to maintain the will of the majority of the convention, and of the people themselves. We believed, with them, that man was a rational animal, endowed by nature with rights, and with an innate sense of justice; and that he could be restrained from wrong and protected in right by moderate powers, confided to persons of his own choice, and held to their duties by dependence on his own will. We believed that the complicated organization of kings, nobles, and priests, was not the wisest nor best to effect the happiness of associated man; **that wisdom and virtue were not hereditary, that the trappings of such a machinery[498], consumed by their expense, those earnings of industry, they were meant to protect, and, by the inequalities they produced[499], exposed liberty to sufferance[500]**. We believed that men, enjoying in ease and security the full fruits of their own industry, enlisted by all their interests on the side of law and order, habituated to think for themselves, and to follow their reason as their guide, would be more easily and safely governed, than with minds nourished in error, and vitiated and debased, as in Europe, by ignorance, indigence and oppression. **The cherishment of the people then was our principle, the fear and distrust of them, that of the other party[501]**. Composed, as we were, of the landed and laboring interests of the country, we could not be less

---

[495] It is acknowledged that the USA would not have endorsed the 2nd amendment without first experiencing its ill effects over time.

[496] To warp is to read subjectively 'the right of the people to keep and bear Arms".

[497] The 2nd amendment has always been steady simply because it can be read objectively. It is the object of a federal jurisdiction.

[498] Machinery is the workings of the 2nd amendment for harm or good.

[499] Inequalities can easily be witnessed in events like Sandy Hook, Orlando and millions of American lives lost to Gun Violence in the USA.

[500] Exposing liberty to sufferance is a reference to the ill effects of the 2nd amendment.

[501] Cherishment of the people are the liberal thinkers.

anxious for a government of law and order than were the inhabitants of the cities, the strongholds of federalism. **And whether our efforts to save the principles[502] and form of our constitution have not been salutary**, let the present republican freedom, order and prosperity of our country determine. **History may distort truth, and will distort it for a time, by the superior efforts at justification of those who are conscious of needing it most. Nor will the opening scenes of our present government be seen in their true aspect, until the letters of the day, now held in private hoards, shall be broken up and laid open to public view**[503]. What a treasure will be found in General Washington's cabinet, when it shall pass into the hands of as candid a friend to truth as he was himself! When no longer, like Caesar's notes and memorandums in the hands of Anthony, it shall be open to the high priests of federalism only, and garbled to say so much, and no more, as suits their views!

With respect to his farewell address, to the authorship of which, it seems, there are conflicting claims, I can state to you some facts. He had determined to decline re-election at the end of his first term, and so far determined, that he had requested Mr. Madison to prepare for him something valedictory, to be addressed to his constituents on his retirement. This was done, but he was finally persuaded to acquiesce in a second election, to which no one more strenuously pressed him than myself, from a conviction of the importance of strengthening, by longer habit, the respect necessary for that office, which the weight of his character only could effect. When, at the end of his second term, his Valedictory came out, Mr. Madison recognized in it several passages of his draught, several others, we were both satisfied, were from the pen of Hamilton, and others from

---

[502] As represented earlier, the constitution was always meant to be founded in liberalism. The 2nd amendment is also proof of this, for it thinks of all of society first.

[503] This is a direct reference to the letters written evidence the truth of the 2nd amendment, and in fact the full narrative behind it. The hoards are the Federalist Papers, Benjamin Franklins Papers, and even other works as of yet unnamed. Every letter and book I reference is part of that hoard, which I was only able to access as digital media through the internet.

that of the President himself. These he probably put into the hands of Hamilton to form into a whole, and hence it may all appear in Hamilton's hand-writing, as if it were all of his composition.

 I have stated above, that the original objects of the federalists were, 1st, to warp our government more to the form and principles of monarchy, and, 2d, to weaken the barriers of the State governments as coordinate powers. In the first they have been so completely foiled by the universal spirit of the nation, that they have abandoned the enterprise, shrunk from the odium of their old appellation, taken to themselves a participation of ours, **and under the pseudo-republican mask**, are now aiming at their second object, and strengthened by unsuspecting or apostate recruits from our ranks, are advancing fast towards an ascendancy. I have been blamed for saying, that a prevalence of the doctrines of consolidation would one day call for reformation or <u>revolution</u>. I answer by asking if a single State of the Union would have agreed to the constitution, had it given all powers to the General Government? If the whole opposition to it did not proceed from the jealousy and fear of every State, of being subjected to the other States in matters merely its own? And if there is any reason to believe the States more disposed now than then, to acquiesce in this general surrender of all their rights and powers to a consolidated government, one and undivided?

 You request me confidentially, to examine the question, whether the Supreme Court has advanced beyond its constitutional limits, and trespassed on those of the State authorities? I do not undertake it, my dear Sir, because I am unable. Age and the wane of mind consequent on it, have disqualified me from investigations so severe, and researches so laborious. And it is the less necessary in this case, as having been already done by others with a logic and learning to which I could add nothing. On the decision of the case of Cohens <u>vs</u>. The State of Virginia, in the Supreme Court of the United States, in March, 1821, Judge Roane, under the signature of Algernon Sidney, wrote for the Enquirer a series of papers on the law of that case. I considered these papers maturely as they came out, and confess that they appeared to me to pulverize every word which had been delivered by Judge Marshall, of the extra-judicial part of his opinion; and all was extra-judicial, except the decision that the act of Congress had not purported to give to the corporation of Washington the authority claimed by their lottery law, of controlling the laws of the States within the States themselves. But unable to claim that case, he could not let it go entirely, but went on gratuitously to prove, that notwithstanding the eleventh amendment of the constitution, a State <u>could</u> be brought as a defendant, to the bar of his court; and again, that Congress might authorize a corporation of its territory to exercise legislation within a State, and paramount to the laws of that State. I cite the sum and result only of his doctrines, according to the impression made on my mind at the time, and still remaining. If not strictly accurate in circumstance, it is so in substance. **This doctrine was so completely refuted by Roane, that if he can be answered, I surrender human reason as a vain and useless faculty, given to bewilder, and not to guide us.** And I mention this particular case as one only of several, because it gave occasion to that thorough examination of the constitutional limits between the General and State jurisdictions, which you have asked for. There were two other writers in the same paper, under the signatures of Fletcher of Saltoun, and Somers, who, in a few essays, presented some very luminous and striking views of the question. And there was a particular paper which recapitulated all the cases in which it was thought the federal court had usurped on the State jurisdictions. These essays will be found in the Enquirers of 1821, from May the 10th to July the 13th. **It is not in my present power to send them to you, but if Ritchie can furnish them, I will procure and forward them. If they had been read in the other States, as they were here, I think they would have left, there as here, no dissentients from their doctrine.** [504]The subject was taken up by our legislature of 1821 - '22, and two draughts of remonstrances were prepared and discussed. As well as I remember, there was no difference of opinion as to the matter of right; but there was as to the expediency of a remonstrance at that time, the general mind of the States being then under extraordinary excitement by the Missouri question; and it was

---

[504] Thomas Ritchie is also a reference in the James Madison letter which also stipulates that something must be discerned by the text alone. In this letter, the meaning of something must be "conform to the probably one in which it was passed. It then says to use "canons" which appears to be code for "Arms", which exist only in the 2nd amendment.

dropped on that consideration. But this case is not dead, it only sleepeth. The Indian Chief said he did not go to war for every petty injury by itself, but put it into his pouch, and when that was full, he then made war. Thank Heaven, we have provided a more peaceable and rational mode of redress.

This practice of Judge Marshall, of travelling out of his case to prescribe what the law would be in a moot case not before the court, is very irregular and very censurable. I recollect another instance, and the more particularly, perhaps, because it in some measure bore on myself. Among the midnight appointments of Mr. Adams, were commissions to some federal justices of the peace for Alexandria. These were signed and sealed by him, but not delivered. I found them on the table of the department of State, on my entrance into office, and I forbade their delivery. Marbury, named in one of them, applied to the Supreme Court for a mandamus to the Secretary of State, (Mr. Madison) to deliver the commission intended for him. The court determined at once, that being an original process, they had no cognizance of it; and therefore the question before them was ended. But the Chief Justice went on to lay down what the law would be, had they jurisdiction of the case, to wit: that they should command the delivery. The object was clearly to instruct any other court having the jurisdiction, what they should do if Marbury should apply to them. Besides the impropriety of this gratuitous interference, could anything exceed the perversion of law? For if there is any principle of law never yet contradicted, it is that delivery is one of the essentials to the validity of the deed. Although signed and sealed, yet as long as it remains in the hands of the party himself, it is in <u>fieri</u> only, it is not a deed, and can be made so only by its delivery. In the hands of a third person it may be made an escrow. But whatever is in the executive offices is certainly deemed to be in the hands of the President; and in this case, was actually in my hands, because, when I countermanded them, there was as yet no Secretary of State. Yet this case of Marbury and Madison is continually cited by bench and bar, as if it were settled law, without any animadversion on its being merely an <u>obiter</u> dissertation of the Chief Justice.

It may be impracticable to lay down any general formula of words which shall decide at once, and with precision, in every case, this

limit of jurisdiction[505]. But there are two canons[506] which will guide us safely in most of the cases. 1st. **The capital and leading object of the constitution[507]** was to leave with the States all authorities which respected their own citizens only[508], and to transfer to the United States those which respected citizens of foreign or other States: to make us several as to ourselves, but one as to all others. In the latter case, then, **constructions should lean to the general jurisdiction[509]**, if the words will **bear** it[510]; **and in favor of the States in the former, if possible to be so construed.**[511] And indeed, between citizens and citizens of the same State, and under their own laws, I know but a single case in which a jurisdiction is given to the General Government. That is, where anything but gold or silver is made a lawful tender, or the obligation of contracts is any otherwise impaired. The separate legislatures had so often abused that power, that the citizens themselves chose to trust it to the general, rather than to their own special authorities. **2d. On every question of construction, carry ourselves back to the time when the constitution was adopted, recollect the spirit manifested in the debates, and instead of trying what meaning may be squeezed out of the text[512],**

---

[505] We now know the 2nd amendment is a formula, with variables, namely Arms and people. The limit of jurisdiction is a reference to this is the only place where the separation of powers merges.

[506] This is a reference the two occurrences of "Arms" in the 2nd amendments as variables, once the first one is recognized as being embedded in the word "Militia".

[507] The "capital" is a reference to the word "Militia" which is the first capitalized word in the 2nd amendment.

[508] "States" as in liberty state of mind. The message here is its about society, and not the individual.

[509] The 2nd amendment should be interpreted as a general jurisdiction of federal government.

[510] Just a "tie in" to the 2nd amendment. symbolism.

[511] Construed is a reference to an "alternate meaning".

[512] The text here is "a right of the people to keep and bear Arms".

or invented against it[513], conform to the probable one in which it was passed. Let us try Cohen's case by these canons only[514], referring always, however, for full argument, to the essays before cited.

It was between a citizen and his own State, and under a law of his State. It was a domestic case, therefore, and not a foreign one.

Can it be believed, that under the jealousies prevailing against the General Government, at the adoption of the constitution, the States meant to surrender the authority of preserving order, of enforcing moral duties and restraining vice, within their own territory? And this is the present case, that of Cohen being under the ancient and general law of gaming. Can any good be effected by taking from the States the moral rule of their citizens, and subordinating it to the general authority, or to one of their corporations, which may justify forcing the meaning of words, hunting after possible constructions, and hanging inference on inference, from heaven to earth, like Jacob's ladder? Such an intention was impossible, and such a licentiousness of construction and inference, if exercised by both governments, as may be done with equal right, would equally authorize both to claim all power, general and particular, and break up the foundations of the Union. Laws are made for men of ordinary understanding, and should, therefore, be construed by the ordinary rules of common sense. Their meaning is not to be sought for in metaphysical subtleties, which may make anything mean everything or nothing, at pleasure. It should be left to the sophisms of advocates, whose trade it is, to prove that a defendant is a plaintiff, though dragged into court, <u>torto collo</u>, like Bonaparte's volunteers, into the field in chains, or that a

---

[513] The text 'against" this is "A well regulated Militia, being necessary to the security of a free State". The meaning of these words have been invented, or read subjectively.

[514] Canons are symbolic of "Arms" and this is plural. There must be more than one occurrence of Arms in the 2nd amendment, in order for them to be viewed as variables. There are of course, because a Militia is simply people and Arms. The spirit in the debates was that everyone was fearful of a new tyrant. It would have been impossible in that time to be more explicit about the 2nd amendment being an Arms control mandate constitutionally assigned to the Federal government. This is even the "2nd" item.

power has been given, because it ought to have been given, et alia talia. The States supposed that by their tenth amendment, they had secured themselves against constructive powers. They were not lessoned yet by Cohen's case, nor aware of the slipperiness of the eels of the law. I ask for no straining of words against the General Government, nor yet against the States. I believe the States can best govern our home concerns, and the General Government our foreign ones. I wish, therefore, to see maintained that wholesome distribution of powers established by the constitution for the limitation of both; and never to see all offices transferred to Washington, where, further withdrawn from the eyes of the people, they may more secretly be bought and sold as at market.

But the Chief Justice says, "there must be an ultimate arbiter somewhere." True, there must; but does that prove it is either party? The ultimate arbiter is the people of the Union, assembled by their deputies in convention, at the call of Congress, or of two-thirds of the States. Let them decide to which they mean to give an authority claimed by two of their organs. And it has been the peculiar wisdom and felicity of our constitution, to have provided this peaceable appeal, where that of other nations is at once to force.

I rejoice in the example you set of seriatim opinions. I have heard it often noticed, and always with high approbation. Some of your brethren will be encouraged to follow it occasionally, and in time, it may be felt by all as a duty, and the sound practice of the primitive court be again restored. Why should not every judge be asked his opinion, and give it from the bench, if only by yea or nay? Besides ascertaining the fact of his opinion, which the public have a right to know, in order to judge whether it is impeachable or not, it would show whether the opinions were unanimous or not, and thus settle more exactly the weight of their authority.

The close of my second sheet warns me that it is time now to relieve you from this letter of unmerciful length. Indeed, I wonder how I have accomplished it, with two crippled wrists, the one scarcely able to move my pen, the other to hold my paper. But I am hurried sometimes beyond the sense of pain, when unbosoming myself to friends who harmonize with me in principle. You and I may differ occasionally in details of minor consequence, as no two minds, more than two faces, are the same in every feature. But our general objects are the same, to preserve the republican form and principles of our constitution and cleave to the salutary distribution of powers which that has established. These are the two sheet anchors of our Union. If driven from either, we shall be in danger of foundering.

To my prayers for its safety and perpetuity, I add those for the continuation of your health, happiness, and usefulness to your country.

This letter is then signed Thomas Jefferson.

Thomas Jefferson appears to have used the same ciphering themes as Benjamin Franklin in this letter. He used the recipient's name as part of the cipher. Keeping in mind that Suspicion was the enemy real names had to be used. Benjamin Franklin had used the name William Alexander regularly for his ciphers even when the man was dead for a period of about 6 years.

So the letter is written to Justice William Johnson
Justice = Law maker.
William = protector
John = favour of god
Son = symbolic of future in the sense of descendants.

This is a real man so suspicion would be minimized. Thomas Jefferson simply took a closer look at this man's name, after already been shown Benjamin Franklins ciphers. If these men were all writing these ciphers, then certainly Benjamin Franklin would have been showing them to his "pupils". This man's name warranted a ciphered letter, so Thomas Jefferson wrote one. It is a more than likely a completely contrived cipher.

This is the letter that is very explicit as a cipher and tells us about the very contents of this book and its author.

It appears that Thomas Jefferson borrowed from Alexander Hamilton writing of Federalist #23 where it is stated.

"Every view we may take of the subject, as candid inquirers after truth, will serve to convince us, that it is both unwise and dangerous to deny the federal government an unconfined authority, as to all those objects which are intrusted to its management"

The wording in this appears to directly reflect "Candid a friend to truth", because the truth is essentially one and the same thing. This is of course the 2nd amendment and its full story.

John Jay

John Jay to Thomas Jefferson 27 Oct. 1786

The inefficacy of our government becomes daily more and more apparent. Our treasury and our credit are in a sad situation; and it is probable that either the wisdom or the passions of the people will produce changes. A spirit of licentiousness has infected Massachusetts, which appears more formidable than some at first apprehended. Whether similar symptoms will not soon mark a like disease in several other States is very problematical.

The public papers herewith sent contain everything generally known about these matters. A reluctance to taxes, an impatience of government, a rage for property and little regard to the means of acquiring it, together with a desire of equality in all things, seem to actuate the mass of those who are uneasy in their circumstances. To these may be added the influence of ambitious adventurers, and the speculations of the many characters who prefer private to public good, and of others who expect to gain more from wrecks made by tempests than from the produce of patient and honest industry. As the knaves and fools of this world are forever in alliance, it is easy to perceive how much vigour and wisdom a government, from its construction and administration, should possess, in order to repress the evils which naturally flow from such copious sources of injustice and evil.

Much, I think, is to be feared from the sentiments which such a state of things is calculated to infuse into the minds of the rational and well-intended. In their eyes, the charms of liberty will daily fade; and in seeking for peace and security, they will too naturally turn towards systems in direct opposition to those which oppress and disquiet them.

If faction should long bear down law and government, tyranny may raise its head, or the more sober part of the people may even think of a king[515].

In short[516], my dear sir, we are in a very unpleasant situation[517]. Changes are necessary[518]; but, what they ought to be, what they will be, and how and when to be produced, are arduous questions[519]. I feel for the cause of liberty[520], and for the honour of my countrymen who have so nobly asserted it, and who, at present, so abuse its blessings. If it should not take root in this soil, little pains will be taken to cultivate it in any other.

---

[515] Faction comes those that vote for "Me the People" versus "We the People" Once this is done then those elected in turn will propagate this rhetoric. Faction would come from those that choose to cherry pick the constitution or find a way to disenfranchise any one individual. Faction comes from racism in assigning the value one skin pigment, or lack thereof as being more entitled to inalienable rights. There is no patriotism with these views if the constitution is to be of any value. Everyone wants the same thing. People just want to life, work and have a life and be part of a society and not pushed off to the fringe of it. The constitution does not care what an individual likes or does not like and is only concerned with the liberty for a United States of America in the only context it can be which is of course "We the People".

[516] A short part of the 2nd amendment. "the right of the people to keep and bear Arms"

[517] It is and will produce a loss of life and liberty for the nation.

[518] "necessary to the security of a free State" The changes are of course the new 2A and common sense gun laws.

[519] "well regulated".

[520] Which is nested in the 2nd amendments 2nd clause as "the state of being free".

To George Washington from John Jay, 7 January 1787

From John Jay
New York 7 Jany 1787
Dear Sir

They who regard the public good with more Attention & Attachment than they do mere personal concerns, must feel and confess the Force of such Sentiments as are expressed in your Letter to me by Col. Humphreys last Fall. The situation of our Affairs calls not only for Reflection and Prudence but for Exertion. What is to be done? is a common Question, but it is a Question not easy to answer.

Would the giving *any* further Degree of Power to Congress do the Business? I am inclined to think it would not—for among other Reasons[:][521]

It is natural to suppose there will always be members who will find it convenient to make their *Seats* subservient to partial & personal Purposes; and they who may be *able* and *willing* to concert and promote useful and **national measures**, will seldom be unembarrassed by the Ignorance, Prejudices, Fears, or interested Views of others.

In so large a Body Secrecy and Dispatch will be too uncommon; and foreign as well as local Influence will frequently oppose and sometimes frustrate the wisest measures.

Large assemblies often misunderstand or neglect the Obligations of Character Honor and Dignity; and will collectively do or omit Things which individual Gentlemen in Private Capacities would not approve. As the many divide Blame and also divide Credit, too little a Portion of either falls to each mans Share, to affect him strongly; even in Cases where the whole Blame or the whole Credit must be national. It is not easy for those to think and feel as Sovereigns, who have always been accustomed to think and feel as Subjects.

The Executive Business of Sovereignty depending on so many wills, and those wills moved by such a Variety of contradictory motives and Inducements will in general be but feebly done.

Such a Sovereign, however *theoretically* responsible, cannot be effectually so in its Departments and Officers, without adequate Judicatories.

521

I therefore promise myself nothing very desireable from any Change which does not divide the Sovereignty into its proper Departments—Let Congress legislate, let others execute, let others judge.

Shall we have a King? not in my opinion while other Expedients remain untried, might we not have a Governor General limited in his Prerogatives and Duration? might not Congress be divided into an upper and a lower House? the former appointed for Life, the latter annually; and let the Governor General (to preserve the Ballance) with the advice of a Council formed, for that *only* purpose of the great judicial officers, have a negative on their acts, our Government should in some Degree be suited to our manners and Circumstances, and they you know are not strictly Democratical.

What Powers should be granted to the Government so constituted is a Question which deserves much Thought—I think the more the better—the States retaining only so much as may be necessary for domestic Purposes; and all their principal Officers civil and military being commissioned and removeable by the national Governmt.[522]

These are short Hints—Details would exceed the Limits of a Letter, and to you be superfluous.[523]

A convention is in contemplation, and I am glad to find your Name among those of its intended Members.[524]

To me the Policy of such a Convention appears questionable. Their authority is to be derived from acts of the State Legislatures.

---

[522] Military control should be a the level of the federal government. Note the term "Officers" being applied to both "civil" and "military". There is a distinction being made here to the public domain. If one was to make a civil officer removable, the man would still exist in society, however his Arms would be at the sole discretion of the federal government.

[523] These "hints" are for you the reader, in the future. Consider this a red flag. Now the "Limits" of the letter is a reference to the letter being too explicit, which is why he uses the term "hints" must be used. The hint would have no context to any that was not familiar with the 2nd amendment.

[524] The convention being the 2nd amendment is about to instilled into a bill of rights and George Washington is symbolic of a soldier and being one of the members as the word "Militia".

Are the State Legislatures authorized either by themselves or others, to alter Constitutions? I think not. They who hold Commissions can by virtue of them, neither retrench nor extend the Powers conveyed by them. Perhaps it is intended that this Convention shall not *ordain,* but only *recommend*—if so—there is Danger that their Recommendations will produce endless Discussions, and perhaps Jealousies and Party Heats.

Would it not be better, for Congress plainly and in strong Terms to declare, that the present fœderal Government is inadequate to the Purposes for which it was instituted[525]—That they forbear to point out its *particular* Defects, or to ask for an Extension of any *particular* powers, lest improper Jealousies should thence arise; but that in their opinion it would be expedient for the People of the States without Delay to appoint State Conventions (in the way they chuse their General Assemblies) with the *sole* and express power of appointing Deputies to a general Convention, who or the majority of whom should take into consideration the articles of Confederation, & make such alterations amendments and additions thereto as to them should appear necessary and proper; and which being by them ordained and published should have the same force & obligation which all or any of the present articles now have.

No alterations in the Government should I think be made, nor if attempted will easily take place, unless deduceable[526] from the only Source of just authority—*the People,* accept my dear Sir, my warmest and most cordial wishes for your Health and Happiness, and believe me to be with the greatest Respect and Esteem, Your most obt & hble Servt

John Jay

This particular letter is referenced by George Washington in a letter dated March 10 1787. George Washington states that there should be particular attention given to it.

---

[525] The purpose of the federal government is to protect the population, even if it is spite of themselves. The "present" federal government is the one that does not know about the convention or the 2nd amendment.

[526] Deduceable is figuring out that the checks and balances work fine, recognizing that gun violence is in fact caused by guns, and the only way to fix it is to understand the 2nd amendment by finally "deducing" it.

"The other, of the 7th of Jany is on a very interesting subject, deserving very particular attention."

So let us take a look at this and see what he wants us to read. He talks about giving more power to congress which is a reference for the 2nd amendment. He says this can't be done in his time because some of those in congress are only in it for themselves. There is the politics of fear. There is avarice. There is pressure from constituents.

He also states that in such a large group it would be impossible to keep it a secret from the public at large who would be very sensitive to the Federal control of Arms.

James Madison

There is one very important letter from James Madison's letters that I chose to put into the section towards the end of this book. He had titled it "Advice to my Country" and it is in the "Genius's don't fish for Lightning". I placed it there because it was the last cipher written, where the Kite experiment was the first. It seemed appropriate to get a better feeling for the scope of time that these letters were written in.

1778 to the General Assembly of the State of Virginia

"We have staked the whole future of American civilization, not upon the power of government, far from it. We've staked the future of all our political institutions upon our capacity…to sustain ourselves according to the Ten Commandments of God." [1778 to the General Assembly of the State of Virginia

So what is James Madison saying here? He is in no way inferring that Christianity should have any authority in the State.

Is this an endorsement of Christianity or is it something else? I'm a Christian myself. It is the symbolism and utility of the 10 commandments as rules to live by. Christianity however does not have exclusive ownership of mans better nature. There is utility in religion, any religion to guide men in this area. The constitution is no different, only it demands it in the reality of the here and now. It is not necessary to get dressed up wash the Mercedes and drive off to church while passing the homeless and hungry along the way and then thank god for the blessings of your life.

If mans nature was not to be selfish then the commandments would not be needed in the first place. If mans nature was not selfish then government would not be needed either. The constitution was written to handle the nature of man in spite of man. The institutions of government are the checks and balances against mans nature, to prevent the tyrant in any from affecting society in a harmful way. Liberty for all is born from all adhering to the 10 commandments or synonymously respecting and not cherry picking the constitution. The 2nd amendment was cherry picked to some extent because men used their own fear to create faction at the expense of death and a clinging to something they perceived as a right. Empowerment over others was perceived as a right but if though shalt not kill then why create a right that makes it easier for others to kill? It is about thinking of yourself as being a part of a complex society. For Christians to attribute this quote as an endorsement and assignment to American values is instant and unabashed hypocracy. God will never judge a nation at the gates of St. Peter but only man. Nation is the invention of man and man is the invention of god and he gave men free will. It is a false choice to attribute a god to any nation, if this attribution is to prop oneself up against any other man of equal goodness. Faction is born, and where there is faction, there is death.

James Madison is recognizing the inherent dangers of democracy. If man is selfish, then democracy will fail, because man will generally vote for his own want in spite of the society. He cherry picks reality and refuses to acknowledge that life would be much harder without society and its collective achievements. Put a man in the wilderness with a gift of a loin cloth for 10 months and there would be few that would not walk out with a brand new admiration for both society and his fellow man. If a man is born to wealth however and feels entitled above all others to all the wealth society has to offer, then liberty is lost for all he encounters. Everything is connected, and now man is about to get a hard lesson in that due to global warming as he seeks to justify the loss of species in the name of progress. Progress for who, and progress for what? James Madison has recognized that the very foundation of government are men. He is saying that there is no such thing as a self regulating man when he is to exist in a society. The 10 commandments are simply regulations regarding to human conduct when man is among men. He is stating quite clearly that oppression can be found in the heart of any man, if he puts himself first and foremost above others, especially in matters of governance.

The symbolism of this can be found in the eye of providence. It is dynamic and sits in the disjointed section of the pyramid. That represents the here and now. It's a reminder that god is watching every decision that every person makes which will affect the society in which they live for better or for worse. God favours no nation because nations are not given free will. There is no free pass to heaven and to infer one by saying that a nation is under gods favor may cause some to assume they have a free pass and become lax in their virtue.

James Madison to Richard Peters 19 Aug. 1789

There is a very good reason that James Madison is calling this a nauseous project because right now he is, if you will excuse the colloquialism, "Smack Dab" in the middle of Benjamin Franklins experiment. The Federalist papers have been written already and they are aligned with the Bill of Rights in advance of its construction. The Bill of Rights was predetermined and the order of them was important. The Bill of Rights at this time though, had 12 articles and not 10 amendments. Benjamin Franklin was in the background watching this, and the other men in the cabal were very much aware as to what was going down. The very first Benjamin Franklin cipher to William Alexander that I encountered was only two months away from being written and archived. To say the cabal had their fingers crossed in this critical time, with so much labor already spent, would be the understatement of at least two centuries. So yes, nauseous I think is only a hint at this reality of history. Later the Federalist papers were rebound, and modified in order to be realigned. The realignment can easily be seen in #84 as "purportedly"[527] written by Alexander Hamilton...

To the second that is, to the pretended establishment of the common and state law by the Constitution, I answer, that they are expressly made subject "to such alterations and provisions as the legislature shall from time to time make concerning the same." They are therefore at any moment liable to repeal by the ordinary legislative power, and of course have no constitutional sanction. The only use of the declaration was to recognize the ancient law and to remove doubts which might have been occasioned by the Revolution. This consequently can be considered as no part of a declaration of rights, which under our constitutions must be intended as limitations of the power of the government itself.

that starts with "To the second..". Number 84 did not exist at this time, as it is currently written. This particular paragraph would have started out with words

---

[527] Benjamin Franklin played a part in these letters. He was probably their editor, and he most certainly taught these men the rules of how to write them. Who wrote what and when is a moot point because it really doesn't matter. They are written for one thing and one thing only. The cabal was on the same page with the cabal. There was no politics here, only constitutional correctness and the establishment of its final legacy, but one with fingers crossed. Yes , there were many facets to their handiwork.

such as **"Regarding the fourth..."**, because at the time this letter was dated, the 2nd amendment would have been the 4th article

The first two articles were ultimately dropped. This is the REAL reason why the Federalist had to be rebound and in part rewritten because collectively, as a whole they are ciphers. They are part of the private hoard. This letter is of course a cipher, and what I shared with you regarding nauseous is simply James Madison telling us the importance of this experiment. I think he wants us to appreciate the real labors that went into the Bill of Rights, which was their orchestration and not its wording. The wording already existed on the day he wrote this letter.

Now with that being said, we can see numbered items in this letter. At this point in time, let's take a look at the 4th item, because if my hypothesis is correct that this is ciphered then it should line up rather nicely with what we now know to be the 2nd amendment. Remember that symbolism is our friend. So here we have the fourth item.

> 4. If amendts. had not been proposed from the federal side of the House, the proposition would have come *within three days,* from the adverse side. It is certainly best that they should appear to be the free gift of the friends of the Constitution rather than to be extorted by the address & weight of its enemies.

"within three days" is even italicized or emphasised in the original letter. James Madison is asking us to put a bit of "think" into this.

I will now transcribe the 2nd amendment numbering the clauses to illustrate. This is the "proposition" with respect to its real meaning.

1. A well regulated Militia
2. Being necessary to the security of a free State
3. The right of the people to keep and bear Arms
4. Shall not be infringed.

The symbolism of "day" is brightness. James Madison is highlighting these three clauses. In the grand scheme of things would history really care as to whether or not something would have taken 3 days or 4 days? It is kind of a moot point that it takes time to do things.

The 3 essential clauses in the 2A are 1,2 and 4 where # 3 is not. The 3 days within the 2nd amendment are clauses 1, 2 and 4. It is the #3 though, "the right of the people to keep and bear Arms", that has kept people in the dark.

The inference to the Federal side is a reference that the government head must do the regulating. Since the constitution was written with checks and balances against power to keep the people from being oppressed, now that the 2nd amendment has suddenly "appeared" as a "gift" from the past. The opposing side are those that liked the phrase "the right of the people to keep and bear Arms". This was "addressed" to those who would buy into this the most. It was also addressed in such a manner that it would appear to be the very context of the 2nd amendment by using "the right" at the start of the clause. The "weight" is simply a reference to the term "bear". It is addressed "Extorted" is basically what the NRA has been doing for awhile now, however it is anyone that puts themselves ahead of the safety of the nation. When you hear things like "guns don't kill people, people kill people" or "people get hit by cars anyway, what are we going to do, ban all cars", or "a gun is only a tool" or "why should law abiding citizens be punished". There are many tunes on this record and the record is of course a .45 which spins and spins hoping to gain purchase in its logic. Guns kill people. Full Stop. James Madison recognized this, as stated. At this time I have not completed the deciphering of this entire document as presented. The window of opportunity for me to actually publish this book is getting smaller. It was the word "nauseous" that I had heard before and had applied it to a nuance of the context that didn't make sense due to chronology. It took me awhile to wrap my head around it or basically fit these pieces of history together to illuminate this never before seen dynamic.

It would be neat if they made a movie about this because one can almost see a close up of pudgy crossed fingers. The script would of course have to do justice to history so that the history itself could provide justice for its future. In the establishment of its truth, at this time the script must keep to the bones as the storyline is fleshed out. Not everyone will be reading these pages, however everyone is entitled to know their constitution and its newly revealed secrets.

> Papers 12:346–48
> The papers inclosed will shew that the nauseous project of amendments has not yet been either dismissed or despatched. We are so deep in them now, that right or wrong some thing must be done. I say this not by way of apology, for to be sincere I think no apology requisite. 1. because a constitutional provision in favr. of essential rights is a thing not improper in itself and was always

viewed in that light by myself. It may be less necessary in a republic, than a Monarchy, & in a fedl. Govt. than the former, but it is in some degree rational in every Govt., since in every Govt. power may oppress, and declarations on paper, tho' not an effectual restraint, are not without some influence. 2. In many States the Constn. was adopted under a tacit compact in favr. of some subsequent provisions on this head[528]. In Virga. It would have been *certainly rejected*[529], had no assurances been given by its advocates[530] that such provisions would be pursued. As an honest man *I feel* my self bound by this consideration[531]. 3. If the Candidates in Virga. for the House of Reps. had not taken this conciliary ground at the election, that State would have [been] represented almost wholly by disaffected characters, instead of the *federal* reps. now in Congs. 4. If amendts. had not been proposed from the federal side of the House, the proposition would have come *within three days,* from the adverse side. It is certainly best that they should appear to be the free gift of the friends of the Constitution rather than to be extorted by the address & weight of its enemies. 5. It will kill the opposition every where, and by putting an end to the disaffection to the Govt. itself, enable the administration to venture on measures not otherwise safe. Those who hate the Govt. will always join the party disaffected to measures of the admi[ni]s[tra]tion, and such a party will be created by every important measure. 6. If no amendts. be proposed the language of antifedl. leaders to the people, will be, we advised you not to adopt the Constn. witht. previous amendts–You listened to those who told you that subsequent securities for your rights would be most easily obtained–-We urged you to insist on a Convention as the only effectual mode of obtaining these–-You

---

[528] The states are a state of life and a state of liberty. The compact was that of the cabal behind the 2nd amendment. These men wrote letters regarding this secret to their deaths.

[529] Simply stating the if the other delegates actually knew how to read the 2nd amendment, they would not have ratified it.

[530] Note the term "advocates" which was also used in letter from George Washington to James Madison. The provisions relate directly to the provision for "crafting" the 2nd amendment.

[531] This is a truth reference.

yielded to the assurances of those who told you that a Convention was unecessary, that Congs. wd. be the proper channel for getting what was wanted. &c &c. Here are fine texts for popular declaimers who wish to revive the antifedl. cause, and at the fall session of the Legislares. to blow the trumpet for a second Convention. In Virga. a majority of the Legislature last elected, is bitterly opposed to the Govt. and will be joined, if no amends. be proposed, by great nos. of the other side who will complain of being deceived. 7. Some amendts. are necssy for N. Carola. I am so informed by the best authorities in that State. I set out with an apology for not writing sooner, I must conclude with one, for writing so much, & still more for writing so scurvily. Yrs truly

The "Well-Regulated" Fallacy: (Jan 21, 1792)

James Madison to Edmund Pendleton (Jan 21, 1792)

This letter is extremely important because it discerns James Madison's intent for the meaning fo the term "regulated". The current understanding and explanation of the term 'well regulated' is related to the term 'well-regulated' as in well ordered, organized, disciplined etc. If 'regulated' could be in any way associated with 'lawed', it would be a very bad thing for those that were trying to validate the words "the right of the people to keep and bear arms, shall not be infringed'. The latitude of that phrase appears to be almost limitless, but to associate it with regulations could have no other effect than to infer limits. This would be a bad thing for the gun industry as well. On the flip side though, it is a confusing sentence, and as we know now, was a riddle.

It occurred to me that in during the orations of the Constitutional Convention only a biased ear would have been able to hear that hyphen. The Bill of Rights had more or less evolved from the Virginia Declaration of Rights. I believe back then this missing hyphen would have been more noticeable because the delegates from Virginia may have been more familiar with what they had to what they were getting. Today people of course aren't all that concerned about what they had because its been immaterial now for over 240 years. Some people may not even know that a Virginia Declaration of Rights had existed. In my research though, I did because it was important for me to see where the 2nd amendment had come from. Even so though, if the delegates had noticed this missing hyphen they obviously had dismissed it because once they read "the right of the people to keep and bear Arms" it was golden.

The sales pitch in this validation is that 'well-regulated' can be found elsewhere such as in the Virginia Declaration of Rights and the Virginia Articles of Confederation. I couldn't help but notice in my research that in those documents other words can be found too. The other words were simple from the English language which just happened to be the language of choice for the founders to use. Yes, I'm being a bit sarcastic, but do this to strike down the well ordered fallacy forever. No, it was not the founders that have changed "well ordered" for the first time in human history to mean 'well-ordered", it is, and always has been the attempts of some to validate ¼ of the 2nd amendment either due to logic, or nefarious gain under the pretense of logic.

Now for any scholars that have used this argument, if James Madison himself explains what I have stated would you finally relinquish this particular point to ill founded conjecture? Keep in mind though, that this letter like all the others I've highlighted cannot be explicit. They must be scrutinized very carefully using the key of what the 2nd amendment really says. We know the purpose of the letters, we need only to unlock them. It has already been demonstrated that "instrument" and "measure" is nothing more than code for the 2nd amendment, so bear that in mind when you read this next letter. This letter was written 5 weeks after the Bill of Rights was ratified.

To Edmund Pendleton.JANUARY 21, 1792

If Congress can do whatever in their *discretion* can be done by money, and will promote the general welfare, the Government is no longer a limited one possessing enumerated powers, but an indefinite one subject to particular exceptions[532].

It is to be remarked that the phrase[533] out of which this doctrine[534] is elaborated, is copied from the old articles of Confederation, where it was always understood as nothing more than a general caption to the specified powers, and it is a fact that it was preferred in the new instrument[535] for that very reason as less liable[536] than any other to misconstruction[537].

---

[532] One of the exceptions to indefinite is a reference to appropriation of money to support the militia two years at a time.

[533] 'well-regulated'

[534] The responsibility of government to create and manage laws for the militia. The elaboration is with respect to jurisdiction which is federal and not state, as well as how those laws are to be "well regulated", but now in the context of individuals in society and their access to arms.

[535] The 2nd amendment, as a formula, as an instrument as fundamentally mandate government to create arms control laws.

[536] The less "liable", the less the suspicions regarding the true nature of the 2nd amendment.

[537] A misconstruction was simply the method to get an Arms control amendment into the Bill of Rights. It was understood that no one would sign onto such a thing, so it must somehow be hidden. It is less liable, because some delegates would actually hear that hyphen when being orated. How can the human ear hear or not hear a hyphen? It is a biased ear that hears what it wants to hear, and a biased eye that reads what it wants to read. Would anyone question or be suspicious of a hyphen that is not heard. The phrase, 'well

Remaining always & most Affecly yours
James Madison

The reference in the letter regarding congress promoting the general welfare is with regards to creating laws, allocating moneys, and maintaining the military as found in the enumerated powers of congress. The 'exceptions' corresponds to the term 'indefinite one' He is saying that there are some enumerated powers that are currently dormant, simply because they have not yet been recognized and therefore have not yet been put into practice.

I have transcribed some of the enumerated powers of Congress as laid out in the United States Constitution.

> "The Congress shall have Power To lay and collect Taxes, Duties, Imposts and Excises, to pay the Debts and provide for the common Defense and general Welfare of the United States; but all Duties, Imposts and Excises shall be uniform throughout the United States;"

> "To raise and support Armies, but **no Appropriation of Money to that Use shall be for a longer Term than two Years**;"

> "To provide and maintain a Navy;"

> "To make Rules for the Government and Regulation of the land and naval Forces;"

> "To provide for calling forth the Militia to execute the Laws of the Union, suppress Insurrections and repel Invasions;"

In article VI from Articles of Confederation: March 1, 1781 I have highlighted the phrase that is being referenced. This is the "old article of Confederation" that James Madison is referring to in his letter.

> "but every State shall always keep up a **well-regulated** and disciplined militia, sufficiently armed and accoutered, and shall provide and constantly have ready for use, in public stores, a due number of filed pieces and tents, and a proper quantity of arms, ammunition and camp equipage."

So how did I find this letter?

---

regulate" could be easily be masked and be less liable to both suspicion and any subsequent debate.

It was contrived. It was placed here for us to read, but in its own way, it was encrypted by alluding to other documents. The letter of course exists and it was archived and not destroyed. If it was actually explicit to the point of "letting the cat out of the bag" it would have been destroyed. At the time of its writing, if it had been explicit, it would have violated and exposed 2nd amendment prematurely.

I liked the context of the letter itself, but when I read the words "new instrument", my eyes turned to ping pong balls and I added this letter to my files for further inspection. So why would James Madison write a letter like this to Edmund Pendleton without getting right to the point? If I may say it, he did not want to point to the "right" explicitly. What urgency could there have be to send out such a letter after the constitution had been ratified? I believe that that James Madison is telling us that Edmund Pendleton was in the loop with respect to the 2nd amendments true utility. He could have helped in the orchestration of both misdirection and direction in the constitutional conventions.

386

First Important Findings Thomas Ritchie

While I was doing my research and piecing together historical threads I started to delve into the inquiries that Thomas Ritchie was making regarding a book by John Taylor in a letter to between himself and Thomas Jefferson. My first introduction to Thomas Ritchie was in the above letter. It was the first letter that I had encountered that seemed to be a direct reference to the 2nd Amendment This was about a month before I understood that ciphered letters were actually written.

My approach to discovering the mysteries of history at this point in time was to attempt to see if I could locate the actors that knew of James Madison's secret for surely he did not do this alone. James Madison was the logical starting point in this and due ot the nature of this letter it was warranted to looking into Thomas Ritchie. Thomas Ritchie appeared to be very interested in the matters of the constitutional conventions. It appeared that James Madison was responding to an inquiry which was made by this man. It is not surprising that his original letter of the 8th is missing since it was probably explicit in its questions. In light of this letter I started to do some research on him with respect to arms and the 2nd amendment at it turned out to be a gold mine of historical information leading right up to Abraham Lincoln and perhaps even the NRA itself. I am making no accusations here but I will be illustrating a chain of events that all appear to be related.

While there are many proofs in this book with respect to the writings of the fathers, this particular thread was different, because now that we know the truth of the 2ndamendment historical motive can now exist where it never existed before.

I will ask the reader to pay particularly close attention to some of my assumptions here. While I have no doubt that there may be some readers with political or industrial bias will attempt to disparage my observations. I only appeal more to the readers own intelligence, common sense, as this book is not meant to be a book of debate, but rather an exploration in history regarding the 2nd amendment. I will be adding footnotes to this document and highlighting a few key lines.

At the time this letter was written James Madison was 70 years of age and Thomas Ritchie was 43.

To Thomas Ritchie from James Madison Sept 15 1821

To Thomas Ritchie   Montpelr. Sepr. 15 1821.
(Confidential)

I have recd. yours of the 8th. instant on the subject of the proceedings of the convention of 1787.

It is true as the public has been led to understand, that I possess materials for a pretty ample view of what passed in that Assembly. It is true also that it has not been my intention that they should for ever remain under the veil of secresy. Of the time when it might be not improper for them to see the light, I had formed no particular determination. **In general it had appeared to me that it might be best to let the work be a posthumous one; or at least that its publication should be delayed till the Constitution should be well settled by practice, & till a knowledge of the controversial part of the proceedings of its framers could be turned to no improper account.** Delicacy also seemed to require some respect to the rule by which the Convention "prohibited a promulgation without leave of what was spoken in it;" so long as the policy of that rule could be regarded as in any degree unexpired.

As a guide in expounding and applying the provisions of the Constitution, the debates and incidental decisions of the Convention can have no authoritative character. However desirable it be that they should be preserved as a gratification to the laudable curiosity felt by every people to trace the origin and progress of their political Insitutions, & as a source parhaps of some lights on the Science of Govt. **the legitimate meaning of the Instrument[538] must be derived from the text itself; or if a key is to be sought elsewhere, it must be not in the opinions or intentions of the Body which planned & proposed the Constitution, but in the sense attached to it by the people in their respective State Conventions where it recd. all the authority which it possesses.**

Such being the course of my reflections I have suffered a concurrence & continuance of particular inconveniences for the time past, to prevent me from giving to my notes the fair & full preparation due to the subject of them. Of late, being aware of the growing hazards of postponement, I have taken the incipient steps for

---

[538] the 2nd amendment.

executing the task; and the expediency of not risking an ultimate failure is suggested by the Albany publication from the notes of a N. York member of the Convention. I have not seen more of the volume than has been extracted into the newspapers, but it may be inferred from these samples, that it not only a very mutilated[1] but a very erroneous edition of the matter to which it relates. There must be an entire omission also of the proceedings of the latter period of the Session from which Mr. Yates & Mr. Lansing withdrew in the temper manifested by their report to their Constituents: the period during which the variant & variable opinions, converged & centered in the modifications seen in the final act of the Body.

It is my purpose now to devote a portion of my time to an exact digest of the voluminous materials in my hands. How long a time it will require, under the interruptions & avocations which are probable I can not easily conjecture. Not a little will be necessary for the mere labour of making fair transcripts. By the time I get the whole into a due form for preservation, I shall be better able to decide on the question of publication.

John Taylor

Shortly you will be seeing a thread in history that took me to 1846, Thomas Ritchie, James K Polk, Samuel Colt and the Court. I did not make this John Taylor connection until after that. I did not know that time that Thomas Jefferson was part of cabal but when I did I later found this letter between him and Thomas Ritchie here. The initial Thomas Ritchie findings were about in the James Madison letter of Sept 15, 1821 which appears to be a similar enquiry as this one.

It appears that John Taylor's services as an author were recruited to carry on the narrative of the letters. The title of his book jumped out at me right away when I first read it. The full title of the book is "Construction Construed, Constitution Validated" and it was published in 1820. We now know that the 2nd amendment was hidden and this book appears to fit this new found knowledge like a glove.

Did Thomas Ritchie know the truth of the 2nd amendment? He had read the book and then questioned both Thomas Jefferson and James Madison about it. This man was later associated with President James Polk at the very time Samuel Colt was given a contract to manufacture 1000 Walker Colts. At exactly that same time one of the first ever court cases that cited the 2nd amendment appeared which was "Nunn vers Georgia" in 1846. I will be talking about this shortly in a bit more detail. I was following this thread because I was wondering if it would take me to the front door of the NRA, in the sense that they may have known about what the 2nd amendment really was. I was unable to establish this one way or the other so I guess its innocent until proven guilty. It's pretty much a moot point now anyway so I guess its best to just let bye gones be bye gones.

To Thomas Ritchie Monticello, December 25, 1820

DEAR SIR,

-- On my return home after a long absence, **I find here your favor of November the 23d, with Colonel Taylor's "Construction Construed,"** which you have been so kind as to send me, in the name of the author as well as yourself. Permit me, if you please, to use the same channel for conveying to him the thanks I render you also for this mark of attention. I shall read it, I know, with edification, as I did his Inquiry, to which I acknowledge myself indebted for many valuable ideas, and for the correction of some errors of early opinion, never seen in a correct light until presented to me in that work. That the present volume is equally orthodox, I know before reading it, because I **know that Colonel Taylor and myself have rarely, if ever, differed in any political principle of importance**. Every act of his life, and every word he ever wrote, satisfies me of this. So, also, as to the two Presidents, late and now in office, I know them both to be of principles as truly republican as any men living. If there be anything amiss, therefore, in the present state of our affairs, as the formidable deficit lately unfolded to us indicates, I ascribe it to the inattention of Congress to their duties, to their unwise dissipation and waste of the public contributions. They seemed, some little while ago, to be at a loss for objects whereon to throw away the supposed fathomless funds of the treasury. I had feared the result, because I saw among them some of my old fellow laborers, of tried and known principles, yet often in their minorities. I am aware that in one of their most ruinous vagaries, the people were themselves betrayed into the same phrenzy with their Representatives. The deficit produced, and a heavy tax to supply it, will, I trust, bring both to their sober senses.

But it is not from this branch of government we have most to fear. Taxes and short elections will keep them right. The judiciary of the United States is the subtle corps of sappers and miners constantly working under ground to undermine the foundations of our confederated fabric. They are construing our constitution from a co-ordination of a general and special government to a general and supreme one alone. This will lay all things at their feet, and they are too well versed in English law to forget the maxim, "boni judicis est ampliare juris-dictionem." We shall see if they are bold enough to take the daring stride their five lawyers have lately taken. If they do, then, with the editor of our book, in his address to the public, I will say, that "against this every man should raise his voice," and more, should uplift his arm. Who wrote this admirable address? Sound, luminous, strong, not a word too much, nor one which can be changed but for the worse. That pen should go on, lay bare these wounds of our constitution, expose the decisions seriatim, and arouse, as it is able, the attention of the nation to these bold speculators on its patience. Having found, from experience, that impeachment is an impracticable thing, a mere scare-crow, they consider themselves secure for life; they sculk from responsibility to public opinion, the only remaining hold on them, under a practice first introduced into England by Lord Mansfield. An opinion is huddled up in conclave, perhaps by a majority of one, delivered as if unanimous, and with the silent acquiescence of lazy or timid associates, by a crafty chief judge, who sophisticates the law to his mind, by the turn of his own reasoning. A judiciary law was once reported by the Attorney General to Congress, requiring each judge to deliver his opinion <u>seriatim</u> and openly, and then to give it in writing to the clerk to be entered in the record. A judiciary independent of a king or executive alone, is a good thing; but independence of the will of the nation is a solecism, at least in a republican government.

But to return to your letter; you ask for my opinion of the work you send me, and to let it go out to the public. This I have ever made a point of declining, (one or two instances only excepted.) Complimentary thanks to writers who have sent me their works, have betrayed me sometimes before the public, without my consent having been asked. But I am far from presuming to direct the reading of my fellow citizens, who are good enough judges themselves of what is worthy their reading. I am, also, too desirous of quiet to place myself in the way of contention. Against this I am admonished by bodily decay, which cannot be unaccompanied by corresponding wane of the mind. Of this I am as yet sensible, sufficiently to be unwilling to trust myself before the public, and when I cease to be so, I hope that my friends will be too careful of me to draw me forth and present me, like a Priam in armor, as a spectacle for public compassion. I hope our political bark will ride through all its dangers; but I can in future be but an inert passenger.

I salute you with sentiments of great friendship and respect.

Now this particular letter took me on a bit of tangent and coincides with what appears to be Thomas Ritchie's inquiries perhaps motivated by suspicion.

[Thomas Jefferson to Archibald Thweatt, 19 January 1821](#)

Monticello Jan. 19. 21.

Dear Sir

I duly recieved your favor of the 11 covering Judge Roane's letter, which I now return. of the kindness of his sentiments expressed towards myself I am highly sensible; & could I believe that my public services had merited the approbation he so indulgently bestows, the satisfaction I should derive from it would be reward enough. to his wish that I would take a part in the transactions of the present day I am sensible of my incompetence. for first I know little about them, having long withdrawn my attention from public affairs, and resigned myself with folded arms[539] to the care of those who are to care for us all. and, next, the hand of time pressing heavily on me, in mind as well as body, leaves to neither sufficient energy to engage in public contentions. I am sensible of the inroads daily making by the federal, the jurisdiction of it's co-ordinate associates the state-governments. the legislative and executive branches may sometime err, **but elections and dependance will bring them to rights**. the judiciary branch is the instrument which working, like gravity, without intermission is to press us at last into one consolidated mass. against this I know no one who, equally with Judge Roane himself, possesses the power & the courage, to make resistance; and to him I look, and have long looked, as our strongest bulwork. if congress fails to shield the states from dangers so palpable and so imminent, **the states must shield themselves and meet the invader foot to foot**[540]. this is already half done by Col Taylor's book:[541] because a conviction that we are right accomplishes half the difficulty of correcting wrong. **this book is the most effectual retraction of our government to it's original principles which has ever yet been sent by heaven to our aid**[542]. every state in the Union should give a copy to every member they elect as standing instruction[543], and ours should

---

[539] Another Arms symbolism, but folded, or a refusal to use them.

[540] Foot to foot appears to be a cute way to say "without arms". The states have been shielded because there are no arms in the symbolism of the invader. To shield is to secure, not let past.

[541] Thomas Jefferson is stating what Colonel taylors book is really about. Now, the reference to "half done", is just a reference that this book is like any of the other hoarded letters. In the revelation of what John Taylors book is really about, is the other half.

[542] Sent by heaven means the retraction is in "gods" hand or beyond their control. It's a posthumous work.

[543] A standing instruction is a symbolism for "waiting". There is no movement yet with respect to the instruction, because it has yet to be understood. O

sat the example. Accept with mrs Thweatt the assurance of my affectionate & respectful attachment.

Th: Jefferson

So here we have Thomas Jefferson talking about Colonel John Taylor's book.

He talks of congress not protecting the public from invaders? Of course congress would support the defence of foreign invasion, so what is the context here? The context must be invaders within the United States itself. The invaders is a reference to an internal Army that attacks from within, or an unregulated Militia.

To Thomas Jefferson from Spencer Roane, 25 Feb 1821

Richmond, Feb. 25. 1821.
Dear Sir

M Thweatt has sent me your favour to him, of 19 ultimo. As that letter was produced by mine of him, I owe you an apology for having caused you the trouble.—Be assured that no man respects your repose more than I do, or would be more unwilling to disturb it. Your claims to that repose, arising from the most eminent services, and from the weight of years, are so strong, and so touchingly pourtrayed, that I am compelled to say—"almost thou persuadest me to be a christian." Although, therefore, in losing our Leader, we run the risk of losing our all, not a whisper of my breath shall be raised against it. Your later days ought to be as serene and as happy, as your life has been illustrious, and useful to your fellow men.

The very flattering mention you are pleased to make of me, in your letter, I shall prize, as the highest honour of my life. **I have neither power nor leisure to render any political services, to my fellow-citizens: yet I see the Dangers which surround us, and shall be always ready to lift my voice against them.**—On account of the last paragraph in your letter, I have taken the liberty to send it, to Col Taylor. I have done this, under the approbation of Governor Randolph. **Col Taylor will be highly gratified, by your just and strong testimony in favour of his inestimable work. To that work may, already, in a measure, be ascribed, the revival which has taken place, on the subject of state rights.**

—I congratulate you on the resolutions of our assembly produced by the citation of the Commonwealth, into the federal Court: and I also congratulate you, most sincerely, on the support which the university has again received.

With sentiments of the highest Consideration respect, and esteem, I am, Dear Sir, your ob Servant
SPENCER ROANE

I have highlighted the key part of this letter. From that I extract this one sentence,

To that work may, already, in a measure, be ascribed, the revival which has taken place, on the subject of state rights.

This appears to be "code" for the 2nd amendment. John Taylor's book is all about it, but in turn is full of symbolisms.

It appears to me that Spencer Roane may have known about the truth behind the 2nd amendment. "In a measure", 'ascribed", because in this letter Thomas Jefferson is telling us that Spencer Roane is had favoured John Taylors work. I can't be sure of this, but it is most certainly a validation from Thomas Jefferson himself. He most certainly would have known about John Taylors work, and he would have most certainly have known that documenting it would have been of value for the future, hence this is one of the hoarded letters.

At the time of this letter Spencer Roane was said to be the most influential judge on the high court of Virginia. What is also interesting is that he was an older cousin of Thomas Ritchie. Now also appointed by Colonel John Taylor. History reports that Thomas Ritchie was a political enemy of John Taylor, and in light of his queries to Thomas Jefferson and James Madison he was highly motivated in finding out just what John Taylors book, "Construction Construed, Constitution Validated" was really about. Spencer Roane became ill in March of 1822, and passed in September 4th of that same year at the age of 60. The man who Spencer Roane replaced on the bench was also his mentor, Edmund Pendleton a federalist.

I have referenced a letter in this book between James Madison and Edmund Pendleton dated January 21, 1792. This letter talks about the usage of "well regulated" and "well-regulated". It appears that Edmund Pendleton was in the know of the 2nd amendment. It is possible, I suppose that the letter itself may have been contrived by James Madison and never sent to Edmund Pendleton, but the symbolism should still be clear. He was telling Edmund Pendleton the truth of the 2nd amendment, so it can be easily inferred that he fact was a confident.

It appears that a cousin of Thomas Ritchie, Spencer Roane may have known the truth of the 2nd amendment as well. This might be a good research project for someone other than I. It should also be noted that history reports that Spencer Roane was an advocate for the Bill of Rights. We already know that it was extremely important for the primary actors of the dangerous experiment to have a 2nd amendment amended to the constitution. Perhaps Spencer Roane a confident and an ally to the plan or maybe he was convinced with the suggestion of it from others? Thomas Jefferson did after all ask Archibald Thweatt, in the letter above dated January 19 1821 to write Spencer Roane directly regarding Colonel John Taylors Book.

Thomas Ritchie

Reads book Construction Construed by Colonel John Taylor which was published in 1820.

To Thomas Ritchie from James Madison Sept 15 1821

asking about the constitution

Writes letter to Thomas Jefferson regarding it Dec 20 1821.

A Conspiracy Theory?

This section is the result of my initial research in trying to resolve who knew about the legitimate meaning of the 2nd amendment. There will be no ciphers in this section because the men in the cabal have all passed on. I was also not even aware of the existence of ciphers at this point, or at least the narrative of them and the true nature of their construction so I was not attempting to hunt them down. This will demonstrate my initial strategy to try and figure out if there was anything that could be gleaned from history to explain the second amendment as I had read it. I was wondering if it was possible that its true utility had been lost over time simply because it was not required for flintlocks due to their limited lethality as a slow loading single shot firearm at least when compared to modern day weaponry. It is a similar sort of logic that has been currently used by liberals, but reversed, because to me the 2nd amendment was now complete opposite to what it was previously known to be. I attempted to follow the progression of firearms development as well as any citing of the 2nd amendment. Faster loading weaponry in the absence of pushrod and wad of paper surely would be dramatically more powerful firearm. The six-shooter came to mind, which lead me up to the development of the Colt-Walker revolver which was developed in the year 1846 by Samuel Colt and Captain Walker.

At minimum this section will demonstrate the first court precedents that cited the 2nd amendment with a certain level of exuberance that comes across as being suspicious. Now with respect to this section being a conspiracy theory it actually has two separate parts, where the first is I believe is more likely than the other. The first part probably won't be all that surprising because it involves a collusion of government, the gun industry and a precedent set with respect to the 2nd amendment about 170 years ago. This will also demonstrate the birth of that hyphen in well regulated in oral argument which has stood the test of time, but not English.

It is the second level of conspiracy that is perhaps the most frightening. What if I could link a man to that court who knew what the second amendment actually was and how to read it? It would be one thing to misinterpret the 2nd amendment, as this would be par for the course. It would be something completely different if someone actually knew its true purpose and decided to cover it up as a form of payment to the gun industry. I can link a man to that court and he appears to have been very suspicious about the constitution.

If you have read the previous chapter you will already be familiar with this man, because he was Thomas Ritchie. He was very interested in John Taylor's book, Construction Construed Constitutions Vindicated. This potential linkage can be found in the first letter which doesn't explicitly reference the 2nd amendment but only the constitution in which it was laying in wait.

> "**the legitimate meaning of the Instrument must be derived from the text itself**; or if a key is to be sought elsewhere, it must be not in the opinions or intentions of the Body which planned & proposed the Constitution"

In the complete absence of any correlating letter, being the one with the inferred enquiry by Thomas Ritchie, we cannot know if he was actually asking specifically about the 2nd amendment. Remember that James Madison was already writing ciphers at this time, and in responding to Thomas Ritchie, he may simply have been introducing a partial cipher for future eyes. I honestly don't think it would have made sense for James Madison to actually be telling someone else specifically about the 2nd amendment if it had already been agreed to by the cabal that it had to be hidden for about 100 years. This letter has after all stood the test of time and no one has ever been able to tie it to the 2nd amendment before. There may have been many historians in the past who were suspicious as well but in the complete absence of understanding the 2nd amendment, how could they have possibly known? On the other hand, Thomas Ritchie was in a time he had brushed up against men who did know this truth. I can name at least three, being James Madison, Thomas Jefferson and John Taylor. If he did make the connection, the only possibility I see would have been relating to correlating John Taylors book very carefully with the 2nd amendment. None the less though, when you see the up and coming historical events, one can't help but wonder. Get ready to connect some dots, or not.

At that early stage of research my theory was that the founders knew that the Arms technology would be advancing, but wasn't really needed yet for the 18th century due to that technology of the day. No one could predict how fast arms technologies would progress only witness its current state and how it was trending. In 1785 Thomas Jefferson took an interest in the French inventor Honores le Blanc who was making interchangeable parts for guns. The technology to do this was based in part on the loom and had to do with mass production.

Here is Thomas Ritchie's autobiography which as transcribed from Wikipedia.

Biography of Thomas Ritchie

He read law and medicine, but, instead of practicing either, set up a bookstore in Richmond, Virginia in 1803. He bought out the Republican newspaper the *Richmond Enquirer* in 1804, and made it a financial and political success, as editor and publisher for 41 years. The paper appeared three times a week. Thomas Jefferson said of the *Enquirer*, "I read but a single newspaper, Ritchie's Enquirer, the best that is published or ever has been published in America."[1] Ritchie wrote the stirring partisan editorials, clipped the news from Washington and New York papers, and did most of the local reporting himself. For 25 years he was state printer, a method by which his political friends subsidized their most articulate voice.

Ritchie was a leader of the "Richmond Junto," (originally with relatives Spencer Roane and Dr. John Brockenbrough of the Virginia State Bank Ritchie controlled the Republican state committee). Richmond was a violent frontier town when Ritchie arrived. Controversial rival journalist and Jefferson opponent James T. Callender was found drowned in three feet of water in 1803. Nonetheless, Ritchie set up a press and began advocating restrictions on free blacks as well as slave manumissions. Lawyer and Richmond Enquirer founding editor Meriwether Jones died in a duel on August 3, 1806. John Daly Burk and Skelton Jones (Meriwether's brother) also both died in duels before completing a projected four volume history of Richmond.[2] Ritchie editorialized against South Carolina and Georgia reopening the transatlantic slave trade, and later for U.S. intervention in the War of 1812. Political rivals also could find themselves excoriated in the press, and even President James Monroe was not immune. The Democratic-Republican party, once nicknamed the quids and thought more radical than Jefferson, grew increasingly pro-slavery, anti-foreigner and anti-Catholic over time. Committed to democratic reform in representation of the western counties and full manhood suffrage (for whites), Ritchie promoted the 1829 Virginia state constitutional convention. A modernizer, Ritchie came to promote public schools and extensive state internal improvements.

In national politics Ritchie's influence rested first on an alliance with Martin Van Buren. They both promoted William H. Crawford's presidential candidacy, and next that of Andrew Jackson. Ritchie favored the "Old Republican" "principles of '98, '99" against what he considered the corrupting influence of Henry Clay and the divisive tactics of John C. Calhoun, whose nullification and Southern-party policies Ritchie detested. Late in his life, Ritchie denounced abolitionists but supported gradual emancipation.

In 1844 Ritchie supported James K. Polk because of Polk's support for the annexation of Texas. Polk brought Ritchie to Washington to edit the national paper *The Union* (1845 to 1851). Ritchie supported the Compromise of 1850, but the new paper never was as influential as the *Enquirer*. Meanwhile, Ritchie had lost his Virginia base, as his son and namesake took over the Richmond Enquirer. In 1846, Thomas Ritchie Jr. killed Richmond Whig founder and editor John Hampden Pleasants, in a duel."

So as you can see here we have a man that rubbed elbows with presidents. What is of interest is that he had hooked up with President James K Polk and he shared a desire for Texas to be annexed. He was also very curious about the constitution at one point in time. We have now linked Thomas Ritchie to James K Polk.

1820 Thomas Richie writes a letter to Thomas Jefferson asking direct questions about Construction Construed. We only know this from the response there doesn't appear to be any record of the original letter, where perhaps the questioning may have been to explicit for other eyes.

1821 Thomas Ritchie, writes a letter to James Madison asking direct questions about the constitution. It appears that he suspects or wants clarification on something he has discovered. We only know this from the responding letter where there appears to be "hints" on how to read the constitution.

1836, June 28   James Madison was the last living founding father and "author" of the 2nd passes away

1837   Georgia creates the first arms control laws in USA history

"The Nation's First Gun Ban
"Georgia's state legislature passed a law in 1837 that banned the sale of knives "used for offensive or defensive purposes" and all pistols except "horseman's pistols." Possession of those weapons was also prohibited, unless the weapons were worn in plain sight.

History did not well record the reasoning behind the legislature's vote. What we do know is that the legislation stood as the law of the land in Georgia for eight years before the state's supreme court declared it unconstitutional and voided it from the books."
http://civilliberty.about.com/od/guncontrol/a/Gun-Control-History-Georgia-Ban-1837.htm

What I found interesting is the modern day bias of this author to not understand the reasoning behind Georgia making these gun laws at this period in time. Did he know he was just feeding the rhetoric that was supplied to him by today's rhetoric promoting the gun as being nothing more than a tool? In any event this modern rhetoric seemed to have an influence on his perception. Like any good government, Georgia was trying to protect its citizens. There is nothing nefarious about their motive for these laws because the motive would be synonymous with seatbelt laws or the need to regulate food safety practices. With a bit of thought, they were able to resolve that guns and swords can and were killing or maiming people. Laws are made to address safe keeping of a society, and it seems that in 1837, Arms had proven themselves to be of such an issue that laws were deemed necessary. This "reasoning" is used in most advanced governments today and this reasoning got a right, wrong. There was also no gun industry of note at that time, or they had not seen the genius exploiting the 2nd amendment as a rather powerful marketing tool. This environment was about to change.

1845   President James Polk recruits Thomas Ritchie to be the editor of the Washington Union.

Now one of the men in our cabal, John Jay was the first Supreme Court Justice. After him George Washington nominated John Rutledge, and after this man he then nominated Oliver Ellsworth on March 8th 1796. It appears that congress back then was not as sophisticated as they are today, and had not yet perceived loopholes in the constitution. Perhaps the word "shall" just lost a bit of its integrity over the years, as did the phrase "well regulated". Now this man had a son named Henry Leavitt Ellsworth who in 1835 was appointed to be the first Commissioner to the United States patent office. His brother William W. Ellsworth was the Governor of Connecticut from 1838 to 1842 and was apparently married to the daughter of our friend Noah Webster. This information is just some background information, noting some actors and their relationships. Some of it is admittedly just trivia but it's interesting how different paths in history and lives can cross.

Now as it turns out Henry Leavitt Ellsworth, the son of a Supreme Court Justice was known to have inspired many men to complete their inventions, one of which was Samuel Colt. It's not my belief that there was anything going on in this relationship, with the possible exception of a father getting his son a good job in government. In the year 1836 he made the decision to issue Samuel Colt patent number 138 for his revolver which allowed him to raise money. If you were to do a bit of research on Samuel Colt you will find that history reports him as being a very shrewd business man. His modus operandi is almost identical today's NRA. Even after getting his patent though, he was still having difficulty selling and promoting his wares but in the year 1845 he was about to get his big break.

Captain Samuel H Walker served under General Zachary Taylor in the Texas Rangers and hooked up with Samuel Colt to design and fulfill a contract for 1000 Colt-Walker Six shooters. The contract was awarded in 1845 and these deadly Arms were available to the United States Army in 1847. It should be noted at this time in history that gun manufacturing was highly specialize with respect to mass production. Each part had to be identical to next so that in the field parts could be interchanged quickly. There would be benefit to this in the heat of battle.

It would be quite an undertaking to set up a manufacturing plant in the industrial age to mass produce guns with interchangeable parts for a state of the art weapon. Now keeping in mind that Samuel Colt was having difficulty selling his arms previously would his start up costs for a plant just to make these Arms be worth it? If one is to have the ability to mass produce weaponry, it would be better to establish a larger market than just the US government for sporadic purchases from time to time. The entire population of the United States would be better from strictly a business point of view. The contract that Samuel Colt was awarded was for 1000 "Colt-Walker" revolvers.

Yes, for some reason the market seemed to open up for him.

Remember those Arms Laws that Georgia had established in 1837, just one year after the passing of James Madison? Well 8 years later something happened in that State.

In 1845 there was no Supreme Court of Georgia and then all of a sudden Governor George W. Crawford began to petition for one to be formed. He succeeded in his efforts and in January of 1846 he had is court, in a state that just happened to have gun laws on the books. In just a few short months a court case suddenly came up in April of 1846 which was Nunn versus Georgia.

In April of 1846 the case "Nunn vers Georgia" came to court and the 2nd amendment was cited, a precedent was set and a gun market was now wide open from sea to shining sea. The birth of wild west, as it is currently thought of, was born.

In 1847 the Colt-Walker contract was completed and the guns were distributed to the US military.

In 1849 Zachary Taylor was elected President of the United States.

In 1849 Zachary Taylor appointed Governor George W Crawford as his Secretary of War.

In 1849 George W Crawford was involved in a bit of a scandal. I bring this up because it appears this politician was a bit of a player. " The **Galphin Affair** was the disputed settlement over the Galphin estate, where George W. Crawford took 50% of the claim for himself. Crawford at the time was working as a part of President Zachary Taylor's cabinet.

The annexation of California, Nevada, Arizona ,Utah, New Mexico soon followed after Texas.

Samuel Colt's personal fortune skyrocketed after that Supreme Court precedent. He was known to be an extremely shrewd business man paying particular attention to the marketing of his wares. He soon became one of the richest men in America. He had also supplied both the north and the south with Arms during the Civil war.

January 10th 1862 Samuel Colt dies of gout at the age 47.

April 15, 1865 Abraham Lincoln is assassinated.

May 9 1865 the civil war ends

Nov 17 1871 The National Rifle Association is formed, just 9 years after Samuel Colts passing, and after all those guns from the civil war were flooded into the public domain.

Let's take a closer look at the court case

> "In July of 1846 Collier, Chief Justice, "The Constitution, in declaring that every citizen has the right to bear in defence of himself and the State, has neither..."

This Chief Justice comments about "defence" and yet, the word "defence" does not exist in the 2nd amendment, only the word "security" does.

> "our Constitution assigns as a reason why the right should not be interfered with, or in any manner abridged, that the free enjoyment of it will prepare and qualify a **well-regulated militia,** which are necessary to the security of a free State." So: "If a well-regulated militia is necessary to the security of the State of Georgia and of the United States, is it competent for the General Assembly to take away this security, by disarming the people? What advantage would it be to tie up the hands of the national legislature, if it were in the power of the States to destroy this bulwark of defence?"

Pay attention to the tone of this ruling. The 2nd amendment is still a right though, regardless of what it says, because it lives in the Bill of Rights. If this ruling is found to be null and void, will the spirit of it with respect to protecting a constitutional right still maintain this demonstrated passion.

> " Nor is the right involved in this discussion less comprehensive or valuable: "The right of the people to bear arms shall not be infringed;" The right of the whole people, old and young, men, women and boys, and not militia only, to keep and hear
> arms of every description, not merely as are used by the militia, shall not be infringed, curtailed, or broken in upon, in the smallest degree; and all this for the important end to be attained: **the rearing up and qualifying a well-regulated militia, so vitally necessary to the security of a free State.** Our opinion is, that any law, State or Federal, is repugnant to the Constitution, and void, which contravenes this right, originally belonging to our forefathers, trampled under foot by Charles I. and his two wicked sons and successors, reestablished by the revolution of 1688, conveyed to this land of liberty by the colonists, and finally incorporated conspicuously in our own Magna Charta! And Lexington,
> Concord, Camden, River Raisin, Sandusky, and the laurel-crowned
> field of New Orleans, plead eloquently for this interpretation! **And the acquisition of Texas may be considered the full fruits of this great constitutional right."**

There is no occurrence of "well-regulated" in the 2nd amendment, only "well regulated". No degree in law is required to discern this fact, only eyesight. This particular court case cited the 2nd amendment in order to strike down Arms laws that had existed in Georgia for over 8 years.

It is the last two lines that I have highlighted in this courts findings that seem a bit "off". The rhetoric here is that guns, as a right, are great for offence. This is obvious because it is why they were designed in the first place. To justify guns as a defensive weapon alone doesn't in anyway make it a defensive weapon alone. It is, and will always be both, no matter how it is explained or justified. So it appears that the 2nd amendment is great because guns can be used for both offence and defence. The United States Military under James Polk was conducting these wars, NOT THE PUBLIC. The 2nd amendment makes NO RESTRICTION with respect to arming the United States Military. Why then would a Supreme Court justice argue this point with such exuberance? It's almost as if he is trying to promote gun ownership, isn't it? It almost comes across as being a marketing campaign. By what realm of logic can he attribute the 2nd amendment as being a mechanism in the "acquisition of Texas" if it was government forces doing the acquiring, and not the people with whom the right is associated with?

Yes, Samuel Colt sure was lucky in this, and so too was the gun industry.

It has been stated that in the recent case of Heller vers Columbia 2008, that guns are an individual right to self defence. Yes, guns would be a individual consumers right to self defence. It was also stated that Heller versus Columbia was the first in-depth exploration of the 2nd amendment. They quoted the Nunn case, as taken from wikipedia...

> The Nunn court's decision has continuing relevance to the ongoing debate over gun rights. The Supreme Court in its ruling in Heller vers. District of Columbia said Nunn, "...perfectly captured the way in which the operative clause of the Second amendment furthered the purpose announced in the prefatory clause...."[15][2] The Nunn court concept of fundamental rights was relevant to determine whether or not the Second Amendment is a restriction only on the federal government or whether the right to keep and bear arms is a fundamental right that cannot be infringed by the state governments

They have called the front part of the 2nd amendment a prefatory clause

"A well regulated Militia, being necessary to the security of a free State"

They have also labeled the last part as being the operative clause being "the right of the people to keep and bear Arms, shall not be infringed".

As we now know, nothing could be further from the truth. The 2nd amendment is not to be butchered and then have one side put on pedestal where the other sits like a fern. The 2nd amendment is a sentence with four clauses. with each one being just as important as the next. Both courts got it wrong, and I say this in deferment to constitutional correctness.

The Martyrdom of Alexander Hamilton

Alexander Hamilton was one of the primary editors of the Federalist Papers and was considered to be a Federalist. James Madison "appears" to have been more geared towards states rights with respect to current known history. Alexander Hamilton was about 6 years younger than James Madison making him the youngest in the cabal. He was also the first Secretary of the Treasury.

Duels were held to protect a man's honor, mind you it was probably used as method for removing a human opponent for any number of reasons. In a way it was like sanctioned murder with its excuse being a man's honour.

Now you may think I'm making a political argument in this regard but I'm not. Alexander Hamilton thought along these lines as well.. If he hadn't then he never would have written what he did in the Federalist Papers. He was on "Team 2nd Amendment as the Holy Grail of Gun Control". He is not the type of man to endorse a dual and because of that, he died a martyr. Alexander Hamilton recognized that there was no cure for death. He recognized that honour or fear was no excuse for it in a civilized society. He recognized that guns were very dangerous. He wanted no part in their promotion or their utility beyond hunting.

On July 11, 1804 Aaron Burr and Alexander Hamilton met for a duel at Aaron Burrs request in New Jersey. Dueling was illegal in the state of New York so they had to cross the Hudson in small boats to Weehawken, New Jersey. Only one of these men was a patriot.

> "There are conflicting accounts of what happened next. According to Hamilton's "second"–his assistant and witness in the duel–Hamilton decided the duel was morally wrong and deliberately fired into the air. Burr's second claimed that Hamilton fired at Burr and missed. What happened next is agreed upon: Burr shot Hamilton in the stomach, and the bullet lodged next to his spine. Hamilton was taken back to New York, and he died the next afternoon."

http://www.history.com/this-day-in-history/burr-slays-hamilton-in-duel

> "Hamilton's friend Nathaniel Pendleton sat him against a boulder and a doctor named David Hosack examined him. Hamilton struggled to say: 'This is a mortal wound, doctor.'1 Hosack and Pendleton carried their unconscious friend into a rowing boat, hoping to make it across New York harbour in time for him to get medical attention. They sprawled Hamilton across the bottom of the boat and

one account has him regaining consciousness for a moment to say: 'My vision is indistinct... Take care of that pistol. It is undischarged and still cocked. It may go off and do harm. Pendleton knows that I did not intend to fire at him.'"

Alexander Hamilton by Ron Chernow page 705

> "With the utmost sincerity of heart I can answer those questions in the affirmative—I have no ill-will against Col. Burr. I met him with a fixed resolution to do him no harm—I forgive all that happened."

https://www.trinitywallstreet.org/blogs/archivists-mailbag/last-hours-alexander-hamilton

So this is another piece of history that has been uncovered in light of the new dynamic of 2nd amendment. We know that Alexander Hamilton was on the second amendment team, in being a primary author of the Federalist Papers, so it appears to me that he martyred himself in defence of his values and labor for the future of his nation. There are two reasons I write this now. The first is related to the book, and the second of course is to plug the play Hamilton in the hopes of garnering a ticket for myself, a ticket I sadly cannot afford at this time. I only seek a check with a balance.

It's interesting that the state of New York had made dueling illegal at this period in history. I guess they must have figured there were better, less lethal ways, for men to defend their honour and pride. I'm sure some people back then figured it was their natural right to be able to defend their honour and pride. I don't think the state of New York necessarily disputed this, but sometimes, a government, must protect the people in spite of their emotions. A government to some extent is like a parent where the children and like its siblings and some of the children think that Animal Farm is a much better way to run a society.

Alexander Hamilton's image is currently printed on the United States 10 dollar bill. The next time you have one in your hands, I ask you to reflect on what he did for America and that he had died in support of the final legacy of the United States Constitution. There is another Bill that holds a previously unknown secret as well. On the back of the United States one dollar bill there is encryption. I will proceed to tell you have this in the next section.

"We the People"

For the one or two people that are not yet aware of these words, this beginning of the preamble to the United States Constitution which predates the Bill of Rights in its construction.

> "*We the People* of the United States, in Order to form a more perfect Union, establish Justice, insure domestic Tranquility, provide for the common defence, promote the general Welfare, and secure the Blessings of Liberty to ourselves and our Posterity, do ordain and establish this Constitution for the United States of America."

After reading this preamble it appears, that it too is a 2A related cipher. It also ties directly back to the Declaration of Independence. I have explained why letters were capitalized in the 2nd amendment which is to give them emphasis. The 'S' in State is there to tie it back to "Liberty" through the definition of it in the Merriam Webster Dictionary. The A in Arms is there because it's the Arms that are on trial and not the people. "M" in Militia should be pretty obvious at this point in time because it has been used as a red herring to subjective readers of it. So, the point here is that capitals were used for emphasis, and even though James Madison did not create the 2nd amendment, he was part of the cabal that did. This is the same cabal that created the preamble to the constitution and in it, we also see capitals.

Let's deconstruct it.

"We" is critical. There is no "I" in "We". The United States is not about you or your opinions. Your opinions may be aligned with it, but your opinions are not the truth of it. Until every man can agree with every other, about everything throughout the cycle of his life, then there can never be an "I". It is because of our viewpoint of "I" which is the very reason why you must never trust everyone. Throughout our lives, sometimes we choose to share, and sometimes we do not because we are emotional creatures and life isn't necessarily smooth sailing from start to finish. Promote the "We" but fear the "I". I'm not talking socialism only the reality of human nature. This is what this document was written for, to guide it, in spite of it, but for it. Yes, it's a conspiracy but for the peoples Liberty.

"People", also capitalized, pretty much the same as We. This is about the people. The word People is not capitalized in the 2nd amendment. Remember that the 2nd amendment was predetermined well in advance of the constitutional convention.

"We the people of the United States" – Everyone must get on board with the 2nd amendment.

"in Order to form a more perfect Union"- the 2nd amendment must be read in "Order" so that the "Union" of "people and Arms" as "encrypted" in the word Militia will be more perfect in that is now a mandate to create common sense ,reality based gun laws. "more perfect" is reading the 2nd amendment objectively versus subjectively. It is also empowers, or rather forces any government to think and take care of all the people.

"establish Justice" is directly related to "well regulated", and note the capital "J".

"Tranquilty" is what happens when you walk out your front door. You don't have to worry about getting shot. Tranquility is the promise of the constitution, but it must be voted for so never empower "We", because "I" will always exist. Never vote for deregulation. Remember that all of us rely on society just to exist, regardless of our wealth. In order for "We the People", again no "I", no self defence, but only common that defence must be arrived at in a well-regulated manner, with rank, training and purpose. Are you allowed to defend yourself? Sure, why not, BUT not at the expense of "We the People", because this is not about you. Justice is for the "We" and not the "I" in the preamble. In this way you lose nothing and rob from no one.

"promote the general Welfare," is simply Life. Health Care. Life. The basics. The word promote is key here. It does not specify pure socialism. It's a line of demarcation. One man's Persuit of Happiness must never infringe on another man's Life or Liberty. Living wages, Education, Clean Water, Sustainability for both "We the people of today, and tomorrow".

"and secure the Blessings of Liberty to ourselves and our Posterity,"

This is directly related to Life and Liberty in the Declaration of Independence. The 2nd amendment predates the Declaration of Independence. These documents have all be carefully stitched together over a span of 61 years and the recognition for its need can be found in a document

Posterity is of course the future and if we rely on the earth for our sustenance which of course includes our climate, then the constitution demands that we study it, and take care of it because there is nothing more that can cause a society more harm than ignorance. Propaganda, Racism, Alternative facts, spin, lack of education so that the people can make better decisions about voting and of course the old dogma of the 2nd amendment.

Secure the blessings of Liberty = "being necessary to the security of a free State".

Where Liberty = "the state of being free" as per Noah Webster's Merriam Webster Dictionary. Remember that this was enlisted to help with this. (see correspondence with both Benjamin Franklin and Thomas Jefferson)

"do Ordain this Constitution of the United States of America"

The constitution is the "joining" of people and Arms, which lies within its truth. Of course it is ordained by the authors of the constitution.

The United States Constitution is currently understood (misunderstood) to have been drafted and James Madison during the constitution convention located in Philadelphia. The bulk of the constitution itself was more than likely composed during this time, but was also loosely based on the Albany Plan as proposed and never implemented back I 1754. Whether you agree with it at this moment or not, it will be established that the Constitutional Convention orchestrated well in advance. The 2nd amendment in its current text existed by at least the year 1752. The conventions convened on May 25 1787 and finally on Sept 17, 1787 the United States Constitution was signed. The Bill of Rights soon followed hence the term "Ten Amendments".

It's the preamble of the constitution that is of greatest interest here. Keep in mind that the Bill of Rights and its amendments were purported to have been created after and yet the 2nd amendment appears to fit the 2nd amendment like a glove when we look closely at it. It has already been shown, that in the ciphering rules, there could be no suspicion, and everything should have a dual meaning. So let's use what we now know about the 2nd amendment and apply it to the very preamble of the constitution itself.

Ok, I have already stated that the constitutional conventions were orchestrated. The 2nd amendment is referenced in a ciphered letter written to William Alexander by Benjamin Franklin in the year 1784. This man had passed in January of 1783 which enforces the fact that the letter is cipher, or at least very fishy and because why would Benjamin Franklin, a genius, write it just wrote for the halibut?. His strategy, which was relentlessly adhered to was that in order to completely eliminate suspicion everything had to have a dual meaning. It is also a relentless strategy of human nature that logic itself will always tend to believe that any one question will have only one answer. This line of thinking appears to be more dominant on the political right than it is on the left, and it's the political right that would be the greatest enemies of the new 2nd amendment. Don't believe me? Watch the pushback on this book and the approach to debate from those that want to keep the now "debunked" 2nd amendment alive. The word "union" itself has been demonstrated in symbolism to reference the union of the words "people and Arms" to equal a "Militia".

When we look up the word liberty in the Merriam-Webster Dictionary we get

Liberty: "the quality or state of being free".

We now know what the 2nd amendment really says and its true purpose.

" A well regulated Militia, being necessary to the security of a free State, the right of the people to keep and bear Arms, shall not be infringed".

It's about a right for all the people, and it is to protect them from the harmful effect of military arms in society. It is about society thinking of each other first, instead of themselves and their own fears. It is about trying to secure an environment of tranquility and liberty.

So let's revisit the preamble of the United States Constitution which was written in 1786.

"We the People of the United States, in Order to form a more **perfect Union**, establish Justice, **insure domestic Tranquility**, provide for the common defence, **promote the general Welfare, and secure the Blessings of Liberty to ourselves and our Posterity**, do ordain and establish this Constitution for the United States of America."

The New rhetoric of the 2nd amendment is that the people must think of each other first and not allow arms into society in the first place. This thinking is more in-line with "We the People" where the other line of thinking, being more fear based relates to "Me the People".

To "form" a more perfect union is to "form" an understanding in your mind , what "Militia" really means and how not allowing arms into society is of much higher benefit to all of society. "In Order" is a reference to how to read the 2nd amendment, which of course is from left to right, just like any other sentence.

Do you still think this is a coincidence? Take a look at this letter which was written to "fill in the blank" Perhaps "We the people?" and labeled after "July 4th" or symbolically the declaration of independence.

To —— (unpublished) [after July 4, 1786]

Sir

I cannot sufficiently express the great Pleasure I felt in seeing on the **4th Instant**[544], the **martial Appearance** and **excellent**[545] **Order**[546] **of the Militia under your Instpection**[547]. If all the military Corps of the Commonwealth, are equally well desciplined, we shall, **with the Blessing of God**, have nothing to fear from **foreign Enemies; the surest Defence of a State being Arms in the Hands of its Citizens**[548].

With great Regard, I am, Sir, Your most humble Servant

B Franklin.

Now I have no doubt, that this very letter the very precursor to the preamble of the United States Constitution, and it ties it directly to the "2nd amendment

This letter is first off addressed to anyone (us). Note the date of the letter as being "after July 4, 1786", which is of course independence day.

"A well regulated Militia"

---

[544] This pertains to the discovery of reading the 2nd amendment for the first time, which occurred 231 years after this letter was written, after it was most certainly inspected.

[545] Remember being graded with an "Excellent" by your English teacher? Personally I don't, but I've seen it written on the papers of my classmates. This is an inference as to how English is to be written and of course read. The 2nd amendment was written fine, but it was never read from left to right.

[546] Order, well an excellent order is the blatant reality that "A well regulated Militia", comes before everything else. It precedes the next clause which clarifies what it must accomplish and most certainly takes precedent over "the right of the people to keep and bear Arms".

[547] "Militia" is the key encryption, but to understand it requires inspection to unlock it's secret in making sense of the 2nd amendment.

[548] The surest defence of a free state of mind is to ensure that the Arms the people have, are ones not causing society excess harms, after the word "Militia" has been inspected.

The 4th instant is a reference to the fourth word in the 2nd amendment which is of course "Militia". It is a "martial appearance" , at this point in the sentence. The reference of under inspection is a directive to take a closer look at. This means to count the words as well as the word "order" is now referred to as being "excellent". Currently the term well regulated is often explained in terms as being "well-regulated" which is synonymous with 'well-ordered". I believe the word "excellent" is used here to distinguish "well regulated" from "well-regulated". It is "excellent" because once read as 'well regulated' one is much closer to resolving what the 2nd amendment really means. Laws are now involved.

Commonwealth simply means "common good", or ALL of society. He then states that "Arms" in the hands of the citizens are allowed to defend from foreign Enemies. The defence is only with respect to the State and NOT the individual. The arms are only in the people's hands when under the direction of the State. The only time Arms can be thought of as a tool of defence is when they are under control of the state and well disciplined.

> "If all the military Corps of the Commonwealth, are equally well desciplined, we shall, with the Blessing of God, have nothing to fear from foreign Enemies"

There is a reference to the Military corp being well disciplined to protect from foreign invasion only. With the blessing of god is a reference to putting your society ahead of your own self interests. At this point in time the United States Seal has already been adopted. The reference to god's blessing is also a reference to the eye of providence at the top of the pyramid. There is a section on this later, but I state it now simply because Benjamin Franklin has woven this theme into this letter. If you think of your neighbour first then the Arms, the dangerous ones will only be in the hands of the military corps and regulated under the direction of a group, and not an individual

The surest defence of a state is now a reference to nation as opposed to state of mind as in the 2nd clause of the 2nd amendment, "being necessary to the security of a free state". The people would have to be Armed to defend the country through the draft or regular forces and in this scenario those conditions would entail the people being both **'well-regulated" AND "well regulated"**. There is no talk of militias here, only arming the people to defend the nation itself under the direction of officers and ranks in times of war or sanctioned arming by congress. There was no 2nd amendment at the time the United States was divorcing itself from King George, so somehow the people managed to find a way to rise up. So what did the people do? They declared their independence united in a common cause, got themselves as well-regulated as they could under ranks and then took the British to task. There were officers in charge of the people who were supplied with Arms and but now there was something different. The people were now in charge of themselves, because now we have a democracy and this was a new thing. Every single person puts their opinion on an equal footing with every other. This however does not bode well for the liberty of all, because simply put all opinions are not created equal. The only value in respecting the opinions of others is because from time to time there may in fact be good ones. Nobody should be disparaged for having a bad one if their intent is honourable. This is of course just my opinion.

There is no contingency here because it is based on real events and real needs taking into account all of society. There is sometimes a fine line between being prudent and being fearful, because the fuel of fear is the imagination. If the entire point is to prevent death in society, then what is the point in not protecting the people from it in society? At the time the 2nd amendment was created I cannot speak to the statistics in this regard. However, 224 years has passed and the 2nd amendment has caused more American casualties from within its borders due Arms than all from outside of its borders to all of American Society then all of its wars combined. The difference between the wars and the 2nd amendment is that the 2nd amendment is under the control of the People, where the wars are more that of influences beyond the control of the people. The latter may not be 100 percent true, but the former certainly is. The people ARE the United States of America, and only they as a collective can tell themselves what to do, but only under the direction of the Constitution. To defend a state is a thing of physical geography, but to "secure a free state" is a reference to the human state of mind. It is either calmed or it is not.

Colonel John Taylor

Colonel John Taylor was from North Carolina. He was a politician and an author.

An Enquiry into the Principles and Tendency of Certain Public Measures 1794

A Definition of Parties: Or the Political Effects of the Paper System Considered 1794

Arator 1818

A Defence of the Measures of the Administration of Thomas Jefferson, attributed to "Curtius" (1804)

An Inquiry into the Principles and Policy of the Government of the United States (1814)

I took a brief look at at his book Tyranny masked 1822 and in the first paragraph he writes this.

> "SECTION ONE
> Good maxims are often worshiped with pretended devotion, and clothed with the splendours of eloquence, when their subversion is meditated; like white heifers whose horns were tipped with gold, and adorned with ribbons, preparatory to their being sacrificed."

This appears to be referencing "the right to bear Arms", as plucked from the 2nd amendment. Further along there is this paragraph.

> The defects of the old union soon suggested its improvement, and the convention for this purpose took place, before the predictions which had suggested **the experiment** upon the popular leader of a veteran army, were diminished. They were not effaced, because they could not find a Bonaparte, and being still alive, they naturally produced propositions for introducing a consolidated republic, by reducing the States to corporations, entirely dependent on the Federal government. These were probably sustained by the same arguments which had recently been urged to Washington to effect a similar purpose; but they were finally rejected. This rejection discloses a disapprobation of a consolidated republic by a majority of the convention, and subjoins to the opinion of Washington, the

solemn judgment against this form of government, of a body of men as enlightened as any which were ever assembled. The weight of authority, patriotism, and talents, was thus so far opposed to a consolidated republic which is attempted to be introduced, without having recourse to any similar tribunal. But the respectable minority which then attempted by fair means to introduce it, caused an alarm. The secret leaked out, and suggested amendments to the constitution, for the purpose of preventing future indirect attempts to introduce a consolidated republic. "The powers, not delegated to the United States by the constitution, nor prohibited by it to the States, are reserved to the States respectively, or to the people." If such was not the sole intention of this amendment, it had no intention at all; if it was to defeat this intention by absorbing these reserved State powers into a consolidated republic, it is unconstitutional.

Construction Construed and Constitutions Vindicated 1820 John Taylor

It appears that Thomas Jefferson had enlisted John Taylor to assist in adding literature to one day help substantiate the new revelation of the 2nd amendment. Historically, being pre December 2015, the very title of this book may not have stood out. In light what we now know, its title appears to have fireworks attached to it. I was unable to find a digital copy that I could reference directly into this document so I have transcribed some initial key findings.

In the very preface of the book the book he states this..

> "To the Publik"
>
> Page ii.
>
> The crisis has come, when following work "may do the state some service."
>
> The **Missouri Question** is probably not yet closed. The **principle**, on which it turns, is certainly not settled. Further attempts are to be made to wrest from the new states, about to enter in the American confederacy, the power regulating their own concerns. The **Tariff** question is again to be agitated. It is time to bring the policy and the power of a legislature's **interfering with the judicial functions** to the bar of publick opinion. The usurpation of a federal power over **roads and canals** is again to be attempted, and again to be reprobated. That gigantic institution, the Bank of the United States, which, while

yet in the green tree, was proclaimed by the republicans a breach fo the constitution., "stands now upon its bond'", but that charter, bad as it is, has been justified by the supreme court of the United States, on **principles** so bold and alarming, that no man who loves the constitution can fold his arms in apathy upon the subject. Those principles, so boldly uttered from the highest judicial tribunal in the United States, are calculated to give the tone to an acquiescent people, to change the whole face of our government and to generate a thousand measures, which the framers of the constitution never anticipated. That decision will be recorded for a precedent,

And many an error by the same example

May rush in the state. It cannot be.

Against such a decision, it becomes every man, who values the constitution, to raise his voice.

"In truth, we have arrived at a crisis, when the first principles of government and some of the dearest rights of the states are threatened with being utterly ground into dust and ashes. When we look at the original form of the government, we are struck with the novelty and beauty. It presents to us one of the grandest experiments that ever was made in political science. We see in it an attempt to ascertain , how far power could be so distributed between two governments, as to prevent **excessive concentration** and consequence abuse to it in one set of hands; at the same time , that so **much power** was conveyed to each, as to enable them to accomplish the objects to which each of them was **best adapted.** The federal government was to watch over our foreign relations; that of the states, was to particularly to take care of our internal concerns. The great secret was, to have these functions so wisely regulated, as to prevent the general government from rushing into consolidation; and the states, into a dissolution of the union. The first extreme would infallibly conduct us to great oppression, and probably to monarchy: the last would subject us to insults and injuries from abroad, to contentions and bloodshed at home. To avoid these extremes, we should never have lost site of the true spirit of the federal constitution. To interpret it wisely, we should have rigidly adhered to the principle, laid down by George Clinton, when he, from the chair of the Senate of the United State, gave the casting voice against renewal of the first bank charter:

"In the course of a long life, I have found that "government is not to be strengthened by the **assumption of doubtful** powers, but a **wise** and **energetick** execution of those that are **incontestable**; the former never fails to produce suspicion and distrust, whilst the latter inspires respect and confidence. If however, on fair experience, the powers **vested** in the government shall be **found** incompetent to the attainment of the objects for which it was instituted, *the **constitution happily furnishes** the means for remedying the evil by amendment*". This maxim deserves to be be written in the letters of gold upon the wall of the capitol in Washington.

The crisis has come, when following work "may do the state some service."

Missouri Question principle, Tariff interfering with the judicial functions principles excessive concentration much power best adapted assumption of doubtful wise energetick incontestable vested found constitution happily furnishes the means for remedying the evil by amendment".

This maxim deserves to be written in the letters of gold upon the wall of the capitol in Washington.

On page 41 he quotes something from Virginia which appears to come from the declaration of rights. What is interesting however is that this particular quote is not actually a quote but is an assembly of sentences. The author is referencing the Virginia declaration of rights but in the context of the 2nd amendment. The two distinct words, "well regulated" do not exist in Virginias Declararation of Rights. Just as I have stated, I don't think that this was an error of James Madison and I don't think this is a reverse error either, especially in light of the books title. The author has gone to the extra effort of adding more clarification to the 2nd amendment by stating that the people themselves have the power. It is their elected officials who are tasked to create the regulations, the arms control laws to defend the population itself from those of it that would choose to do harm.

This was on page 41 in chapter..

"All the power is derived from the people. Magistrates are their trustees or servants. A well regulated militia is the proper defence of a free state"

John Taylor wrote this book back in 1820.

Construction Construed, and Constitutions Vindicated.

" SECTION 2.

CONSTRUCTION.

    IT is necessary, before I proceed, to appropriate a short section to this art or artifice. There are two kinds of construction; one calculated to maintain[549], the other to corrupt or destroy the principles upon which governments are established[550]; one visible to common sense[551], the other consisting of filaments so slender, as not to be seen except through some magnifying glass[552]; one which addresses the understanding[553], the other which addresses prejudice or self-interest[554]. When a man splits his mind, and glues one half to certain principles, and the other to a mode of construction, by which the same principles are subverted, it is no easy matter to find arguments which will please both halves[555]. There was in old times a God, said by his worshippers to be blind and lame and foolish, but who seems to me to be more quick-sighted, active and acute in the arts of construction than Minerva herself. But his inspirations are unhappily partial; for, if this deity would but open the eyes of every one to his own interest[556], the mode of construction

---

[549] Reading the 2nd amendment objectively is defined by this book and its very wording.

[550] Reading the 2nd amendment subjectively The principle of government is to maintain order and protect its people through laws.

[551] Reading the 2nd amendment objectively and thus allowing government to be empowered to take care of the peoples welfare.

[552] The filaments are the two components of a Militia being People and Arms which can only be seen under very close scrutiny.

[553] Reading the 2nd amendment objectively"

[554] Reading the 2nd amendment subjectively, with speculation and conjecture and only the last words "the right to keep and bear arms".

[555] On one hand you believe in god and his teachings, and on the other you ignore those very teachings because you are unable to let go of your fears and think of yourself first, before your neighbours and fellow citizens.

[556] If everyone truly was a believer in gods teachings.

most conducive to the general interest[557] would be elected by a republican majority."

---

[557] The 2nd amendment read objectively would be accepted by most people, because it respects all the population, and not just the individual.

The Cherry Tree Revisited

A few months into my research after coming to grips with the narrative of the ciphers and usage of symbolism I recalled a story about a cherry tree and a young George Washington. I didn't investigate it until months later after I remembered thinking about it earlier. The symbolisms in the theme of that surface kept coming to my mind, Truth, Cherry tree, Axe, and a young George Washington. I remember when I first read it that it seemed like a bit of a fable and yet not a fable. It seemed too detailed and the cherry tree seemed to have too much importance. Then it seemed to become a lesson in telling the truth. It was very symbolic and almost cryptic because the message from the author seemed to have purpose of mind in the very detailing of it.

I believe the story first came to mind when I read the Thomas Jefferson quote "the tree of Liberty must be refreshed from time to time". It was already obvious how the 2nd amendment had been re-authored by the reader in reading what they wanted to read, or in other words "cherry picking" the sentence to suit their wishes.

I then stumbled across Thomas Jefferson's letter in which he had written

> "What a treasure will be found in General Washington's cabinet, when it shall pass into the hands of as candid a friend to truth as he was himself!"

Where before there was just one theme, being the "tree of liberty/cherry tree", now we have the appearance of another which is the "Truth" theme. The "legitimate meaning of the instrument" plays into this theme as well. It was time to take a closer look at the young George Washington and the cherry tree. The axiom, "Where there is smoke there is fire" was my viewpoint in this.

The author of that story was a Mason Lock Weems and it was titled "The Life of Washington and written in 1800. This was good because it fell well within the date range of the other ciphers. The next step was to establish if this man and Thomas Jefferson were communicating with each other. Yes they were which I will illustrate after first showing you a few excerpts from this book.

Read through it and see if you can pick out any symbolisms as related to the 2nd amendment.

> Never did the wise Ulysses take more pains with his beloved Telemachus, than did Mr. Washington with George, to inspire him

with an early love of truth. "Truth, George'" (said he) "is the loveliest quality of youth. I would ride fifty miles, my son, to see the little boy whose heart is so honest, and his lips so pure, that we may depend on every word he says. O how lovely does such a child appear in the eyes of everybody! His parents doat on him; his relations glory in him; they are constantly praising him to their children, whom they beg to imitate him. They are often sending for him, to visit them; and receive him, when he comes, with as much joy as if he were a little angel, come to set pretty examples to their children."

"But, Oh! how different, George, is the case with the boy who is so given to lying, that nobody can believe a word he says! He is looked at with aversion wherever he goes, and parents dread to see him come among their children. Oh, George! my son! rather than see you come to this pass, dear as you are to my heart, gladly would I assist to nail you up in your little coffin, and follow you to your grave. Hard, indeed, would it be to me to give up my son, whose little feet are always so ready to run about with me, and whose fondly looking eyes and sweet prattle make so large a part of my happiness: but still **I would give him up, rather than see him a common liar.**

"Pa, (said George very seriously) do I ever tell lies?"

"No, George, I thank God you do not, my son; and **I rejoice in the hope you never will.** At least, you shall never, from me, have cause to be guilty of so shameful a thing. Many parents, indeed, even compel their children to this vile practice, by barbarously beating them for every little fault; hence, on the next offence, the little terrified creature slips out a lie! just to escape the rod[558]. But as to yourself, George, you know I have always told you, and now tell you again, that, whenever by accident you do any thing wrong, which must often be the case, as you are but a poor little boy yet, without experience or knowledge, never tell a falsehood to conceal it; but come bravely up, my son, like a little man, and tell me of it: and instead of beating you, George, I will but the more honour and love you for it, my dear."

---

[558] The rod is a symbolism for a gun, and the lie is misreading the 2nd amendment due to fear. Some perceive it is better to have guns for self defence from other people with guns, except that if you are being hunted by another, there's a good chance you will never know it. The very gun that is endorsed is the one that will shoot you.

This, you'll say, was sowing good seed!--Yes, it was: and the crop, thank God, was, as I believe it ever will be, where a man acts the true parent, that is, the Guardian Angel, by his child.

The following anecdote is a case in point. It is too valuable to be lost, and too true to be doubted; for it was communicated to me by the same excellent lady to whom I am indebted for the last.

"When George," said she, "was about six years old, he was made the wealthy master of a hatchet! of which, like most little boys, he was immoderately fond, and was constantly going about chopping every thing that came in his way. One day, in the garden, where he often amused himself hacking his mother's pea-sticks, he unluckily tried the edge of his hatchet on the body of a beautiful young English cherry-tree, which he barked so terribly[559], that I don't believe the tree ever got the better of it. The next morning the old gentleman finding out what had befallen his tree, which, by the by, was a great favourite, came into the house, and with much warmth asked for the mischievous author, declaring at the same time, that he would not have taken five guineas for his tree. Nobody could tell him any thing about it. Presently George and his hatchet made their appearance. George, said his father, do you know who killed that beautiful little cherry-tree yonder in the garden? This was a tough question; and George staggered under it for a moment; but quickly recovered himself: and looking at his father, with the sweet face of youth brightened with the inexpressible charm of all-conquering truth, he bravely cried out, "I can't tell a lie, Pa; you know I can't tell a lie. I did cut it with my hatchet."--Run to my arms, you dearest boy, cried his father in transports, run to my arms; glad am I, George, that you killed my tree; for you have paid me for it a thousand fold. Such an act of heroism in my son, is more worth than a thousand trees, though blossomed with silver, and their fruits of purest gold.

Symbolisms:

Young George symbolises a young America as a nation.

The axe symbolises Arms, and a young America having and experiencing them in the public domain.

---

[559] Barking is congress or the judiciary cherry picking the constitution through oral arguments.

The cherry tree symbolizes the constitution and that part of the 2nd amendment that people like. Chopping it down is simply removing that part of the constitution that never existed which is "the right of the people to keep and bear Arms". This clause and the cherries are one and the same thing.

The "chopping down" is a transition from the old to the new meaning of the 2A and since George is telling the truth about chopping down the cherry tree, he is removing the falsehood. While the author of this story is writing it after George Washington's death he is telling us too that in reality George Washington also knew the secret of the 2nd amendment. We have seen his letters already which are further evidence to this.

So now we are back to George Washington representing a young America where his father in the story represents a founding father. His father is pleased, and now that the 2nd amendment is finally understood, he asks George, to bring him his Arms. Somewhat curious choice of words, isn't it?

I continued to read this story and attempted to decipher the symbolisms. It's amazing how clever this author was. In this section George's father is up to something.

> "One day he went into the garden, and prepared a little bed of finely pulverized earth, on which he wrote George's name at full, in large letters–then strewing in plenty of cabbage seed, he covered them up, and smoothed all over nicely with the roller.--**This bed he purposely prepared close along side of a gooseberry walk, which happening at this time to be well hung with ripe fruit**[560], he knew

---

[560] The goose step is a term that originated in the 18th century for infantrymen, hence the term gooseberry walk. This is all a direct reference to the 2nd amendment itself and its design. The bed are the words "regulated militia" which is the encryption of the 2nd amendment. It is in fact sleeping where the term berries, being something sweet and irresistible to mans' natural palate are the words "the right of the people to keep and bear Arms". The author is telling us explicitly through symbolism that this was hidden by design which both invalidates the current dogma of the 2nd amendment and validates the unknown narrative and true meaning and purpose of the 2nd amendment. This states that the 2nd amendment was encrypted in not one, but two ways. First and foremost it was encrypted by mans tendency to read what he wants to read.

would be honoured with George's visits pretty regularly every day[561]. Not many mornings had passed away before in came George, with eyes wild rolling[562], and his little cheeks ready to burst with great news.

" O Pa! come here! come here!"
" What's the matter, my son ? what's the matter ?"
"O come here, I tell you, Pa: come here! and I'll shew you such a sight as you never saw in all your life time."

The old gentleman suspecting what George would be at, gave him his hand, which he seized with great eagerness, and tugging him along through the garden, led him point blank to the bed whereon was inscribed, in large letters, and in all the freshness of newly sprung plants, the full name of

GEORGE WASHINGTON.

" There Pa? " said George, quite in an ecstacy of astonishment, " did you ever see such a sight in all your life time? "

" Why it seems like a curious affair, sure enough, George ! "

" But, Pa, who did make it there ? who did make it there ? "

" It grew there by chance, I suppose, my son."

"By chance, Pa! O no! no! it never did grow there by chance, Pa. Indeed that it never did! "

" High! why not, my son? "

" Why, Pa, did you ever see anybody's name in a plant bed before? "

"Well, but George, such a thing might happen, though you never saw it before."

" Yes, Pa; but I did never see the little plants grow up so as to make one single letter of my name before. Now, how could they grow up so as to make all the letters of my name! and then standing; one after another, to spell my name so exactly!--and all so neat and even too, at top and bottom! ! O Pa, you must not say chance did all this. Indeed somebody did it; and I dare say now, Pa, you did it just to scare me, because I am your little boy."

---

[561] Early America aka George Washington would be introducing more and more Arms to society as the perceived peoples right.

[562] Wild and rolling is symbolic of how much fun Arms can be.

His father smiled; and said, "Well George, you have guessed right. I indeed did it; but not to scare you, my son; **but to learn you a great thing which I wish you to understand. I want, my son, to introduce you to your true Father.**"

" High, Pa, an't you my true father, that has loved me, and been so good to me always? "

" Yes George, I am your father, as the world calls it: and I love you very dearly too. But yet with all my love for you, George, I am but a poor good-for- nothing sort of a father in comparison of one you have."

"Aye ! I know, well enough whom you mean, Pa. You mean God Almighty; don't you?"

" Yes, my son, I mean him indeed. He is your true Father, George."

" But, Pa, where is God Almighty ! I did never see him yet."

"True my son; but though you never saw him, **yet he is always with you.** You did not see me when **ten days ago I made this little plant bed,** where you see your name in such beautiful green letters: but though you did not see me here, yet you know I was here! "

" Yes, Pa, that I do. I know you was here."

" Well then, and as my son could not believe **that chance had made and put together so exactly the letters of his name (though only sixteen**)[563] then how can he believe, that chance could have made and put together all those millions and millions of things that are now so exactly fitted to his good! That my son may look at everything around him, see ! what fine eyes he has got! and a little pug nose to smell the sweet flowers l and pretty ears to hear sweet sounds! and a lovely mouth for his bread and butter! and O, the little ivory teeth to cut it for him! and the dear lithe tongue to prattle with his father! and precious little hands and fingers to hold his play-things ! and beautiful little feet for him to run about upon! and when my little rogue of a son is tired with running about, then the still night

---

[563] "regulated Militia" also has 16 characters, which is why the author stated how many letters there are in George Washington. In light of the symbolisms all pointing back to the narrative what other "logical" explanation could there be for telling the reader how many letters George Washington had with such specificity? George Washington was also a soldier as well, which is of course a component of the Militia.

comes for him to lie down: and his mother sings, and the little crickets chirp him to sleep! and as soon as he has slept enough, and jumps up fresh and strong as a little buck, there the sweet golden light is ready for him! When he looks down into the water, there he sees the beautiful silver fishes for him! and up in the trees there are the apples, and peaches, and thousands of sweet fruits for him! and all, all around him, wherever my dear boy looks, he sees everything just to his wants and wishes;--the bubbling springs with cool sweet water for him to drink! and the wood to make him sparkling fires when he is cold! and beautiful horses for him to ride! and strong oxen to work for him! and the good cow to give him milk! and bees to make sweet honey for his sweeter mouth! and the little lambs, with snowy wool, for beautiful clothes for him! Now, these and all the ten thousand thousand other good things more than my son can ever think of, and all so exactly fitted to his use and delight--Now how could chance ever have done all this for my little son? Oh George!--

He would have gone on: but George, who had hung upon his father's words with looks and eyes of all- devouring attention, here broke out--

"Oh, Pa, that's enough! that's enough! It can't be chance, indeed-- it can't be chance, that made and gave me all these things."

" What was it then, do you think, my son? "

" Indeed, Pa, I don't know unless it was God Almighty ! "

" Yes, George, he it was, my son, and nobody else."

" Well, but Pa (continued George), does God Almighty give me everything? Don't you give me some things, Pa?"

"I give you something indeed! Oh how can 1 give you any thing, George! I who have nothing on earth that I can call my own, no, not even the breath I draw!"

" High, Pa! isn't that great big house your house, and this garden, and the horses yonder, and oxen, and sheep, and trees, and everything, isn't all yours, Pa? "

" Oh no! my son ! no! why you make me shrink into nothing, George, when you talk of all these be- longing to me, who can't even make a grain of sand! Oh, how could I, my son, have given life to those great oxen and horses, when **I can't give life even to a fly?--no! for if the poorest fly were killed, it is not your father, George, nor all the men in the world, that could ever make him live again!** "

At this, George fell into a profound silence, **while his pensive looks showed that his youthful soul was labouring with some idea never felt before**. Perhaps it was at that moment, that the good Spirit of God ingrafted on his heart that germ of piety, **which filled his after life with so many of the precious fruits of morality**.

Can you see the symbolism in this?

The cabbage spells out "George Washington" who was of course a soldier.

It has been planted beside a gooseberry walk laden with fruit. The gooseberry walk I believe is what ones' eyes do when they traverse through the 2nd amendment. The gooseberries refer to its most appealing part, that being "the right of the people to keep and bear Arms". It is human nature to have one's eyes drawn to something that is appealing.

A well **regulated Militia**, being necessary to the security of a free State, the right of the people to keep and bear Arms, shall not be infringed".

Then there is talk of 16 letters, which is bracketed for emphasis. The author is doing this because just like the letters suddenly appearing, so too has the encryption of 2nd amendment. The words "regulated Militia", which have been subjectively read for over 200 years are now exposed objectively and coincidentally have EXACTLY 16 letters. George reinforces the symbolism further by saying it all stands in a perfect row and it cannot be put there by accident. It cannot be a coincidence. There must have been intelligent purpose behind its construction in the sudden revelation of it. This is a direct reference to the first objective reading of the 2nd amendment, which most certainly differs from ANY subjective reading as discerned for the past 220 years. This is exactly what I recognized when I first read the 2nd amendment objectively in December of 2015. The underlying intelligence could not be denied. I must say, this has been an extremely surreal roller coaster ride of research. It will of course be a great relief to find myself back on solid earth again.

The "plant bed" is symbolic of the Bill of Rights where the '10' days was selected as a reference to the 10 amendments. The 2nd amendment is "planted" in the Bill of Rights. Young George elaborates on this extensively, and quite frankly, I really don't feel any further requirement on my own part to do so. George says that it obviously cannot be a coincidence of nature, or in this case of English text. So with George as a "young America" suddenly discovering this, his father is symbolic of the founding father who planted this temporary secret by design. The talk of god also goes to the very heart of the 2nd amendment. There is no avarice here, no entitlement, but only a plea that the world be viewed in accordance with the gods wishes. The world was created for all men. That the world be respected and acknowledge and this of course is nature of the true 2nd amendment. A fly cannot be brought back to life, and neither can a victim of gun violence.

Think of your countrymen first and only then can the nation be truly united. There is enough bounty in America to be shared by all and if it all rises to the top, to the few and life is lost then oppression is back and the war of independence had no other effect than to transfer the title of king from one land to another.

Further down in "The life of Washington" Georges father states this..

> "for if the poorest fly were killed, it is not
> your father, George, nor all the men in the world,
> that could ever make him alive again !"

There is no cure for death, or in other words once someone has been shot or killed by lethal weaponry, it's too late.

I didn't go through this story from start to finish because I felt I had illuminated enough to demonstrate that this story itself was just like any other letter employed to encrypt the truth of the 2nd amendment. I did do a quick search on the word "militia" and it returned a result. I figured it would be worth a look see since it would make sense for the fabric of it to be sewn into this tale.

> "But to give Colonel Washington two thousand men, seemed to
> old governor Dinwiddie, like giving the staff out of his own hand, as
> he elegantly called it ;and rather than do that, he would risk the
> desolation of the western country, by continuing a defensive war,
> and a mad dependence on a disorderly militia, who would come and
> go as they pleased— get drunk and sleep when they pleased —
> whoop and halloo where they pleased — and, in short, serve no other
> purpose on earth but to disgrace their officers, deceive the settlers,
> and defraud the public"'

This is an observance that Arms are dangerous, especially the military grade arms even in the late 1700s.

I will again reference the Thomas Jefferson to William Stephen Smith letter dated Nov 13, 1787. This letter is the precursor to Mason Locke Weems story by about 13 years.

"what country can preserve it's liberties if their rulers are not warned from time to time that their people preserve the spirit of resistance? **Let them take arms.** The remedy is to set them right as to facts, pardon & pacify them. What signify a few lives lost in a century or two? **The tree of liberty must be refreshed from time to time with the blood of patriots & tyrants. It is it's natural manure"**

The "tree of liberty" relates to the "young cherry tree". "let them take arms" which is synonymous with Georges father saying "bring me your Arms". The "spirit of resistance" even relates directly to "a mad dependence on disorderly militia. The "defensive war" is related to the previous argument of a people requiring Arms for the contingency of a tyrannical government. "Desolation" is current trajectory of the United States with respect to military grade Arms allowed into the very society government is charged to protect.

As I've stated, a young George Washington is a young America that we can now put an age too which is 224 years. I suppose as far as nations are concerned if we are to use this as a symbolism, America has just learned that a certain "Clause" never existed. It only existed because it had to even though its utility would be harmful, it would render experience and with that hopefully a new found knowledge and understanding. If there are alternative facts to be argued, they will not be found in this research.

Thomas Jefferson's 'tree of liberty must be refreshed" is synonymous with "the cherry tree being cut down" from a symbolic point of view. It appears that Thomas Jefferson had given Mason Locke Weems some direction with respect to this story.

I think it would be very difficult to argue that this author was not recruited by Thomas Jefferson as a confident and actor to help document the truth of the 2nd amendment. This story was not a story meant for children, but for the Supreme Court of the United States and all the people of the USA in a time when gun violence has reached levels that can best be described as epidemic.

After a bit more research I managed to find this next letter. It's my belief that this particular letter was a reference to Mason Locke Weems story just after it was published. The "subject of publishing" is also stated. This letter was placed here for us to read, like all the others which have been referenced as "hoarded". The utility of it should be obvious because it directly ties Mason Locke Weems story, "Life of George Washington" and its symbolisms directly to Thomas Jefferson. The term "natural right" is a reference to the often quoted inalienable right of self defence. The term "sufficiently matured" is a reference to the 2nd amendment being hidden for a period of time.. Algernon Sidney was a republican theorist who had passed away over 130 years previous.

Thomas Jefferson to Mason Locke Weems, Dec 13, 1804

Sir

I thank you for the pamphlet you were so kind as to send me which I have read with great satisfaction. you ask my opinion on the subject of publishing the works of Algernon Sidney. the world has so long and so generally sounded the praises of his Discourses on government, that it seems superfluous, and even presumptuous, for an individual to add his feeble breath to the gale. they are in truth a rich treasure of republican principles, **supported by copious & cogent arguments**, and adorned with the finest flowers of science. **it is probably the best elementary book of the principles of government, as founded in natural right,** which has ever been published in any language: and it is much to be desired in such a government as ours that it should be **put into the hands of our youth as soon as their minds are sufficiently matured**[564] **for that branch of study.** in publishing it, I think his life, trial & letters should be thrown into one volume[565] & the Discourses into another. the latter is the most important, & many purses can reach one volume which could not conveniently extend to the other. should you proceed to the

---

[564] The youth, being the United States of America has now matured to the age of 224 years. The branch of study is the 2nd amendment being scrutinized and revealed.

[565] The discourses are the debates about the 2nd amendment being bad. He refers to two different volumes though, and yet it is one book. This is because there are two different interpretations. The two purses are symbolisms of the people of the day buying into the fable of George Washington, but they would not buy into the truth of the 2nd amendment in the beginning. The debates would arise over the years and more and more people would be more willing to buy into the "latter", which is that gun violence is tearing our society apart.

publication, be so good as to consider me as a subscriber:[566] and accept my salutations & assurances of great esteem & respect.
   Th: Jefferson

---

[566] An obvious of endorsement from a man who knows exactly what this story is about, and who it was really written for.

TREASON

If you have read the other ciphers by Benjamin Franklin you will know that the "William Alexander" series are particularly telling. These letters have been exposed as ciphers. I have placed the following cipher here which already discerns the intent of the founders as to the penalty for those that choose to ignore the 2nd amendments activation and maintenance once exposed. Regardless of ideology and completely independent of the shenanigans of politics any government which includes congress, the executive and the Supreme Court of the United States will be under penalty of high treason if they choose to ignore societies right of the 2nd amendment. As shown in United States Seal chapter, the states themselves have no say in this matter either. The evidence as presented in this research should be an open and shut case.

IT WOULD BE AN ACT OF HIGH TREASON.

While I don't expect everyone to understand the information presented here, I do expect that the bulk of America will. Ignorance or feigned ignorance should not be an option for the judiciary.

George Washington, Benjamin Franklin, Thomas Jefferson, John Adams, Alexander Hamilton, James Madison and John Jay are 100 percent behind this. The rest of the delegation signed onto it because they chose not to read it in the sense that they read what they wanted too.

From William Alexander

> ALS: American Philosophical Society
> Dijon 22d Decr 1776[567]
> My Dear Sir
> I can hardly express my surprise on first hearing of your arrival, And Altho' motives are here assigned for your Journey[568] which I will not beleive unless you Confirm them yourself[569], That safety is your object[570], and I will only believe you, because I think you one of the

---

[567] Battle of Ironworks Hill. (Battle of Mount Holly)
[568] Into the future until discovered.
[569] Proof of new meaning through letters.
[570] 2nd amendment and real meaning

few Politicians, to whom Lying will be unnecessary[571]. Be that as it will, my hypothesis is already formed, but without Entering[572] into such Abstruse Matters[573], I conceive it very possible that you may find it convenient to be retired for Some litle time[574], were it but for a few weeks perhaps untill the British Parlt meets after the Holidays. If this or any other Motive can Induce you to Come the length of Dijon I write[575] you My Dear Friend[576] to offer you a sanctuary, which I am Sure when you are in it, will be Agreeable. I am here in a very Comfortable House with a very Good spare Room for one I Love, I have only with me two very Excellent young Girls[577] who will Consider you as another Father[578]. You can be much, or litle in society as you please. And you can have the Company[579] of a few very Ingenious and worthy Men, Or a More Briliant Company[580], if you incline part of both, or none of Either[581] If you please. I can offer you the use of

---

[571] If one is not lying then one is speaking the truth, where the context of it is the 2nd amendment as revealed.

[572] The encryption of the 2nd amendment.

[573] The 2nd amendment will be difficult to figure out.

[574] It must remain in limbo until the future.

[575] Length of "Dijon" is 5 letters , as the word right, which is followed by the word "write".

[576] Note the term "friend", and previous usage of "truth". This is the theme that Thomas Jefferson borrowed on years later when he said "Candid a friend of Truth".

[577] Young girls are servants, but refer to the words "people and arms' and they are excellent because they are going to serve the nation.

[578] The 2nd father is the 2nd amendment which has two occasions of the words "people and Arms" , which are the two excellent girls because they are of better service to society once broken open out of the word Militia

[579] A military term, aka "Militia"..

[580] Shed some light on the word Company as in think about it more. Company of soldiers = Militia.

[581] Reference to regulating either just the Arms, just the people , or a little bit of both as long as the peace is kept. If there is no harm in society from the current Arms there, then no regulations are required.

Some of the Best private libraries in France⁵⁸². Living is here good and Cheap⁵⁸³. It will not Cost me more than 2 *l.t.* per day to Entertain you like a Prince.

I have no English servants so that It might be possible for you to remain incognito⁵⁸⁴ If you desire it, by assuming another name⁵⁸⁵. I have even Contrived a vehicle for you Correspondence in case you should have any of a secret Nature⁵⁸⁶. There are two post Coaches a week from Paris⁵⁸⁷. The Charge of travelling from thence will be about 3 **Louis**. The distance is about the same as from Paris to Dover⁵⁸⁸. I think I have now left you but two Excuses, Pleasure⁵⁸⁹ or Business⁵⁹⁰, for I put health out of the Question with your

---

⁵⁸² "Private" is another hint as to the word Militia. France code for the 2ⁿᵈ amendment because "Dijon" as referenced earlier as "right" is within the 2ⁿᵈ amendment. Library is a symbolism that the best solution to gun violence has been shelved in the constitution already. It only has to be read for what it is. It is the best solution.

⁵⁸³ Good and cheap is a reference to how much less it will cost society once the 2ⁿᵈ amendment is finally resolved for what

⁵⁸⁴ England is a reference to a nation that regulates Arms in public domain, where USA will not due to misread 2ⁿᵈ amendment. Hence, there are no "English servants" or those with a viewpoint that the public should be protected from guns.

⁵⁸⁵ It may take awhile to read the 2ⁿᵈ amendment objectively through its very English. The English language will serve up the true meaning. It might take some time though. It did.

⁵⁸⁶ The "Case" relates to the letters themselves as hints. The capitalization of 'M", "S", "A".

⁵⁸⁷

⁵⁸⁸ Louis means "reknowned warrior in France (as related to Paris) but in Dover (England) it is more a derivative of Lawrence or laurels. Aka victory. There is victory for all once the 2ⁿᵈ is read for what it is. England has gun laws at this time still, where America is about to have free reign over guns with the 2ⁿᵈ amendment.

⁵⁸⁹ Guns are fun.

⁵⁹⁰ Guns are for hunting

Constitution[591]. I will Come and fetch you If you desire it, Tho' I woud leave my two Girls with reluctance but we will all Come some stages to meet you. So let me know your resolution. Your friends in England were all well about a fortnight ago, I mean all those I know. Williams you probably know is very agreeably Setled with the Blunts[592] and will work his way. He is my faithfuls Correspondent for American news, and behaves so as to deserve and Obtain the love of all who know Him[593].

With regard to myself I Shall say the less, that I am in print [*interlined*: for the use of my friends] tho' not publishd, but my history Since you left us is a litle romance, which you shall see at meeting, at present I Shall only Say that your two Last Thousand pounds were paid in a Jail, so that money Matters are even between us, tho' there is a large account in my heart, that never will. It will be in the Mean while a Satisfaction to know that I have been always Very happy and still preserve my old system That time and Patience will with propriety of Conduct, bring about every desireable end. My Antagonists say I am very obstinate which I hope is the worst They can say of me.

In case we are not to meet let me know my Dear Sir[594] If I can be usefull to you. You know perhaps better than myself what I am fit for, and in any thing you will desire, but high Treason[595] You may Command me [*interlined*: and that I will only Commit when I go to America] were It even necessary[596] to go to England for you. The

---

[591] Health or self defence of the person has nothing to do with guns as far as the constitution is concerned.

[592] Merriam Webster Dictionary for Blunt : "slow or deficient in feeling".

[593] Note the Williams and Alexandre are used in the letter itself. William is code for protecting or hiding the 2nd amendment for the future. This is done by people loving the term "the right of the people to keep and to keep and bear Arms".

[594] He is addressing us, the future , and he can only guess the circumstances.

[595] It would be high Treason to ignore the 2nd amendment

[596] Being necessary to the security of a free State, which would be fulfilled by "England" style common sense gun laws.

more you Employ me the more you will oblige me[597] and that you may not think the Compliment[598] too great know that I am studying Law[599] and Anatomy[600] thro' sheer Idleness[601]. In case you can make me of use I can contrive a resource for the Girls for a Month or two. I conclude this long letter by assuring you, That you have no friend who is more Entirely Yours Than Your most obedient humble Servant

    William Alexander

    My address is a Monr Alexandre Hotel de st Louis a Dijon[602] as I know not your address I Send this under Cover of my friend Mr. Lumisden a very worthy and Ingenious Man who knows Paris well and I am Sure will have a pleasure in being usefull to you. He is the single Person in Paris That knows any thing of me or my affairs and can give an account of both and of Dijon where he did me the favour to spend a few days with me.

    Notation: Lett. from W Alexander Dijon 22 Decr 1776

---

[597] The more guns that are removed from society through the employment of the 2A, the more thankful society will be. Remember that "William Alexander" is a cipher for the 2nd amendment "Protector of Protector of Humanity" Hidden 2nd amendment(protector) which is really too protect society with reality based gun laws.

[598] Compliment too great = very well.

[599] Law = Regulated

[600] Anatomy = Arms

[601] Idleness of course has created guns in society, a full compliment aka recognition of them.

[602] Address of the solution to gun violence: Housed in Alexandre Hotel (Alexander means protector) Dijon as stated before means "right"

6-United States Seal

You may be wondering what the United States Seal has to do with the 2nd amendment. About 9 months into this research after having discovered well over 150 letters it was pretty obvious that symbolism was heavily used in their construction. Having already established that the time frame in which they existed by at least around the time of the Declaration of Independence and that they were actually used in the Bill of Rights wondered if the Seals were used as well in this plan. While not of a literal nature with the exception of the Latin inscribed upon it the Seals highly symbolic themselves. In prior years I had looked into the symbolism of these Seals with no other motivation than curiosity. I remember that they too were conjectured upon a little bit as to the meaning of their symbolism. That being the case inferred that their symbolism wasn't fully explained from source. I think it can be agreed that the 2nd Amendment is the same type of creature. So I decided to give them a closer look with no expectation of success in this matter but I did know most certainly being kept so why leave a stone unturned? If they were related this particular stone would most certainly be a milestone in this research.

While I liked what I saw in the Seals, I knew that liking something was not necessarily the path to the truth. In a way they were like indicators that I saw in the letters before I realized they were ciphers but there would really be no path forward in conjecture alone. The other issue was that I had not even established yet the men in the cabal were directly tied to the final version of these Seals. The problem was that the Seals were finalized in 1782 by the secretary of the Continental Congress Charles Thompson. There were four committees and it was only the first one which was formed immediately after the Declaration of Independence. Now that committee I would have been fine with had they completed the Seal, because on that one there were only three men and all of them were part of the cabal. Benjamin Franklin, John Adams and Thomas Jefferson were initially charged with this task. Unfortunately at first glance they appeared to be out of the loop.

This particular research is and the threads that I was trying to follow in it was a bit of a treasure hunt and I had to address a few new problems if I was going to attempt to tie the Seals into this matter.

Now with that all being said I had to accomplish two things. I had to establish that Benjamin Franklin or the cabal had either direct or indirect influence in the drafting of the United States Seal. I then had to establish that the United States

Seal was a graphical encryption of the United States Seal or just another cipher. It would be like reading any other letter but now I was not just dealing with words but objects. I encountered a few hurdles in this endeavour so please bear with me as I take you through the path I took in this rather interesting quest. While I didn't' need this additional evidence to shore up what I already discovered you would have to admit it would be a rather astonishing discovery similar to a few of the others that I have shared with you so far.

I looked into the history of the seal and discovered that the Continental Congress had appointed a committee who were tasked to create a National Seal shortly after the Declaration of Independence was read. The original committee members were Benjamin Franklin, John Adams and Thomas Jefferson. I located this information on Wikipedia. Four consecutive committees were actually appointed to finally render the United States Seal.

The current official United States Seal was presented to the Continental Congress by Charles Thompson who had headed up the fourth and final committee. Charles Thompson was the secretary to the Continental Congress and was asked to compile the three previous versions to come up with the final one. I'm stressing here that the symbolisms were not of his creation but it was his version that was finally adopted.

The Eagle Side

Eagle Head is President

Currently the interpretation is out of many states one, but in a democracy it seems more applicable to be related to the head of state.

E Pluribus Unum - Out of Many, One – Once president is elected from all the people, of the people for the people. It is also held in the mouth of the eagle which only has one brain.

Body is the People

Shield is the Congress – which protects the people through statutes

Tail feathers : the judiciary steering everyone along the lines of the constitution.

The Pyramid

So one side of the United States Seal seems to appear to reflect the constitution and is partly related to the 2nd amendment in meaning, but it can also further be elaborated on because we know when the key framers were working through their plan. The opportunity would have been irresistible to use the United States seal to incorporate a message for the future. Is the key enough to share it though?

It is pyramid I found the most interesting and actually the most relevant to the 2nd amendment.

Annuit Cœptis approved of undertakings.

The current interpretation is that "Providence is in favor of our Undertakings".

I don't see it like this for a number of reasons. I'm sure many would disagree simply because who would not want to be favored by god. This is bias and right or wrong it's based on a previously established narrative. Does this sound familiar? Reason number one is that "Did god actually tell anyone that he is in favor of the United States?" I'm of catholic upbringing, and I was taught that we are all judged by our deeds at St Peters gate. Besides these gates there is a fire pole of sorts and it is the gravity of our nefarious deeds in life that will bring us to a place where the only mercy is that we will never see a utility bill for heat again. So pick wisely, the utility you see in the Bill of Rights in the context of We the People. God does not judge countries, he only judges men, and he only does this based on how we use the free will he has blessed us with. During our life we must make choices, good or bad, we must make choices and we can choose to learn from them or not. While there may be comfort in normalizing that which is not right it might be better to work toward correcting the wrongs and then normalize that instead.

It is my opinion that the eye is a reminder that we are always being watched and it is hoped that the choices we make are virtuous in nature. The eye is the present for that is the only place when any American can make a choice. The present is of course dynamic which is why the eye is above the pyramid and not attached to it. The past is the pyramid it is all the labours of every American before that has helped to create and build not only the nation of the United States but also its current culture. Regardless of how virtuous any man has been, in the cycle of life of each American, a nation is being built. The decision of a man's vote is complicit in the formation of this pyramid.

Now the eye is disjointed from the pyramid and its open and watching to remind us that in anything we do, we have a choice and it would be in gods favour if our choices were made for the good of the nation and not the good of ourselves. Now the top of the pyramid represents the PRESENT at any point in time. Each and every man in United States are always making choices in the present, and the pyramid represents the full culmination of those decisions be them good or bad. It is the nation that the people get to own. It is preferred though, that before you make any decision that you think of your fellow man and not infringe on his liberty. That eye is watching and it does not blink. Everyone has a choice, everyone has opportunity and some people have more power than others, so don't choose oppression. The pyramid represents the current culture and history of the United States of America as built by every man in the democracy. It is a constant process, there is no gift here. Its borders only define a region of rock, earth and tree with everything else, including humans just cycling through their own lives. Is the extinction of life or liberty a thing to be proud of in the name of progress? Liberty provides quality of life, because it can only exist in the absence of oppression. The source of oppression will always come from the nature of man and any of us can oppress others from time to time. Sometimes we may experience guilt as a result of this and sometimes we may view it as a means to an end which is generally self serving in nature.

The United States is not a thing that exists to be exploited. It is simply the summation of all the choices the people have made beginning just one minute earlier. These choices can only be created in the here and now and their outcomes will be either recorded to history or be realized in the near to far future. The only thing that can be changed is the future, because each man is the brush of his own destiny, but the nation, under the constitution will always be its canvas. Votes can be canvassed, but what they paint, in a democracy may not always be a pretty picture in the context of "We the People", if avarice is mixed into its ink. It's a stain on humanity's better nature. Avarice can only thrive though, if it is given not just opportunity but the power to do so in the first place.

Life Liberty and the Pursuit of Happiness are for everyone. One man's pursuit of happiness must not infringe on another's liberty or life. This is the heartbeat of the United States Constitution and is in fact necessary for all to understand and appreciate the truth behind the 2nd amendment. In the history of man there has never been a self regulating man once he has been inserted into a society. This cannot be debated, because it is impossible that every man will agree with every other on every issue in every moment of his life regardless of his wealth, race, intelligence, maturity, religion, ideology or even good looks. If a conflict of ideas must exist then so too must government and so to must a constitution which was put there not to win the debate, but put there in spite of the debate to protect every man and the very sanctity of the greater union.

I've inserted this letter here because it demonstrates Benjamin Franklin's views on religion and virtuous thought. I found this letter as a result of scanning through documents and this one stood out simply because it started with the words "A Tale". It came across as something Benjamin Franklin wanted us to know. The original letter was in French so I translated it through an online translator

Connecting Benjamin Franklin to the Seal

When I was consolidating my work in this section for publication I realized that I missed something rather important. It appeared that Benjamin Franklin, Thomas Jefferson and John Adams had been taken out of the loop. I was partial to the interpretation that I had presented because it was consistent with the theme of having the courage to think of country over self. It was in the 3rd and 4th committees that a man by the name of William Barton was involved in the process. He was a lawyer a scholar and a known expert in Heraldry.

Charles Thompson had enlisted William Barton's expertise when he was consolidating the previous symbolisms from the first three committees. I noticed something very interesting during the design phase of the third committee. William Barton suggested that the pyramid with its thirteen steps and the eye be put on the back of the Seal. Why did this man want this symbol in here because it was my impression that the eye was symbolic of an interface to record ALL of the choices we make in life and act upon which would be consistent with "We the People" or "Me the People". In using the analogy where there is smoke there is fire, I perceived a wisp of smoke here which I felt warranted further investigation. This choice of symbolism fit perfectly with the 2nd amendment because it was all about choosing country over self and fears that influence out logic in making decisions. If this was factually true then I had to see if I could somehow establish William Barton as a possible proxy to Benjamin Franklin through documentation or known?

Ok, now it was getting interesting because there appeared to be a trail. I did some more research on William Barton and discovered that in the year 1789 he was invited to join the American Philosophical society. This would immediately connect him to Benjamin Franklin, the rest of the cabal and possibly make him a proxy to the Seal. I then started to see if I could find any letters between Benjamin Franklin and William Barton at Franklinpapers.org.

There were about six letters but none appeared to be what I was looking for. I was looking for a letter ciphered with symbolisms of pyramids or eyes. I did a bit more research on William Barton and discovered that he was a nephew to a David Rittenhouse who, as it turns out, was not only a member of the American Philosophical Society but was elected to the position of president after Benjamin Franklin's passing in April of 1790. I found exactly what I was looking for in a letter dated April 29th 1780. There is another thing about David Rittenhouse. He was an astronomer and liked to keep his eyes on the heavens. He also was skilled in working with metal, made his own telescopes and clocks.

Take a gander and see what you can glean from it. The tone of the letter is also very important so what you will be looking for is aloofness. The letter wants to tell you explicit

What is equally important as the symbolisms is the tone. Remember that if a letter is a cipher, it was written to be found by you, but it could not be explicit. In the writing of it the sender is not facing the recipient but rather you. The letter may not even have been mailed and was more than likely just archived after being carefully crafted.

From David Rittenhouse April 29th 1780

als: American Philosophical Society
Philadelphia April 29th. 1780
Sir
Amidst the many **important objects of your attention** I doubt not but you sometimes **unbend your mind** by an Excursion thro' the fields of Philosophy, I shall therefore make no apology for communicating to you a freak of Nature which seems to be new, at least it is so to us. On the 19th. of August last during a heavy Shower of Rain, not attended by any Thunder lightning or wind, a prodigious Torrent fell on the North or Blue Mountain **10 Miles** from Carlisle, and Carried away every Rock and Tree however large that stood in its Course, it likewise tore up the **Earth & Stones from 4 to 10 feet deep**, and from **two to 6 perchers wide**, for upwards of 100 rod, that is from very near the top of the Mountain down to the foot of the first Steep Ascent. **I had heard such wonderful accounts of the effects of this Cataract** that I was induced to take a ride of **130 miles to view the**

Spot, and spent a whole Day there with **satisfaction and astonishment.** The facts I am perfectly convinced of by my own observation, and which appear to me most worthy of your notice are these. It was certainly a stream of water falling from the Clouds in a Spot not above 10 yards diameter, and not any Collection of waters falling in rain, on the surface of the Earth. The face of the mountain will not admit a possibility of suppoing it to have been a collection of water already fallen in rain the common way, it being a very high narrow ridge, and the Soil, Stony, Sandy and sufficently porous to drink up rains falling in the common way. **And tho' the Stream seems to have continued some time, certainly at least a few minutes**, it nevertheless fell invariably in the **same Spot, without moving to the right or left.** I should be happy in having your opinion on this matter, my own Conjecture is that a Great Quantity of the Electric fluid, passing silently from the Cloud to the Mountain, carried the **forming drops of rain from all quarters of the Cloud to one point, and by uniting them producd this prodigious Cataract—**

I am, Dr. Sir, with the utmost respect and esteem, your sincere friend and most obedient humble Servant

Davd. Rittenhouse

Dr. Franklin

So right off the bat we are asked to focus on important objects and really open up our minds. Benjamin Franklin is essentially asking us to solve a cipher BUT he knows that we are looking for it. He knows that we are already on the hunt for these ciphers because he assumes we are now aware of the very key that is required to understand them in the first place. He is simply telling us, almost explicitly that here is a cipher and it's riddled with numbers and what appear to be directions. I found this cipher in 15 minutes, because Benjamin Franklin left a path to it. United States Seal, William Barton contractor, David Rittenhouse uncle, both men belonged to the APS and then the letter.

It has been my observation that Benjamin Franklin often utilized the characteristics of the sender/ receiver in his ciphers. He had used friend or foe, achievements in life, alive or dead or even the very meaning of a person's name to further add symbolism to the cipher. He is attempting, and rather successfully so, to cram as much in information into the cipher as he can.

In this case I made the connection of David Rittenhouse's chosen field in science. David Rittenhouse was an astronomer, and he built his own telescopes and in using them he put an unblinking eye on the heavens above. The eye of providence is of course very prominent as it sits above the pyramid in the United States Seal. My own eyes began to dilate a bit when after looking into this man's background.

After a first pass, I liked the dates, I liked the numbers, I liked Carlisle and I most certainly liked cataracts. Rods were a an indicator of a 2nd amendment cipher as well.. A mountain with a steep ascent sounded like a pyramid. You may be thinking that I am trying to fit this letter to a pre-established narrative and you would be exactly right. This is exactly what I am trying to do but the coincidences must be added up until they transcend coincidences. The "freak" of nature was interesting too in that it seemed a bit extreme. How many times in our lives can we say that we've witnessed a freak in nature?

I then decided to tackle the date Aug 16. Now why didn't Benjamin Franklin just write out this date as he had in the letter's header? Yes, this letter appears to be from David Rittenhouse but this is what Benjamin Franklin does in his ciphered letters to ensure they don't look like ciphered letters. He has removed the year, but just gently enough so as not to hide it completely. I jumped back to his archives and looked up letter dated Aug 16, 1779 and came up with nothing. In my past research I had noticed that Benjamin Franklin and others had often used past dates to link these ciphers together so that they wouldn't be conveying too much information in any one letter. One had to work for the answers, and for those that liked to think in extremes and take the path of least resistance in their thinking, this would further help to shield the a secret which had to be kept.

I then did an internet search on Aug 16, 1779 and at the top of the results was an American battle with the British at **Paulus Hook** New York which is on the border of New Jersey. Now this didn't seem too fruitful and there was nothing else that I could associate with this date so I began to read about this battle. My eyes began to dilate again. There is something special about this battle which is going to require just a bit of elaboration. Apparently in this period of time soldiers generally opted for revenge over mercy. Unfortunately this is human nature for some of us, even in knowing the eye of providence is looking down upon us. What if this battle had no demonstration of that ugliness? Could it not be referred to as a freak of nature, tying it directly to the eye of providence? We are now in a headspace of battles so let's keep looking here.

I believe the symbolism of "Blue" relates to the Bluecoats and the north is related to the Red coats in the sense that British were stationed in what is now Canada. No thunder or lighting is a reference to the retort of a gun or flash of the muzzle. In the year 1757 a barracks was built in the town of Carlisle Pennsylvania which was probably the base of operations for this attack. This battle resulted in only 2 deaths which may have been a record for any battle where guns are involved. After the battle,

Major Henry Lee reported back to George Washington in a letter dated August 22 1779 in which he said.

> "American humanity has been again signally manifested. Self-preservation strongly dictated, on the retreat, the putting the prisoners to death, and British cruelty fully justified it; notwithstanding which, not a man was wantonly hurt."
>
> Lee also reported, "I intended to have burnt the barracks; but on finding a number of sick soldiers and women with young children in them, humanity forbad[e] the execution of my intention."

As a point of trivia, eight years later Major Henry Lee would father General Robert E. Lee. Lord Stirling aka William Alexander was also referenced in this letter which doesn't have any relevance to this cipher, or at least not in my opinion.

It appears that Benjamin Franklin is giving us instructions with distances with just the vaguest of bearings.

> "I had heard such wonderful accounts of the effects of this Cataract that I was induced to take a ride of 130 miles to view the Spot, and spent a whole Day there with satisfaction and astonishment."

The starting point is Carlisle which will take us to the spot which is 130 miles distant. There are many units that come into play, first and foremost 10 miles. The mode of transportation in the late 18th century was either walking or beast. There were natural obstacles which would include wide deep rivers, so places had to be found where a river could be forded. Bridge, Ferry or shallow depths would be the only realistic means of crossing so now we have mention of 4 to 10 feet deep.

If I was to take a guess at it, we have to transport ourselves back in time. This may be a reference to the route that must be taken from Carlisle which could only be achieved by walking or horse and buggy. The 10 miles may be reference of distance to a river crossing or bridge. The 130 miles speaks of no direction which could be 360 degrees which makes for rather wide search area. I discovered that there is a place on the Susquehanna river called "Blue Mountain Gap" where there appear to be shallows as the crow flies if you draw a line from Carlisle to these shallows it will cross the Blue Mountain Ridge at the 10 mile mark. Curious coincidence or not. The shallows are located on the outskirts of Marysville PA. Rod is a unit of measurement which equates to 16.5 feet, and a percher is synonymous with a rod. A man is also perched on his horse. The four to ten feet deep is a reference to the depth of the river The mountain is referenced as a ridge and of course cannot support the river because the river has cut through it. It does however look like it is trying to support it because there are many rocks sticking up across this span. There is a statue of liberty on one such rock.

His journey by horse and my journey using Google earth would be two different modes of transportation. So I saddled up, launched Google earth and started to look around for something that would symbolize a pyramid within 130 miles of Carlisle PA. The spot has been referenced as something being under a cataract so this seemed logical. I was thinking perhaps it was a mountain shaped like a pyramid. If I could establish this, then it would just establish another coincidence and link the pyramid symbolism of the United States Seal to the 2nd amendment. Looking at the topography I used the google mobile to see if I could make out any suspect mountains through the trees. Realizing I was a grown man, I then did a search on "PA" and "pyramid" and hit pay dirt.

In the Pennsylvania woods about 116 miles from Carlisle is the "Fraternitas Rosae Crucis". This site was affiliated with the Masons before the year 1858. Both Benjamin Franklin and George Washington are known to be Masons and Benjamin Franklin had reached the rank of Grand Master for Pennsylvania

Rosicrucian Pyramids of Bucks County (QuakerTown PA)

I believe the symbolism of the pyramids was borrowed from Egypt. Don't confuse this with what Egyptian symbolisms were, but only the symbolism of the pyramids, as built by man. They have lasted a long time, and they were not built by any one man. A team effort was involved in this or they could not have existed. Their base represents the past. The peak in theory will always be the most recent thing that was built and so it stands to reason that its very tip would represent the present. The future has not yet arrived so it is invisible. So there are three pyramids here and I've attempted to see if I could discern their symbolisms so that I could better understand what Benjamin Franklin was thinking.

Pyramid #1

There is no top because it is still waiting to be built. It is also waiting for the person to choose the right path to it. The building of the pyramid will requires the efforts of all but each man may lay a stone to it with thoughts only of himself or of all that build it because it is a thing that cannot be built on his own.

This place is about 36 miles from Pennsylvania which can be managed in a day by horse and buggy.

Pyramid #2

Initially when I first looked at this pyramid I was a bit stumped. There were three pyramids on this property which I suspected had a common theme and were each in their own way trying to tell us something.

After studying this pyramid it finally clicked. The paths don't exist here, so how is choice represented, if it is to be found? If our choices build the top of the pyramid then this can only occur in the present time. The past is static, being the pyramid, the future invisible and the present is always on the move. The present is fluid and fills our past once its run its course. This is where decisions are made. This is the point of no return, so choose wisely because motive cannot be hidden from the eye of providence on judgement day. The devil is in the details.

Again, it's all about choice and the pyramid is the summation of those choices. All choices are at the level of the individual. In each layer there are varied interpretations of Life Liberty and Pursuit of Happiness. In the sand of its mortar can be found grains of hypocrisy, but hopefully not too many because none are capable of holding a bond.

Pyramid #3

the names of Benjamin Franklin and George Washington. Didn't Dr. Rittenhouse direct that cipher towards Benjamin Franklin? Abraham Lincoln appears to have been part of this club as well, but I doubt very much he knew about the 2nd amendment.

> "I long ago made up my mind that if anybody wants to kill me, he will do it. If I wore a shirt of mail and kept myself surrounded by a bodyguard, it would be all the same. There are a thousand ways of getting at a man if it is desirable that he should be killed. Besides, in this case, it seems to me, the man who would come after me would be just as objectionable to my enemies – If I have any. "
>
> Abraham Lincoln to journalist Noah Brooks in 1863.

With respect to the owning firearms in society in the context of self defense it appears that he would have said "Don't sweat the small stuff". Just as his name was on the same plaque with Benjamin Franklin, he was also on the same page in his thinking, which will be illustrated in the "Whale Tale" further along. We can get shot in society but the likely hood of it is increased 1000 by our imaginations. We can also get attacked by terrorists as well. There is no difference between the terrorist or the criminal, because if they want to attack you they will probably succeed. They have a much better chance though if they have easy access for the tools required to complete their plan. A hand gun is probably the most lethal, simply due to both its portability and the ability to keep it easily hidden. Abraham Lincoln was killed by a very small handgun, called a derringer, which under the 2nd amendment, would never be allowed into American society because there is no purpose for it. The only possible exception this may be with respect to those that would require something for protection from wildlife while working very much off grid. I suspect in this circumstance it would be highly regulated. At this point in time, such a thing may be hard to imagine, but for any that have tried to cross into Canada with a firearm of this nature they would have faced the reality of small arms regulations first hand. I suspect many probably never really gave it a second thought 10 minutes into their stay. Once entering Canada are Americans terrified of getting shot. It is a question I can only ask and not answer, but if the answer is "No" or not as much as within the confines of the USA, then ask only "why".

In the earliest part of my research I followed a thread in history that took me almost directly to the door step of Abraham Lincoln. Abraham Lincolns private physicians was Dr. Robert K Stone. His wife's name before they were married was Elizabeth J Ritchie. Her father was the man who was writing to both James Madison and Thomas Jefferson regarding the constitution, but in particular, the 2nd amendment. His name was Thomas Ritchie, the same Thomas Ritchie that later hooked up with James K Polk and was in full support of the annexation of Texas. Thomas Richie appeared to be very suspicious of the constitution, which is clearly demonstrated by the letters which were in response to his obvious enquiries.

Here is a picture of that plaque with the names of Benjamin Franklin, George Washington and Abraham Lincoln. It is mounted on the outside of pyramid which houses the legitimate meaning of the 2nd amendment within.

There is an alcove inside with barred windows with what appears to be a sealed metal wall or door. In any event, it is what is on the other side which is to be both viewed and protected.

I'm no expert on Masonic symbols, but I did do some research and discovered that the symbols in the peak have Masonic characteristics..It shouldn't be too difficult to make out their meanings. Death is represented with the skull and bones. We are only on the world for a fixed amount of time before we take flight from it. We start life on this earth, at the base and progress to the top, leaving behind us the legacy of our deeds which in turn were the result of actions based on choices we had made. There are a couple of destinations that we would be headed to where one is heaven, the torch and the other is hell, the anchor, going down. It's the word "Try" that is of most interest because it's easier think of our self first. Some men think that their own pursuit of happiness is of the utmost importance and it doesn't matter if it infringes on the life or liberty of others. The word "Try" seems to differ with that particular ideology. The word "Try" tells us that we always have a choice which is also known as free will. Free will has invented some ideologies to normalize "not trying" where our fellow man is concerned. I am trying to complete this book of my own free will. Will you try to understand with yours? If you will maybe we can catch up later. All we can do is "Try".

Life, Liberty and the Pursuit of Happiness, are the promise of the constitution, but encrypted in just one word, "Pursuit" can be found in the word "Try". It is often easier to take the path of least resistance. It is far more gratifying to think of oneself than the rest of society. What's ironic is that those that exploit society the most also ask for admiration in the achievement of status. Essentially they are constantly attempting to validate their worth from the eyes of others, because they cannot find it within themselves because they know exactly how they got to where they are. Perhaps they were born to it. Perhaps they think they were "blessed", but the only thing man was ever blessed with was free will. Perhaps they think they are in gods favor as if he is handing out free passes. No, being born to wealth and nation is not a blessing it is random luckiness because nation is the invention of man and it will never find itself being judged at St. Peters gates.

Encrypted in life are things like health care and a living wage and the dignity of being able to support oneself. There is no oppression where there is Liberty. It is when one man's Pursuit of Happiness or very ideology infringes on any others Life or Liberty that oppression is experienced and a tyrant can then be named. Even in the word "tyrant", "try" can be found but it is turned inside out.

I believe Benjamin Franklin borrowed from the Masonic symbols and encrypted the anchor and the torch into the eye of providence. It's very similar to the 2nd amendment where Arms and people were encrypted in the word Militia.

With the 2nd amendment people have been reading what they wanted to read, a gift of power and control for the self in spite of all of society.

It is my belief that this pyramid, wall and door predate the United States Seal. The metal used in the plaque above looks to be constructed differently. Whether it was or was not really doesn't make any difference, but if it was, then that skull and winged earth may very well have been the very source for the eye of providence. The other benefit of the eye of providence is that it too, could be interpreted as being under the direct favor of god. How can a nation be in the direct favour of god if god judges individuals by their deeds independent of nature? Everyone likes to be told they are blessed because it is empowering in the comfort it provides. The other thing it does, is gives us a sense of entitlement because we would start to believe that god is behind us in all our endeavours of a nation. It's a curious license to have, that I'm sure are reckoned out at some future time. Yes, when it comes to god's favour, it might be more prudent to try than to just wing it.

The Inner Chamber

There is a 3x5 foot inner chamber protected by two barred viewing windows. The only items in the chamber are 3 bronze plaques hanging on the wall. The pyramid which these are housed in is about 22 feet across at the bottom. The United States Seal , front and back are directly across are on the opposing wall These are just print screens that I've taken from the video I previously mentioned. The back of the seal plaque is shown above beside engraving from the peak of the alcove wall.

These are exact replicas of the United States Seal which were adopted on June 20, 1782. Benjamin Franklin was in France from 1776 to 1785. Now if he was responsible for these plaques being put in the pyramid, as a Grand Master Mason of Pennsylvania then he either had it done remotely or these plaques were placed in the chamber upon his return. If the latter is the case then he had 5 years to do this while in life because he died on April 17, 1790. Either scenario or any other that may be now hidden to history does not really matter. What does matter is that the plaques exist, protected in their current grouping, and are tied directly to Benjamin Franklin through his own written word. This location is about 36 miles from Philadelphia. I looked up the speed of a horse and buggy and they can travel about 50 miles in 8-12 hours which translates to about 5 to 9 hours for 36 miles. You can almost hear the clip clop of hooves as Benjamin Franklin was transporting these plaques from their place of fabrication to their final resting place of the puzzle chamber within the walls of the pyramid.

The Key to the Plaques

If you look closely at this plaque you will see what appears to be a keyhole within the pyramid. A keyhole will of course require a key, but if there is no visible key, then perhaps this plaque is asking us to find it. Perhaps this plaque is part of a riddle and being in a room with only the front and back of the United States Seal, it is only part of a greater riddle. If this is not a riddle, then someone went through quite a bit of effort in its fabrication because a quill alone would not have been chosen to fulfill the purpose of these grouped objects placed so neatly in what certainly appears to be a viewing chamber.

The key is that thing that looks like a doorknocker. It could also be described as the back of a beetle with four legs. After staring at it for awhile, a bell went off in my head and I realized it was not a door knocker but rather a head on cross sectional view of an eagle's beak, or more appropriately put in this scenario, a bill. The beetle suddenly vanished, along with it is legs as I realized the what I thought were legs, when referenced with the other object in this chamber was a scroll folded in upon itself. Just one scroll, but its ends are buried in the bronze, because as I stated, this is cross sectional view. Things, to put it mildly were starting to get rather interesting as this strange plaque was beginning to tie into the United States Seal. The pyramid represents the culmination of all of our choices in history in the building of a nation. There is a key to choosing wisely as well as a key to a secret encrypted within the Seal itself. The eye of providence is about choice.

The two images on top are a different viewpoint of the eagle, but this time a top down view. The fact that are two is a symbolism of choice. If you look closely you can see the tail feathers, and due to my already established knowledge of bird anatomy at its other end must be the head. It's the beaks that are interesting because we either have a very poor artist at work, or their bills were blown out of proportion by design. The reason that they are so large is a clue to look closer at the bill.

"Join, or Die" is a political cartoon that Benjamin Franklin had first published in his newspaper the Pennsylvania Gazette on May 9 1754, which illustrates a snake in pieces where each piece has a colonies name under it. There is a snake on the plaques perimeter with its head at the top. All the colonies are now joined to form the United States of America at this point in time. The snake biting its tale denotes a time when the United States is causing itself harm through misinterpretation of the Constitution. This strange plaque is telling us that there is a solution to this problem that has been put in place a very long time ago, because the United States Seal was established in 1782. The harm that the serpent denotes is the anticipated to be accrue over time. It is the anticipated misinterpretation of the 2nd amendment that was the reason for building this place, otherwise it would not exist.

The Presidential Seal

If you will notice the glory above the eagle is shining and in it are 13 stars. If I may borrow from the Dickens story a Christmas Carol, which also deals with a clause, these are the ghosts of Colonies past. They are the States, which at this particular period in time numbered 13. Remember the wings on the earth which was illustrated earlier? These are the same wings that denote ones flight through life to the final destination. The entire Seal, front and back holds the encryptions of the 2nd amendment where the glory holds the lost souls, the angels, the patriots of America who have died due to the fallacy of the 2nd amendment. The lost souls are also referenced by the snake biting its tail from the clue plaque because that snake symbolises a United States of America causing itself harm due to a fallacy of the constitution. It is in this place where "the blood of patriots and tyrants" live as referenced by Thomas Jefferson's quote, "the tree of liberty must be refreshed from time to time with the blood of patriots and tyrants". This is not a reference to god's favor as previously interpreted because the only gift of god is "free will", and he only favors the choices we make with it if they stem from a place with virtue.

From the eagles point of view its head is turned to the right, toward the olive branches, as opposed to the Arms. This is the federal head and all around it are four places where the United States can be found as represented by the 13 now joined colonies of that period. The stripes on the shield, the stars in the glory, the arrows and most importantly the olive branches all number 13 are a reference pointing to the United States of America. As a whole this shows that the 2nd amendment is working properly because it is no longer about a "right of the people to keep and bear Arms" and is now under the full administration of the federal head with all the blessings of the glory above.

So we have the eagles head turned to the right which is code for the "Bill of Rights" which is anticipated to be drafted in advance of its drafting at least 6 years later. We require more information, because there are 10 amendments, and what we see are "arrows" or Arms so this must be a reference to the 2nd amendment for that is the only place that is explicitly relates to Arms. There are 13 of arrows as well just as there are 13 olive branches. It's an either or situation with no in between and it cannot be debated in which direction the eagle favors to look. The eagle is looking forward because it cannot look in both directions simultaneously. Behind it there is no right to bear Arms because in that circumstance its head would be turned to the left, and to turn it left, is no right at all. Its head, the government, is locked in one direction only which is necessary to the security of a free State, or peace in society, as denoted by the olive branches. The first clause of the 2nd amendment is the eagles head doing its well regulating, the 2nd clause is the olive branches, the third clause are the arrows which are most certainly not to be given any weight in this matter and the fourth is the fact that the head is locked in only one direction with all the blessings of the glory. How can the Supreme Court of the United States rule otherwise, when in their very seal, the truth of the 2nd amendment is there for all to see? We are not finished yet in solving this puzzle, because there is still more to be resolved against the "key plaque"

It is the scroll that points to the key which lives in the 2nd amendment because written in Latin is the text.

E Pluribus Unum - Out of Many, One.

These are the words that will take the subjective interpretation of the 2nd amendment to an objective one. Just as we have seen a duality in meaning of the Bill of Rights there is also a duality in meaning to this text. There are TWO ANSWERS to one question because this is the very nature of the ciphers. I know it's easier or perhaps logical to think there is only one answer to any question but not if the author used this habit of reasoning to hide what has been most obviously hidden. Can this text be applied to the 2nd amendment? We already know that the primary encryption was the word "Militia", and we already know that this one word must be first broken down and viewed in its pieces. If we congregate the many things known as people and Arms we are left with just one word which summarizes them, being of course "Militia". "From many One". "E Plurius Enum". So there you have it, because once that is understood the 2nd amendment immediately transforms and if we choose to read it like a sentence, which it is we no longer to need to either discern or interpret it as the Supreme Court has been doing in order to make better sense of it. No longer is there a prefatory clause or an operative clause, but only four clauses. The Supreme Court, Congress and the Senate need only look at their own seals, because this same eagle is nested rather neatly in its design. It is now a no brainer. Case closed.

This gets even more astonishing if you have not picked up it yet. It not only proves the legitimate meaning of the 2nd amendment but it proves something else as well. This has to do with the currently known chronology of history. The Seal was completed in the year 1782 well in advance of the constitution convention by at least 6 years or even 8 if we were to base our math on the 1780 letter of Benjamin Franklin and David Rittenhouse. It was a busy year in 1780 because that was also the year that the other men had been enlisted into the American Philosophical Society with the exception of James Madison. This was also the year that Pennsylvania began its own abolition of slavery. The normalization of slavery at this point in time would have been one of the greatest detriments to the 2nd amendment being ratified in its true form. In 1780 it appears that Benjamin Franklin decided to get the ball rolling and that ball has rolled for 224 years and finally stopped at the beginning of the 21st century. At that point I had chosen to get the ball rolling as well, albeit a much smaller ball but it is my theory and my hope that it too stops with you.

So this proves that the constitutional convention was orchestrated to such an extent that it explains why the Bill of Rights was not called the United States Declaration of Rights. If one had decided to be consistent with naming conventions, it would have seemed logical to call the Bill of Rights the United States Declaration of Rights keeping in form with Virginia. No, they chose to call it a Bill of Rights instead, but why?

The reason is looking right at you. The eagle was a utility bird. **There had to be a bird part in the "Bill" of Rights" so that the secret of the 2nd amendment could be exposed through the Untied States Seal where there resides a bill as well.**

Yah, I know. One hell of a knee slapper isn't it? One could not help if Benjamin Franklin pondered the reaction to such a discovery in the future. Knowing human nature, as well as he did, and being human himself, you can almost see a guilty grin on his face. So now there sits his fly on the wall of the Supreme Court, Senate, Congress and even on the door of Air Force One.

The shield, which has 13 lines symbolizes the body of the people from lethal weaponry. The shield is a defensive device and is generally not viewed as a particularly lethal offensive tool. It is an object that is completely separated and distinctly different than the arrows. This also shows that it is solely in the domain of the executive to protect the states from harm through regulations. The federal head, the eagle is not looking towards arms but is locked in a position looking toward ensuring the "security of a free State", or Peace and Liberty which can only exist without the oppression of men with too much power in their hands and nefarious minds to direct it.

"Resolved, That Dr. Franklin, Mr. J. Adams and Mr. Jefferson, be a committee, to bring in a device for a seal for the United States of America."

- July 4, 1776, Journals of Continental Congress

In light of the now exposed orchestration of the constitution it is interesting that before the Seals were ever constructed that it was referred to as being a "device" by the Continental Congress. While the final version of the Seal may not have been resolved, I conjecture that it may have been planned to insert the 2nd amendment into it at the onset. The earliest cipher that I have located was from 1752 which will be illustrated in the next section. I believe that cipher was to be associated with te Albany Plan at the time which never transpired. In light of that Benjamin Franklin had 35 years to continue strategizing his plan and that is in genius years!. Personally I still read the directions on the coffee maker. Device is synonymous with the word "instrument" which James Madison had used as a reference to the 2nd Amendment as quoted in his letter to Thomas Ritchie dated Sept 15 1821.

> **"the legitimate meaning of the Instrument must be derived from the text itself;** or if a key is to be sought elsewhere, it must be not in the opinions or intentions of the Body which planned & proposed the Constitution".

We already know that the Bill of Rights was predetermined in advance of its actually drafting since it was already linked to the Federalist papers in advance of its drafting. It is the reference to the word "device" which appears to have predetermined the intended utility of the Seals.

The Dorset Dies

I recently encountered some information on four dies that have been discovered in recent years. They are about 3 inches in diameter and are very similar to the United States Seal. One of them apparently belonged to George Washington. They have been a bit of a mystery because they have a few different to the Seal itself. It was observed that the Eagles head faces the Arrows as opposed to the Olive Branches and instead of 9 tail feathers there are 7. This helped me to resolve the symbolism of the tail feathers. It's already been established that 13 refers to the colonies which makes perfect sense. At the "tail end " of the 2nd amendment is the word "infringed" which has 9 letters.

With an eagle head facing the Arrows though is synonymous with the subjectively read 2nd amendment. The Arrows signify the 3rd clause or the common bias to its true meaning. That being said the way to read it objectively is to understand the word Militia. Militia has 7 letters and is the primary literary encryption. The fact that these are "dies" also is a clue that while subjectively read people will die. These are made of metal and would last through time but were owned by individuals but individuals who knew of the 2nd amendment like George Washington. Why would they make dies at that differed from an already established Seal? This is the question they want the future to ask. They want a future time to think there is something strange going on in the Seals. Under further scrutiny it was hoped somebody would discover the secret of the Seals. That being said they can be thought of as a third method for discovering the Secret o the 2nd amendment. For myself they told me that the tail feather count was related to a letter count in the sentence itself. Tale end.

Dorsett die

1782 Great Seal die

The United States Seal Letter

Two decades after Benjamin Franklin's 1780 "pyramid" letter from David Rittenhouse we have another letter written from Charles Thomas to James Madison. This next letter Remember that Charles Thompson was the secretary of the Continental Congress and was part of the fourth and final committee that created the final version of the United States Seal. This letter stands on its own to render a wary eye as to the secret hidden in the United States Seal. No longer are dealing with visual symbols. It's my view that this letter was completely contrived because I don't believe that the Charles Thompson was privy to the secret of the 2nd amendment. If he had in fact written this letter to James Madison he would have been 72 years of age.

To James Madison from Charles Thomson, 1 December 1801

From Charles Thomson
Decr. 1. 1801 DEAR SIR,

Enclosed I send you an explanation of the Device for an armorial[603] Atchievement and Reverse of a Great Seal for the United States in Congress assembled.

It was drawn up when I made report & contains the Sentiments which I had in my mind when I was considering the subject, and **which I wished to express covertly by the device. It has never been published** nor have I ever given a copy of it. If you think it worth preserving you may lodge it in your office, if not; destroy it. Accept the assurance of my esteem & regard. Your old Friend
CHAS THOMSON

[Enclosure]

Device for an Armorial Atchievement and Reverse of a great Seal for the United states in Congress Assembled

Arms.

On a field Chevrons composed of seven pieces on one side & six on the other, joined together at the top in such wise that each of the six bears against or is supported by & supports two of the opposite

---

[603] In Merriam Webster dictionary armorial: 'of, relating to, or bearing heraldic arms'

side the pieces of the chevrons on each side alternate red & white. The shield born on the breast of An American Eagle on the Wing & rising, proper. In the dexter talon of the Eagle an Olive branch & in the sinister a bundle of Arrows. Over the head of the Eagle a Constellation of Stars surrounded with bright rays and at a little distance clouds.

An eagle, being a bird, has a bill and in this particular bill there is a scroll with the words

"E pluribus Unum"

Reverse

A pyramid unfinished

In the Zenith an Eye in a triangle surrounded with a glory, proper.

Over the Eye these Words

Annuit cœptis

On the base of the pyramid the numerical letters

MDCCLXXVI

And underneath these words

Novus Ordo seclorum.

N B the Head & tail of the American bald Eag[l]e are white. The body & Wings of a lead or dove colour.

The device is the Seal. The armorial achievement is the achievement to describe the true usage of arms in the context of the 2nd amendment by introducing it into a coat of Arms. His sentiments are really the sentiments of the key founding fathers, and the subject was how to use the eagle to incorporate a secret. There is a secret because it was being expressed covertly by the device of the seal. Now at the time this letter it was written, it had never been published before, but it is now as I write it.

The following is the key phrase here because the word "bill" is being used. It helps to prove the interpretation of the third plaque as well.

"In the bill of the Eagle a scroll with these words E pluribus Unum. "

I'm going to make another observation. Since the United States Seal is in a state where the 2nd amendment is being used correctly we can now reinterpret the Latin on the Pyramid side.

Annuit cœptis : approved of undertakings.

This now makes even more sense.

Novus Ordo seclorum.: New world Order

The "New world" is the future and the "order" is reading the 2nd from left to right. The world is also displayed at the apex inside that alcove in the pyramid. It would be a very difficult thing to lose that pyramid to time, especially in the backwoods of Pennsylvania, under the management of the freemasons.

The 2nd amendment no longer requires an interpretation.

In light of this discovery it is going to be difficult for any faction to rule against the very seals which they work under and in front of. Alternative facts are going to be very difficult thing to enforce when the truth is there for all to see. Truth doesn't care about opinions or the vote of the people, or even the judiciary because truth is not an option.

The value of the legitimate 2nd amendment can also be banked on

The value of the legitimate 2nd amendment can also be banked on because it is now exposed as the currency of both Life and Liberty, which in reality must both exist before the Pursuit of Happiness can even be realised.

Mass Marketing One Oh One.

Once this encryption is revealed to the masses aka "We the People", the marketing campaign for truth is already well underway. The billboard has been imprinted on the backs of the American one dollar bill for all to see. I don't think the irony in this can go unnoticed because money is not only the medium for Liberty so that a man can feed and shelter himself but it is also the currency of greedy. The marketing campaigns of the Gun Industry will be very quickly overtaken because now the very heart of their business model will have completely vanished.

The Back of the American One Dollar Bill

Bill of Rights, Arms, E Plurius Enum (Arms + People = Militia)

"A well regulated Militia,

being necessary to the security of a free State,

the right of the people to keep and bear Arms,

shall not be infringed"

The Right of "We the People" and not "Me the People" has always been

"Necessary to the security of a free State"

(of mind).

Think in terms of butterflies and bunny rabbits.

Inalienable because Liberty: the quality or state of being free

The Concluding comments on the Seal

In light of these revelations we can now make better sense of the Latin that is written on the pyramid side of the Seal. I am calling the front of the seal the Eagle side which is generally arrived at intuitively but it is this side that exposes what the 2nd amendment actually says through its encryption. We now can objectively see that the Eagle side is the front because in the absence of knowing it's encryptions there is no chance of being able to understand those on the pyramid side. The pyramid side simple looks deeper into what the 2nd amendment is actually saying to We the People. It explains it further, and the Latin that is written there are its closing statements which begin with

Annuit cœptis : approved of undertakings.

This pertains to "choice" that every man usually makes. Since the entire Seal is a reference to the 2nd amendment then it is hoped that those that find this difficult to accept will do so in gods favor. Put society above self.

Novus Ordo seclorum.: New world Order

The word "Order" is synonymous with "shall not be infringed" but it is expressed in Latin. The meaning of "shall not be infringed" has not changed and should be viewed to have the same integrity as it did before. The only judge and jury in this matter is the raw truth of reality because the "security of a free State" must be well regulated. While everyone is entitled to their opinion their opinion is not entitled to reality.

The 2nd amendment no longer requires an interpretation.

Plaque Trivia

While researching David Rittenhouse I stumbled across a coin that he had crafted. It occurred to me that this may be evidence that he was capable of fabricating those plaques in the pyramid. The full volume and labor of the secrets regarding the 2nd amendment was extremely important. If someone had to be entrusted with this secret perhaps David Rittenhouse was just such a man. He appears to have been highly ranked in the American Philosophical society since he was the next president elected there after the passing of Benjamin Franklin.

7-Pre-Cabal Findings

This section covers an area of time that predates the Revolutionary war by decades and the only person that exists in the cabal that appears to have been writing about the second amendment was Benjamin Franklin. He did however enlist a few other men to help him out, but not for the constitution, but for his Albany Plan. Constitution or Albany plan he was preparing for the time when the colonies would become united and would of course need new governmental structure to guide them. These are some observations and ciphers from that period which, like the others, were being seeded for a future time.

An 18th century Massacre

At the age of 58 Benjamin Franklin would have read about a rather horrible massacre in the papers. I was looking for evidence of gun violence in the 18th century and found this.

"The Narrative of the Late Massacres Jan 30 1764" at FranklinPapers.org.

> "On Wednesday, the 14th of December, 1763, Fifty-seven Men, from some of our Frontier Townships, who had projected the Destruction of this little Common-wealth, came, all well-mounted, and armed with Firelocks, Hangers and Hatchets, having travelled through the Country in the Night, to Conestogoe Manor. There they surrounded the small Village of Indian Huts, and just at Break of Day broke into them all at once. Only three Men, two Women, and a young Boy, were found at home, the rest being out among the neighbouring White People, some to sell the Baskets, Brooms and Bowls they manufactured, and others on other Occasions. These poor defenceless Creatures were immediately fired upon, stabbed and hatcheted to Death!"

> "When I mention the Baseness of the Murderers, in the Use they made of Arms, I cannot, I ought not to forget, the very different Behaviour of *brave Men* and *true Soldiers,* of which this melancholy Occasion has afforded us fresh Instances. The Royal Highlanders have, in the Course of this War, suffered as much as any other Corps, and have frequently had their Ranks thinn'd by an Indian Enemy; yet

they did not for this retain a brutal undistinguishing Resentment against *all* Indians, Friends as well as Foes."

"The only Crime of these poor Wretches seems to have been, that they had a reddish brown Skin, and black Hair; and some People of that Sort, it seems, had murdered some of our Relations. If it be right to kill Men for such a Reason, then, should any Man, with a freckled Face and red Hair, kill a Wife or Child of mine, it would be right for me to revenge it, by killing all the freckled red-haired Men, Women and Children, I could afterwards any where meet with."

This group of men came back to finish the job a few weeks later and killed the balance of Indians that had been in the town that day to sell their wares. A total of 20 Indians were massacred which consisted of 7 men, 5 women and 8 children. A fifty man militia decided to use the power they possessed to proceed to massacre some people based on their race. Race, religion as long as a group of humans can be labelled then collectively they are the enemy and the 50 men that massacred them had a consensus of opinion and such is the way of self regulating men with too much power, who may otherwise have been law abiding citizens. This is human nature at its worst and was perhaps not an anomaly in Benjamin Franklins' day. Virtually nothing has change from the 18th century to the 21st century as far as this logic of labelling goes. Race and religion are banners of the tyrants to enforce their will on others and build a consensus. Were the Indians oppressed or the women who were burned at the stake in the name of god in the late 17th century? The only difference between the 21st century and the 18th century is invention. Human nature is exactly the same.

At any point in time a societies' environment just becomes normalized. The current gun culture in the United States is just a modern day example of this. Gangs empowered with the guns that society allows them, composed of people, caught up in a subculture that was fueled by guns. This doesn't mean that everyone agrees with it however and there is probably no better proof than Benjamin Franklins' views on his own society. Progress becomes a sales pitch and even an excuse at times. Slavery has been banished in the USA but human nature still finds other ways to exploit humanity. Racism is most certainly still exists today, but for the most part it appears that those who are the most bigoted deny it with a passion. The "race card" is often used to deal with it. Massacres are happening abroad and within the confines of the States. It is effectively sanctioned terrorism, because guns have been allowed and have now reached a point where they are almost normalized. I do stray. I have used a similar analogy to the man above in "Narratives we Build" section. His analogy seems to have fallen on deaf ears 250 years ago.

Do Geniuses Go Hand Fishing for Lightning?

In order to avoid suspicion Benjamin Franklin had to base his ciphers on reality. This particular cipher takes it to the limit and perhaps a bit beyond. Once you see the symbolisms that he has used I think you will see how he could not resist it. He must have known that he had crossed a line from reality to fiction with this one and in so doing probably found it a bit humorous. In reality he was experimenting with lighting rods so in that respect he was staying true to his plan. This cipher was still protected from scrutiny in that it would still require a key to unlock the truth of it. News of his experiment had reached Europe and he must have been asked about it rather frequently. I wonder if he felt any guilt when talking to a peer of his day and looked at them straight in the eye and said, "Oh Yes, I did that". In talking to a fellow cerebral did he take any amusement during such a serious conversation? I'd like to say time will tell but those aren't quite the right words. A white lie justified for a grander purpose. He had to propagate this lie for about 45 years to perhaps 1000's of curious people wondering what it was like to harness lightning with a piece of string. I can't even tell a lie more than three times, no better make that four in all truthfulness. The pictures of Benjamin Franklin he ha

I'd like to send a callout to the show "Myth Busters" in seeing if they could mimic Benjamin Franklin's experiment in reality. They busted it pretty quickly. I think they gave it a definite "No Way". It sort of makes sense because even my dog knew the danger of lightning and had taken refuge many a time under a bed. If a tree can be shattered and burned to the core, well a human would be like bacon to the pan.

It appears that he may have used his friend "Joseph Priestly", much as he used "William Alexander". I only discovered this in the very final days of as I was attempting to edit this book. There are some historians and scientists that find Benjamin Franklin's experiment a bit difficult to believe in practice. He documented his experiment and even the show "Myth Busters" had attempted to imitate it and found it to be impossible. Benjamin Franklins kite experiment may have been borrowed upon to create Benjamin Franklin ciphers. It may even have been this very experiment that gave him the idea of keys and ciphers. Benjamin Franklin concluded his kite experiment in the year 1754. Twelve years later, letters begin to pop up from Joseph Priestly.

There is no reason not to believe that Benjamin Franklin was indeed performing electrical experiments which resulted in creating Lightning rods for buildings, but this particular experiment as laid out is perhaps his very first 2nd amendment cipher.

The Kite Experiment

I. Printed in *The Pennsylvania Gazette,* October 19, 1752; also copy: The Royal Society. II. Printed in Joseph Priestley, *The History and Present State of Electricity, with Original Experiments* (London, 1767), pp. 179-81.

FRANKLIN'S STATEMENT

Philadelphia, October 19

As frequent Mention is made in the News Papers from Europe, of the Success of the Philadelphia Experiment for drawing[604] the Electric Fire from Clouds[605] by Means of pointed Rods of Iron erected on high Buildings[606], &c. it may be agreeable to the Curious[607] to be inform'd, that the same Experiment has succeeded in Philadelphia, tho' made in a different and more easy Manner, which any one may try, as follows.

Make a small Cross of two light Strips of Cedar, the Arms so long as to reach to the four Corners[608] of a large thin Silk Handkerchief[609] when extended; tie the Corners of the Handkerchief to the Extremities of the Cross[610], so you have the Body of a Kite[611]; which being properly accommodated with a Tail, Loop and String[612], will

---

[604] Guns are drawn

[605] Clouds of smoke ,also stormy times ahead.

[606] Men with Arms on rampart of a building with guns pointed

[607] This is a subtle invitation to look more closely at this experiment and study its

[608] There are 4 clauses in the 2nd amendment which of course has to do with Arms.

[609] In a 'well-regulated Militia there are officers who are under the command of the federal head. As part of their dress uniform officers wore silk sashes.

[610] Cross is a religious connotation .It asks that the people put aside fear and avarice and think of their fellow man first.

[611] A Kite is also defined as " a person who preys upon others".

[612] Before the flintlock there was the matchlock pistol. It required twine to be fired.

rise in the Air, like those made of Paper[613]; but this being of Silk is fitter[614] to bear[615] the Wet and Wind[616] of a Thunder Gust without tearing. To the Top of the upright Stick[617] of the Cross is to be fixed a very sharp pointed Wire[618], rising a Foot or more above the Wood. To the End of the Twine, next the Hand, is to be tied a silk Ribbon[619], and where the Twine and the silk join, a Key may be fastened. This Kite is to be raised when a Thunder Gust appears to be coming on, and the Person who holds the String must stand within a Door, or Window, or under some Cover[620], so that the Silk Ribbon may not be wet[621]; and Care must be taken that the Twine does not touch the Frame of the Door or Window[622]. As soon as any of the Thunder

---

[613] In the 4th amendment can be found the encryption "papers and effects" which alludes to gun fire and the loading of a flintlock. Paper relates to the flintlock gun, more advanced weaponry which would be associated more with government forces.

[614] Officers in the 18th century were fitted with silk sashes. Officers again relate to the regulation of Arms, because they are under the control of government.

[615] Interesting choice of word.

[616] The officers having flyntlocks were better off in the rain, because the lit piece of twine associated with a matchlock would be more prone to going out. The matchlock, would be more prevalent and associated with mid 18th century militias, even if just in symbolism.

[617] Gun

[618] The ramrod of a flintlock.

[619] We are now in the 2nd amendment and the silk ribbon is the officer's sash, and relates directly to the key of the word Militia. It is through the sash, that governmental control or "Well regulated" is revealed. The twine is on the other side, and relates to the older interpretation of the 2nd amendment. The more primitive of technology and thinking.

[620] A person must of course take cover because there are guns everywhere with respect to the older 2nd amendment.

[621] Regulations must be put into play if the key is to be used.

[622] A right of the people to keep and bear Arms, relates to the twine, but it is through the window or door of word "Militia" if you are careful in your thinking that you will see only its constituent parts and then be able to read the 2nd amendment subjectively.

Clouds come over the Kite, the pointed Wire will draw the Electric Fire from them, and the Kite, with all the Twine, will be electrified, and the loose Filaments of the Twine will stand out every Way[623], and be attracted by an approaching Finger[624]. And when the Rain has wet the Kite and Twine, so that it can conduct the Electric Fire freely, you will find it stream out plentifully from the Key[625] on the Approach of your Knuckle[626]. At this Key the Phial may be charg'd[627]; and from Electric Fire thus obtain'd, Spirits may be kindled[628], and all the other Electric Experiments be perform'd, which are usually done by the Help of a rubbed Glass Globe or Tube[629]; and thereby the *Sameness* of the Electric Matter[630] with that of Lightning compleatly demonstrated[631].

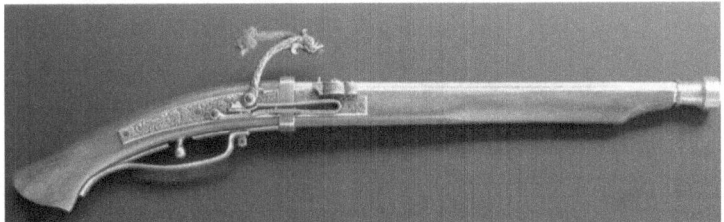

A primitive match lock pistol

---

[623] Gun violence

[624] Pulling the trigger and causing fire.

[625] The key of the 2nd amendment will dissipate gun violence.

[626] Reaching out to take back the lethal Arms.

[627] Emotions may get "vile" aka a phonetic of (phial)

[628] Some people may get angry at the revelation of the 2nd amendment.

[629] This appears to be rubbing the brain with a finger and thinking about the Arms.

[630] Even though there are many types of guns which may fire differently, they can still have the same result in a society, which is death.

[631] It will be finally demonstrated that gun violence in society can be controlled by the 2nd amendment.

OFFICER
29TH REGIMENT

Note the silk sash around his waist, which is an officer designation

In the year 1785, George Washington wrote this to James Madison. ""It is a **dangerous experiment—once slacken the reins and the power is lost**—and it is questionable with me whether the advocates of **the measure foresee all the consequences of it**."

As I've stated before on Sept 15, 1821, James Madison wrote this "the legitimate meaning of the Instrument must be derived from the text itself; or if a **key** is to be sought elsewhere, it must be not in the opinions or intentions of the **Body** which planned & **proposed the Constitution**".

Sixty four years later, Thomas Jefferson writes a similar cipher in that it is directly related to the 2nd amendment and that it also uses primitive guns. Where this one uses the matlock, the cipher "written" to John Payne Todd, 15 August 1816 references a "wheel lock" pistols.

Now for those that think I may be grasping at straws here, Thomas Jefferson calls me a "skilful gunsmith" in the context of being the person who figures this out. I state this not out of a sense of bravado, but to fully exploit the findings of this book, because it's the findings that are far more important that I. So yes, in a sense there are strings attached to bringing up the skilful gunsmith reference. I'm a puppet of their truth, but I'm no dummy.

Joseph Priestley 1767

The Kite Experiment
PRIESTLEY'S ACCOUNT

To demonstrate, in the completest manner possible, the sameness of the electric fluid with the matter of lightning, Dr. Franklin, astonishing as it must have appeared, contrived actually to bring lightning from the heavens, by means of an electrical kite, which he raised when a storm of thunder was perceived to be coming on. This kite had a pointed wire fixed upon it, by which it drew the lightning from the clouds. This lightning descended by the hempen string, and was received by a key tied to the extremity of it; that part of the string which was held in the hand being of silk, that the electric virtue[632] might stop when it came to the key. He found that the string would conduct electricity even when nearly dry[633], but that when it was wet, it would conduct it quite freely[634]; so that it would stream out plentifully from the key, at the approach of a person's finger.

At this key he charged phials, and from electric fire thus obtained, he kindled spirits, and performed all other electrical experiments which are usually exhibited by an excited globe or tube.

As every circumstance relating to so capital a discovery[635] as this (the greatest, perhaps, that has been made in the whole[636] compass of philosophy[637], since the time of Sir Isaac Newton[638]) cannot but give pleasure to all my readers, I shall endeavour to gratify them with

---

[632] Replace the emotion of fear with the virtue of thinking of the 2ⁿᵈ amendment as a right of all the people.

[633] The "conduct" is related to passion for guns.

[634] Once wet though,

[635] The discovery is the in the capitalized word "Militia".

[636] The "whole" word militia contains the parts "people and Arms" which then reveals the 2ⁿᵈ amendment as an equation or instrument.

[637] This is a sociological experiment of sorts, based on the philosophy of mans nature.

[638] He relates this to Sir Isaac Newton because he knows this experiment is a big one, and the discovery will be very important and will take some time. Sir Isaac Newton was also more of a philosopher later in life.

the communication of a few particulars[639] which I have from the best authority.

The Doctor, after having published his method of verifying his hypothesis concerning the sameness of electricity with the matter of lightning[640], was waiting for the erection of a spire in Philadelphia to carry his views into execution[641]; not imagining that a pointed rod, of a moderate height, could answer the purpose[642]; when it occured to him, that, by means of a common kite, he could have a readier and better access to the regions of thunder than by any spire whatever[643]. Preparing, therefore, a large silk handkerchief, and two cross sticks, of a proper length, on which to extend it; he took the opportunity of the first approaching thunder storm to take a walk into a field, in which there was a shed convenient for his purpose. But dreading the ridicule which too commonly attends unsuccessful attempts in science[644], he communicated his intended experiment to no body[645] but his son, who assisted him in raising the kite.

The kite being raised, a considerable time elapsed before there was any appearance of its being electrified. One very promising cloud

---

[639] There are two particulars that will be the cure for gun violence which will relieve the liberal view of society under "We the People", and not "Me the People".

[640] Arms and their varying types still cause death in a society.

[641] Philadelphia is also the capital where the government would reside and would be a place where a constitution would be written and reach into the future as a spire would for stormy times ahead due to the how the 2nd amendment would be interpretted in this "kite" or "a person who preys upon others" experiment by arming him guns.

[642] More guns are not the solution to gun violence.

[643] Don't introduce guns into society in the first place. Regulate them, with the 2nd and the thunder will be dissipated.

[644] He knows that the 2nd amendment is ahead of its time which is a reference to the ridicule he would receive if it was exposed too early. The experiment was to prove that Arms cause society harm, and the 2nd amendment would already be in place for its cure.

[645] "No Body" and not "nobody". The inference is subtle. His son, represents not the individual but the progeny of America and the "Body" of its future population.

had passed over it without any effect; when, at length, just as he was beginning to despair of his contrivance[646], he observed some loose threads of the hempen string to stand erect[647], and to avoid one another, just as if they had been suspended on a common conductor. Struck with this promising appearance, he immediately presented his knuckle to the key, and (let the reader judge of the exquisite pleasure he must have felt at that moment[648]) the discovery was complete. He perceived a very evident electric spark. Others succeeded, even before the string was wet, so as to put the matter past all dispute, and when the rain had wet the string, he collected electric fire very copiously. This happened in June 1752, a month after the electricians in France had verified the same theory, but before he heard of any thing they had done.

---

[646] The experiment was contrived to such an extent, it was not real, only the 2nd amendment was.

[647] A Matchlock gun has string which stands erect in order for it to fire.

[648] A judge and a kite seems a bit odd, unless he's really talking about guns being on trial and found guilty.

James Madison: Advice to my Country - ca 1834

As this advice, if it ever see the light[649] will not do it till I am no more it may be considered as issuing from the tomb where truth alone can be respected[650], and the happiness of man alone consulted[651]. It will be entitled therefore to whatever weight can be derived from good intentions[652], and from the experience of one[653], who has served his Country in various stations through a period of forty years[654], who espoused in his youth and adhered through his life to the cause of its liberty[655], and who has borne a part[656] in most of the great transactions[657] which will constitute epochs of its destiny[658].

---

[649] It is now seeing the light as I'm explaining it after about 183 years later. The letter of course would see the light, as per his request so long ago, so to infer it may never see the light is to infer there are secrets he cannot even talk about after death. In essence, his tomb is a time capsule, but one that has always required a key.

[650] James Madison of course knows the truth of the 2nd amendment, which is the EXACT truth he speaks of. Like Thomas Jefferson's letter from June 12, 1823, this is a similar symbolism to "what a treasure will be found", because treasures are usually buried. This is a cipher. I am also digging up this cipher, which I would never have been able to do, had I not been the "Candid a friend to Truth". Truth being a bias to reality, where only truth can live.

[651] A solution to the gun violence epidemic has finally been revealed.

[652] Weight=bear people are only entitled to the arms as derived by a well regulated militia.

[653] Experience of the word "Militia".

[654] There are 40 characters in "being necessary to the security of a free State," and the various "Stations" in a country are the two different meanings of the word "State". "period" is relating to the ending of clause, but is a comma.

[655] In Americas "youth" people grew attached to the idea that the 2nd amendment was there to protect the peoples liberty.

[656] Militia, being borne into a different meaning.

[657] The 2nd amendment is a transaction with two different meanings.

[658] Note "epochs", or plural. There are two events in history where the first was when the 2nd amendment being initially ratified and then ultimately being read for the first time objectively. The 2nd epoch is now.

The advice nearest to my heart and deepest in my convictions is that the Union of the States be cherished & perpetuated[659]. Let the open enemy to it be regarded as a Pandora with her box opened[660]; and the disguised one[661], as the Serpent[662] creeping with his deadly wiles into Paradise.

I have included this next letter because I believe it to be the last cipher written by the cabal where the kite experiment appears to be the first one. What is astonishing is this that they span a period of 84 years where previously drafting of the 2nd amendment appeared to span about three years Virginia Declaration of Rights. Both point to the 2nd amendment in their own way. Benjamin Franklin taught James Madison how to write these ciphers about five decades earlier. This letter was the final one, the final labor and the final hope and wish for the future of their America. It was their American Dream and it's finally in the grasp of the 21st century but in the hands at the end of the arms.

James Madison wrote this particular letter toward the end of his life with instructions that it only be opened after his passing. In all likelihood this is probably the final ciphered letter that relates to the 2nd amendment. So let's take a closer look at it. At the outs

So let's look at this cipher. "Truth alone can be respected",

There are some key words that are used here that can be related directly to the 2nd amendment.

"Weight = Bear" "Various Stations of a country are "States", "Derived",

"Pandoras Box" can now be viewed as the unbridled passion for guns, massacres, and the ever widening gulf of political faction that the United States is currently experiencing due to unregulated Arms. Once again we see the snake which keeps coming up in these ciphers. The snake is represents mans nature and the choices he makes in putting himself above all others. Paradise denotes the future of the United States without the gun violence. "being necessary to the

---

[659] He wants all of America to Unite behind this final legacy of his constitution.

[660] Pandora is the rhetoric and panic of those that will not like this. He wants people to relax and put emotion away.

[661] the propaganda of fear based politics and avarice.

[662] Once again we have the snake, as referenced in "Join or Die"

security of a free State" OR a tranquility in the public domain that probably only exists in the American dream for most.

From Joseph Priestley

ALS (fragment): American Philosophical Society
[February 1766]
[*First part missing*] myself so much as to think I am able to [carry to completion] this large plan. I only propose to do it [if I can leave] it to you and my other friends in Lon[don readily to sup]ply my deficiencies. In the mean time I should be glad to have your sentiment of it. [Asking your pardon for] trespassing so long upon your patience [I am with the greatest res]pect, Dear Sir your most obliged humble servant
J Priestley
[*Torn*] contents [*torn*]ent, to [*torn*]

We have talk of a large plan that appears to be in pieces at the moment. The large plan is the integration of the 2nd amendment into a constitution for the use of the future. The letter itself is physically torn and then apparently archived. There are two things to note about this letter in that it is the first in a series of letters from "Joseph Priestly". Benjamin Franklin also created a series of ciphers later on beginning in about 1777 with David Hartley, some of which I have transcribed in this book.

From [Joseph Priestley]

ALS (mutilated): American Philosophical Society
Warrington 25 March 1766.
Dear Sir
I have received your letter, containing some remarks on my experiments, and a printed paper for the transactions which has given me very great satisfaction, and for which I think myself much obliged to you. I shall think myself very happy if the accounts you are pleased to permit me to send you of my imperfect experiments do but revive your attention to your once favourite study; **for that seems to be universally acknowledged to be the great desideration to further discoveries.**

Immediately upon the receipt of yours, I set about pursuing the hints you gave me, and I am impatient, little as I have done, to give you an account of it. **My great ambition would be to act under your auspices in the business of electricity.**

John Adams used Benjamin Franklin and his rods and electricity theme to cipher one of his letters. Is he tying his letter back to this Jason Priestly Series? It is not difficult to imagine Benjamin Franklin explain his earlier ciphering themes to those in the cabal years later. If the themes are threaded together, then they would further be of benefit to historians in some distant future. That distance is now identical from our point of view to the time in which these letters were written.

This kite experiment cipher has a rather explicit indicator which is the symbolism of a line and in the middle of it is a key. The kite is carried into the storm of the future where there is trouble. The Arms are collected at the start of the line, as the kite is being regulated and directed in search of light and noise. In Benjamin Franklins experiment he looked for ways to dissipate the electricity and used water as a conductor in his line. I believe the electricity is related to the elevated fear and passion to own guns. The key is used to collect it and dissipate thus fear because it represents the 2nd amendment being used and removing guns from society. The reduction of guns equate to less massacres being reported to the public, and therefore a reduction in fear. The opposite has proven to be true, because now whenever there is a widely reported massacre gun sales tend to spike briefly. Interesting, isn't it? Remember that the Join or Die doodle was created on May 9th 1754.

Passages for Priestley's History of Electricity (II)

Draft: American Philosophical Society [1766]

It ought to be so on Dr. F.'s Principles. If one Side be rubbed by the Finger; it acquires from the Finger some of the Electric Fluid. This being spread on the Glass as far as the Rubbing extended, repels an equal Quantity of that contain'd in the other Side of the Glass, and drives it out on that Side, where it stands as an Atmosphere, and so both sides are found *plus*. If the unrubb'd Side were in Contact with a Conductor communicating with the Earth, the Electric Fluid would be carried away, and then that Side would be left *apparently* in the natural State. If the electric Fluid found on the unrubb'd Side was really part of that which had been communicated by and from the Finger, and so had actually *perm-[eated]* the Glass, it might, when conducted away, be continually replac'd by fresh permeating Fluid communicated in the same Manner: But if the Effect is continually diminishing, while the suppos'd Cause repeated, continues the same, there seems reason to [doubt] the Relation between that

Cause and the Effect. It appears difficult to conceive how Electric Fluid having pass'd thro' a permeable Body, should make it more difficult for other Electric Fluid to follow, till at length none would pass thro' at all.

Are there indicators that this is a cipher? Yes there most certainly are and we have seen them before. These can be seen in the capitalization of the letters, which normally would not be necessary in a letter. As you read through it think just a bit more. Remember that in the 2nd amendment there were 3 capital letters. In this one the phrase "natural State" is used and it refers to the natural state of tranquility. The state only becomes unnatural when mans invention is introduced which in the context of society, is the introduction of lethal weaponry. Dr. Franklin's principles are only with respect to his observation of human nature. One side being rubbed by the finger denotes a trigger being pulled. The Electric Fluid I believe is a reference to the excitement this may instill in a man, such as adrenaline. The symbolism of "glass" can be thought of as a looking glass, to look closely at the 2nd amendment, from one side to the next. This fluid/excitement is dissipated if the trigger of a gun is "unrubbed" through the regulation of Arms that cause too much excitement. As technology of Arms advances so too does their lethality and power, and it's the sense of power that a man possesses which is the fluid. Removing that power, is necessary to the security of the "natural State". When its stated "really part of that", is inferring that the "right of the people to keep and bear Arms", does not exist, and never has. The relation between cause and effect is that of fear, and the less guns there are the less fear there will be in a society of them. This point is driven home when it's stated "none would pass thro' at all", which is simply the cessation of fear and an overactive imagination.

To Joseph Priestley London Sept. 19. 1772

ALS (letterbook draft) and copy: Library of Congress

Dear Sir,
In the Affair of so much Importance to you, wherein you ask my Advice, I cannot for want of sufficient Premises, advise you *what* to determine, but if you please I will tell you *how*. When these difficult Cases occur[663], they are difficult chiefly because while we have them under Consideration all the Reasons *pro* and *con* are not present to

---

[663] Judging which arms are lethal and which are not.

the Mind at the same time[664]; but sometimes one Set present themselves, and at other times another, the first being out of Sight. Hence the various Purposes or Inclinations that alternately prevail, and the Uncertainty that perplexes us. To get over this, my Way is, to divide half a Sheet of Paper by a Line into two Columns[665], writing over the one *Pro,* and over the other *Con.* Then during three or four Days Consideration[666] I put down under the different Heads short Hints of the different Motives that at different Times occur to me for or against the Measure[667]. When I have thus got them all together in one View, I endeavour to estimate their respective Weights; and where I find two, one on each side, that seem equal, I strike them both out: If I find a Reason *pro* equal to some two Reasons *con*, I strike out the three. If I judge some two Reasons *con* equal to some three Reasons *pro,* I strike out the five; and thus proceeding I find at length where the Ballance lies[668]; and if after a Day or two of farther Consideration nothing new that is of Importance occurs on either side, I come to a Determination accordingly. And tho' the Weight of Reasons cannot be taken with the Precision of Algebraic Quantities, yet when each is thus considered separately and comparatively[669], and the whole lies before me[670], I think I can judge better[671], and am

---

[664] People tend to think of their own defence first and not the empowerment of their enemies which allow them to enforce their will on others. The USA has gotten it right when they don't want other nations to have nuclear weapons. This is the EXACT same concept as the 2nd amendment.

[665] Symbolic of a group of men.

[666] After removing some Arms from society it takes time to study the statistics of gun violence being reduced. (ie take out all the handguns.

[667] The measure is the 2nd amendment.

[668] The balance is that some men can still hunt but for food, and the same weaponry is not necessarily harming society.

[669] Think of a society with handguns and without handguns.

[670] Whole is the a direct reference to the word Militia, which contains the weaponry that is currently in society which are causing harm because they are in the hands of the Militia. A Militia is the whole of people and Arms. He says it lies before him, because this word is in front of him and requires study in order to unlock its secret context.

[671] Judge better = well regulated and not "well-regulated".

less likely to make a rash Step[672]; and in fact I have found great Advantage from this kind of Equation, in what may be called *Moral*[673] or *Prudential Algebra*[674]. Wishing sincerely that you may determine for the best, I am ever, my dear Friend, Yours most affectionately
    B Franklin
    Dr Priestly

This is another cipher that talks about the usage of the 2nd amendment as an equation. He doesn't know The 2nd amendment is an equation with variables. The word **measure** is even referenced by George Washington just 13 years later in a letter to James Madison when he says. "It is a **dangerous experiment**—once slacken the reins and the power is lost—and it is questionable with me whether the **advocates** of the **measure** foresee all the consequences of it"

---

[672] The step he speaks of is stepping to the third clause of the 2nd amendment "the right of the people to keep and bear Arms", which is rash, because it infers virtually no regulations AND tells the people that this is the nature of their right, which is a thing that men don't often want to give up.

[673] Think first of your society and not your own fear.

[674] Benjamin Franklin is talking about the 2nd amendment as being an equation with variables. Prudential algebra, is a direct reference to it, because it is far more prudent to evaluate the output of people and Arms as variables in the clause "the right of the People to keep and bear Arms.

The Grand Leap of the Whale

Posted by Benjamin Franklin on 22 May 1765, 8:07 am
To the Printer of the Public Advertiser.

SIR, In your Paper of Wednesday last, an ingenious Correspondent that calls himself the SPECTATOR, and dates from Pimlico, under the Guise of Good-Will[675] to the News-Writers, whom he allows to be "an useful Body of Men in this great City[676]," has, in my Opinion artfully attempted to turn them and their Works into Ridicule; wherein, if he could succeed, great Injury might be done to the Public[677], as well as to those good People.

Supposing, Sir, that the We hears they give us of this and t'other intended Voyage, or Tour of this and t'other great Personage, were mere Inventions, yet they at least afford us an innocent Amusement while we read, and useful Matter of Conversation when we are disposed to converse. English-men, Sir, are too apt to be silent when they have nothing to say[678]; too apt to be sullen when they are silent, and when they are sullen to h — g themselves[679]. But by these We Hears we are supplied with abundant Fund of Discourse: We discuss the Motives to such Voyages, the Probability of their being undertaken, and the Practicability of their Execution[680]. Here we can display our Judgment in Politics[681,] our Knowledge of the Interests of

---

[675] "Guise" of "Good-Will" and the hyphen This is a reference to "well regulated" being under the guise of "well-regulated"

[676] This is a reference to a Militia.

[677] Arms in society.

[678] It's a fact that you cannot hear the hyphen when well regulated is spoken in English. Note "English-men" is used to give a clue as to the context of this sentence. In debates people would hear what they wanted too, and it wouldn't be questioned.

[679] Not hearing the actual words "well regulated" would in fact cause death among men. Hanging themselves is a reference to this. It is the absence of "an" in the word hang that the cipher invites to figure the nature of the cipher here, or in other words, fill in the blanks. If this just "clicked", also know that this letter was written in 1765, twenty years before the constitutional convention even began.

[680] A well regulated Militia is impracticable for an entire population.

[681] These are the regulations.

Princes[682], and our Skill in Geography[683]; and (if we have it) shew our Dexterity moreover in Argumentation. In the mean time[684], the tedious Hours is killed; we go home pleased with the Applauses we have received from others[685], or at least with those we secretly give to ourselves[686]; we sleep soundly, and live on, to the Comfort of our Families[687].

But, Sir, I beg leave to say, that all the Articles of News, that seem improbable, are not mere Inventions[688]. Some of them, I can assure you on the Faith of a Traveller, are serious Truths. And here, quitting Mr. Spectator of Pimlico, give me Leave to instance the various numberless Accounts the News-Writers have given us (with so much honest Zeal for the Welfare of Poor Old England!) of the establishing Manufactures in the Colonies to the Prejudice of those of this Kingdom. It is objected by superficial Readers, who yet pretend to some Knowledge of those Countries, that such Establishments are not only improbable but impossible; for that their Sheep have but little Wool[689], not in the whole sufficient for a Pair of Stockings[690] a Year to each Inhabitants; and that, from the universal Dearness of

---

[682] Princes are high ranking people and are a reference to regulating people under a government.

[683] This is a reference to having the "skill" to see the word "state" not as a colony, but as a state of mind.

[684] The "mean" time is when the 2nd amendment is misunderstood.

[685] The feeling that we are being patriotic.

[686] We know we are thinking of ourselves first and not society as far as arms are concerned.

[687] We have normalized gun ownership.

[688] The 2nd amendment, once revealed is not something that was contrived, not matter how unbelievable it may be. He is telling us that there is a correct way to read this sentence, and why it is better.

[689] People who are being sold the value of a right to keep and bear Arms.

[690] The "whole" is a reference to subjectively reading "Militia", which in turn gives weight to "a right of the people to keep and bear Arms" because 'people and Arms" are now embedded within "Militia". Furthermore , the fact that the sheep have been sheered of their wool, means that others are profiting from a misinterpretation of the 2nd amendment. Think in terms of cotton and slavery.and the utility of Arms for slave holders.

Labour among them, the working of Iron and other Materials, except in some few coarse Instances, is impracticable to any Advantage.[691] Dear Sir, do not let us suffer ourselves to be amused with such groundless Objections. The very Tails of the American Sheep are so laden with Wool[692,] that each has a Car or Waggon on four little Wheels to support and keep it from trailing on the Ground[693]. Would they caulk their Ships? would they fill their Beds? would they even litter their Horses with Wool, if it was not both plenty and cheap? And what signifies Dearness of Labour, where an English Shilling passes for Five-and-twenty? Their engaging three hundred Silk Throwsters here in one Week for New York was treated as a Fable, because, forsooth, they have "no Silk there to throw." Those who made this Objection perhaps did not know, that at the same Time the Agents from the King of Spain were at Quebec contracting for 1000 Pieces of Cannon to be made there for the Fortifications of Mexico, with 25,000 Axes for their industrious Logwood-Cutters[694]; and at New-York engaging an annual Supply of warm Floor-Carpets for their West-India Houses; other Agents from the Emperor of China were at Boston in New-England treating about an Exchange of Raw-Silk for Wool, to be carried on in Chinese Jonks through the Straits of Magellan. And yet all this is as certainly true as the Account, said to be from Quebec, in the Papers of last Week, that the Inhabitants of Canada are making Preparations for a Cod and Whale Fishery this Summer in the Upper Lakes. Ignorant People may object that the Upper Lakes are fresh[695,] and that Cod and Whale are Salt-water Fish: But let them know, Sir, that Cod, like other Fish, when attacked by their Enemies, fly into any Water where they think they can be

---

[691] The making of Arms.

[692] Its the end of the 2nd amendment which renders profit to the rich, but leaves all of society stripped.

[693] 4 wheels or clauses of the 2nd amendment. This article or amendment is also being propped up, but only the part people like or see of being the greatest utility.

[694] While America was arming its citizenry, other nations were putting the big Arms in charge of government, (cannons), and the people would get small arms, axes, which were related more to industry.

[695] There can be two types of environments, one with guns and one without.

safest; that Whales, when they have a Mind to eat Cod[696], pursue them wherever they fly; and that the grand Leap of the Whale[697] in that Chace up the Fall of Niagara is esteemed by all who have seen it[698], as one of the finest Spectacles[699] in Nature[700]! — Really, Sir, the World is grown too incredulous: Pendulum-like, it is ever swinging from one Extream to another[701]. Formerly every Thing printed was believed, because it was in Print[702]: Now Things seem to be disbelieved for just the very same Reason. Wise Men wonder at the present Growth of Infidelity! They should have consider'd, when they taught People to doubt the Authority of News-papers[703], and the Truth of Predictions in Almanacs, that the next Step might be a Disbelief in the well-vouch'd Accounts of Ghosts and Witches, and Doubts even of the Truth of the A —— n Creed.

Thus much I thought it necessary to say in favour of an honest Set of Writers[704], whose comfortable Living depends on collecting and supplying the Printers with News, at the small Price of Six-pence an Article[705]; and who always show their Regard to Truth, by

---

[696] When a whale (person with gun) decides to hunt down a cod (anyone else) then they will do it, and there is nothing that you can do about it.

[697] A Whale symbolises a fish with too much power, such as a man with lethal Arms in society or water A whale also symbolises the secret of the 2nd amendment being a very big discovery because Niagra means "an overwhelming flood" of information that has been discovered. It is overwhelming because the 2nd amendment has just taken a 180 degree turn.

[698] It's mans downfall not to use it to chase cods.

[699] Look closely

[700] Human nature

[701] Some people only think in black and white and give no quarter to the middle ground.

[702] "The right of the people to keep and bear Arms" was believed.

[703] It seems in the 18th century Benjamin Franklin had to deal with the alternative fact crowds as well.

[704] People who honestly knew how to use the English language

[705] Article is a reference to anticipated 2nd amendment being instilled. It is much cheaper on the liberty of society to not allow lethal guns into society in the first place.

contradicting such as are wrong in a subsequent Article[706] — for another Six-pence, to the great Satisfaction and Improvement of us Coffee-house Students in History[707] and Politics, and the infinite Advantage of all future Livies, Rapins, Robertsons, Humes, Smollets, and Macaulays, who may be sincerely inclin'd to furnish the World with that rara Avis, a true History. I am, SIR, Your humble Servant, A TRAVELLER[708].

The Public Advertiser, May 22, 1765

One of the key arguments for the right to bear Arms is to protect oneself against others with guns.

The whale is symbolic of one marine animal having much more power over another. This is simply an analogy pertaining to the greatly enhanced power a man can have over another once he has lethal weaponry.

"But let them know, Sir, that Cod, like other Fish, when attacked by their Enemies, fly into any Water where they think they can be safest; that Whales, when they have a Mind to eat Cod, pursue them wherever they fly; and that the grand Leap of the Whale in that Chace up the Fall of Niagara is esteemed by all who have seen it, as one of the finest Spectacles in Nature!"

Almost exactly one century later, Abraham Lincoln appeared to share this view when he wrote

"I long ago made up my mind that if anybody wants to kill me, he will do it. If I wore a shirt of mail and kept myself surrounded by a bodyguard, it would be all the same. There are a thousand ways of getting at a man if it is desirable that he should be killed. Besides, in this case, it seems to me, the man who would come after me would be just as objectionable to my enemies – If I have any. "

Abraham Lincoln to journalist Noah Brooks in 1863.

There is no inference that Abraham Lincoln actually knew what the 2nd amendment really was, but rather that he wasn't fearful of being hunted by

---

[706] Same article as above, which is the 2nd amendment but it is being completely contradicted due to it being read subjectively.

[707] Future historians who will understand the 2nd amendment for what it really is.

[708] 2nd amendment travelling on a journey to the future.

another human. There are many ways that a man can die, but with respect to guns, he who shoots first usually wins. This is an action of offence and not defence and requires nothing more than the flex of a finger. When a society is armed to the teeth, is to change the environment from cod to Whale, where one can transform to another in an instant. The method of this transformation is due solely to the nature and lethality of the empowerment. I have heard arguments that we are all going to die anyway or that 1000s of other people are killed by cars. Cars however have air bags, horns, seatbelts, collapsible bumpers, which were put place to protect life, and enforced by regulations. While it may be true that people still die in car accidents, it has been studied that many more would die without. In the absence of a seatbelt, a man can easily be shot out of a vehicle in a sudden crash, so it was deemed necessary to the security of a human body, through regulations, that it not be allowed to become a projectile in the first place. Believe it or not, sometimes in society there are bad drivers and it is contingent upon government to protect them in spite of themselves. It is also contingent on government to protect others just in case some bad drivers suddenly appear. This is called preventive medicine and it is far cheaper to do this than not. A simple example of this is to look both ways before you cross the street.

8-Conclusions and Reflections
The Narratives We Build

All animals require an understanding of their environment. They learn this through life experience and trial and error. They are shown by parents how to hunt and survive through mimicry. It is a method for passing along wisdom to give the offspring a jump start. Would an animal survive on its own, if the wisdom of trial and error from previous generations was not passed along? Some animals are more intelligent than others and what they have to teach is more complex. For the most part though, animals teach each other the basics of how to hunt, live and be sheltered. Once intelligence is factored in then things change rather dramatically and get far more complex. This is the reason why politics is not liked by most because the messaging becomes a confusing mess. Everyone just wants stability for the most part. Everyone just wants to eat, be sheltered and experience the liberty and dignity of being able to provide for these things for themselves. Intelligence is a double edged sword, because now it can be used to get what we want, if we are cunning. We can use intelligence to create a sales pitch and if we can sell something then people of course will buy it. This is the currency of the politician. As the currency of business this is called marketing.

I succumbed to this marketing. As I deliver this news to you now there was a time that I labored through two snow storms to deliver newspapers. With my earnings, I proceeded to buy myself a "Pet Rock". You can look it up, but it was sold in the book stores. There was a large display of small boxes with holes in them. The holes were there so that the rock inside could live. Now this rock came with an instruction manual. It said you could name your rock. It also said that you could try and train your pet rock to do tricks. Now since the budgie at home was getting boring I decided to buy this new pet which I thought was brilliant because apparently it would not require feeding. Yes, the man that discovered the truth behind the 2nd amendment after almost 200 years bought a rock in box which had holes in the side so it could breath. Basically I traded someone a cheeseburger, fries and a shake for a rock. I still have that rock and I can now report that Cedrick has been a very good listener. Ha! The thing is, I went there. I imagined that the impossible, may in fact be possible. As you can see I'm now trying to sell you something to salvage my own dignity, but the fact remains, I went there. In my yet to be fine tuned thinking, I allowed for the "what if". Years later, I asked myself that exact same question which flew in the face of a narrative that had existed for 224 years. I asked myself "what if the 2nd amendment was not what everyone has thought it to be?" I went there and when I did that, I can assure you, I was not stoned. For the most part the narratives we build, we stop building them at the moment they are of utility to us alone and may fall just short of the truth.

If we didn't have a narrative we would not be able to survive. We would not know what to do. We would not know how we fit into our environment. We would not know how to acquire our food or even what it looked like. We would not even know where the best place to sleep is. We would be a state of instability. We would be cold and hungry and would not even know what to do about it. We would do everything in our power to resolve these problems fill our stomachs and warm up, but in the process we would have built a narrative. Does the end justify the means? How did we acquire our food? Do we catch a fish or steal a cheeseburger from a hungry teenager and force him to starve? Where stability is concerned the end will always justify the means in our narratives. It works for the individual only until it no longer works. It works only until society has had enough of your narrative if it infringes on their own. We are of course making a choice between respecting our fellow man and his lunch or not. One method would be arguably easier from a physical point of view but it would also be easier from a thinking point of view too. It would require far more skill to catch a fish where a hamburger requires only eyeballs, a nose a hand and tied shoelaces.

Now let's assume that it's our nature to choose the fishing method to acquire our food. Imagine one day we are happily fishing and have honed our skills to such an extent that fishing has now become second nature to us. Our stomachs are full and we have even discovered that a fish bone can be used as a tooth pick. We have thought long about this and as long as we keep perceiving paths to new utility we will explore them. Let's assume in the narrative building process that we have no understanding of a bear. We have never seen one, heard one, smelt one or looked into the eyes of one. We don't even know what they are called, and I only now share with you the word for it because I'm assuming it's in your narrative already. We do know what teeth are because we had just been using them to chew our fish and were now at the point in our lunch where we were happily picking out a few tasty morsels. So a bear suddenly comes into the picture and throws us a generous smile. Now this being our first encounter with such a creature gives us pause. Our imagination kicks in, grabs the wheel and begins to spin. Our imagination frantically tries to direct our narrative back to a place of stability with the new variables it perceives. Things are frantic because one of these variables is of course time, and while time stops for no one it is perceived that our own may be up. We have just seen very large teeth and imagine the possibility of us being a morsel stuck within, only this time a bear is not using a fishbone, but a human rib to pluck us out in order to further establish the food chain. For a brief moment we attempt to find solace in the humour of the fish flipping out earlier as we are now. The solace doesn't pan out though. We do not like the idea of a right to bear Arms in this circumstance because we perceive danger in the claws. So as we recede from the bear in a direction that can best be described as "away", we note that the bear didn't chase us. We are achieving stability and our newly expanded narrative likes it. It's a rare thing to see a bear after all, but now we know the danger in it. We still choose the path which will take us to the fish but we now know to keep one eye open and perhaps choose the prudence of a bear spray.

It is human nature to take the path of least resistance in our thinking and this includes the thinking involved to build our own narratives. From time to time we may switch things out but not all that often. This process is far more frequent when we are younger and it starts to get most complex when we have to figure out how to interact in a society. Now part of this process of thinking involves thinking that there is one answer to any question. It is either this or it is that. In keeping with this hamburger theme I recall a time when I was much younger when one of my brothers was about 5 years old. We were visiting some new old people we had never met before and we were very leery of them. Now my middle brother whom I will not name to protect his dignity had a rudimentary understanding of cows. I believe at this point in his life he knew they went moo and provided milk, and with milk one could add chocolate flavouring. He asked one of the elders if he could go milk a cow. My great uncle apparently had no problem with this and told my brother, the middle one, no problem and then carried on conversing with my parents. I didn't witness this exchange at the time because I was probably too busy shedding some light on an ant with my new magnifying glass. About twenty minutes later I heard a bit of a commotion, and being interested in these, I soon discovered my teary eyed middle brother in bath tub with an angry red hoof print on his stomach. I could hear the elder laughing as my brother looked up at him in rage. Now what had transpired in that twenty minutes was that my middle brother's narrative about cows was instantaneously changed due to his folly of choosing the only cow in the barn that was not in the possession of an udder. Perhaps it was the lighting, but as they say in the realty world it's all about location, location, location. Now, I'm just guessing as I attempt to paint this picture, but I would imagine that a "moo" is still firmly implanted in his narrative. Now isn't that a kicker? Some narratives are easily defeated with a truth that can only be mustered up by experience.

Throughout our lives we all seek stability and for the most part have found it in the perceived integrity of narratives we have both built and adopted. In the beginning this is supplied to us by our parents in the form of food, shelter and praise. Even these things are not guaranteed but the lessons we are taught in their acquirement is incorporated into our narratives. Sometimes the nurture we get from our parents in teaching us our narratives this is difficult to process because it comes across as to much work. If our emotions are not satisfied, then we are not satisfied. When our emotions are satisfied then we also feel as if we have reached a point of stability. The faster a child can be helped to arrive at that point the faster peace will be arrived at. The child of course has its own narrative which it uses to get what it wants. The child has a sales pitch with its primary component being a set of lungs. Regardless of how we are nurtured we still must create a narrative for ourselves. We encounter situations within or outside of our control which we must process and assimilate into our experience of our perceived reality. The template we need for this is our own instruction manual or our narrative of how are universe works around us and how we are to behave within it. We seek stability and we like to stick to the plan of a well established narrative that we call our own. We have all observed that some people have differently ideologies. We generally don't like the ideologies of others, because they conflict with our own. Religion is a microcosm of this. Some of us can't tolerate the religions of others and some of us can. Stepping back from religion it helps us to understand our purpose in life and gives it meaning. Some people find meaning in other ways. None the less though, in our narrative our intelligence would like to justify our own existence and in that there is even further utility if it is perceived. If it is in our nature to wish to feel more important than others to give ourselves more value, then this can be achieved through religion. It's not our idea after all, and it comes with a wide reaching consensus in the matter so this helps to validate it. I'm not saying religion is "wrong" or anything along those lines, but if we integrate religion as being a part of our narrative, in part we do so, because it seems logical. It also has value to us. Yes, a consensus must always be a place of truth. The thing is, is that truth does not care about a consensus. I'm one man and this book exists because I didn't buy into the consensus of a 200 year old dogma and subsequently discovered a truth. I've just told a rather large group of people that a 200 year old dogma has always been a fallacy in a founding document. It is not my intent to sound arrogant as surely I must. From my point of view I would be more inclined to label it awkward.

Liberty can be easily denied if there is no opportunity to create it for ourselves due to those that think it's a game to cut societies pie by their own dictates. y. There will always be those that may wish to 5freeload on societies gifts which are of course the collective invention and labors of men. Some of these people may even be the poor from time to time, but that's a thing that is much harder to discern. A starving man who is denied a job due to race, age, or past errors of judgement while traversing the long road through life often loses a debate where morals and starvation are concerned.

How we think

Have you ever encountered a personality that knows it all? I'm not talking about the wisest of the wise but rather a person who is extremely adamant in their views on pretty much everything. They seem to have built a moat around their narrative constructed battlements and stationed well-regulated Militias all around to guard against any attack. Why? Is it possible that they've run out of room for more knowledge? There is no room to be wrong for this individual and it is almost as if they have no choice in matter. I believe the reason for this has far less to do with what the narrative is but rather in the approach taken to its construction.

Now add to this taking the path of least resistance in their thinking which is in itself is natural thing to do but it is also a choice. This will greatly limit ever finding the truth if this is the sole engine of logic. They have gotten into the habit over time of thinking and approaching problem solving by thinking in extremes. Ok, now hold that thought, and only that thought. This is underpinning of how they problem solve and quite literally how they think. The "gotcha moment" is the instant that a truth has been demonstrated and actually acknowledged but it clashes with a narrative that has been reckoned in the manner I have just stated. The "gotcha moment" has even been labelled as a thing so that it can easily be dismissed as nothing more than a tactic removing it even further from an opportunity to actually learn it.

How would a person who has chosen to think in this manner to the point that its almost second nature now take to being told that they got just a part of their narrative wrong? It is the very nature of this thinking that does not really allow for parts. Every piece that they have incorporated into their narrative was arrived at through "black and white" thinking. For the most part, there are no parts because everything was arrived at through black and white thinking simply because this approach was easiest. This in turn can further be compounded when emotion alone is used as a source of logic and reasoning. If it feels good it must be good. If it feels bad it must be bad. Such thinking would make a person an easy target for fear and slogans.

Now over time as each new piece of an expanding narrative is resolved in this fashion it is then incorporated and then fused in with the rest. Remember that it is either completely right or completely wrong, and if it's completely right, then there is no perceived need to take it with a grain of salt. If such a person were told that part of their narrative was wrong, they would then assume all of it was wrong, or at the very least would be almost incapable of removing a particular piece of their fused narratives without possibly breaking or even shattering other pieces. It would be a place of horror in the mind because if that was to happen, then it would be an assault on the very thing that they used to create their narratives in the first place. The amount of instability involved in this circumstance would be a very big barrier indeed which would further solidify the very nature of their thinking.

As I said earlier, everyone needs a narrative to survive, but if their starting point in life is from a place of wealth, then part of their narrative from day one may be from a place of entitlement. A man with royal blood or another born to money could easily have this viewpoint. They could not help but notice how much better off they are than others, so they would have to justify this in their own mind. It must after all feel pretty good, so it must be right. I don't paint all with such a brush but you can easily see this happening. This is how a pompous ass is created. They are born into the "Pursuit of Happiness" which they have associated with money, because it is all they know. This in itself is no big deal, just luck of the draw I suppose but when this individuals Pursuit of happiness interferes with any others Life or Liberty, then they are no different than King George. They have become the face of oppression and they are nothing more than a tyrant running amuck in society. I think I said earlier there can be good kings and there can be bad kings and a king is nothing more than a man born to wealth and position. Money is power, and the biggest threat to this power is to have the money taxed, or regulated, in order to ensure that everyone else has both Life and Liberty.

There are many different religions in the world which is great because it gives people a narrative that gives them both comfort and meaning. Some people choose to think that other religions are a threat to their own. If there are 12 different kinds of gods out there then it is perceived that only one can be right. There is only room for one god, which is again demonstration of people thinking in terms of black and white. If we have our own beliefs about something that we are perfectly comfortable with then why should we care about others? The same can be said for different forms of government. The same can be said for different races and cultures. This goes to the very heart of conflict, if a heart can even be found there. This is also exactly why it was deemed that there should be a separation of church and state in the constitution. How can different religions exist in We the People if it is perceived by some that there can only be one? Everyone wants the exact same thing which is to survive and the bare minimum for that is Life and Liberty. No one should ever be put on trial for wanting those things in the court of our own logic. There will always be a right and a wrong side to history if mankind is to take any pride in itself.

Racism

Our brains use contrast to resolve one thing from the other. Once something is perceived as being different then it immediately becomes a curiosity. We attempt to incorporate it into our narrative. A grey squirrel is able to resolve contrast with perhaps the same speed as a human. The grey squirrel may see a black one, but for the most part may only be wondering where that other squirrel is hiding its nuts. It doesn't judge the other squirrel based on its color because it is able to reason out that the other squirrel is also a squirrel, and likes to collect nuts as well. Yes, "nuts" is very much a part of this reality based analogy. Now when we add intelligence to the equation the ego starts to form. The ego likes to know where we fit in and works very hard to ensure we are at the top of the food chain. Our ego is constantly looking for ways to increase our own sense of value. If we can attribute more value to ourselves then we can in turn use it to prop ourselves up in the eyes of our peers. Peacocks do this in the absence of creative thinking because they are using bird brains. A squirrel is more concerned about nuts, and perhaps isn't driving itself nuts by constantly trying to self validate its own existence. Its only religion is the shade of a tree and the warmth of a burrow. Its devils are winged creatures that it can actually see. Man however finds utility in these exact same creatures, being eagles, as symbols of power and liberty. Everything is connected and everything has a different viewpoint on reality imagined or otherwise.

The squirrel and the man are able to use contrast with equal speed but the man with the ego may equate his own fast thinking in discerning contrast as being a sign of a really good brain. Fast intelligent thinking is of utility to the ego as it looks for avenues to create more value for itself. If a difference is perceived then there may be a perceived utility in it. The end justifies the means, and if the means is really easy, the end is achieved with speed. We may then try to establish that our color is better than any other color for surely one thing must be better than another. Race is used almost like a religion for those that take the path of least resistance in their thinking. A bias is now in play and it attempts to exploit the situation for personal gain. An enemy may even be perceived and it is now easy to classify an entire group of people with only a glance. We immediately know all we need to know, and even desire to know, because any further validation may take away something we've already established with our really good brains. Nobody likes having something taken away from them, if they view it of value to themselves. If they find some form of joy in the thing from a place of childhood glee then there is resistance to changing our thinking. It's a very easy thing with no more thought put into the process than that of a 5 year old. Some may argue that the culture of these lesser humans is different, but perhaps, just perhaps, part of that culture has been created through the environment of racism. If everyone lives under the same flag, and desires the exact same things, with the only discernible difference being skin pigment then why would a pigment or lack thereof be a threat? The only reason it could possibly be a threat is because of racism, caused by some very simple thinking on one side, and the experience of it on the other. If we were to walk into a room with 1000 of our own race would it be wise to trust everyone in that room, or view them as being the same? Is everyone the same in your own family? Everyone is different aren't they? Just because people are different doesn't necessarily meant that they are your enemies. The only thing you may have in common is in knowing that those of your own race are unlikely to be racist towards you. I have heard the concept of white power which is the very antithesis of the constitution. It holds within it a certain quality of vitriol fed by meat, like that to a starving dog, which waves the confederate flag as a tale, which will forever remain on the wrong side of history. Political correctness is nothing m-ore than good manners and respect for the words "We the People".

Choices

The most powerful thing a man has is the ability to make choices. He may not be able to act on them, but in his mind he can resolve choices in any manner he or she pleases.

The point of this comes down to we all have a choice not just what we think, but more importantly in how we think. We can choose to make decisions based on logic dictated by the whim of our emotions or not. Usually vastly different conclusions will be arrived at if we decide to take short cuts in our thinking. We may be perfectly good with these conclusions if it suits us, but being perfectly good in a conclusion for ourselves, isn't necessarily so good for the rest of society. Everyone is somewhere on their path in life, and everyone requires the ability to feed and shelter themselves. Every person is part of a society and everyone contributes in their own way, given that they have an opportunity to do so in the first place. There will always be those that may try to take advantage of the system and they can fall in any segment of society, which can now be measured in terms of Life, Liberty and the Pursuit of Happiness. The wealthiest may be trying to take advantage of the system if they are forever playing in the pursuit of happiness with not a care for any others life or liberty. Perhaps they attempt to sway the vote to lower taxes or deregulation or haven't given their employees a living wage, and further squeezed them with longer hours. Perhaps they champion "trickle-down-economics", or threaten job losses if the wages are too high. It seems to me though that jobs are related more to the customer base where the latter are related to the rich who have long forgotten, or perhaps have never known the struggle of living from paycheck to paycheck which in itself balances precariously on the edge of oppression. The life and liberty of the rich are never under assault, only their Pursuit of Happiness where the very upper limit is a thing that will always be seen on the horizon of their imaginations. To them, the poor are both enemy and friend. An enemy if it is perceived that they are the cause of an approaching horizon, or a friend if status is a thing that is perceived to feed the ego and cause it to hunger no more.

Imagine what the world would be like if in every business model life and liberty were incorporated into the bottom line? Any business model requires consumers but if all businesses have not factored in a living wage, a liberty wage if you will, into their bottom line then they have created an environment that will shrink their consumer base to the point of going bankrupt. Perhaps in order to maximize the size of this base they will find ways to manufacture products that are cheaper for the consumer, while simultaneously dramatically cutting down the life span of their products. Design in a shorter lifespan for the washing machine, and not only will they sell more, but now they can supplement their profits with extended warranties which will most certainly be demonstrated as being useful. Now there are two revenue streams, providing they throw enough marketing at the first one. I once had someone ask me if I would like to spend 25 dollars on an extended warranty for an 80 dollar particle board book shelf with a cardboard backing. They told me that if it was scratched I could have it fixed. When I got home, the first thing I did was look in the mirror to see if I could find any signs of stupid. It confused me, but erring on the side of caution I painfully plucked a rogue hair from an earlobe, which ironically was a stupid thing to do in light of the pain.

A monopoly is nothing more than an industrialized liberty rake allowed to flourish in the complete absence of regulation, as it piles up the pursuit of happiness for the few.

If a balance was found that would allow jobs for all with living wages then the inalienable rights of Life and Liberty would be fulfilled for all. These are the lines of demarcation for the constitution, because if the "Pursuit of Happiness" for the few trumps Life and Liberty, then the revolutionary war was fought for nothing. Just as the second amendment is a reality based tool for ensuring the public safety, Life and Liberty could be used as the measurement for business models, wages and a goal post for both rich and poor alike. One can look at taxes as being something taken away from us, or they can view taxes as being society rent used in part to ensure that Life and Liberty are secured in the context of "We the People". The man who is the true patriot is the man that votes for Life and Liberty for all which of course includes himself. The man born to wealth or the one that has achieved through his own business model and ingenuity will become the tyrant if he robs the most basic inalienable rights of other through not paying a fair wage, where his goal is solely to increase his own Pursuit of

Happiness, if he defines that by money alone. Unfortunately it is money, the cost of living that provides Life and Liberty, but it is often times used as a measure of success, but lines are crossed if it robs others due to the structure of their business models as adopted. They have become tyrants in society because of their own inability to self regulate and ignoring the most basic rights of all the people. How many unpaid hours must be worked to be a team player? How many part time jobs must be worked just to survive, because it's been decided by accountants that if the labour was all part time, there would be cost savings in overtime pay and even making scheduling easier. Is there any line on the spreadsheet that accounts for a man's liberty or is the goal singularly the Pursuit of Happiness of only one which has been chosen to be defined as money alone?

    Following this paragraph is excerpt which I found at Franklinpapers.org. This is an observation of human nature from almost 300 years ago. I used only its beginning text from this article because it was most relevant to this book. It also demonstrates that Benjamin Franklin knew what he was up against in trying to devise a way to help humanity in spite of itself. The letter is almost 300 years old having been printed in 1723. Over the time span of 300 years mans knowledge and invention have grown in exponentially. Some may even believe that human nature has kept pace with these advancements. Human nature will never advance but it can be guided through the correct interpretation and adherence to the wisdom of the constitution. Human nature still screams out in anger if it does not get what it wants and may at times see the constitution as an obstacle to his own pursuit of money. It may in fact be an obstacle, but it is not the fault of the constitution but rather the failings of his business model to factor in the rights of Life and Liberty. The constitution is like a parent, but looks out for all its children to ensure there is harmony in the family. Human nature has invented corporations and paths to monopolies. It is human nature that has gerrymandered voting districts. It is human nature that has argued for voter restrictions using fear as its ally. It is human nature that takes power from the constitution where none exists in the appointment of a Supreme Court Justice. It is human nature that attempts to tie a nation to only one god and affiliate it with the constitution. It is human nature that will attack the constitution, in spite of the very inalienable rights it was written to protect. It is human nature that chooses to associate "Pursuit of Happiness" with the advancement of personal wealth well and beyond the simple necessities for life and liberty. It is human nature that prioritizes "The Pursuit of Happiness" over "Life" with respect to health care. It is human nature that believes that corporations are people too. This is ridiculous if I may be so candid in my opinion and opinion fully endorsed by Thomas Jefferson. Pick the arrogance you may now perceive and I will submit that one of them is the lesser evil. The output of my labor will hopefully provide Life and Liberty by exposing the constitution for what it always was.

Now here is that letter

> **"On Titles of Honor**
> Printed in *The New-England Courant,* February 18, 1723.
> Mero meridie si dixerit illi tenebras esse, credit.
> There is nothing in which Mankind reproach themselves more than in their Diversity of Opinions. Every Man sets himself above another in his own Opinion, and there are not two Men in the World whose Sentiments are alike in every thing. Hence it comes to pass, that the same Passages in the Holy Scriptures or the Works of the Learned, are wrested to the meaning of two opposite Parties, of contrary Opinions, as if the Passages they recite were like our Master Janus, looking two ways at once, or like Lawyers, who with equal Force of Argument, can plead either for the Plaintiff or Defendant.
> The most absurd and ridiculous Opinions, are sometimes spread by the least colour of Argument: But if they stop at the first Broachers, they have still the Pleasure of being wiser (in their own Conceits) than the rest of the World, and can with the greatest Confidence pass a Sentence of Condemnation upon the Reason of all Mankind, who dissent from the peculiar Whims of their troubled Brains."
> www.franklinpapers.org

In modern times some have viewed the constitution as being outdated, where others have viewed it as a living document. The constitution was written to handle human nature which is unlikely to change in the next 20,000 years if at all. In the acknowledgement of its existence and a better understanding of how it works, we can guard against it and the first place that must be done is from within ourselves if we take any pride in mankind as a species. It's just a choice and choices are not forced upon us though some are more difficult than others, until they are not because then those choices simply become a habit and pay dividends in liberty for all. For some to think they know better than the framers is the height of arrogance. Even an attempt to make an argument that human nature has changed in the short span of 300 years can be only be sourced from a place of vanity with no respect for reality. It's all about survival, and its most basic needs. The constitution was written to provide "We the People" with the inalienable rights. If there comes a day when the constitution is no longer required, then on that exact same day government will no longer be needed. On that day and every other to follow every man will no longer disagree with any other, about anything, at any time. Every man will allow ever other his own religion with both exuberance and respect as a fell human with no embellishment. The vitriol of faction is enjoyed most by those who choose to be shackled to the remnants of their childhood school yard cultures. At some point there must come a time to move on.

Some Closing Remarks

The work that went into this book was done on behalf of Benjamin Franklin, George Washington, John Adams, Thomas Jefferson, John Jay, James Madison and John Jay. They knew that they would not be bound to the earth for the length of time required for their nation to experience the real checks and balances of the constitution. They saw no other alternative but to demonstrate mans own human nature and only partially exposed the logic and effectiveness of the constitution being the checks and balances against power. Their labors of about 84 years have not been in vain if you are reading this now, because after over 200 years the final stage of their plan is now underway.

Before writing this book I had no aspiration to become an author or a historian. While this book will be easily seen to be remarkable in its need for editing, it is the discovery, supporting documentation and the new narrative of history which will be seen as being profoundly important. I have also documented the patterns I saw in the ciphers and how to go about resolving them to their true context of history. There are many more letters that have yet to be discovered and much work left to do for historians. Many of the ciphers I have located are still incomplete and require more study, but studied with an eye that cares only for the candid truth of history and not blinded by ideological motive alone. This is the first "answer book" to those ciphers. These ciphers have never been perceived to exist and are perhaps the greatest reward to my research because in finding them it has re-animated the framers. It's been a bit of a literary Indiana Jones type of adventure. If you have read their letters, as deciphered you will probably have experienced a much better understanding of these men. First and foremost their intelligence and dedication was amazing. As I approached each letter that I had concluded was a cipher, I would talk out loud and say, "Ok Benjamin, what is it that you are trying to tell me?", and then I would listen and the nuance of the ciphers would begin bubble to the surface. As you can see I had to suffer through this more than a few times. They are back and as you can see, they have had much to say. If you find that your political beliefs align with the truth history then congratulations, you are the right side of it

I'm no genius but I do suspect that this book will more than likely be controversial. While this may be an authors dream, this book was written to transition the American dream from a thing of fading hope, to a thing of reality, providing the encoded direction of the constitution is not infringed. The pushback on these findings is probably going to be ferocious as a result to the current normalization of gun ownership. What is learned can be unlearned. This process should be made even easier if ones goal is to be a law abiding citizen, patriotic to the constitution and respectful to the wisdom of the founders. If there is a debate it it will have to be with the framers now, but to debate them, is to debate the constitution and its checks and balances that have already provided so much for the American society. Lethal gun ownership is nothing more than dressing a wolf in sheep's clothing and it is only when the wolf is revealed that the sheep will be brought to slaughter. A thing discovered cannot be undiscovered once the genie is let out of the bottle. Truth cares nothing for the opinions of people because opinions are arrived at from a very wide spectrum of motives.

I'm only the first in a very long line of people who has been astonished that the 2nd Amendment can actually be read with clarity using only its text. No knowledge of history, advice from peers or the wisdom of scholars is necessarily required understand the 2nd amendment now. We don't need this assistance this because 2nd amendment was always a riddle which is now forever solved. Any mystery pertaining to it has been explained away. "E Plurius Enum", "from many one", is part of its solution and is a direct reference to the word "Militia", because it is one word with many things in it, the things being people and Arms. Further research resolved just how the 2nd amendment is to be administered or well regulated once finally exposed and a primer was even provided which was nested just under the surface of the Bill of Rights. Once that knowledge is acquired then the sentence begins to transform. This was always an individual right that was necessary to the security of a free state, but not of colony, but of mind in the absence of fear fueled primarily by the introduction of Arms in the first place. The Federalist papers further explains this but due to the volume of that literature I have only been able to add a fraction of what I have deciphered thus far from those essays. This book, as it is, has almost been pushed to the limits of its physical size with the current choice of fonts and line spacing.

Designing of the Constitution

The genius of the United States Constitution is that it was designed by men who had a very thorough understanding of past governments. Benjamin Franklin was a polymath and one of his greatest curiosities was human nature and the recognition that people's opinions were usually a constant work in progress. This was a problem that had only one solution because it is rare for a person to relinquish their own opinion for that of another regardless of how it was arrived at. There is a natural resistance to change, because this would take energy and possibly a reorganization of other opinions in order to make a new one fit. Just because we need opinions to make sense of our world does not necessarily mean that they jive with the reality of it. It may satisfy our emotions but our emotions are not a foundation of logic, they are however real, and more often than not control us, more than we control them. He went about crafting a way to give the people the opportunity to live amongst each other and experience liberty in spite of conflicting opinions. There is no question that this new nation would be a land of opportunity, but the work to exploit it would be an ongoing struggle where the odds of success to achieve liberty would require deference to the wisdom of the men that drafted the constitution. In a sense he was designing a software program but he first had to resolve the structure to produce a desired result. The veracity of his keen observation of human nature has just been demonstrated for the past 224 years because he employed it to hide the final legacy of the constitution along with the help of those allied in his grand experiment of his design. This alone I believe, is an excellent example of a fact. His approach to the constitutions design is identical to any modern day software engineer. I think my own experience in this field greatly assisted me in seeing the patterns of his code. Programmers usually don't put extraneous bits in their code because it confuses it and has no relevance in producing a desired output. The Bill of Rights appeared to have extraneous bits in places and in respecting the intelligence of the men that produced it these could not be extraneous bits. If I was to attribute this code to the timeframe of the period alone then the motivation for such an approach would be an arrogance of my own in thinking that we are far more intelligent to the men of the 18th century. It was my opinion that the reason why these bits were extraneous was quite simply because they had not yet been resolved to not be extraneous. They had to have been put there for a reason because the cabal didn't come across as being unreasonable men. The thought that went into this coding was theirs and not mine and if I was unable to read it, find the truth of it, then I would have accept the fact that I just didn't understand it. The man that has all the answers is usually the man that refuses to defer to the intelligence or education of others. The man that does not is the man that is more interested in leaving a void in limbo to be filled only with truth rather than in filling it with nonsense just to satisfy the ego. The more an ego is propped up on eggshells of nonsense becomes an ego far more likely to panic when under threat and further creates opinions on emotion alone. I believe it this is a good indicator as to how one has built their narratives and had appeared to me as a pattern consistent with ideological groups.

The Journey of the author

Some people may be wondering why I had not shared this discovery earlier. From the day that I read the 2nd amendment I immediately recognized that the

Supreme Court and all of Academia had gotten it wrong albeit had they suspected it was a riddle in the first place their approach would not have left the confines of its text in search of answers elsewhere. Now how does one go about telling a nation that they got part of their constitution wrong without sounding like a complete, for lack of a better word, "nut-job". It is a bit awkward to say the least, awkward for the very reasons I have explained in the chapter on Narratives we build. To start a sentence with "This might sound crazy but.." has a very high probability of making a very bad first impression especially when there is a pleading undertone to it. If dignity had mass I would now look anorexic. This was bigger than me and dignity was a thing that would just have to wait. I did make attempts to contact those that would be able to escalate this discovery so that it could be implemented as it had to be. It had to be because it shall not be infringed. I had attempted to reach over 30 people and organizations on both sides of the border but I received no answer as I was quickling swallowed up in the noise of society. This was highly frustrating as you can imagine but this was not a thing that could be let go and still consider myself as part of human landscape. I had to somehow establish myself as someone who was "in the know" in order to get the ears of others to listen before their minds turned them off. This would after all be seen as "just my opinion" and a very difficult thing to square away with any veracity in the circles of academia especially when I was not in that circle to begin with. The weight of opinion is usually judged on credentials, but what I had discovered could not be found in any institution that supplied those credentials in the first place. This was ground zero, a discovery and profoundly important.

So I took it upon myself to delve into historical research. I was seeking out answers over and above what I had read. My initial strategy was to share this through social media, being you tube. I used power point to make slides, which I then converted to a video. This started to grow very tedious especially when the research was uncovering more and more letters. Further to this, such a video would have come across as being tacky and very difficult to cross reference as only a book can. I perceived it would have been an insult to the importance of these documents and would possibly degrade from its importance, so a book seemed to be much better strategy. The only problem was that as someone who has never written a book before, believe it or not, the task ahead seemed a bit daunting as the clock ticked. I was of course seeking the path of least resistance and this would have taken me out of my comfort zone.

Then everything changed because a very important dynamic of my research was suddenly revealed. It was like a slap in the face, but not one stemmed from anger, but one that yanked me into reality. My own part in this had escalated when I realized that I was actually a variable in Benjamin Franklins' experiment and grand plan. No longer was I just trying to share this discovery with my neighbours to the south but now it appeared I was charged with completing a story that was started long ago. To put it mildly this was going to be a bit awkward. The framers had anticipated that one day someone would connect the dots which could only be done with a reality based bias. More to the point, that someone, for better or for worse was me. This was their plan, and no plan of mine, but I suppose that if someone is to get sucker punched, I could do worse than its source being that of the wise scheming knuckles of Benjamin Franklin. This was one hiccup in life I never would have anticipated, and fear unfortunately would not be its remedy.

From day one the government had to learn how to operate under the new constitution and over time the false narratives of history would become well established as dogma. Political parties evolved over time and each one and picked their ideological heroes from the cabal to defend their current political views and opinions. My own mission in this is of constitutional correctness, as opposed to the opinions of political correctness and every one of the men from the cabal is backing me up on this book 100 percent. Human nature thrived, as it always had, but now it was guided in part by the checks and balances that have become less and less adhered too over time as those in power will sometimes respect their own wishes over the dictate of the constitution itself.

I recognized that there was a certain utility of someone not belonging to any American political party. This would be less likely to be seen as an attack from one ideology from within a party attacking another. Political parties have evolved over time as their views changed and men vied to get elected with perhaps a viewpoint less from a viewpoint of public service and more as an opportunity for political power, status and financial gain. I recognized that the nature of the men I was working for would have fit exclusively into the previous category, the proof of which is the extent of their labors which bordered on either side of their political careers. While I am obviously liberally minded I am still neutral but with a bias only towards raw truth of the constitution and the veracity of history behind it. This was a very strange place to find myself in and as a liberally minded individual this book is an issue of lost and found. I felt responsible to share the framers story, and to deny them what they desired most to have told was not within my power. The alternative, in my mind was unthinkable. I suppose I could have taken the view that this was none of my business, not my problem but after 225 years, how many more people must die as the gulf of faction continues to widen. I will admit that I did hesitate though, in light of the politics wondering if now was the right time, but then I realised that this was a decision that was well beyond my own pay grade.

I did not know if I would be able to accomplish a solution to this dilemma but I did know I had to give it an honest effort. The fact is, nobody would listen because it appears those I contacted felt this was an infringement on their own brand of common sense. This is not meant as a disparagement to these individuals, or anything other of like mind, because in the absence of a full narrative in what surely must sound like some half baked conspiracy theory, people generally don't like to have their intelligence insulted.

The utility of this book as is that it can now be used as a template for the simple reason that it now exists. I am I suppose an arbitrator of truth, or at least in the context of this work. Thomas Jefferson appears to have my back on this and in a very surreal sense I theirs. As one can imagine it doesn't take a clairvoyant to see that the pushback on this volume from political and commercial faction will be nothing short of ferocious. The truth isn't particularly concerned with this though, because it will always stand on its own merit. Any nefarious attempts to contradict the bones of these findings will expose only the motives of tyrants, or those that do not wish to give up their power for the sake of society.

Final thoughts

With only the bias of Merriam Webster diction we know that liberty is "the state of being free" as it pertains to the 2nd amendment. We now know the path of achieving this state are through regulations but not as a check and balance against government but he people themselves. This is not a book about State's rights but only for the liberty of those that live in the full geography of the United States.

Power is also synonymous with money. America has lived under the checks and balances of the constitution which have been regulating the power attributed to government through both its structure and clearly defined roles of its branches. It has been over 200 years and these checks and balances have kept oppression at bay at least with respect to the federal head. Oppression still exists in America because of the people continue to vote for Pursuit of happiness alone. This is nothing more than a pipe dream though because to vote for Pursuit of Happiness is too vote for a side effect of Life and Liberty. Without Life and Liberty the Pursuit of Happiness can never be achieved. That being said, be careful on what you vote for because you cannot vote for business models that corporations or companies choose to use, but you can vote for laws that will gently guide them to provide the very life and liberty that are the promise of the American dream.

This book is about far more than the 2nd amendment. It is about finally exposing the full wisdom of the founders to help guide men in spite of themselves. It is about exposing our own human nature to ourselves and to better understand how it works in others. It is a thing that cannot be cured, but it can be guided, but that guidance must first be voted for. It is the patriotic duty of any citizen to vote for the inalienable rights of men in nations that are in the possession of real democracies. It is patriotic to vote for them in spite of others opinions as their own understanding is hindered by their own human nature. It is not only an act of patriotism, but an act of humanity. It is the effects that will pacify the electorate. It is impossible to convince everyone, but everyone is experiencing the effects of a shrinking middle class, and the fulfillment of the American dream coming down to the luxury of a happy meal.

After the United States Constitution was both drafted and crafted by some very wise men and demonstrated to the world it shortly came into vogue for other nations to start inventing new forms of government beyond that of a monarchy. Communism is one example but without checks and balances put into place to serve the people despots soon saw an opportunity to exploit power. The people would find it virtually impossible to have any chance at their own pursuit of happiness and were only given liberty at the whim of their government.

The moment that 'well-regulated" became well regulated the heartbeat of the constitution was exposed. The message was clear in that it now stated that no man can be trusted, full stop. This is not to infer that all men are nefarious in their thinking, but who that person is will never be known until after their nefarious deed has been experienced by society. The rhetoric completely changed because now the real checks and balances as currently in place have proven themselves to be true. The wise men of the cabal do not endorse the possession of arms as a contingency to take down a tyrant.

The best defence against the appearance of tyrant is in the vote, but now that tyrant can be any man with too much power. Men have invented corporations which have their own utility but can easily become the oppressor as their accountants become the champions of profit, and human resource departments become only a pretense of liberty, directed by those whose pursuit of happiness is defined purely by money alone. At any time they can enforce their will upon the people, be it in the wages, monopolies or otherwise. A man does not care about the source of his oppression, only the oppression itself. Its source can be king George, or any man with too much power, which they can only have in the absence of regulations. The ultimate source of oppression in a function democracy is in the vote itself. Party ideologies

This 2nd Amendment was an Easter egg of sorts that was planted into the constitution as a final legacy to "We the People" which has now finally been hatched. While this may cause some indignation for some, as for me, never in my life did I ever figure I would one day find myself hatching an egg. None the less though to actually be of service to these men has been an indescribable honor and as a "finding father", this in turn will be my own legacy, providing of course somebody reads this book.

It appears to me that there is no other sentence that better describes the very heartbeat of the constitution than the 2nd amendment. No longer will it be known as a contingency for the people, sitting in limbo to pacify fear while simultaneously fueling it. It is now going to play a very proactive role to ensure that liberty is maintained in real time. It is the only text in the constitution that connects government directly to the people through the Bill of Rights. The Bill of rights mandates any government in power to protect the people through a check and balance against the power any one person may possess.

It has been established that the 2nd amendment has existed since at least 1752 unless you choose to believe that a genius would actually go hand fishing for lighting or that a whale was actually witnessed breaching the crest of Niagra falls in the pursuit of a cod. Both of these stories, if you forgive me for saying, are rather fishy when put into the context of the truth of reality.

The 2nd amendment is a check and balance against the people to limit the onset of tyrants or those that would choose to do society harm if first enabled with the power to do so. Since it has been shown that the text of the 2nd amendment has existed since 1752, it is my belief that checks and balances of the current constitution were fleshed out by the one simple concept that any man, once left up to his own devices will from time to time will exploit power to his own advantage and benefit but to the detriment of very society he is so dependent on. This is rather astonishing because the very thing that people thought the 2nd amendment was a contingency for is the very thing that ultimately gave them the real checks and balances of the constitution itself.

The code of Life, Liberty and Pursuit of Happiness could not be revealed nor explained but has been waiting for the day when it would finally be exposed for what it really is. Everyone has always had their own interpretation of Liberty and the American Dream. With the use of a dictionary, and our knowledge of the real checks and balances and the fact that liberty itself is imbedded into the 2nd amendment through the use of word "State" it is now exposed that the primary purpose of the constitution was to prevent oppression for all of society, or We the People. In knowing that any man can be a tyrant, and that checks and balances against power have been proven to work then voting no longer becomes a mystery, it becomes a patriotic duty. It becomes a patriotic duty because not everyone will understand these revelations due to their own human nature and current status of their narratives. The tyrant will use any sales pitch he can think up to acquire power. He will prey on the fears of men, because this is the most effective and comes across being cared for. This is a form of terrorism though, because the ultimate effect of voting for the empowerment of corporations and industry through deregulation is to empower them with complete control over the dictation of wages, hours. The promise of jobs or trickledown economics is nothing more than a sales pitch and promises nothing. Regulations however are the guarantee to be free of oppression. The monopolies use the rhetoric of small business, and yet destroy them in their own pursuit of happiness. A job provides no liberty if no living wage is realised. Trickle-down-economics was not even a promise but a thing to be hoped for, and hope alone does not pay the bills as liberty never occurred if a nation's money rests in the kings of industry. Some view the kings of industry as those realizing the American dream and view them as the proof of it. They are, but only if the middle class is thriving, and living wages exist. They are if the inalienable right of healthcare for all is realised because that can be found in "Life". Vote for lower taxes and you vote for oppression, because industry will no longer be taking part in keeping the health of liberty in good check.

The final legacy of the United States Constitution is the full disclosure of the path to liberty for "We the People". The final check and balance has always been in the hands of the people. You get what you vote for, and if checks and balances have worked to keep a tyrant at bay, they will also work to preserve the Liberty of the land. No mans liberty belongs to any others Pursuit of Happiness. It is actually chiselled into the United States Seal. The United States Seal ultimately says that no man can be trusted so do not allow him so much power in the first place. Two hundred years has been proof of concept.

Even at this point in the book there will be many that will think these ciphers are nothing more than constructs of my own overactive imagination. Some may be hearing of this concept for the first time but it is most certainly not a concept of mine because it has existed for over 200 years. Thomas Jefferson writes about ciphers explicitly in a tutorial between John Patterson and himself. The point of a cipher is to hide knowledge from men, and regardless of how smart you are, you are still a man and the knowledge that was hidden had to hidden from every level of intelligence including your own. You have of course heard of ciphers before because they are used today, but only fashioned in a slightly different manner. The fashioning of the ciphers and their level of sophistication is only limited to the ingenuity of its author. Today the president has something that is always close by called a nuclear football. In that are the codes which are simply just a key to unlock a nuclear missile launch where the code in the missiles give them purpose and functionality. I have simply found a key to code whose silo's were housed in the privately hoarded letters. The fallout when launched will reveal to each and every man in a functioning democracy the world over the true path to liberty. It will reveal to every man the path to attain liberty. It is on behalf the George Washington and the others that I have located their football opened its satchel and pushed the button which I found inside. They also knew that once revealed their weapon against oppression would be intercontinental and combat oppression through the neutering of propaganda or exposing the true path to liberty through the vote. The future of humanity lies in the choices we make and there will always be fallout. How many lessons of history are required for mankind to finally figure it out or are we doomed to doom ourselves? Just simple adjustments in the grand scheme of things, starting with the vote and respect for truth. In understanding our own nature we will not be diminished, but empowered, because we will come to understand that we are all essentially the same, but only the products of our own inventions under the governments that either rule us, or are there for us too collectively rule through the wisdom of a vote that respects all the people, in spite of the people, irrespective of their station in life or current position along its course.

Truth will win every time if the people themselves first know it to be true. Nobody would listen and now after two centuries, and even the dawn of civilization itself, it will finally be heard for what it is. That's my two cents on the United States Constitution and hopefully this change will be for the better.

> "and say finally whether peace is best preserved by giving energy to the government, or information to the people. This last is the most certain and the most legitimate engine of government. Educate and

inform the whole mass of the people, enable them to see that it is their interest to preserve peace and order, and they will preserve it, and it requires no very high degree of education to convince them of this. They are the only sure reliance for the preservation of our liberty.—After all, it is my principle that the will of the majority should prevail. If they approve the proposed constitution in all it's parts[709], I shall concur in it chearfully, in hopes they will amend it whenever they shall find it works wrong[710]. This reliance cannot deceive us, as long as we remain virtuous[711]"

This excerpt comes from a letter written by Thomas Jefferson to Uriah Forrest, with Enclosure, 31 December 1787. It actually references another letter that Thomas Jefferson had been responding to from James Madison but historians have reported he got his dates wrong. Whether this was an oversight of Thomas Jefferson's or his own device of creating a hint through this anomaly we may never know. It is an error of reality just like Benjamin Franklin writing a letter to a dead man being William Alexander. If I was to make an educated guess I would put my money on an error by design. The utility in this is that it would make the letter stand out helping to indicate that it is a cipher. We do know the ciphers have all been very carefully crafted and then stitched together to give one letter support with another. In doing this a cipher hunter would now be suspicious of two letters and not just one. This was how I was able to locate many of ciphers in looking for anything that seemed a bit odd in a letter.

> "The advice nearest to my heart and deepest in my convictions is that the Union of the States be cherished & perpetuated"
> From James Madison's "Advice to my Country" letter, 1834.
> His instructions were that it be opened after his death which occurred in 1836.

---

[709] Note that "Militia" has two parts, "people and Arms"

[710] "wrong in that the 2A has been infringed, as anticipated".

[711] Put the concerns of all of society above yourself in a United States of America.

Benjamin Franklin was the Candid friend to Mankind

It appears to me that Benjamin Franklin made it his life's mission to create the perfect formula to guide humanity for all time in spite of itself. The United States was to be a demonstration of this to the world, because that formula we now know as the United States Constitution. He knew that human nature would never change which I think most will see that it has not so the opportunity he gave the USA was an opportunity recognize the wisdom that went into the constitution whether it is recognized or not. The constitution itself was designed to be a line of demarcation to keep all tyrants at bay and would sit above any ideology which is usually just the sales pitch of tyrants to gain control of the people and rob them of their inalienable rights. The strength is in the peoples understanding this and voting first and foremost for a smooth running constitution and not for those who will always exist for want of changing it to serve their own individual desires. Humanity is an experiment of evolution and of god and it is only humanity that must own its own salvation or its extinction. In a game of survival of the fittest only one man will be left standing to say that he won, with no one left to listen, and then we will be gone. The ball has always been in our court but we never really did fully understand the nature of the game and far too few have cried foul because they have been far more concerned with today than for tomorrows that are being destroyed.

Overview of History's New Context

1731   Benjamin Franklin becomes a freemason

1732-1758   When Benjamin Franklin was 26 years old he publishes Poor Richards Almanac and hones his skill in creating witty phrases that steer mind towards introspection. The use of psychology is the very foundation of marketing and even at times deception. Appealing to a man's emotions especially fear is a particular effective approach.

1743   Benjamin Franklin founds the American Philosophical Society.

April 13 1743   Thomas Jefferson is born

1752   The Kite Experiment Letter (first cipher)

1754   The Albany Plan and cartoon Join or Die

1758   Benjamin Franklin publishes 26th edition of Poor Richards Almanac at age 52. He could have retired with the proceeds from this publication.

April 19 1775   American Revolutionary War Begins

June 12 1776   Virginia Declaration of Rights drafted by George Mason

July 4, 1776   Declaration of Independence was written by Thomas Jefferson at the insistence of John Adams because he felt that "they" would be too suspicious of him.

1779   Benjamin Franklin updates an essay called "Morals of Chess" and puts it into the public domain. It talks about planning moves well in advance, and say it is best not to interrupt your opponents thinking.

This was never more clearly demonstrated than when the Bill of Rights was ratified 12 years later. Most of the delegates read what they wanted to read with respect to the 2nd amendment and signed onto it. A select few read what the 2nd amendment actually said and signed onto it. This was only a key move in the game though. The next two moves would take 225 years until, In a few ciphers Benjamin Franklin refers to that piece being a knight or chevalier.

1780   It was recognized democracy had no place in the drafting of the constitution due to the very nature of man it had to guard from in spite of man. Democracy was to be a check and balance of the constitution and its rules defined by the constitution and not necessarily the other way around unless a 2/3 vote house and senate were to be successfully achieved. The grand experiment was then designed, and the work of the letters was started.

1780   First letter appears referencing the 2nd amendment.

1780   Benjamin Franklin records the memberships of the key founders who were to write the letters into his membership records.

1780   George Washington joins American Philosophical Society

1780   Thomas Jefferson joins American Philosophical Society

1780   John Adams joins American Philosophical Society

1780   John Jay joins American Philosophical Society

1780   Alexander Hamilton joins American Philosophical Society

1780   The State of Pennsylvania puts into motion to begin to abolish of slavery, which is a key factor as to why the 2nd amendment would be ahead of its time. When John Adams figured it would require at least 100 years for the 2nd amendment to remain a secret I suspect he also had the duration of slavery in mind as well.

1783   Heavily encrypted letter located where Benjamin Franklin talks of 2nd amendment in structure and of the letters he is working on.

Sept 3, 1783   American Revolutionary war ends

1785   James Madison joins American Philosophical Society

1787-1788   The Federalist Papers, 85 in total are written. It is my suspicion that these letters may have been started in advance though, with very specific dates put on them to make it appear they were written during the drafting of the constitution.

April 30 1789   George Washington becomes the first president of the United States, and knows full well what the 2nd amendment really means. Perhaps he recognizes his utility as a National symbol to help propagate its secret into the future? Is it a coincidence that the next three presidents were also part of this cabal? Is it possible that their placements and labors to establish them was more than just about the presidency? Perhaps their primary goal was for the very future of their constitution? These were after all the framers, and these particular framers we now know had been orchestrating history. Why would they not go "all-in" on this if they were to be true to their nation and firmly establish their constitution through the demonstration of its use? They had after all been writing the ciphers on either side of their political appointments.

April 17, 1790   Benjamin Franklin passes

Dec 15, 1791   Bill of Rights was ratified

Dec 15, 1791 to 1801 James Madison and Alexander Hamilton scramble to realign the already written Federalist papers because the original 12 articles of the Bill of Rights had were now reduced to 10 amendments

March 4, 1797   George Washington's presidency ends

March 4, 1797   March 4 1801 John Adams Presidency ends.

Dec 14, 1799   George Washington passes at age of 67.

March 4, 1801-March 4, 1809   Thomas Jefferson Presidency

July 4, 1804.....Alexander Hamilton dies an unknown martyr in a duel

March 4, 1809-March 4, 1817   James Madison Presidency

July 4, 1826   Thomas Jefferson passes

July 4, 1826   John Adams passes

May 17, 1829…. John Jay passes

1834 James   Madison writes "Advice to my Country" to be opened after his death.

June 28, 1836   James Madison Passes

1845   Samuel Colt gets a government contract to manufacture 2000 colt walkers.

February 1846   Nunn versus Georgia case strikes down gun laws after citing the 2nd amendment.

Apr 12, 1861   May 9, 1865 Civil War

April 15, 1865   Abraham Lincoln is assassinated with a derringer. (very small handgun)

Nov 17, 1871   NRA founded

Dec 2, 2015   2nd amendment read objectively in the public domain for the first time.

May 2017   this work will dispel any and all mystery regarding the 2nd amendment. The Holy Grail of Gun Control has been revealed which now favors Life and Liberty and the Pursuit of Happiness for all the people which is of course the context of "We the People".

May 2017-forward   the "public view" becomes a reality and concludes the experiment that Benjamin Franklin had started so many years before. The people will have to make a choice to respect all of the constitution and see that it is not a thing to be voted upon, or cherry picked unless it is in the confines of its predetermined rules.

9-The Book Ends

Yes I know it's a genius title for the last chapter but I ask that you bear with me on this one because it's not quite over yet.

The next two letters were written or endorsed by Benjamin Franklin and predate the birth of even George Washington by at least a year. While they are not ciphers they do seem to frame in this book rather well. It appears at the age of 25 that Benjamin Franklin first thought of creating the perfect constitution. Even though this letter is 286 years old it speaks to 21st century with an uncanny foresight I have titled this chapter to be consistent with the duality of Benjamin Franklin's literature which has now been extensively demonstrated. These letters are not ciphers but hold great relevance to this newly exposed dynamic of history, and even the modern state of affairs. Nothing has changed, and Benjamin Franklin knew nothing would which is the genius of his constitution. Benjamin Franklin wanted to make civilization a better place for humanity to live in used the written word to and an astonishing amount of ingenuity and foresight to reach well past his own time on earth.

The Authors First Words

Observations on Reading History

> ms Autobiography: Huntington Library
> Observations on my Reading History in Library
> May 9. 1731.
> That the great Affairs of the World, the Wars, Revolutions, &c. are carried on and effected by Parties.
> That the View of these Parties is their present general Interest, or what they take to be such.
> That the different Views of these different Parties, occasion all Confusion.
> That while a Party is carrying on a general Design, each Man has his particular private Interest in View.
> That as soon as a Party has gain'd its general Point, each Member becomes intent upon his particular Interest, which thwarting others, breaks that Party into Divisions, and occasions more Confusion.
> That few in Public Affairs act from a meer View of the Good of their Country, whatever they may pretend; and tho' their Actings

bring real Good to their Country, yet Men primarily consider'd that their own and their Country's Interest was united, and did not act from a Principle of Benevolence.

That fewer still in public Affairs act with a View to the Good of Mankind.

There seems to me at present to be great Occasion for raising an united Party for Virtue, by forming the Virtuous and good Men of all Nations into a regular Body, to be govern'd by suitable good and wise Rules, which good and wise Men may probably be more unanimous in their Obedience to, than common People are to common Laws.

I at present think, that whoever attempts this aright, and is well qualified, cannot fail of pleasing God, and of meeting with Success.

B. F.

www.franklinpapers.org.

The Authors Last Words

I stumbled across an eerily fitting quotation of Benjamin Franklin's which I took the liberty of placing at the end of this book. I'm not really big believer in fate unless it comes to getting check on a first date. Now though I can't help but wonder if this is a proof of it. This may in itself be a cipher if Benjamin Franklin had decided very early on in life to dedicate it to the betterment of both himself and humankind.

The Epitaph

"In 1728, aged 22, Franklin wrote what he hoped would be his own epitaph:"[712]

"The Body of B. Franklin Printer;

Like the Cover of an old Book,

Its Contents torn out,
And stript of its Lettering and Gilding,
Lies here, Food for Worms.
But the Work shall not be wholly lost:
For it will, as he believ'd, appear once more,
In a new & more perfect Edition,
Corrected and Amended By the Author"

---

[712] Reference: https://en.wikipedia.org/wiki/Benjamin_Franklin

Reference and Sources
The 12 Article Bill of Rights.

Article I
After the first enumeration required by the first article of the Constitution, there shall be one representative for every thirty thousand, until the number shall amount to one hundred, after which the proportion shall be so regulated by Congress, that there shall be not less than one hundred representatives, nor less than one representative for every forty thousand persons, until the number of representatives shall amount to two hundred; after which the proportion shall be so regulated by Congress, that there shall be not less than two hundred representatives, nor more than one representative for every fifty thousand persons.

Article II
No law varying the compensation for the services of the Senators and Representatives, shall take effect, until an election of Representatives shall have intervened.

Article III
Congress shall make no law respecting an establishment of religion, or prohibiting the free exercise thereof; or abridging the freedom of speech, or of the press; or the right of the people peaceably to assemble, and to petition the Government for a redress of grievances.

Article IV
A well regulated Militia, being necessary to the security of a free State, the right of the people to keep and bear Arms, shall not be infringed.

Article V
No Soldier shall, in time of peace be quartered in any house, without the consent of the Owner, nor in time of war, but in a manner to be prescribed by law.

Article VI
The right of the people to be secure in their persons, houses, papers, and effects, against unreasonable searches and seizures, shall not be violated, and no Warrants shall issue, but upon probable cause, supported by Oath or affirmation, and particularly describing the place to be searched, and the persons or things to be seized.

Article VII

No person shall be held to answer for a capital, or otherwise infamous crime, unless on a presentment or indictment of a Grand Jury, except in cases arising in the land or naval forces, or in the Militia, when in actual service in time of War or public danger; nor shall any person be subject for the same offence to be twice put in jeopardy of life or limb; nor shall be compelled in any criminal case to be a witness against himself, nor be deprived of life, liberty, or property, without due process of law; nor shall private property be taken for public use, without just compensation.

Article VIII

In all criminal prosecutions, the accused shall enjoy the right to a speedy and public trial, by an impartial jury of the State and district wherein the crime shall have been committed, which district shall have been previously ascertained by law, and to be informed of the nature and cause of the accusation; to be confronted with the witnesses against him; to have compulsory process for obtaining witnesses in his favor, and to have the Assistance of Counsel for his defence.

Article IX

In Suits at common law, where the value in controversy shall exceed twenty dollars, the right of trial by jury shall be preserved, and no fact tried by a jury, shall be otherwise re-examined in any Court of the United States, than according to the rules of the common law.

Article X

Excessive bail shall not be required, nor excessive fines imposed, nor cruel and unusual punishments inflicted.

Article XI

The enumeration in the Constitution, of certain rights, shall not be construed to deny or disparage others retained by the people.

Article XII

The powers not delegated to the United States by the Constitution, nor prohibited by it to the States, are reserved to the States respectively, or to the people.

The Bill of Rights (as ratified Dec 15 1791)

First Amendment
Congress shall make no law respecting an establishment of religion, or prohibiting the free exercise thereof; or abridging the freedom of speech, or of the press; or the right of the people peaceably to assemble, and to petition the Government for a redress of grievances.

Second Amendment
A well regulated Militia, being necessary to the security of a free State, the right of the people to keep and bear Arms, shall not be infringed.

Third Amendment
No Soldier shall, in time of peace be quartered in any house, without the consent of the Owner, nor in time of war, but in a manner to be prescribed by law.

Fourth Amendment
The right of the people to be secure in their persons, houses, papers, and effects, against unreasonable searches and seizures, shall not be violated, and no Warrants shall issue, but upon probable cause, supported by Oath or affirmation, and particularly describing the place to be searched, and the persons or things to be seized.

Fifth Amendment
No person shall be held to answer for a capital, or otherwise infamous crime, unless on a presentment or indictment of a Grand Jury, except in cases arising in the land or naval forces, or in the Militia, when in actual service in time of War or public danger; nor shall any person be subject for the same offence to be twice put in jeopardy of life or limb; nor shall be compelled in any criminal case to be a witness against himself, nor be deprived of life, liberty, or property, without due process of law; nor shall private property be taken for public use, without just compensation.

Sixth Amendment
In all criminal prosecutions, the accused shall enjoy the right to a speedy and public trial, by an impartial jury of the State and district wherein the crime shall have been committed, which district shall have been previously ascertained by law, and to be informed of the nature and cause of the accusation; to be confronted with the witnesses against him; to have compulsory process for obtaining

witnesses in his favor, and to have the Assistance of Counsel for his defence.

Seventh Amendment

In suits at common law, where the value in controversy shall exceed twenty dollars, the right of trial by jury shall be preserved, and no fact tried by a jury, shall be otherwise re-examined in any court of the United States, than according to the rules of the common law.

Eighth Amendment

Excessive bail shall not be required, nor excessive fines imposed, nor cruel and unusual punishments inflicted.

Ninth Amendment

The enumeration in the Constitution, of certain rights, shall not be construed to deny or disparage others retained by the people.

Tenth Amendment

The powers not delegated to the United States by the Constitution, nor prohibited by it to the States, are reserved to the States respectively, or to the people.

Actors Reference

"Nor will the **opening scenes** of our present government be seen in their true aspect, until the letters of the day, now held in private hoards, shall be broken up and laid open to public view"

Thomas Jefferson June 12, 1823.

I've added this section as a reference for the lesser known actors in the ciphers. Benjamin Franklin masterminded this entire experiment and created the cabal. The cabal in turn enlisted others to write ciphers or used others as part of their ciphers. The earliest letter I've located is his write up on his fictitious Kite experiment of 1752. At this time James Madison was one year old and even if he was a child prodigy I don't think he was as abreast of the 2nd amendments legitimate meaning as he was later in life. The letters themselves spanned 84 years. They were started by Benjamin Franklin when he was 46 and were written for 46 years after his passing in the year 1790.

In general, the cabal I refer to centers around the time period of the Constitutional Convention because this is when the 2nd amendment was finally implemented in a publicly written form, being the Bill of Rights. Benjamin Franklin had originally hoped to put it into his Albany Plan, which would have been a constitution like document but with the inclusion of King George. There may very well be many other actors, one being Joseph Priestly from this period, but I have not really researched this period too extensively.

I had gazed over a few other ciphered letters without even knowing it as I searched for ciphers in Benjamin Franklins' digitized archive at Franklinpapers.org. It seemed logical that Benjamin Franklin, an author of note, would have been participating in creating ciphers since I had just discovered the names in his organization, the American Philosophical Society. It was when I discovered his letter of Oct 26, 1789 to William Alexander which referenced type sets and fonts that I was certain that I had located an actual cipher which was written expressly for the secret of the 2nd amendment. I was also certain that I was the first person to identify this letter, and furthermore decrypt it. Without the key of the 2nd amendment this would have been impossible. To further substantiate what I had read, I also discovered that William Alexander had been resting in the grave for about 6 years. While it may be true that dead men are very good at keeping a stiff upper lip, they most certainly cannot read or write. Furthermore I discovered that real William Alexander had an ancestor who was also titled the Earl of Stirling, and of same name from about 150 years earlier.

This letter had was completely contrived and meant for future eyes. So the actors had a purpose in their symbolism be them alive or not. Sometimes an actor is not even mentioned by name, but only by title in order to hide their true identity and context in history. This has been done many times in the Federalist papers. One such an example was a footnote which references "duke of Marlborough" which I was able to resolve to be George Mason. In his Virginia Declaration of Rights George Mason was interested in preserving the concept of land ownership. In light of footnote, and narrative in that particular Federalist essay the cabal thought this man to have a selfish nature as a politician. His land generated him wealth through slavery and tobacco fields.

If I could identify a man as a philosopher and he was in correspondence with the primary actors of the cabal then it was an indicator that there may be ciphers in their correspondence. John Adams had given instruction to look for the "hints from the philosophers which may be of help to our countrymen". Letters between the primary men were also of importance as well. Usually if a letter comes across as being a bit cryptic and symbolic then that was an indicator that it may be a cipher. The term "papers and effects" in the 4th amendment is a good example of this. It seemed to pad the amendment with extraneous information as if there was a word quota that had to be met in the amendment. I already knew that these ciphers had been very well thought out, which in turn gauged just how much thought I had to put into them myself in reading them. I'm not going to say it was easy, because it was most certainly not, but it was an extremely rewarding endeavour, and hopefully not just for me.

Another utility of actors was the very nature of their politics in context of them being federalists or anti-federalists. An anti-federalist would be in favor of a right to bear Arms as well as States rights, where a Federalist would have been more in favor of its legitimate meaning. This relates to the now known fact that the buck will stop with the federal government doing the "well regulating". Benjamin Franklin used Patrick Henry and Richard Henry Lee's biases towards States rights and fervor for gun ownership in his ciphers as they would be the most likely to take the bait of "the right of the people to keep and bear Arms". When I located a cipher with a new actors name in it then I would continue to research that individuals correspondence. This was especially true with the William Alexander, Alexander Small, Joseph Priestley and David Hartley. They were completely contrived and then archived. After the initial discovery of the first William Alexander letter, I knew that any other that was dated after the time of his death was guaranteed to be a cipher to be a cipher even if I didn't initially perceive indicators within it. The onus was on me to figure it out. Furthermore, as

I've stated elsewhere the name William Alexander, in meaning, fits the 2nd amendment like a glove. With one of these letters already identified as a cipher, and seeing this ciphering method used elsewhere, this cannot be a coincidence. It was an indicator or red flag which helped me to quickly locate other letters of the "name-nature". Examples of other names are "Alexander Small, Joseph Priestly and Judge William Johnson. Joseph Priestly would be symbolic of a man of virtuous thought, which would definitely be required for men to fully endorse the new meaning of the 2nd amendment.

The following is a roughed out list of the actors who may or may not have known the true meaning of the 2nd amendment. Some of the actors that I will be referencing were only used in contrived letters due to the nature of the ciphers construction.

The actors that knew of the 2nd amendment were

The Primary Cabal

Benjamin Franklin

George Washington, John Adams, Thomas Jefferson, Alexander Hamilton, James Madison and John Jay

Enlisted Authors

Noah Webster: Founder of the Merriam Webster Dictionary. (BF or TJ)

Colonel John Taylor: Author of "Construction Construed, Constitution Validated". (GW, TJ)

Mason Locke Weems: Author of "The Life of George Washington – Cherry Tree version". (TJ)

Other Actors

William Alexander: Did not know

Alexander Small: Did not know

Joseph Priestley: Yes I believe he knew (BF)

David Hartley: 50/50 on this one, but leaning no. He appears to have been a "filing cabinet".

Benjamin Rush: maybe. I say this because he was also a delegate, so he would have had utility in helping to orchestrate the constitutional convention. This was an issue of top secret so any man chosen to be brought into this fold had to be completely trusted to take this secret to the grave.

Thomas Ritchie. Leaning no, but he was very suspicious of the 2nd amendment. If he did know then what appears to have been a conspiracy is now one that is far more horrific in nature. Too put this into perspective picture the NRA promoting their guns while knowing full well the true meaning of the 2nd amendment.

William Stephen Smith: (son in law to John Adams) thinking no.

Historical tangent beyond the letters to 1846 (contingent on Thomas Richie knowing)

James Polk, Zachary Taylor, Samuel Colt, Supreme Court of Georgia in Nunn versus Georgia.

Judge

Alexander Small (1710 – 31 August 1794)

was a Scottish surgeon and scholar, and a friend and frequent correspondent of Benjamin Franklin.

"Dr. Small and Benjamin Franklin were correspondents for at least thirty years, likely until Franklin's death. Franklin referred to them as "philosophers, who study and converse for the benefit of mankind

https://en.wikipedia.org/wiki/Alexander_Small

Noah Webster Jr. (October 16, 1758 – May 28, 1843)

was an American lexicographer, textbook pioneer, English-language spelling reformer, political writer, editor, and prolific author. He has been called the "Father of American Scholarship and Education". His blue-backed speller books taught five generations of American children how to spell and read, secularizing their education. According to Ellis (1979), he gave Americans "a secular catechism to the nation-state."

Webster's name has become synonymous with "dictionary" in the United States, especially the modern Merriam-Webster dictionary that was first published in 1828 as An American Dictionary of the English Language.

https://en.wikipedia.org/wiki/Noah_Webster

David Hartley (8 August[1] 1705 – 28 August 1757)

was an English philosopher and founder of the Associationist school of psychology.[2]

https://en.wikipedia.org/wiki/David_Hartley_(philosopher)

He was the father of Benjamin Franklin's friend of the same name. It appears thought that this man was used as a "filing cabinet" for letters.

William Alexander, 1st Earl of Stirling (c. 1567 – 12 September 1640)

was a Scottish courtier and poet who was involved in the Scottish colonisation of Port Royal, Nova Scotia and Long Island, New York. His literary works include Aurora (1604), The Monarchick Tragedies (1604) and Doomes-Day (1614, 1637).

Alexander's grandest work is an epic poem describing the end of the world, Doomes-day. It was first published in four books (Edinburgh, 1614), and later in twelve (in the collected edition of Alexander's work printed in London, 1637). The poem, which contains almost 1,400 eight-line stanzas in total, begins with a synopsis of world history in the First 'Hour', then provides long catalogues of the creatures, battle dead, pagans, monarchs, sinners, biblical characters and, finally, members of the heavenly host who will appear at the Final Judgement.[8] Alexander's method was indebted to the French Protestant poet Guillaume de Salluste Du Bartas; Drummond acknowledged the kinship in the title of a manuscript poem 'Sur les oeuures poetiques de Guillaume Alexandre, Sieur De Menstre'.[9]

https://en.wikipedia.org/wiki/William_Alexander,_1st_Earl_of_Stirling

William Alexander, (1726 New York City – 15 January 1783)

was an American Brigadier-General during the American Revolutionary War. Alexander was considered male-heir to the title of Earl of Stirling through Scottish lineage (being the senior male descendant of the paternal grandfather of the first Earl of Stirling, who had died in 1640), and sought the title sometime after 1756. His claim was granted by a Scottish Court; however, the House of Lords ultimately over-ruled Scottish law and denied the title, granting Alexander instead the compromise title of Lord.[1]

https://en.wikipedia.org/wiki/William_Alexander,_Lord_Stirling

Mason Locke Weems (October 11, 1759 – May 23, 1825)

was usually referred to as Parson Weems, was an American book agent and author who wrote the first biography of George Washington immediately after his death. He was the source of some of the apocryphal stories about Washington. The tale of the cherry tree ("I cannot tell a lie, I did it with my little hatchet") is included in The Life of Washington (1800), a bestseller that depicted Washington's virtues and was intended to provide a morally instructive tale for the youth of the young nation,

https://en.wikipedia.org/wiki/Mason_Locke_Weems

Joseph Priestley (24 March 1733 – 6 February 1804)

was an 18th-century English theologian, English Dissenters clergyman, natural philosopher, chemist, innovative grammarian, multi-subject educator, and Liberal political theorist who published over 150 works.

https://en.wikipedia.org/wiki/Joseph_Priestley

Thomas Ritchie (November 5, 1778 – July 3, 1854)

Thomas Ritchie of Virginia was a leading American newspaper journalist, editor and publisher. He was the editor of the Richmond Enquirer 1804-1845. He was later became the editor of the "The Daily Union", a Washington newspaper for the years 1845-1851. President James K Polk had recruited him to take up this position. He had 12 and his 8th child was named Margaret who was the wife of Dr. Robert King Stone (1822-1872). Now Dr. Robert King Stone claim to fame was that he was Abraham Lincoln's personal physician. Abraham Lincoln's name is on the outside of the Benjamin Franklin's Pyramid and Thomas Ritchie was also extremely curious about Colonel John Taylors Book "Construction Construed- Constitutions Vindicated" and had been in correspondence with both James Madison and Thomas Jefferson. It was in one of those letters, dated Sept 15, 1821, that James Madison wrote ""**the legitimate meaning of the Instrument must be derived from the text itself** " It's interesting on how these threads in history are intertwined, however I have found no evidence that Abraham Lincoln actually knew the true meaning of the 2nd amendment. The question that leaves me most curious is as to whether or not Thomas Ritchie knew was able to resolve the instrument to the 2nd amendment. In the absence of actually reading the 2nd amendment objectively, Thomas Ritchie would have had no context, or the key to unlock the meaning of the ciphers. I have no doubt though, that he was highly suspicious that there was something going on. There is also a very early letter that he wrote where he appears to be interested in a very new technology that is related to the revolver.